Advances in Computer Vision and Pattern Recognition

More information about this series at http://www.springer.com/series/4205

Hong Cheng

Sparse Representation, Modeling and Learning in Visual Recognition

Theory, Algorithms and Applications

Springer

Hong Cheng
University of Electronic Science
and Technology of China
Chengdu, Sichuan
China

ISSN 2191-6586 ISSN 2191-6594 (electronic)
Advances in Computer Vision and Pattern Recognition
ISBN 978-1-4471-7251-2 ISBN 978-1-4471-6714-3 (eBook)
DOI 10.1007/978-1-4471-6714-3

Springer London Heidelberg New York Dordrecht

Softcover reprint of the hardcover 1st edition 2015

Printed on acid-free paper

Springer-Verlag London Ltd. is part of Springer Science+Business Media (www.springer.com)

Preface

Over the past decade, sparse representation, modeling, and learning has emerged and is widely used in many visual tasks such as feature extraction and learning, object detection, and recognition (i.e., faces, activities). It is rooted in statistics, physics, information theory, neuroscience, optimization theory, algorithms, and data structure. Meanwhile, visual recognition has played a critical role in computer vision as well as in robotics. Recently, sparse representation consists of two basic tasks, data sparsification and encoding features. The first task is to make data more sparse directly. The second is to encode features with sparsity properties in some domain using either strictly or approximately K-Sparsity. Sparse modeling is to model specific tasks by jointly using different disciplines and their sparsity properties. Sparse learning is to learn mapping from input signals to outputs by either representing the sparsity of signals or modeling the sparsity constraints as regularization items in optimization equation. Mathematically, solving sparse representation and learning involves seeking the sparsest linear combination of basic functions from an overcomplete dictionary. The rationale behind this is the sparse connectivity between nodes in the human brain.

The necessity and popularity of sparse representation, modeling, and learning are spread over all major universities and research organizations around the world, with leading scientists from various disciplines. This book presents our recent research work on sparse representation, modeling and learning with emphasis on visual recognition, and is aimed at researchers and graduate students. Our goal in writing this book is threefold. First, it creates an updated reference book of sparse representing, modeling, and learning. Second, this book covers both the theory and application aspects, which benefits readers keen to learn broadly sparse representation, modeling, and learning. Finally, we have provided some applications about visual recognition, as well as some applications about computer vision. We try to link theory, algorithms, and applications to promote compressed sensing research.

This book is divided into four parts. The first part, Introduction and Fundamentals, presents the research motivation and purpose, and briefly introduces the definition of spares representation, modeling, and learning, as well as its applications on visual recognition. The second part, Sparse representation, Modeling and Learning, which includes sparse recovery approaches, robust sparse representation and learning, efficient sparse representation and modeling, introduces large-scale visual recognition, and situations of efficient sparse coding and sparse quantization. The third part, Visual Recognition Applications, which includes feature representation and learning, sparsity-induced similarity, and sparse representation and learning-based classifiers, is the result of combining pattern recognition and compressed sensing. In different SRLCs, sparsity could be used in sample similarity, histogram generation, local feature similarity, and nearest neighbor classifiers. The fourth part, Advanced Topics, discusses the topic beyond the sparse—low-rank representation which is known as two-dimensional sparse representation. Additionally, Mathematics fundamental, and Computer Programming Resources are included in the appendices.

Most of this book refers to our research work at University of Electronic Science and Technology of China, and Carnegie Mellon University. I would like to offer my deep respect to Jie Yang at Carnegie Mellon University who supported my research during my stay at this university, as well as Zicheng Liu at Microsoft Research for his deep discussions with me. I would like to express my sincere thanks to Nan Zhou, Jianmei Su, Yuzhuo Wang, Ratha Pech, Saima who have provided immense help with preparation of figures and with the typesetting of the book. Springer has provided great support throughout the final stages of this book. I would like to thank my commissioning editor, Simon Rees, for his support. Finally, I would like to thank my wife, Xiaohong Feng, who has been supportive of me to write this book.

Chengdu, China
February 2015

Hong Cheng

Contents

Part III Visual Recognition Applications

Mathematical Notation

$\mathbb{R}$	Real numbers
$\mathbb{R}^D$	Vector space of real valued D dimensional vectors
$\mathbb{R}_K^D$	The space of K-sparse vector in $\mathbb{R}^D$
$\mathbb{B}_K^D$	The space of binary K-sparse vector built from $\{0, 1\}$
$\mathbb{T}_K^D$	The space of K-sparse vector built from $\{-1, 0, 1\}$
$\boldsymbol{x}$	(Sparse)sampling coefficients
x_i	ith element of vector $\boldsymbol{x}$
$\lvert \cdot \rvert$	If applied to a number, absolute value
$\langle \boldsymbol{x}, \boldsymbol{y} \rangle$	The inner product of $\boldsymbol{x}, \boldsymbol{y}$, $\sum_i x_i y_i$
$\boldsymbol{y} = A\boldsymbol{x}$	Linear system equation
$\boldsymbol{y} \in \mathbb{Y}$	Sample/observation and sample/observation space
A	Dictionary/codebook
$A_{i.}$	ith row of matrix A
$A_{.j}$	jth column of matrix A
A_{ij}	The ith row jth column element of matrix A
I_n	Identity matrix of size n
$E(\cdot)$	Expected value of a random variable
$N(\boldsymbol{\mu}, \Sigma)$	Gaussian with mean μ and covariance Σ
N	The number of feature vectors
D	The number of feature vector dimensions
$\lVert \mathbf{x} \rVert_{\ell_p}$	For a vector ℓ_p-norm or ℓ_p seminorm defined as $(\sum_i \lvert x_i \rvert^p)^{\frac{1}{p}}$
$\lVert \boldsymbol{x} \rVert_{\ell_0}$	ℓ_0-norm of a vector. Number of nonzero elements in $\boldsymbol{x}$
$(a)_+$	a if $a > 0$ and zero otherwise
$\mathrm{sgn}(\cdot)$	Sign of a number
K	K-sparse
C	The number of classes
c	The index of a class

λ	Lagrange multiplier
$(.)^T$	Matrix transpose
$(.)^\dagger$	The Moore-Penrose pseudoinverse
e, ε	Noise term and its $\ell_2 - norm$
$\mathbf{1}$	A vector with all the elements are 1 ($[1, 1, \cdots, 1]^T$)

Part I
Introduction and Fundamentals

Chapter 1
Introduction

1.1 Sparse Representation, Modeling, and Learning

1.1.1 Sparse Representation

Sparse representation consists of two basic tasks, data sparsification and encoding features. The first task is to make data more sparse directly. Moreover, data sparsification is to project original data into a potentially either same-dimensional or higher-dimensional latent space, which guarantees the minimum distance between before-projection and after-projection features [18]. The second task is to encode features with sparsity properties in some domain using either strictly or approximately K-sparsity. First of all, sometimes features are either sparse or compressible in nature. Sparse features mean that only K-coefficients have large magnitude and others are zero. K is much smaller than the dimension of coefficients vector. In other words, the coefficients vector has only K nonzero entries. Compressible features mean that the coefficient vectors in certain codewords are composed of a few large coefficients and other coefficients are of small value. Of course, the compressible features are not sparse ones. However,if we set small coefficients to zero, the remaining large coefficients can represent the original features with certain loss, called sparse quantization. For example,the gradient of a piecewise constant signal is sparse in the time domain. Natural signals or image are either sparse or compressible in the discrete cosine transform (DCT) domain. More generally, most signals/data are dense, such as image intensity, scene depth mapping, and action/gesture trajectories. However, even dense signals/features could be sparse in another domain. The relationship of sparsity between different domains follows the fundamental law of signal resolution for sparse signal representation, uncertainty principal (UP). This is similar to Heigenberg's UP in quantum mechanics, and a fundamental limit to the sparsity properties of data in different domains. Moreover, if signals/features are sparse but not strictly K-sparse, we can use K-sparse to approximate those signals/features, called sparse quantization. Sparse quantization is a basic way to code signals/features for

H. Cheng, *Sparse Representation, Modeling and Learning in Visual Recognition*,
Advances in Computer Vision and Pattern Recognition,
DOI 10.1007/978-1-4471-6714-3_1

efficient representation and modeling, such as for patch description [8] and visual recognition [9].

1.1.2 Sparse Modeling

Sparse Modeling is to model specific tasks (e.g., visual recognition tasks) by jointly using different disciplines and their sparsity properties. This is rooted in statistics, physics, information theory, neuroscience, optimization theory, algorithm and data structure, matrix theory, machine learning, and signal processing, shown in Fig. 1.1.

There are many applications of sparse modeling, such as regression [54, 66, 80], classification tasks [14, 78], graphical model selection [3, 50, 56], sparse M-estimators [52, 57], and sparse dimensionality reduction. Sparse modeling is a particularly important issue in many applications of machine learning and statistics where the main objective is to discover predictive patterns in data which would enhance our understanding of underlying physical, biological, and other natural processes, beyond just building accurate 'black-box' predictors. Common examples include biomarker selection in biological applications [80], finding brain areas predictive about 'brain states' based on fMRI data [12], and identifying network bottlenecks best explaining end-to-end performance [15]. Moreover, efficient recovery of high-dimensional sparse signals from a relatively small number of observations is the main focus of compressed sensing [11, 22, 41], and also is a rapidly growing and extremely popular area of signal processing.

More interestingly, sparse modeling is directly related to various computer vision tasks, such as image separation [6], image restoration and denoising [23], face recognition [73, 79], image superresolution [43, 76], recommendation systems [5], EEG analysis [19], text classification [6, 46], subspace methods [25], label propagation [17], and human activity recognition [16].

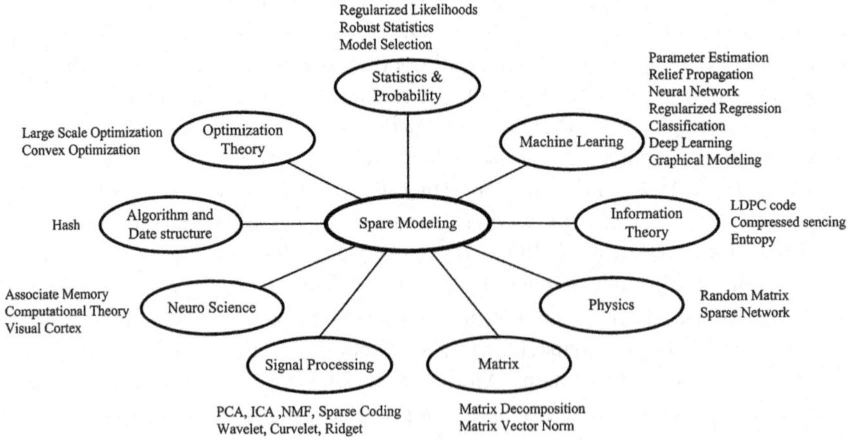

Fig. 1.1 The corresponding knowledge of sparse modeling

1.1.3 Sparse Learning

Sparse learning is to learn mappings from input signals/features to outputs by either representing the sparsity of signals/features or modeling the sparsity constraints as regularization items in optimization equations. Given a specific application, sparse learning is based on both sparse modeling and sparse representation. In general, sparse learning has two branches *supervised sparse learning* and *unsupervised sparse learning*. The most famous work in sparse unsupervised learning is the *sparse feature learning*, such as dictionary learning [40, 49, 68], feature learning and matrix factorization [21, 61, 70, 81]. By adding the sparse constraints in feature learning, it can extract the representative features. Another work in sparse unsupervised learning is *sparse subspace clustering* [24, 25], which uses the sparse representation to cluster the data and get extremely good results. The *supervised sparse learning* is to learn the parameters with the training data with labels which can be used for classification.

The most famous work in *supervised sparse learning* is the *sparse regression* [13, 30, 58], which is widely used in medical diagnosis. Another one is the *Sparse Bayesian Learning* [67, 71, 72] which was first proposed by M. E. Tipping et al. [67] used in relevance vector machine (RVM), which adds a sparse constraint prior distribution to the parameters to learn a sparse parameter vector. It can provide more accurate prediction model than support vector machine (SVM).

1.2 Visual Recognition

1.2.1 Feature Representation and Learning

1. Feature Categories

In visual recognition, there are various features extracted from pixel intensities. We will introduce some basic features of images/videos, such as edges, interesting points, saliency, and histogram of oriented gradient.

Edge

Edges are the discontinuity of intensity in some direction. Thus, we can detect edges by localizing the pixels with large derivative values. The large value means a sharp change in an image. More details, the discontinuities in image brightness are likely to correspond to discontinuities in depth and surface orientation, changes in material properties, and variations in scene illumination.

The edge pixels are at local maxima of gradient magnitude. The pixel gradient can be computed by convolving with Gaussian derivatives, and the gradient direction is always perpendicular to the edge direction, shown in Fig. 1.2. In the ideal case, an edge detector may result in a set of connected curves that indicate the boundaries of objects, surface markings, and surface orientation [4]. Thus, the

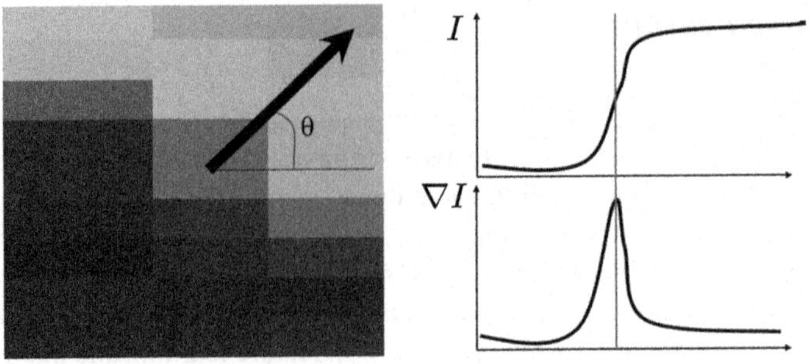

Fig. 1.2 The gradient direction (*left*) and the relation between edge and image

edge detection may significantly reduce the amount of pixel intensities and filter unimportant information, while only preserving the important structural properties of an image. This procedure is a kind of data sparsification.

The edge detection can be divided into two categories, *search-based* and *zero-crossing based*. The *search-based* approaches usually use a first-order derivative to compute the strength of the edge, and then search a local maximum direction of the gradient magnitude. The *zero-crossing based* approaches search for zero crossing in a second-order derivative to find edges, such as the zero-crossings of Laplacian or the zero-crossings of a nonlinear differential expression. Before edge detection, we need to smooth the image first, typically using Gaussian smoothing. J. Mairal et al. use sparse representation for class-specific edge detection problem [48]. In this approach, two dictionaries are trained for each specific class, one of which corresponds to the "Good edges" for this class, and the other corresponds to the "Bad edges" for this class. Figure 1.3 shows us that different directions of derivatives can generate different edges.

Interest Point

Interest points are the junctions of contours in images and can be characterized as follows [59]:

- It is clear and well-defined in concepts, scales, and image spaces;
- Its local image structure is rich;
- It is *stable* under local and global perturbations in the image domain as illumination/brightness variations, such that the interest points can be reliably computed with high degree of reproducibility;

Mathematically, we can localize the interesting points using local displacement sensitivity within a window. In detail, we define a shift change of intensity between a pixel and its neighboring pixels within this window. Furthermore, we have a bilinear approximation using first-order Talyor approximation. Thus, the Harris matrix in the bilinear approximation describes the distribution of intensity within the window, and thus can be used to detect interesting points. Furthermore, 2D interesting point detection can extend to 3D cases, a.k.a spatial temporal interesting points (STIPs) [45].

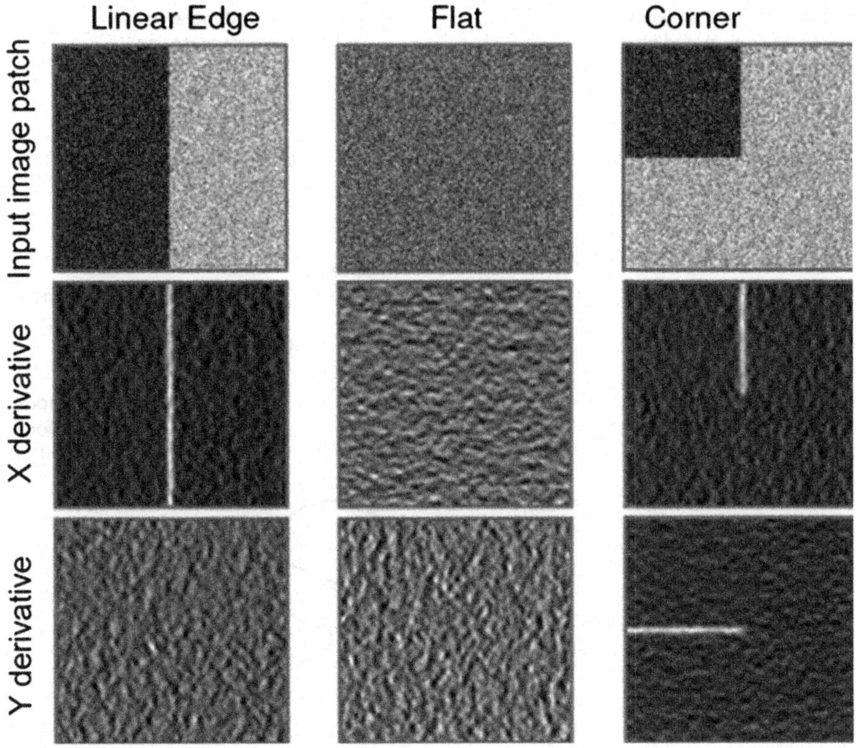

Fig. 1.3 The edges corresponding to different direction of derivatives

Visual Saliency

One of the most severe problems of perception for either humans or machines is information overload [32]. It is challenging especially for machines to process all the information from peripheral sensors all the time. The neural system of humans is good at making decisions on which part of the available information is to be selected for further, and which parts are to be discarded. This procedure, selection, and ordering process is called selective attention. Detecting and recognizing objects in unknown environments is an important yet challenging task, especially for machines. Visual saliency approaches guide the attention of people/machines to some positions in images/videos in a computational procedure. Typical features used in visual saliency are color, gradient, and contrast for distinguishing salient regions from the rest. Upon those features, we can generate various saliency mappings using visual saliency approaches. Moreover, saliency mappings root in feature integration theory (FIT) [69], and its framework are shown in Fig. 1.4.

The saliency map consists of two basic models, top-down and bottom-up. The visual saliency involves feature learning and saliency computation. The top-down visual saliency is driven by expectation and tasks while bottom-up visual saliency

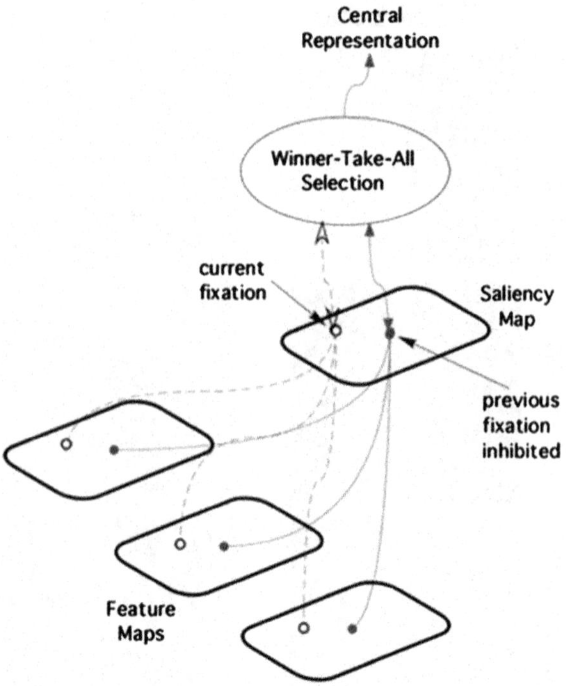

Fig. 1.4 The basic saliency map model as proposed by Koch and Ullman [44]

is determined by feature properties in the context. Moreover, according to the mathematical models of visual saliency, we can divide saliency algorithms into five kinds, i.e., local contrast models [39], information maximization models [10], graph-based models [33], low-rank matrix recovery models [62, 74], and spectral residual models [37]. As we may know, visual saliency is widely used in mobile robots [63], visual recognition [77], and text detection from images/videos [38, 42, 60].

Gradients

In mathematics, gradient is the derivative of a function in one dimension to a function in several dimensions, which means the change of function. It can model many physical phenomena in images/videos, such edges, interest points, and saliency since gradient encodes edges and local contrast very well. The rationale behind this is the human visual system is very sensitive to gradients. Thus, the image/video gradient is important in various computer vision tasks, such as human detection [20], local descriptors [47], and high-resolution [64]. Image/video gradients include two kinds of information, magnitude and orientation. The former denotes how quickly the images/vidoes are changing while the latter tells us the direction in which the images/videos is changing most rapidly.

The first important application of image gradients is human detection [20]. Histogram of Oriented Gradients (HOG) is the dense local feature for describing one image, and is widely used in object detection. The core idea of HOG is that the

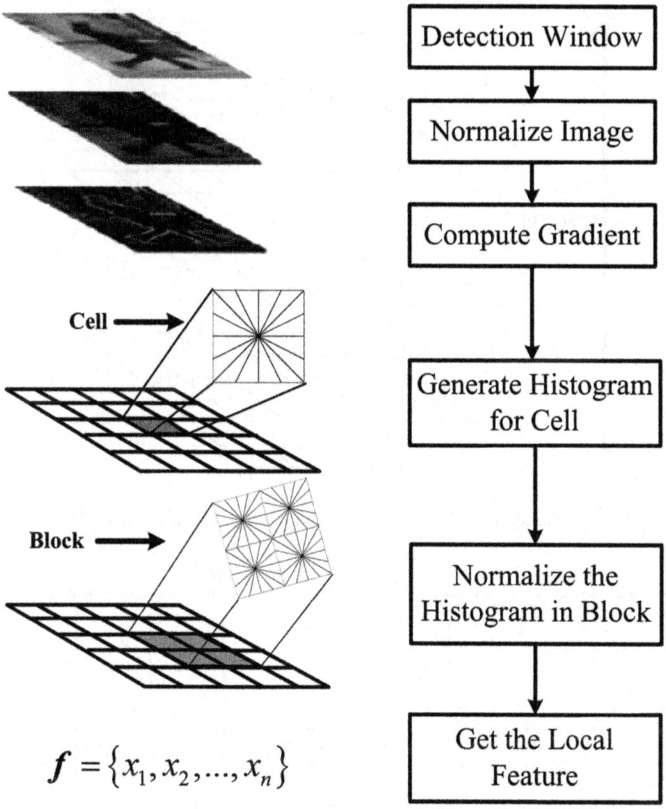

Fig. 1.5 The flowchart of how to get HOG feature

local appearance and shape of one patch can be represented using the distribution of gradient. The merit of HOG is that it has good invariable property for changes in illumination and geometry. The flowchart of how to get the HOG feature is illustrated in Fig. 1.5.

One more application of HOG is scale invariant feature transform (SIFT) in image matching and classification. It is similar to HOG feature. Compared to HOG, the SIFT is not the dense local feature in one image. They are obtained by searching the extreme point in scale spaces as shown in Fig. 1.6. Moreover, Fig. 1.7 shows the procedure of generating the signature of SIFT.

2. *Feature Learning*

Feature learning is a set of techniques in machine learning that learn a transformation of "raw" inputs to a representation that can be effectively exploited in either supervised or unsupervised learning tasks. The main goal of feature learning is to learn good representations from data by eliminating irrelevant features while preserving the useful features for object detection, recognition, classification, or

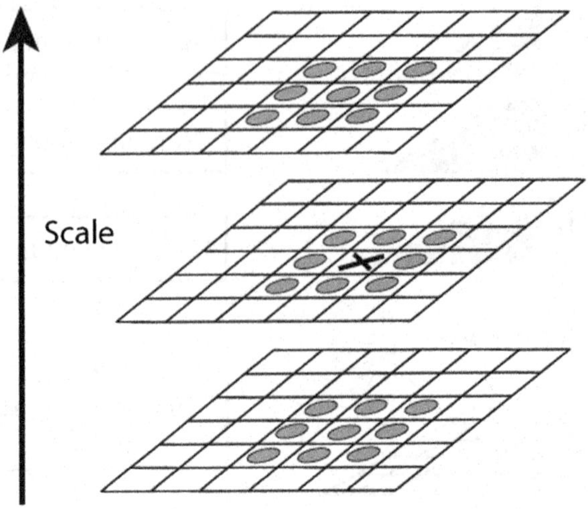

Fig. 1.6 The SIFT is obtained by searching the extreme point in scale space [47]

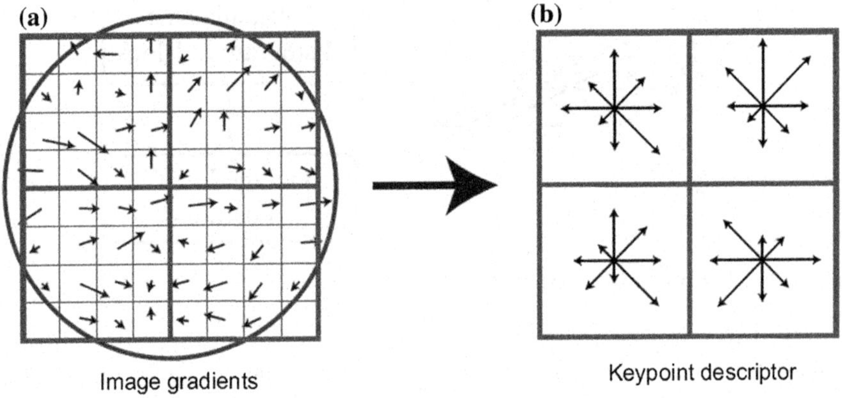

Fig. 1.7 The procedure of calculating the signature of SIFT gives an interesting point: **a** The magnitude and orientation of image gradients; **b** The SIFT descriptor [47]

prediction. Roughly, feature learning can be divided into two categories, unsupervised and supervised. Typical unsupervised learning consists of PCA/SPCA/RSPCA, K-means, mean shift, KSVD, and expectation maximization (EM), and supervised learning consists of neural networks, support vector machines (SVMs), restricted Boltzmann machines (RBM), and linear discriminant analysis. Among these algorithms, sparse feature learning is more and more popular in the computer vision and machine learning committee, such as sparse SVM, recursive feature elimination. Moreover, deep learning (a.k.a deep representation learning) is widely used in visual recognition, such as face recognition and image classification.

1.2.2 Distance Metric Learning

Distance Metric Learning is to learn a distance metric for input feature spaces in either supervised or unsupervised way. Learning a good distance metric in feature space is critical for various computer vision tasks, such as image classification and content-based image retrieval. For example, the retrieval quality of content-based image retrieval (CBIR) systems is known to be highly dependent on the criterion that is used to define similarity between images. Also, it has motivated significant advancement in learning good distance metrics from training data. Moreover, in the K-nearest-neighbor (KNN) classifier, one of the key issues is to select a good distance measure for the specific task. The previous work [34–36, 51] has shown that good distance metric learning can improve the performance of KNN classifier, which is better than the standard Euclidean distance.

Much effort has been made on distance metric learning over the past few years. We can divide distance metric learning into two categories depending on the availability of the training examples: *supervised distance metric learning* and *unsupervised distance metric learning*. In supervised learning, training samples are cast into pairwise constraints: the equivalence constraints where sample pairs belong to the same classes, and inequivalence constraints where pairs of samples belong to different classes. The supervised distance metric learning uses two different strategies, the *global learning*, and the *local learning*. The first strategy learns the metric in a global sense, i.e., to satisfy the constraints of all the training samples pairwise simultaneously. The second strategy is to learn the distance metric in a local setting, i.e., only to satisfy the local pairwise constraints. The main idea for unsupervised distance metric learning is to learn an underlying low-dimensional manifold where geometric relationships between most of the observed data are preserved. The *sparse induced similarity* is an unsupervised distance metric learning method [17], which uses sparse representation as a distance metric.

1.2.3 Classification

1. The Nearest Neighbor Classifier

The *Nearest Neighbor Classifier* (NNC) is a nonparametric approach and also the oldest yet best one, especially for large-scale visual recognition. Nearest neighbor rule is a suboptimal procedure. Its use will usually lead to an error rate greater than the minimum possible, the Bayes error rate [53], shown in Fig. 1.8. We can see that $P^* \leq P \leq P^*(2 - \frac{c}{c-1}P^*)$, where P^* is the Bayesian probability of error rate, P is the nearest error rate. The critical issues are to choose the proper distance measure and efficient NN searching.There are many alternative distance measures to use in NNCs, such as Euclidean distance, Gaussian kernel similarity, sparsity-induced similarity [17], and distance metric learning. Moreover, for large scale NN

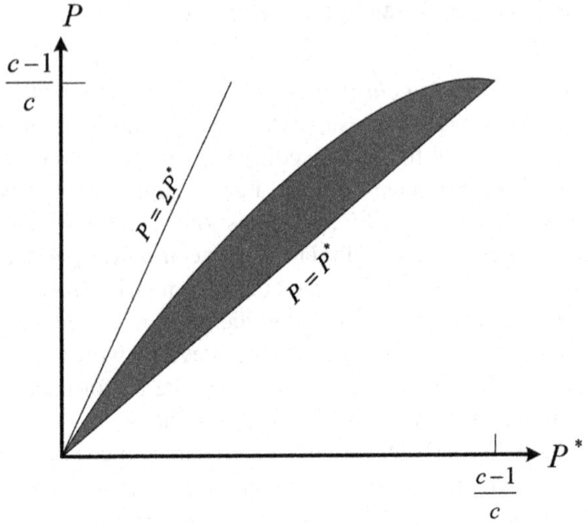

Fig. 1.8 The nearest neighbor error rate. P^* is the Bayesian probability of error rate, P is the nearest neighbor error rate

searching, we can use approximate nearest neighbors [1] to speed up the searching procedures.

2. The Bag of Feature Approach

In computer vision, the bag-of-features (BoF) approaches are widely used in image classification, by treating local image features as visual words [27]. In principal, a BoF is a vector of occurrence counts of a vocabulary of local image features.

There are three steps in the BoF model: (1) Feature detection; (2) Feature description; (3) Codebook generation. A definition of the BoF model can be the histogram representation based on independent features [27]. This image representation method is first used in content-based image indexing and retrieval (CBIR) [55]. Feature representation methods deal with how to represent the patches as numerical vectors. These vectors are called as the local descriptors. A good descriptor should be insensitive with intensity, rotation, scale, and affine variations. One of the most famous descriptor is scale-invariant feature transform (SIFT) in image classification [55]. The SIFT converts each patch to be a 128-dimensional vector. After this step, the image is represented as a collection of vectors of the same dimension. If we want to represent the image in BoF model, we need to generate the "codebook" which is used to quantize each local descriptor to be one word of the codebook. One simple method is using K-means clustering over all the vectors to generate the codebook. The number of the clusters is the codebook size. Thus, each patch in an image is mapped to a certain codeword by computing the similarity with each word in codebook and the image can be represented by the histogram of the codewords. The BoF model is illustrated visually in Fig. 1.9.

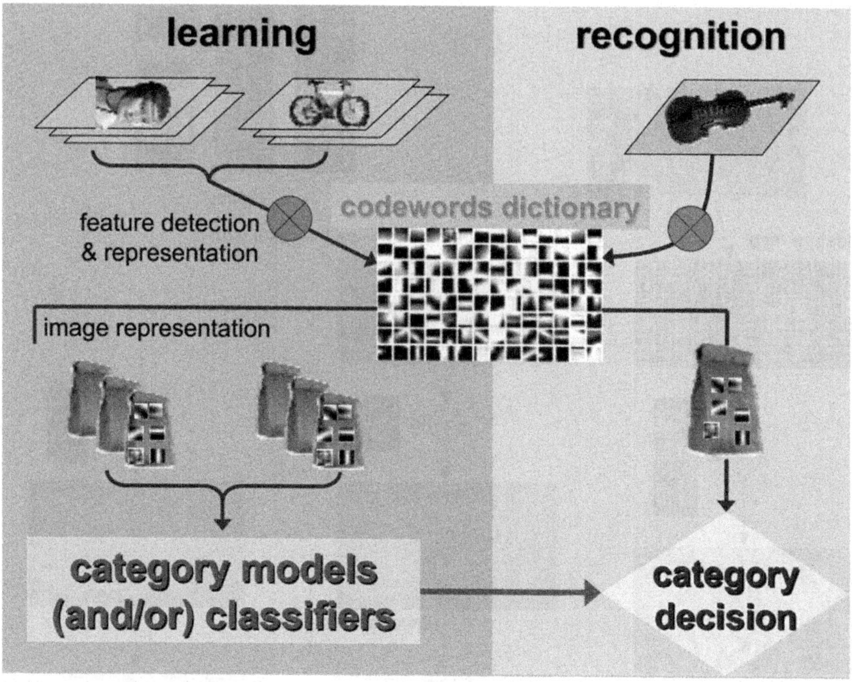

Fig. 1.9 The BoF model [27]

3. Deformable Parts Model

Traditional object recognition approaches, such as SVM, NN, BOF, face a big challenge in detecting and recognizing generic objects from nonrigid categories. The reason behind this is that those approaches do not model highly variable objects explictly. Toward this end, deformable part models (DPMs) provide a framework of multiscale deformable parts [28]. In details, star models are used in modeling object parts, and consist of a root filter and a set of part filters. For seeking the optimal star model, we evaluate the score of each star models at a particular position and scale within an image. Moreover, we can calculate the scores of both root and part filter by the dot product between a filter and a subwindow of a feature pyramid from the input image. The flowchart of DPM is illustrated in Fig. 1.10.

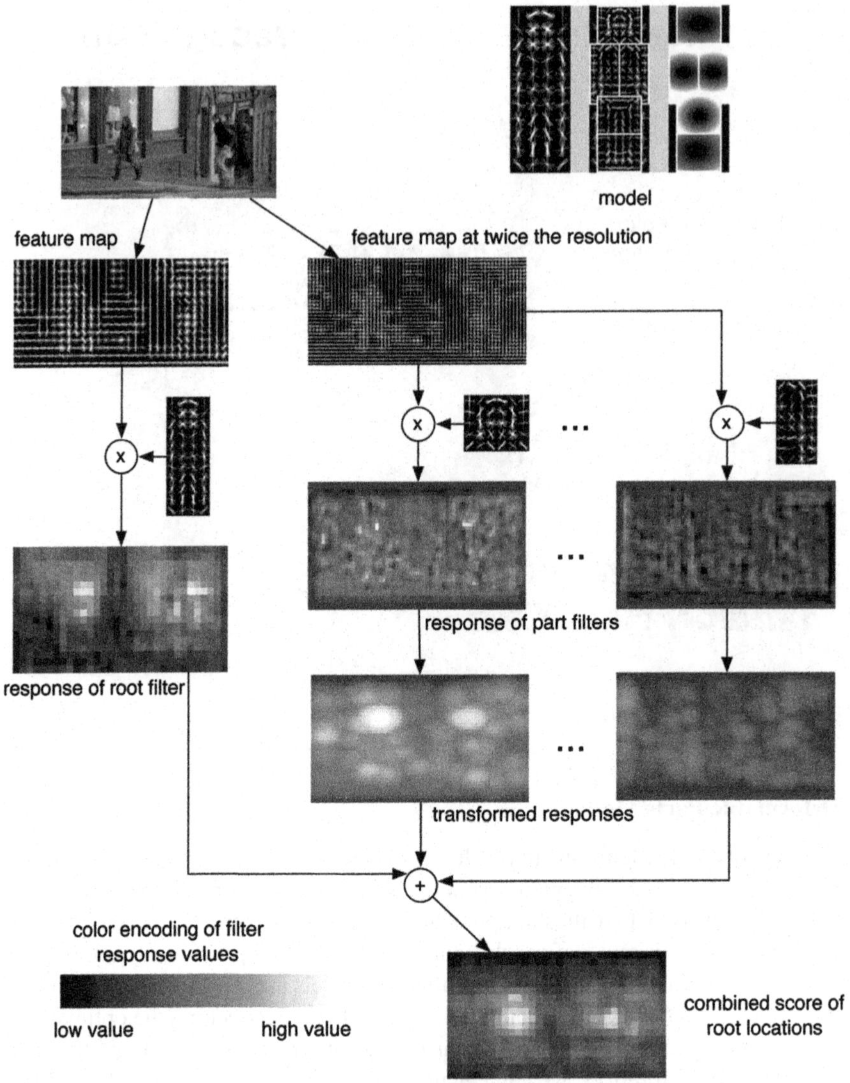

Fig. 1.10 The matching process at one scale. Responses from the root and part filters are computed at different resolutions in the feature pyramid. The transformed responses are combined to yield a final score for each root location. We show the responses and transformed responses for the "head" and "right shoulder" parts. Note how the "head" filter is more discriminative. The combined scores clearly show two good hypothesis for the object at this scale [28]

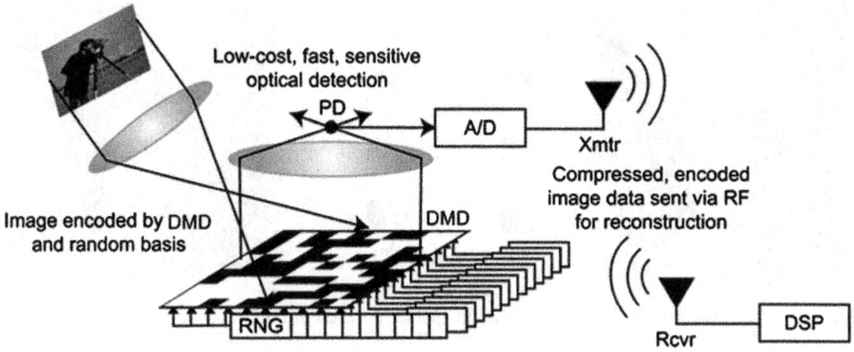

Fig. 1.11 The structure of single-pixel camera

1.3 Other Applications

1.3.1 Single-Pixel Cameras

Rice University used the Compressed Sensing method to create a single-pixel camera. This camera directly acquires random projections of a scene without first collecting the pixels. The structure of the single pixel camera is illustrated in Fig. 1.11.

1.3.2 Superresolution

Superresolution (SR) is a technique that can enhance the resolution of an image. It can overcome some of the inherent resolution limitations of the imaging sensor and allow better utilization of growing capability of high-resolution displays. The task of SR is to recover the original high-resolution image by fusing the low-resolution images, based on reasonable assumptions or prior knowledge about the observation model that maps the high-resolution image to low-resolution one [76], shown in Fig. 1.12. The constraint of SR problem is that the reconstructed image should be able to reproduce the low-resolution image (original image) after applying the same model. Because we do not know blurring operators, the insufficient number of low resolution images, and the resolution from the reconstruction constraint is not unique; the SR image reconstruction is generally a severely ill-posed problem. There are various regularization methods to constraint the ill-posed problem, such as [7, 26, 31]. The performance of reconstruction-based SR may greatly degrade when the desired magnification factor is large or the number of available input images is small. In these cases the reconstruction image may be too smooth and lacks important high-frequency details [2].

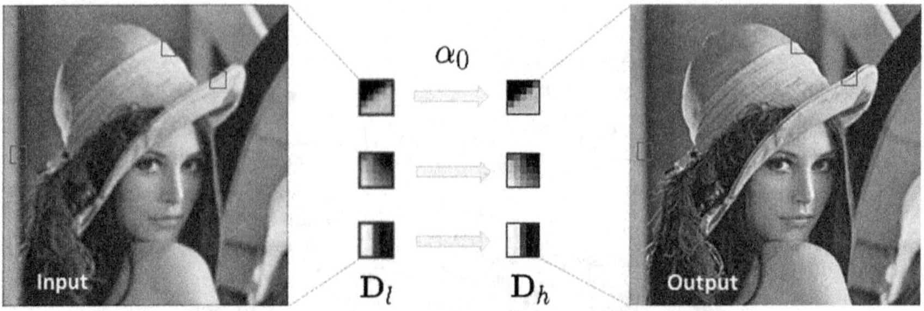

Fig. 1.12 The flowchart of superresolution via sparse representation [76]

Another branch of the SR method is based on machine learning techniques, which attempts to capture the correlation between low-resolution and high-resolution image patches. W. T. Freeman et al. [29] proposed an example-based learning method that applies to generic images where the correlation between low-resolution and high-resolution is learned by Markov Random Field (MRF) solved by belief propagation. J. Sun et al. [65] extend this approach using the primal sketch priors to enhance blurred edges, ridges and corners. H. Chang et al. use locally linear embedding (LLE) from manifold learning, assuming similarity between the two manifolds in the high-resolution and the low-resolution patch space. Using this method, more patch patterns can be represented by a smaller training database. However, it often results in blurring effects, due to over or under-fitting. In order to overcome this problem, J. Yang et al. [75] proposed an adaptive choosing neighbors method based on sparse representation and producing superior results. However, it is too time-consuming to sparse coding over large patch dictionary. The core idea of the SR based on sparse coding is using the low-resolution and high-resolution pairs to jointly train the low-resolution dictionary D_l and high-resolution dictionary D_h. The low-resolution image patch $\boldsymbol{y}$ can be sparse represented under the dictionary D_l to get the sparse representation $\boldsymbol{\alpha}$, and we can use this sparse representation $\boldsymbol{\alpha}$ to reconstruct the high-resolution image patch under the high-resolution dictionary D_h.

References

1. Arya, S., Mount, D.M., Netanyahu, N.S., Silverman, R., Wu, A.Y.: An optimal algorithm for approximate nearest neighbor searching fixed dimensions. J. ACM **45**(6), 891–923 (1998)
2. Baker, S., Kanade, T.: Limits on super-resolution and how to break them. IEEE Trans. Pattern Anal. Mach. Intell. **24**(9), 1167–1183 (2002)
3. Bani Asadi, N., Rish, I., Scheinberg, K., Kanevsky, D., Ramabhadran, B.: Map approach to learning sparse Gaussian Markov networks. In: IEEE International Conference on Acoustics, Speech and Signal Processing (2009)
4. Barrow, H.G., Tenenbaum, J.M.: Interpreting line drawings as three-dimensional surfaces. Artif. Intell. **17**(1), 75–116 (1981)

5. Bell, R.M., Koren, Y.: Lessons from the netflix prize challenge. ACM SIGKDD Explor. Newsl. **9**(2), 75–79 (2007)
6. Berry, M.W., Browne, M., Langville, A.N., Pauca, V.P., Plemmons, R.J.: Algorithms and applications for approximate nonnegative matrix factorization. Comput. Stat. Data Anal. **52**(1), 155–173 (2007)
7. Bishop, C.M., Tipping, M.E.: Bayesian image super resolution. US Patent 7,106,914 (2006)
8. Boix, X., Gygli, M., Roig, G., Van Gool, L.: Sparse quantization for patch description. In: IEEE CVPR (2013)
9. Boix, X., Roig, G., Leistner, C., Van Gool, L.: Nested sparse quantization for efficient feature coding. In: ECCV. Springer (2012)
10. Bruce, N., Tsotsos, J.: Saliency based on information maximization. In: Advances in Neural Information Processing Systems (2005)
11. Candès, E.J.: Compressive sampling. In: Proceedings of the International Congress of Mathematicians (2006)
12. Carroll, M.K., Cecchi, G.A., Rish, I., Garg, R., Rao, A.R.: Prediction and interpretation of distributed neural activity with sparse models. NeuroImage **44**(1), 112–122 (2009)
13. Cawley, G.C., Talbot, N.L.: Gene selection in cancer classification using sparse logistic regression with bayesian regularization. Bioinformatics **22**(19), 2348–2355 (2006)
14. Chan, A.B., Vasconcelos, N., Lanckriet, G.R.: Direct convex relaxations of sparse SVM. In: ICML (2007)
15. Chandalia, G., Rish, I.: Blind source separation approach to performance diagnosis and dependency discovery. In: ACM SIGCOMM Conference on Internet Measurement (2007)
16. Cheng, H., Liu, Z., Hou, L., Yang, J.: Sparsity induced similarity measure and its applications. IEEE Trans. Circuits Syst. Video Technol. (2012)
17. Cheng, H., Liu, Z., Yang, L.: Sparsity induced similarity measure for label propagation. In: IEEE ICCV (2009)
18. Cho, K.: Simple sparsification improves sparse denoising autoencoders in denoising highly noisy images. In: ICML (2013)
19. Cong, F., Phan, A.H., Zhao, Q., Huttunen-Scott, T., Kaartinen, J., Ristaniemi, T., Lyytinen, H., Cichocki, A.: Benefits of multi-domain feature of mismatch negativity extracted by non-negative tensor factorization from EEG collected by low-density array. Int. J. Neural Syst. **22**(06), 1–19 (2012)
20. Dalal, N., Triggs, B.: Histograms of oriented gradients for human detection. In: IEEE CVPR (2005)
21. d'Aspremont, A., Bach, F., Ghaoui, L.E.: Optimal solutions for sparse principal component analysis. J. Mach. Learn. Res. **9**, 1269–1294 (2008)
22. Donoho, D.L.: Compressed sensing. IEEE Trans. Inf. Theory **52**(4), 1289–1306 (2006)
23. Elad, M., Aharon, M.: Image denoising via sparse and redundant representations over learned dictionaries. IEEE Trans. Image Process. **15**(12), 3736–3745 (2006)
24. Elhamifar, E., Vidal, R.: Sparse subspace clustering. In: IEEE CVPR (2009)
25. Elhamifar, E., Vidal, R.: Sparse subspace clustering: Algorithm, theory, and applications. IEEE Trans. Pattern Anal. Mach. Intell. **35**(11), 2765–2781 (2013)
26. Farsiu, S., Robinson, M.D., Elad, M., Milanfar, P.: Fast and robust multiframe super resolution. IEEE Trans. Image Process. **13**(10), 1327–1344 (2004)
27. Fei-Fei, L., Fergus, R., Torralba, A.: Recognizing and learning object categories. CVPR Short Course **106**(1), 59–70 (2007)
28. Felzenszwalb, P., McAllester, D., Ramanan, D.: A discriminatively trained, multiscale, deformable part model. In: IEEE CVPR (2008)
29. Freeman, W.T., Pasztor, E.C., Carmichael, O.T.: Learning low-level vision. Int. J. Comput. Vis. **40**(1), 25–47 (2000)
30. Friedman, J.H.: Fast sparse regression and classification. Int. J. Forecast. **28**(3), 722–738 (2012)
31. Hardie, R.C., Barnard, K.J., Armstrong, E.E.: Joint map registration and high-resolution image estimation using a sequence of undersampled images. IEEE Trans. Image Process. **6**(12), 1621–1633 (1997)

32. Harel, J., Koch, C., Perona, P.: Saliency map tutorial (2012)
33. Harel, J., Koch, C., Perona, P.: Graph-based visual saliency. In: Advances in Neural Information Processing Systems (2006)
34. He, J., Li, M., Zhang, H.J., Tong, H., Zhang, C.: Manifold-ranking based image retrieval. In: ACM International Conference on Multimedia (2004)
35. He, X., King, O., Ma, W.Y., Li, M., Zhang, H.J.: Learning a semantic space from user's relevance feedback for image retrieval. IEEE Trans. Circuits Syst. Video Technol. **13**(1), 39–48 (2003)
36. He, X., Ma, W.Y., Zhang, H.J.: Learning an image manifold for retrieval. In: ACM International Conference on Multimedia (2004)
37. Hou, X., Zhang, L.: Saliency detection: a spectral residual approach. In: IEEE CVPR (2007)
38. Imamoglu Konuskan, F.: Visual saliency and biological inspired text detection. Ph.D. thesis, Technical University Munich & California Institute of Technology (2008)
39. Itti, L., Koch, C., Niebur, E.: A model of saliency-based visual attention for rapid scene analysis. IEEE Trans. Pattern Anal. Mach. Intell. **20**(11), 1254–1259 (1998)
40. Jenatton, R., Mairal, J., Bach, F.R., Obozinski, G.R.: Proximal methods for sparse hierarchical dictionary learning. In: ICML (2010)
41. Ji, S., Carin, L.: Bayesian compressive sensing and projection optimization. In: International Conference on Machine Learning (2007)
42. Karaoglu, S., Van Gemert, J.C., Gevers, T.: Object reading: text recognition for object recognition. In: ECCV. Springer (2012)
43. Kato, T., Hino, H., Murata, N.: Sparse coding approach for multi-frame image super resolution (2014) arXiv preprint
44. Koch, C., Ullman, S.: Shifts in selective visual attention: towards the underlying neural circuitry. In: Matters of Intelligence (1987)
45. Laptev, I.: On space-time interest points. Int. J. Comput. Vis. **64**(2–3), 107–123 (2005)
46. Liu, Y., Jin, R., Yang, L.: Semi-supervised multi-label learning by constrained non-negative matrix factorization. In: Proceedings of the National Conference on Artificial Intelligence, vol. 21, p. 421 (2006)
47. Lowe, D.G.: Distinctive image features from scale-invariant keypoints. Int. J. Comput. Vis. **60**(2), 91–110 (2004)
48. Mairal, J., Leordeanu, M., Bach, F., Hebert, M., Ponce, J.: Discriminative sparse image models for class-specific edge detection and image interpretation. In: ECCV. Springer (2008)
49. Mairal, J., Sapiro, G., Elad, M.: Multiscale sparse image representationwith learned dictionaries. In: IEEE ICIP (2007)
50. Meinshausen, N., Bühlmann, P.: High-dimensional graphs and variable selection with the Lasso. Ann. Stat. **34**, 1436–1462 (2006)
51. Müller, H., Pun, T., Squire, D.: Learning from user behavior in image retrieval: application of market basket analysis. Int. J. Comput. Vis. **56**(1–2), 65–77 (2004)
52. Negahban, S., Yu, B., Wainwright, M.J., Ravikumar, P.K.: A unified framework for high-dimensional analysis of m-estimators with decomposable regularizers. In: Advances in Neural Information Processing Systems (2009)
53. Och, F.J.: Minimum error rate training in statistical machine translation. In: Proceedings of the 41st Annual Meeting on Association for Computational Linguistics (2003)
54. Park, M.Y., Hastie, T.: L1-regularization path algorithm for generalized linear models. J. R. Stat. Soc. **69**(4), 659–677 (2007)
55. Qiu, G.: Indexing chromatic and achromatic patterns for content-based colour image retrieval. Pattern Recognit. **35**(8), 1675–1686 (2002)
56. Ravikumar, P., Wainwright, M.J., Lafferty, J.D., et al.: High-dimensional ising model selection using $\ell 1$-regularized logistic regression. Ann. Stat. **38**(3), 1287–1319 (2010)
57. Rish, I., Grabarnik, G.: Sparse signal recovery with exponential-family noise. In: Compressed Sensing and Sparse Filtering (2014)
58. Ryali, S., Supekar, K., Abrams, D.A., Menon, V.: Sparse logistic regression for whole-brain classification of fMRI data. NeuroImage **51**(2), 752–764 (2010)

59. Schmid, C., Mohr, R., Bauckhage, C.: Evaluation of interest point detectors. Int. J. Comput. Vis. **37**(2), 151–172 (2000)
60. Shahab, A., Shafait, F., Dengel, A., Uchida, S.: How salient is scene text? In: IAPR International Workshop on Document Analysis Systems (2012)
61. Shen, H., Huang, J.Z.: Sparse principal component analysis via regularized low rank matrix approximation. J. Multivar. Anal. **99**(6), 1015–1034 (2008)
62. Shen, X., Wu, Y.: A unified approach to salient object detection via low rank matrix recovery. In: IEEE CVPR (2012)
63. Siagian, C., Itti, L.: Biologically inspired mobile robot vision localization. IEEE Trans. Robot. **25**(4), 861–873 (2009)
64. Sun, J., Xu, Z., Shum, H.Y.: Gradient profile prior and its applications in image super-resolution and enhancement. IEEE Trans. Image Process. **20**(6), 1529–1542 (2011)
65. Sun, J., Zheng, N.N., Tao, H., Shum, H.Y.: Image hallucination with primal sketch priors. In: IEEE CVPR (2003)
66. Tibshirani, R.: Regression shrinkage and selection via the lasso. J. R. Stat. Soc. **58**, 267–288 (1996)
67. Tipping, M.E.: Sparse bayesian learning and the relevance vector machine. J. Mach. Learn. Res. **1**, 211–244 (2001)
68. Tosic, I., Frossard, P.: Dictionary learning. IEEE Signal Process. Mag. **28**(2), 27–38 (2011)
69. Treisman, A.M., Gelade, G.: A feature-integration theory of attention. Cogn. Psychol. **12**(1), 97–136 (1980)
70. Wang, L., Cheng, H., Liu, Z., Zhu, C.: A robust elastic net approach for feature learning. J. Vis. Commun. Image Represent. **25**(2), 313–321 (2014)
71. Williams, O., Blake, A., Cipolla, R.: Sparse bayesian learning for efficient visual tracking. IEEE Trans. Pattern Anal. Mach. Intell. **27**(8), 1292–1304 (2005)
72. Wipf, D.P., Rao, B.D.: Sparse bayesian learning for basis selection. IEEE Trans. Signal Process. **52**(8), 2153–2164 (2004)
73. Wright, J., Yang, A.Y., Ganesh, A., Sastry, S.S., Ma, Y.: Robust face recognition via sparse representation. IEEE Trans. Pattern Anal. Mach. Intell. **31**(2), 210–227 (2009)
74. Yan, J., Zhu, M., Liu, H., Liu, Y.: Visual saliency detection via sparsity pursuit. IEEE Signal Process. Lett. **17**(8), 739–742 (2010)
75. Yang, J., Wright, J., Huang, T., Ma, Y.: Image super-resolution as sparse representation of raw image patches. In: IEEE CVPR (2008)
76. Yang, J., Wright, J., Huang, T.S., Ma, Y.: Image super-resolution via sparse representation. IEEE Trans. Image Process. **19**(11), 2861–2873 (2010)
77. Yang, L., Zheng, N., Yang, J., Chen, M., Chen, H.: A biased sampling strategy for object categorization. In: IEEE ICCV (2009)
78. Zhu, J., Rosset, S., Hastie, T., Tibshirani, R.: ℓ_1-norm support vector machines. Adv. Neural Inf. Process. Syst. **16**(1), 49–56 (2004)
79. Zhuang, L., Chan, T.H., Yang, A.Y., Sastry, S.S., Ma, Y.: Sparse illumination learning and transfer for single-sample face recognition with image corruption and misalignment (2014) arXiv preprint
80. Zou, H., Hastie, T.: Regularization and variable selection via the elastic net. J. R. Stat. Soc. **67**(2), 301–320 (2005)
81. Zou, H., Hastie, T., Tibshirani, R.: Sparse principal component analysis. J. Comput. Graph. Stat. **15**(2), 265–286 (2006)

Chapter 2
The Fundamentals of Compressed Sensing

2.1 Sampling Theorems

Definition 2.1.1 Sampling is a fundamental way to represent and recover the continuous signals (analog domain) in the field of signal processing.

The Sampling theorem connects continuous signals and discrete signals. Figure.2.1 shows the procedure of the ideal sampling.

Theorem 2.1.1 (Nyquist Sampling Theorem [28]) *If a signal $x_a(t)$ is confined to be $[0, w_{max}]$ cycles per second, the signal can be reconstructed without loss by sampling it at more than $2w_{max}$ cycles per second as*

$$x_a(t) = \sum_{\infty}^{\infty} x(n) \frac{\sin \pi(2w_{max}t - n)}{\pi(2w_{max}t - n)} \tag{2.1}$$

where $x(n) = x_a(\frac{n}{2w_{max}})$.

For example, if one has a signal which is perfectly band limited to a band of f_0 within a time interval of T seconds, then one can reconstruct all the information in the signal by sampling it at discrete time as long as their sample rate, namely Nyquist rate, is greater than two times their bandwidth signal ($2f_0$), known as Nyquist frequency. In case the bandlimit is too high or there is no bandlimit at all, the reproducing will derive imperfect result, named aliasing. Anyway, one can make an assumption that the signal has bandwidth B cps (cycle per second) with tiny values outside the interval T.

H. Cheng, *Sparse Representation, Modeling and Learning in Visual Recognition*,
Advances in Computer Vision and Pattern Recognition,
DOI 10.1007/978-1-4471-6714-3_2

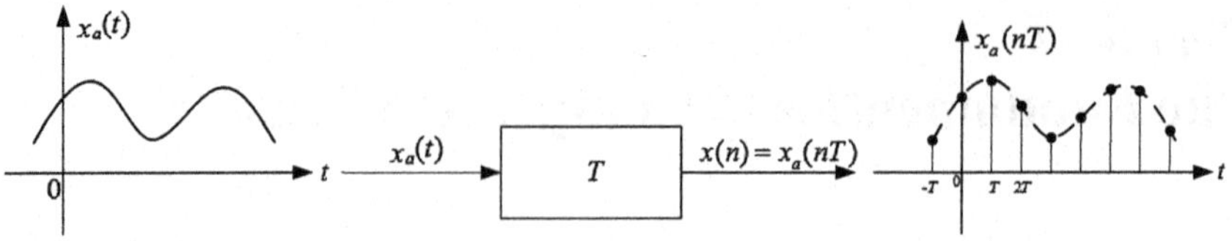

Fig. 2.1 The procedure of ideal sampling

Definition 2.1.2 (*Compressive Sampling*) If a signal $x_a(t)$ is compressible (i.e., K-sparse), we can have

$$x = \sum_{i=1}^{N} S_i \psi_i = \psi S \tag{2.2}$$

Thus, we can have compressive measurements via linear random procedure

$$y = Ax = A\psi S = \Theta S \tag{2.3}$$

where A or Θ is an $X \times N$ measurement matrix, a good measurement matrix can preserve the information in x, and one can recover x using various sparse recovery approaches in Chap. 3.

Compressive Sampling is to use linear random projection techniques to efficiently acquiring and reconstructing a compressible signal.

In general, the Nyquist-Shannon Sampling theorem only assumes the signal is band limited, and one can recover it without loss by sampling at $2w_{max}$. While compressive sampling depends on sparsity prior of the signal. Thus, Nyquist-Shannon sampling theorem ignores the sparsity prior. As a result, one has to increase Nyquist rate to guarantee the completion of the signals. This could be extremely worse in imaging systems (Fig. 2.2).

Fig. 2.2 Dimensionality reduction from 2D circles to 1D [28]

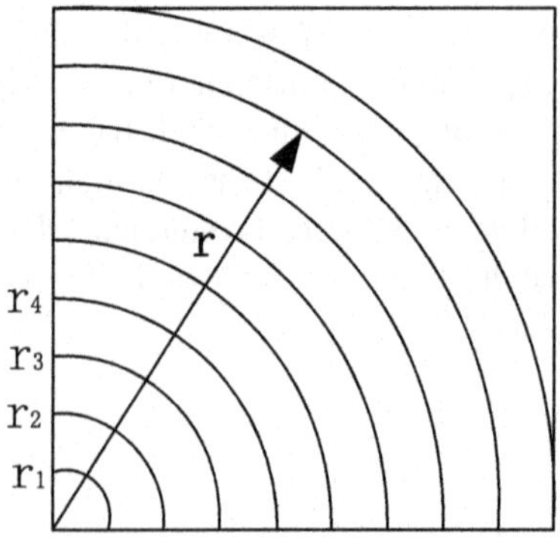

2.2 Compressive Sampling

As mentioned in previous section that Nyquist-Shannon sampling theorem is one of the tenet in signal precessing and information theory. It is worthwhile to restate the theorem here that: in order to perfectly reconstruct a signal, the number of samples needed is dictated by its bandwidth, i.e., the length of the shortest interval which contains the support, the spectrum of the signal. However, in the last few years, the "Compressive Sampling" has been the alternative theory and has emerged in the field of signal processing as well as information theory. The theory, basically, follows the concept of neural network in human brain which perceives information from outside world sparsely. With a small number of representation of the signal, human can most perfectly reconstruct the signal. Compressive sampling, similarly, shows that super-resolved signals and images can be reconstructed from far fewer data or measurements than what is usually considered important.

Compressive sampling has drawn much attention from research community in different fields ranging from statistics, information theory, coding theory, to theoretical computer science. We are going to summarize a few examples of compressive sampling in the real applications. JPEG2000 exploits the fact that many signals have a sparse representation, meaning that one can reconstruct, store, or transmit only a small numbers of adaptively chosen transform coefficients rather than all the signals samples. Another example can be illustrated in a digital camera. Instead of storing millions of imaging sensors, the pixels, it encodes the picture on just a few hundred kilobytes. In radiology, and biomedical imaging one is typically able to obtain far fewer data about an image of interest than the number of unknown pixels. Moreover, in wideband radio frequency signal analysis, a signal to be obtained at a rate which is much lower than the Nyquist rate because current Analog-to-Digital converter is limited. It is very obvious that typical signals have some structure; therefore, they can be compressed efficiently without much perceptual loss.

Mathematically, compressive sampling can be formulated as undersampled measurement problem as follows. Given a signal y_k, we aim to reconstruct a vector $x \in \mathbb{R}^N$ from linear measurements y as

$$y_k = \langle x, \varphi_k \rangle, \quad k = 1, \ldots, K, \quad or \quad y = \Phi x. \tag{2.4}$$

We are now trying to acquire information about the unknown signal by sensing x against K vectors $\varphi_k \in \mathbb{R}^N$. We are interested in the case that $K \ll N$ (underdetermined), where we have more unknown signal values than measurements. At first glance, the problem seems impossible. Sparse recovery techniques, discussed later in Chap. 3, will make the problem feasible.

2.2.1 Random Projection and Measurement Matrix

Johnson-Lindenstrauss lemma [23] has been a classic result of concerning low-distortion embeddings of points from high-dimensional into low-dimensional Euclidean space. The lemma is widely used in compressive sensing, manifold learning, dimensionality reduction, and graph embedding. Suppose we have n points $u_1, \ldots, u_n \in \mathbb{R}^d$, where d is large. We are going to map φ that $\mathbb{R}^d \longrightarrow \mathbb{R}^k$, where $k \ll d$, such that for each $i, j, 1 \le i < j \le n$, we have $(1-\varepsilon)||u_i - u_j||^2 \le ||\varphi(u_i) - \varphi(u_j)||^2 \le (1+\varepsilon)||u_i - u_j||^2$. The Johnson-Lindenstrauss lemma gives a randomized procedure to construct such a mapping with $k = O(\varepsilon^{-2} \log n)$. The embedding is a linear projection into a random k-dimensional subspace.

1. Random Projection

Random Projection is to use a random matrix $A \in \mathbb{R}^{n\times m}$ whose rows have unit length to project data from the high-dimensional data space $\boldsymbol{x} \in \mathbb{R}^m$ to a low-dimensional data space $\boldsymbol{v} \in \mathbb{R}^n$

$$\boldsymbol{v} = A\boldsymbol{x}, \tag{2.5}$$

where $n \ll m$. Ideally, we expect that A will provide a stable embedding that can preserve the distance between all pairs of original data in high-dimensional space to the embedded data points in the low-dimensional space. Luckily, the Johnson-Lindenstrauss lemma asserts that with high probability the distance between the points in a vector space is approximately preserved if they are projected onto a randomly selected subspace with suitably high dimension. Refer to [1] for details.

Baraniuk et al. [2] even proved that the random matrix A satisfying the the Johnson-Lindenstrauss lemma will also satisfy the restricted isometry property in compressive sensing. Thus, if the random matrix A in Eq. (2.5) satisfies the Johnson-Lindenstrauss lemma, we can recover x with minimum error from v with high probability if x is compressive such as audio or image. In other words, we can guarantee that v preserves most of the information which x possesses.

2. Random Sparse Measurement Matrix

Traditionally, we always use the random Gaussian matrix $A \in \mathbb{R}^{n\times m}$, where $a_{ij} \sim N(0,1)$ as the measurement matrix which satisfy the RIP condition. However, the matrix of this type is dense; so the memory and computational loads are still large when m is large. Zhang et al. [33] proposed a sparse random measurement matrix which consumes little memory is consumed and can greatly reduce the computation in data projection. The entries of sparse random measurement matrix can be defined as

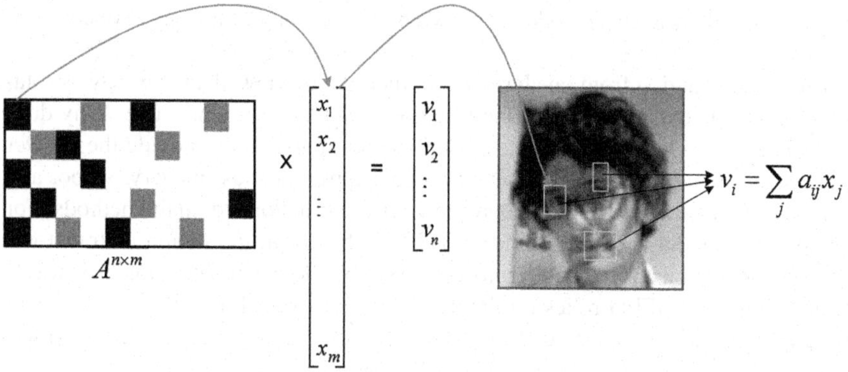

Fig. 2.3 Generating a compressive feature v from high-dimensional

$$a_{ij} = \sqrt{s} \times \begin{cases} 1 & \text{with probability } \frac{1}{2s} \\ 0 & \text{with probability } 1 - \frac{1}{s}. \\ -1 & \text{with probability } \frac{1}{2s} \end{cases} \tag{2.6}$$

Li et al. [25] showed that for $s = O(m)$ $(\boldsymbol{x} \in \mathbb{R}^m)$, then this matrix is asymptotically normal. Even when $s = m/\log(m)$, the random projections are almost as accurate as the conventional random projections where $a_{ij} \sim N(0, 1)$. In [33], they use $s = m/4$ to compress the data in visual tracking and get very good performance.

The process of data compressing by sparse random measure matrix is intuitively illustrated in Fig. 2.3, graphical representation of compressing a high-dimensional vector $\boldsymbol{x}$ to a low-dimensional vector $\boldsymbol{v}$. In the matrix A, dark, gray, and white rectangles represent negative, positive, and zero entries, respectively. The blue arrows illustrate that one of nonzero entries of one row of A sensing an element in $\boldsymbol{x}$ is equivalent to a rectangle filter convolving the intensity at a fixed position of an input image [33].

2.2.2 *Sparsity*

Sparsity, simply, means that the original signal is dense in a particular basis, however, after transformation into other convenient basis ψ, the coefficients under ψ offers a concise summary. Sparsity or compressibility has played and continue to play a fundamental and important role in many fields of science. Sparsity provides a solution in signal efficient estimations; for example, thresholding or shrinkage algorithms depend on sparsity to estimate the signal. Moreover, it leads to dimensionality reduction and efficient modeling. Sparsity even leads to signal compression where the precision of a transform coders depends on the sparsity of the signal one wishes to decode.

The transformation from one basis to another can be viewed analytically as rotation of coordinate axes from the standard Euclidean basis to a new one. Why does it make sense to change coordinates in this way? Sparsity can provide the answer to such question. Take a look at several media types such as imagery, video, and acoustic, they all can be sparsely represented using transform-domain methods. For example, the media encoding standard JPEG is based on the notion of transform encoding, which means the data vector representing the raw pixels samples is transformed. Basically, JPEG relies on the discrete cosine transform (DCT)—a variant of the Fourier transform, while JPEG2000 based on the discrete wavelet transform (DWT).

The DCT of media content, technically, has transformed coefficients, which are quite large at the first several, but the rest are very small. Putting the those small coefficients to zeros and approximating the large coefficients by quantized representations will yield an approximate coefficient sequence which can be efficiently used to reconstruct the signal in a few bits. The approximate coefficient sequence can be inverse transformed to obtain an approximate representation of the original media content. On the other hand, the DWT has relatively few large coefficients, which are not necessarily at the first ones. Letting the small coefficients to zeros, and quantizing the large ones can obtain a sequence to be efficiently stored, and later inverse transformed to provide an approximate representation of the original media content. For many types of image content, JPEG2000 outperforms JPEG, while fewer bits are needed for a given accuracy or approximation. Thus, the success of DWT in image coding has close relationship to sparsity image content.

In short, sparsity of representation plays an important role in widely used techniques of transform-baseed image compression. It is also a driving factor for other important signal and image processing problems, including image denoising and image deblurring. Remarkably, it has been shown that a better representation is the one that is more sparse, i.e., less number of nonzero value.

2.2.3 Structured Sparsity

From the sparse representation research community point of view [30], sparsity has been roughly divided into two types. One is the pure or flat or unstructured sparsity which can be achieved by ℓ_0-norm, or ℓ_1-norm regularizer. Another is structured sparsity which usually can be obtained by different sparsity-inducing norms such as $\ell_{2,1}$-norm, $\ell_{\infty,1}$-norm, group ℓ_1-norm, and so on. In the flat sparsity or simply sparse representation, when regularizing with ℓ_0-norm, or ℓ_1-norm, each variable is selected individually, regardless of its position in the input feature vector, therefore, that existing relationships and structures between the variables, e.g., spatial, hierarchical or related to the physics of the problem at hand, are totally ignored. However, those properties are very important or may improve the predictive performance in many applications.

Taking advantage from the prior knowledge has been shown effective in various applications. In neuroimaging based on functional magnetic resonance (fMRI) or magnetoencephalography (MEG), sets of voxels allowing to discriminate between different brain states are expected to form small localized and connected areas. Similarly, in face recognition, robust performance to occlusions can be improved by considering as features, sets of pixels that form small convex regions of the face which is beyond the capability of ℓ_1 regularization to encode such specific spatial constrains.

Such problems need the design of sparsity-inducing regularization schemes which are capable of encoding more sophisticated prior knowledge about the expected sparsity patterns.

2.3 ℓ_0, ℓ_1 and ℓ_2 Norms

In signal processing community, signals as real-valued functions which are divided into either continuous or discrete, and either infinite or finite. Norms play an important role on subspaces, and then we introduce the normed vector spaces. In this section, we shall consider the ℓ_0-norm, ℓ_1-norm, and ℓ_2-norm, and present the identities about them. First, we shall give the definition of the ℓ_p-norm

Definition 2.3.1 (*ℓ_p-norm*) $\boldsymbol{x}$ is a N-dimension vector, the ℓ_p-norm can be defined by the following formulation:

$$\|\boldsymbol{x}\|_{\ell_p} = \left(\sum_{i=1}^{N} |x_i|^p\right)^{\frac{1}{p}}. \tag{2.7}$$

By the definition of the ℓ_p-norm, we can easily define the ℓ_0-norm, ℓ_1-norm and ℓ_2-norm. When $p = 1$, we can define the ℓ_1-norm as follows:

$$\|\boldsymbol{x}\|_{\ell_p} = \begin{cases} \left(\sum_{i=1}^{N} |x_i|^p\right)^{\frac{1}{p}}, & p \in [1, \infty) \\ \max_{(i=1,2,\ldots,N)} |x_i|, & p = \infty \end{cases} \tag{2.8}$$

Note that the standard inner product in R^N leads to the ℓ_2-norm $\|\boldsymbol{x}\|_{\ell_2} = \sqrt{< x, x >}$. But, we should note that the ℓ_0-norm is not really a norm because it does not have some properties of the norm, it is defined as follows:

$$\|\boldsymbol{x}\|_{\ell_0} = |supp(x)| = \lim_{p \to 0} \|\boldsymbol{x}\|_p^p. \tag{2.9}$$

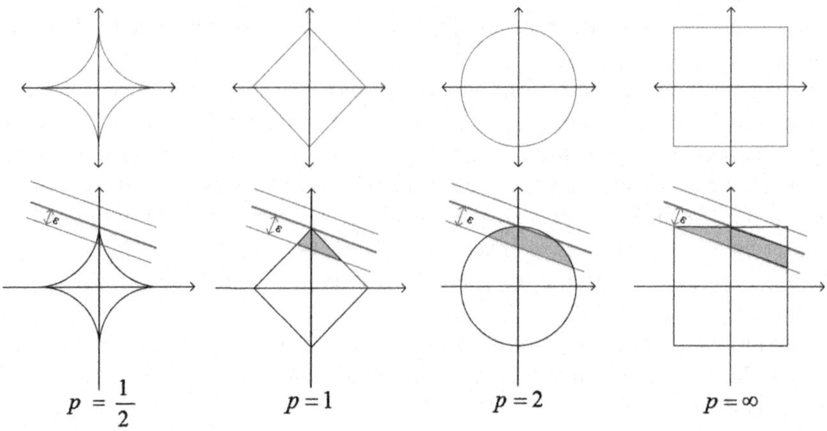

Fig. 2.4 The feasible region of $\|x\|_{\ell_p} = 1$ with $p = \frac{1}{2}$, 1, 2 and ∞, respectively

That means, the ℓ_0 is used to count the nonzero elements number of vector $\boldsymbol{x}$. The ℓ_p-norm with $p = \frac{1}{2}$, $p = 1$ and $p = 2$ can be seen intuitively in Fig. 2.4.

From the Fig. 2.4, we can see that when $0 < p < 1$ the ℓ_p-norm is not smooth and the vertex of the ℓ_p-norm at the coordinate axis; so it can be used as the regularization term to get the sparse solution. However it is nonconvex, so, it is not suitable to get the global optimal solution. When $p > 1$ the ℓ_p-norm is convex and smooth, it can be used as regularization term to get the global optimal solution. However, it is smooth and not suitable to get the sparse solution. Only in the situation $p = 1$, ℓ_p-norm both keep the convex and sparse properties; we would like to point out that not only the directive ℓ_1-norm is used to seek the sparse solution, but also the log-sum of ℓ_1-norm is used [31, 34]. Moreover, the log-sum of ℓ_1-norm is same as the ℓ_0 in principal. Shen et al. provided a rigorous justification for its optimization problem and the iterative reweighted method [31].

We can use norms to measure the residuals in many engineering problems. For example, we want to approximate $x \in R^N$ using $\widetilde{x} \in A$, a one-dimensional affine space. Then we can formulate the approximation error suing an ℓ_p-norm an $\text{argmin}_{x \in A} \|\boldsymbol{x} - \widetilde{\boldsymbol{x}}\|_{\ell_p}$. From the Fig. 2.4. We can see that different norms results in different residuals. The procedure of seeking the optimal $\widetilde{x}$ is equivalent to grow on ℓ_p spark centered on x until it intersects with A. Note that laver p correspondents to more even residual among the coefficients while smaller p correspondents to more an evenly distributed of residuals. $\widetilde{x}$ is proved to sparse in latter case which has some amazing properties in high dimensions.

2.4 Spark and Singleton Bound

As we known from the Chap. 1, the sparse representation problem is used to solve the underdetermine problem $Ax = y$. This problem has infinite solutions, so we need to add a prior to get the unique solution. The prior knowledge that we add is the assumption that solution is sparse, so we add a $\|x\|_{\ell_0}$ regularization term to constrain the sparsity of solution. In order to study the uniqueness of solution, a key property we need to know is the *spark* of matrix A, which is mentioned in [15]. The rank of a matrix A is defined as the maximal number of columns A that are linearly independent, and its evaluation is a sequential process required L steps. However, calculation spark(A) quires a combinational process of 2^L steps.

Definition 2.4.1 (*Spark*) The *spark* of matrix A is the smallest possible number of its columns which are linearly dependent as

$$Spark(A) = \min_{x \neq 0} \|x\|_{\ell_0}, s.t. \quad Ax = \mathbf{0} \tag{2.10}$$

Definition 2.4.2 (*The Singleton Bound*) The highest spark of an matrix $A \in \mathbb{R}^{D\times N}$, $(D < N)$ is less than or equal to $D + 1$ [24].

The *spark* gives the simple criterion for the sparse solution of the $Ax = \mathbf{0}$ problem. The solution must satisfied that $\|x\|_{\ell_0} \geq spark(A)$ to avoid trivial solutions. By the definition of spark, we can get the Theorem 2.4.1 as follows:

Theorem 2.4.1 (Uniqueness-Spark) *If a system of linear equations $Ax = y$ has a solution x^* obeying $\|x^*\|_{\ell_0} < spark(A)/2$, this solution is necessarily the sparsest possible [18].*

As we know the definition of *spark*, computing the spark of a matrix is a NP-hard problem, so, we need to find a simpler way to guarantee the uniqueness. The simplest way is to use the mutual-coherence of matrix A, which is defined as follows:

Lemma 2.4.1 (Mutual-Coherence) *The mutual-coherence of matrix A is the largest absolute normalized inner product between different columns from A. The mutual-coherence is defined as [18]*

$$\mu(A) = \max_{1\leq i,j\leq N,\ i\neq j} \frac{|A_{.i}^T A_{.j}|}{\|A_{.i}\|_{\ell_2} \cdot \|A_{.j}\|_{\ell_2}}. \tag{2.11}$$

We can note that the mutual-coherence is used to characterize the dependence of the matrix columns. The mutual-coherence of the unitary matrix is zero. The $D \times N$ matrix A with $D < M$, and the mutual-coherence of this matrix is strictly positive, so we want the smallest value in order to make the matrix A as close as possible to the unitary matrix. So, we can use the mutual-coherence to find the lower bound of the spark, which is very hard to get.

Definition 2.4.3 (*Spark Lower Bound*) For any matrix $A \in \mathbb{R}^{D\times N}$, the following relationship holds [18]:

$$spark(A) \geq 1 + \frac{1}{\mu(A)} \tag{2.12}$$

By the Theorem 2.4.1, we get the uniqueness about mutual-coherence.

Definition 2.4.4 (*Uniqueness-Mutual-Coherence*) If a linear system of equations $Ax = \boldsymbol{y}$ has a solution $\boldsymbol{x}^*$ obeying $\|\boldsymbol{x}\|_{\ell_0} < \frac{1}{2}(1 + 1/\mu(A))$, this solution is necessarily the sparsest possible [18].

2.5 Null Space Property

The previous section tells us, if we want to recover a K-sparse signal, what condition about the spark and mutual-coherence of the sensing matrix we needed. In this section, we shall talk about the condition of sensing matrix from null space aspect, if we want to recover a K-sparse signal or approximately sparse signals. First, let us give the definition of the null space,

Definition 2.5.1 (*Null Space*) The null space of matrix A is denoted as follows:

$$\mathcal{N}(A) = \{z : Az = \mathbf{0}\}. \tag{2.13}$$

From the Theorem 2.4.1, we know $Spark(A) \in [2, D+1]$. Therefore, it requires that $D \geq 2K$, if we want to recover a k-sparse signal. However, not all the signal is so sparse as we want. In some situations, we only have to deal with the approximately sparse signals, so we need to consider more restrictive conditions on the null space of A [11]. Suppose that $\Lambda \subset \{1, 2, \ldots, N\}$ is the subset of indices and $\Lambda^c = \{1, 2, \ldots, N\}/\Lambda$, $\boldsymbol{x}_\Lambda$ is the vector $\boldsymbol{x}$ with setting index Λ^c to be zero, $\sum_K = x_i$, $\|\boldsymbol{x}\|_0 \ll k$.

Definition 2.5.2 (*Null Space property*) A matrix A satisfies the **Null Space Property** (NSP) of order k if there exists a constant $C > 0$ such that [14],

$$\|h_\Lambda\|_{\ell_2} \leq C\frac{\|h_{\Lambda^c}\|_{\ell_1}}{\sqrt{K}} \tag{2.14}$$

holds for all $h \in \mathcal{N}(A)$ and for all Λ such that $|\Lambda| \leq K$.

From the definition of NSP, we can see that vectors in null space of A should not be concentrated on small subset of indices. By the NSP, we can give the conclusion about how to measure the performance of sparse recovery algorithm when dealing with general nonsparse signal $\boldsymbol{x}$. We define $\Delta : \mathbb{R}^D \rightarrow \mathbb{R}^N$ as the recovery algorithm,

$\Sigma_K = \{x : \|x\|_{\ell_0} \leq K\}$, and $\sigma_K(x)_p = \arg\min_{\hat{x}\in\Sigma_K} \|x - \hat{x}\|_{\ell_p}$. The algorithm condition is as follows:

$$\|\Delta(Ax) - x\|_{\ell_2} \leq C\frac{\sigma_K(x)_1}{\sqrt{K}}. \tag{2.15}$$

This algorithm can exactly recover the K-sparse signals, and also have a degree of robustness to non-sparse signals which depends on how well the signals are approximated by the K-sparse signals [11]. Then we shall give the theorem about NSP and the recovery algorithm.

Theorem 2.5.1 ([11]) *Let $A : \mathbb{R}^N \to \mathbb{R}^D$ denote a sensing matrix and the $\Delta : \mathbb{R}^D \to \mathbb{R}^N$ denote the arbitrary algorithm. If the pair (A, Δ) satisfies Eq. (2.15) then A satisfies the NSP of order $2K$.*

2.6 Uniform Uncertainty Principle, Incoherence Condition

In this section, we aim to introduce uncertainty principle proposed by Donoho and Stark [16, 17]. The UUP is a fundamental law in compressed sensing for signal representation and ℓ_1 uniqueness proof. First of all, the UUP is a fundamental law of signal resolution for sparse signal representation. In other word, we can represent a signal in a sparse way but it is strictly limited by this principle. Second, the NP is used to proof the ℓ_1 uniqueness.

From the previous section, NSP is a necessary condition for Eq. (2.15), which guarantees the algorithm can recover the K-sparse signal and ensures a degree of robustness to approximate the non-sparse signal. But NSP does not consider about the noisy situation. If the signals are contaminated, we should consider about other stronger conditions. Candes and Tao [7] had introduced the uniform uncertainty principle (UUP). It aims to define the "Restricted Isometry Property (RIP)" of the sensing matrix A, which plays a very important role in compressed sensing. First, we need to know what is the *Uncertainty Principle* which is given as follows:

Theorem 2.6.1 (Uncertainty Principle [16]) *The time domain signal $y \in \mathbb{R}^D$ has the sparsity K_t under the transformation $y = A_t x_t$, where A_t is the identity matrix, and the Fourier transform $\overline{y} \in \mathbb{R}^D$ has the sparsity K_w under the transformation $\overline{y} = A_w x_w$. Then, the two sparsity parameters should satisfy*

$$K_t K_w \geq D \geq \frac{1}{\mu^2}, \tag{2.16}$$

and

$$K_t + K_w \geq 2\sqrt{D} \geq \frac{2}{\mu}, \tag{2.17}$$

where μ is the maximum correlation of the two bases A_t and A_w which is defined as

$$\mu := \max_{i,j} \left\{ |\langle A_{t(.i)} A_{w(.j)} \rangle| \right\} \tag{2.18}$$

The *Uncertainty Principle* tell us that any signal cannot be sparsely represented in both domains simultaneously. If the sparsity in one domain is fixed, i.e., K_t, then, the sparsity level obtainable in the other domain shall be limited, i.e., $K_w \geq \frac{2}{\mu} - K_t$. By the uncertainty principle, Candes et al. propose the *Uniform Uncertainty Principle* which is the fundamental knowledge of compressed sensing.

Definition 2.6.1 (*Uniform Uncertainty Principle (UUP)* [8]) We can say a measurement matrix or sensing matrix A satisfy the *Uniform Uncertainty Principle* with oversampling factor λ if for every sufficiently small $\alpha > 0$, the following statement is true with probability at least $1 - O(N^{-\rho/\alpha})$ for some fixed positive constant $\rho > 0$: for all subsets T such that

$$|T| \leq \alpha \cdot K/\lambda, \tag{2.19}$$

the sensing matrix A obeys the bounds

$$\frac{1}{2} \cdot \frac{K}{N} \|\boldsymbol{x}\|_{\ell_2}^2 \leq \|A\boldsymbol{x}\|_{\ell_2}^2 \leq \frac{3}{2}\frac{K}{N} \|\boldsymbol{x}\|_{\ell_2}^2, \tag{2.20}$$

holding for all signals $\boldsymbol{x}$ with support size less or equal to $\alpha K/\lambda$.

Definition 2.6.2 A matrix A satisfies the Restricted Isometry Property of order K if there exists a $\delta_K \in (0, 1)$ such that

$$(1 - \delta_K)\|\boldsymbol{x}\|_{\ell_2}^2 \leq \|A\boldsymbol{x}\|_{\ell_2}^2 \leq (1 + \delta_K)\|\boldsymbol{x}\|_{\ell_2}^2, \tag{2.21}$$

holds for all K-sparse vector $\boldsymbol{x}$, where δ_K is called K-restricted isometry constants.

The RIP condition provides the basic condition for the compressed sensing theory. If the matrices satisfies the RIP condition, many good things are guaranteed such as the ℓ_1 recovery is equivalence with ℓ_0 recovery. If a matrix A satisfies the RIP of order $2K$, then the Eq. (2.21) can be interpreted as the matrix A approximately preserves the distance between any pair of K-sparse vector, thus we can use this matrix to recover the K-sparse signal. We can note from the definition of RIP condition that if matrix A satisfies the RIP of order K with constant δ_K, then for any order $K' < K$ the matrix A also satisfies the RIP of order K' with constant $\delta_{K'}$. Needell and Tropp [27] also present that if the sensing matrix A satisfies the RIP with a very small constant, then the matrix A also satisfies RIP of order γK for certain γ, with a worse constant. This property is presented as follows:

Lemma 2.6.1 *Suppose that A satisfies the RIP of order K with constant δ_K. Let γ be a positive integer. Then A satisfies the RIP of order $K' = \gamma \lfloor \frac{K}{2} \rfloor$ with constant $\delta_{K'} < \gamma \cdot \delta_K$, where $\lfloor \cdot \rfloor$ denotes the floor operator.*

In many cases, the signal is non-sparse but it can be represented as sparse signal under some specific orthogonal basis; for example, $\boldsymbol{s} = \Psi \boldsymbol{x}$, where, $\boldsymbol{s}$ is non-sparse signal and Ψ is the orthogonal basis, $\Psi^T \Psi = \Psi \Psi^T = I_N$. The $D \times 1$ measurement vector $\boldsymbol{y}$ can be expressed as

$$\boldsymbol{y} = \Phi \boldsymbol{s} = \Phi \Psi \boldsymbol{x} := A\boldsymbol{x}, \tag{2.22}$$

where Φ is $D \times N$ sensing matrix.

Definition 2.6.3 (*Incoherence Condition*) The Incoherence Condition can be defined as the rows of Φ should be incoherent to the columns of Ψ.

We can note that if Φ and Ψ could not satisfy the incoherence condition, for example, in the extreme case, selecting the first D column of Ψ as the D rows of Phi we can get

$$\Phi \Psi = \begin{bmatrix} 1 & & & \\ & 1 & & \\ & & \ddots & \\ & & & 1 \end{bmatrix}. \tag{2.23}$$

We can easily find that this matrix $\Phi \Psi$ can never satisfy the RIP condition. We can use the i.i.d. Gaussian to construct the sensing matrix which has been proved that it will be in coherent to any basis.

2.7 ℓ_1 and ℓ_0 Equivalence

The RIP [7] is used to prove the equivalence between ℓ_1 and ℓ_0-norm in sparse signal recovery. It has been proved in [7] that the solution of dual ℓ_0 minimization problems

(1) Sparse Error Correction: Given $\boldsymbol{y} \in \mathbb{R}^N$, $A \in \mathbb{R}^{N \times M}$ $(N > M)$,

$$\boldsymbol{x}^* = \arg\min_{\boldsymbol{x}} \|\boldsymbol{y} - A\boldsymbol{x}\|_{\ell_0}, \tag{2.24}$$

(2) Sparse Signal Reconstruction: Given $\boldsymbol{z} \in \mathbb{R}^D$, $B \in \mathbb{R}^{D \times N}$ $(D < N)$,

$$\boldsymbol{w}^* = \arg\min_{\boldsymbol{w}} \|\boldsymbol{w}\|_{\ell_0} \quad \text{s.t.} \quad \boldsymbol{z} = B\boldsymbol{w}, \tag{2.25}$$

are the same as the solutions of problems

$$\boldsymbol{x}^* = \arg\min_{\boldsymbol{x}} \|\boldsymbol{y} - A\boldsymbol{x}\|_{\ell_1}, \tag{2.26}$$

$$\boldsymbol{w}^* = \arg\min_{\boldsymbol{w}} \|\boldsymbol{w}\|_{\ell_1} \quad \text{s.t.} \quad \boldsymbol{z} = B\boldsymbol{w}, \tag{2.27}$$

if the error $\boldsymbol{e} = \boldsymbol{y} - A\boldsymbol{x}$ or the solution $\boldsymbol{w}$ is sufficiently sparse. Y. Sharon et al. [29] verify the equivalence between ℓ_1 and ℓ_0 minimization problem by the algorithm. First, they give the definition of "*d-skeleton*" as follows:

Definition 2.7.1 (*d-Skeleton* [29]) The "d-skeleton" is defined as the collection of all the d-dimensional faces of the standard ℓ_1-ball $B_1 \doteq \{\boldsymbol{v} \in \mathbb{R}^m : \|\boldsymbol{v}\|_{\ell_1} \leq 1\}$. We can denote $SK_d(B_1)$:

$$SK_d(B_1) \doteq \{\boldsymbol{v} \in \mathbb{R}^N : \|\boldsymbol{v}\| = 1, \|\boldsymbol{v}\|_{\ell_0} \leq d + 1\}. \tag{2.28}$$

By the definition of d-skeleton, they can prove the proposition as follows:

Proposition 2.7.1 *For every $\boldsymbol{x}_0 \in \mathbb{R}^M$ and $\boldsymbol{y} \in \mathbb{R}^N$, the following implication holds*

$$\|\boldsymbol{y} - A\boldsymbol{x}_0\|_{\ell_0} \leq T \quad \Rightarrow \quad \boldsymbol{x}_0 = \arg\min_{\boldsymbol{x}} \|\boldsymbol{y} - A\boldsymbol{x}\|_{\ell_1} \tag{2.29}$$

if and only if

$$\forall \boldsymbol{v} \in SK_{T-1}(B_1), \quad \forall \boldsymbol{z} \in \mathbb{R}^M \backslash \boldsymbol{0}, \quad \|\boldsymbol{v} + A\boldsymbol{z}\|_{\ell_1} > 1. \tag{2.30}$$

We can note that the Eq. (2.29) is what we needed. But this proposition asks us to check starting from $T = 1, 2, \ldots$ until the condition (2.30) eventually fails. Even more, it asks us to check every point on the d-skeleton. Then, they propose the proposition which tells us an equivalent condition that does not require search over $\boldsymbol{v}$, and only involves checking a finite set of points in $span(A)$.

Proposition 2.7.2 *Let $A \in \mathbb{R}^{N \times M}$ and $d \in \mathbb{N} \cup 0$ be given and assume the rows of A are in general directions, i.e., any M rows of A are independent. The following holds:*

$$\forall \boldsymbol{v} \in SK_d(B_1), \quad \forall \boldsymbol{z} \in \mathbb{R}^M \backslash 0 \quad \|\boldsymbol{v} + A\boldsymbol{z}\|_{\ell_1} > 1 \tag{2.31}$$

if and only if for all subsets $I \subset Q \doteq \{1, \ldots, N\}$ containing $M - 1$ indices, all subsets $J \subset Q \backslash I$ containing $T = d + 1$ indices, and for some $\boldsymbol{y} \in \mathbb{R}^N$ such that

$$\boldsymbol{y} \in span(A) \backslash 0, \quad \forall i \in I \quad y_i = 0, \tag{2.32}$$

the following holds:

$$\sum_{j \in J} |y_j| < \sum_{j \in Q \backslash J} |y_j|. \tag{2.33}$$

2.8 Stable Recovery Property

In this section, we shall give some conclusions which can present RIP condition's necessity for signal $\boldsymbol{x}$ recovery from the measurements $A\boldsymbol{x}$, and even more it is necessary for stable recovery in case of noise [13]. Stable recovery stems from two issues. First of all, signals are not strictly sparse in practice. The small portion of the signal has large magnitude while the rest are close to zero but not exactly zero. Thus, there exits model error in a sparse model. Second, there always exit noise in the signal measured from sensors.

Definition 2.8.1 Let $A : \mathbb{R}^N \rightarrow \mathbb{R}^D$ denotes the sensing matrix and $\Delta : \mathbb{R}^D \rightarrow \mathbb{R}^N$ denotes the recovery algorithm. We say that the pair (A, Δ) is C-stable if $\forall \boldsymbol{x} \in \Sigma_k$ and $\forall \boldsymbol{e} \in \mathbb{R}^D$, we have that

$$\|\Delta(A\boldsymbol{x} + \boldsymbol{e}) - \boldsymbol{x}\|_{\ell_2} \leq C\|\boldsymbol{e}\|_{\ell_2}. \tag{2.34}$$

This definition tells us that if the measurements add some small amount of noise, the impact on the recovered signal should not be arbitrarily large. Next, we shall give a theorem which demonstrates that any recovery algorithm can stably recover the signal from noisy measurements requires that A satisfy the lower bound of RIP condition with a constant determined by C [13].

Theorem 2.8.1 *If the pair (A, Δ) is C-stable, then*

$$\frac{1}{C}\|\boldsymbol{x}\|_{\ell_2} \leq \|A\boldsymbol{x}\|_{\ell_2} \tag{2.35}$$

for all $\boldsymbol{x} \in \Sigma_{2K}$.

We can note that when $C \rightarrow 1$, the sensing matrix A can satisfy the lower bound of RIP condition with $\delta_K = 1 - 1/C^2 \rightarrow 0$. Thus, if we want to reduce the impact of the noise in the recovery algorithm, we must let sensing matrix A to satisfy the lower bound of RIP condition with a smaller δ_K.

Another aspect we need to consider is the dimension of the measures, and how many measurements are necessary to achieve the RIP. Now, we ignore the impact of the δ and only focus on the dimensions of the problem (D, N and k) then we can get a simple lower bound, which is proven in [13].

Theorem 2.8.2 *Let A be an $D \times N$ matrix that satisfies the RIP of order $2K$ with constant $\delta \in (0, \frac{1}{2}]$. Then*

$$D \geq CK \log\left(\frac{N}{K}\right), \tag{2.36}$$

where $C \approx 0.28$.

1. The Relationship Between the RIP and the NSP

Finally, we shall give the conclusion that when the matrix satisfies the RIP, it also satisfies the NSP, in other words, the RIP is strictly stronger than the NSP.

Theorem 2.8.3 *Suppose that sensing matrix A satisfies the RIP of order* $2K$ *with* $\delta_{2K} < \sqrt{2} - 1$. *Then A satisfies the NSP of order* $2K$ *with constant*

$$C = \frac{\sqrt{2}\delta_{2K}}{1 - (1 + \sqrt{2})\delta_{2K}}. \tag{2.37}$$

The prove detail of this theorem can be found in [19].

2. Signal Recovery via ℓ_0 and ℓ_1 Minimization

Let us consider the original problem that we want to solve the linear underdetermined problem $\boldsymbol{y} = A\boldsymbol{x}$ with constraint $\boldsymbol{x}$ as sparse as possible. The problem can be naturally solved by the following optimal equation:

$$\boldsymbol{x}^* = \arg\min_{\boldsymbol{x}} \|\boldsymbol{x}\|_{\ell_0} \quad \text{s.t.} \quad \boldsymbol{y} = A\boldsymbol{x}. \tag{2.38}$$

The performance of above method can be analyzed in [10, 22] which is under the appropriate assumptions on A, but we still do not have a sufficient method to solve this problem, because $\|\cdot\|_{\ell_0}$ is nonconvex and minimizes $\|\boldsymbol{x}\|_{\ell_0}$ is a NP-hard problem [26].

One of the tractable method is approximate ℓ_0-norm by ℓ_1-norm which preserves the sparsity and convex properties, and the reason can refer to Sect. 2.3.

$$\boldsymbol{x}^* = \arg\min_{\boldsymbol{x}} \|\boldsymbol{x}\|_{\ell_1} \quad \text{s.t.} \quad \boldsymbol{y} = A\boldsymbol{x}. \tag{2.39}$$

So, this problem is computational tractable and can be treated as a linear programing problem [9]. The following theorem is very remarkable. It consider about the case that $x \in \Sigma_K$ and if the sensing matrix A satisfies the RIP condition which only need $O(k\log(N/K))$ measurements, we can recover the K-sparse signal exactly.

If we only consider about the noise free case, we can get the following Lemma and Theorem.

Lemma 2.8.1 *Suppose that A satisfies the RIP of order* $2K$, *and let* $h \in \mathbb{R}^N$, $h \neq 0$ *be arbitrary. Let* Λ_0 *be any subset of* $\{1, 2, \ldots, N\}$ *such that* $|\Lambda_0\| \leq K$. *Define* Λ_1 *as the index set corresponding to the K entries of* $h_{\Lambda_0^c}$ *with largest magnitude, and set* $\Lambda = \Lambda_0 \bigcup \Lambda_1$. *Then*

$$\|h_\Lambda\|_{\ell_2} \leq \alpha \frac{\|h_{\Lambda_0^c}\|_{\ell_1}}{\sqrt{K}} + \beta \frac{|\langle Ah_\Lambda, Ah\rangle|}{\|h_\Lambda\|_{\ell_2}}, \tag{2.40}$$

where

$$\alpha = \frac{\sqrt{2}\delta_{2K}}{1-\delta_{2K}}, \quad \beta = \frac{1}{1-\delta_{2K}}. \tag{2.41}$$

By the Lemma 2.8.1 we can get the Lemma 2.8.2.

Lemma 2.8.2 *Suppose that A satisfies the RIP of order $2K$ with $\delta_{2K} < \sqrt{2}-1$. Let $\boldsymbol{x}, \hat{\boldsymbol{x}} \in \mathbb{R}^N$ be given, and define $h = \hat{\boldsymbol{x}} - \boldsymbol{x}$. Denote Λ_0 as the index set corresponding to the K entries of $\boldsymbol{x}$ with largest magnitude and Λ_1 the index set corresponding to the K entries of $h_{\Lambda_0^c}$ with largest magnitude. Set $\Lambda = \Lambda_0 \bigcup \Lambda_1$. If $\|\hat{\boldsymbol{x}}\|_{\ell_1} \leq \|\boldsymbol{x}\|_{\ell_1}$, then*

$$\|h\|_{\ell_2} \leq C_0 \frac{\sigma_k(\boldsymbol{x})_1}{\sqrt{k}} + C_1 \frac{|\langle A h_\Lambda, A h\rangle|}{\|h_\Lambda\|_{\ell_2}}, \tag{2.42}$$

where

$$C_0 = 2\frac{1-\left(1-\sqrt{2}\right)\delta_{2K}}{1-\left(1+\sqrt{2}\right)\delta_{2K}}, \quad C_1 = \frac{2}{1-\left(1+\sqrt{2}\right)\delta_{2K}}. \tag{2.43}$$

The Lemma 2.8.2 shows us that if the sensing matrix satisfies the RIP, the error bound of the general ℓ_1 minimization algorithm. If we consider about the problem of Eq. (2.39), the specific bounds is given by Theorem 2.8.4 as follows:

Theorem 2.8.4 *Suppose that sensing matrix A satisfies the RIP of order $2K$ with $\delta_{2K} < \sqrt{2}-1$. Then the solution $\boldsymbol{x}^*$ of problem of Eq. (2.39) obeys*

$$\|\hat{\boldsymbol{x}} - \boldsymbol{x}\|_{\ell_2} \leq C_0 \frac{\sigma_K(\boldsymbol{x})_1}{\sqrt{K}}. \tag{2.44}$$

Right now, we consider the noisy case, because in the real-world systems the measurements always contaminated by some form of noise. We consider the worst situation to uniformly bound the noise [6].

Theorem 2.8.5 ([5]) *Suppose that A satisfies the RIP of order $2K$ with $\delta_{2K} < \sqrt{2}-1$ and let $\boldsymbol{y} = A\boldsymbol{x} + \boldsymbol{e}$ where $\|\boldsymbol{e}\|_{\ell_2} \leq \varepsilon$. The solution $\boldsymbol{x}*$ to Eq. (2.39) obeys*

$$\|\boldsymbol{x}^* - \boldsymbol{x}\|_{\ell_2} \leq C_0 \frac{\sigma_K(\boldsymbol{x})_1}{\sqrt{K}} + C_2\varepsilon, \tag{2.45}$$

where

$$C_0 = 2\frac{1-\left(1-\sqrt{2}\right)\delta_{2K}}{1-\left(1+\sqrt{2}\right)\delta_{2K}}, \quad C_1 = 4\frac{\sqrt{1+\delta_{2K}}}{1-\left(1+\sqrt{2}\right)\delta_{2K}}. \tag{2.46}$$

This theorem tells us that even in the noisy case, if the sensing matrix satisfies the RIP condition, the ℓ_1 algorithm also can recover the signal stably.

2.9 Information Theory

Information theory is an interdisciplinary branch of applied mathematics, computer science, and electrical engineering. The field was remarkably developed by Claude E. Shannon in his theorem in finding fundamental limits on signal processing operations, e.g., compressing, storing and communicating data. Since then it has been emerged in many applications such as natural language processing, cryptography, biology, statistical inference, information retrieval, and so on. Information theorem, mathematically, based on statistics and probabilistic theory.

2.9.1 *K-sparse Signal Model*

Definition 2.9.1 Signal modeling is the process of representing signals, with respect to an underlying structure of the signal's fundamental behavior, by some set of parameters.

Signal modeling is used in many applications including signal compression, prediction, reconstruction, and understanding. In signal compressive applications, rather than storing original signal, one needs to store a set of parameters, whose sizes are much smaller than the original signals, and can be used to reconstruct the original signal or at least as close as possible to the original signal. Usually, to reconstruct the signal, one needs to design a filter as shown in Fig. 2.5. In other words, the problem can be simply defined as given observations $X[n], n = 0, \ldots, N-1$ and filter order m and n, find the parameters of $H(z)$ such that the modeled output, $y[n] = h[n]$.

In the field of digital signal processing, the input–output relation of a linear time-invariant (LTI) system is given in the z domain by

$$Y(z) = \frac{B(z)}{A(z)}X(z) = H(z)X(z) \tag{2.47}$$

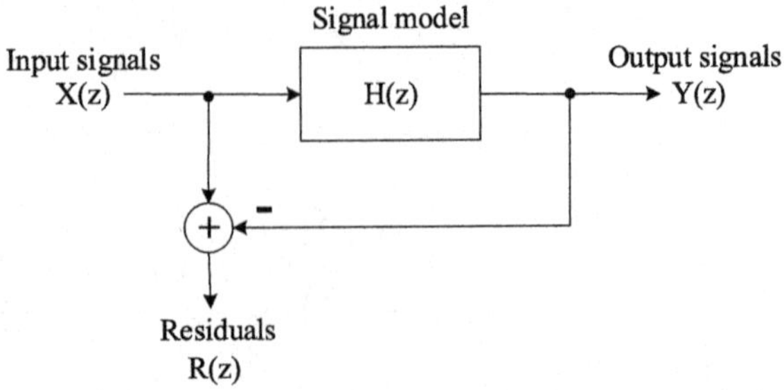

Fig. 2.5 A basic model for signal conversion

where $H(z)$ is filter response, $A(z)$ and $B(z)$ are polynomials. Therefore, $H(z)$ can be relaxed to

$$H(z) = \frac{\sum_{i=1}^{n} b_n z^{-n}}{\sum_{j=1}^{m} b_m z^{-m}} \tag{2.48}$$

Various models have been proposed in the literatures, e.g., AutoRegressive (AR), Moving Average (MA), AutoregRessive-Moving Average (ARMA), and low-rank or sparse model which is the main topic of the book.

We are now interested in vector x with K nonzero entries, i.e., K-sparse vector. We denote the indices of those nonzero entries of the vector x by $t = (t_1, t_2, \ldots, t_K)$, and name it as index profile. Moreover, each entry $t_k \in \{1, 2, \ldots, N\}$ denotes the index of a nonzero entry in x. Let S_t be the set of all feasible index profile. Its size can be defined as

$$|S_t| = \binom{N}{k} \tag{2.49}$$

We set the values of the K nonzero entries into a vector $s = (s_1, s_2, \ldots, s_K)$, and name it value profile which can be determined from a distribution. For instance, we could use Gaussian, Bernoulli, or a hybrid distribution. We use a p.d.f $f_s(s)$ to denote a VP distribution. For an example of complex valued Gaussian multivariate random vector, the p.d.f is obtained by

$$f_s(s) = \frac{1}{\pi^N |C_s|} \exp\left[-\frac{1}{2}(s - \bar{s})^* C_s^{-1} (s - \bar{s})\right] \tag{2.50}$$

where $\bar{s} := E\{s\}$ is the mean vector of the Gaussian multivariate s and $C_s := E\{(s - \bar{s})(s - \bar{s})\}$ is the covariance matrix.

In the case that support set size of vector x is smaller than or equal to K, the hybrid distribution should be used to overcome such problem. The index profile set S_t should include all feasible index profile whose size is smaller than or equal to K. Therefore, the size of the index profile set is equal to the number of points in a Hamming sphere of size K as

$$|S_t| = V_2(N, K) = \sum_{k=0}^{K} \binom{N}{k}. \tag{2.51}$$

Finally, we obtain the number of nonzero entries, k as a random variable with the following distribution

$$f_K(k) = \frac{\binom{N}{k}}{V_2(N, K)}. \tag{2.52}$$

To obtain a hybrid distribution, one could use the two distribution from Eqs. (2.49) to (2.51).

2.9.2 The Entropy of K-sparse Signals

In the field of information theory, entropy is the average amount of information contained in a message, i.e., events, samples, or characters drawn from a distribution or data stream. Entropy of a discrete variable X is a measure of the amount of uncertainty associated with the value of X.

Definition 2.9.2 The entropy $H(X)$ of a discrete random variable X is defined by

$$H(X) = -\sum_{x \in X} px(x) \log p(x). \tag{2.53}$$

The entropy is expressed in bits, therefore, the log is to the base 2. In case the logarithm is based in p, the entropy is defined as $H_b(X)$. Entropy does not depend on the value of random variable X, but depends on its probabilities. As entropy is a measure of unpredictability of information content, let us have a look at an example to get more intuitive understanding about it.

Now consider a coin-tossing problem. If the coin is fair which means when the probability of heads is the same as the probability of tails, then the entropy of the coin toss is as high as it could be. Obviously, there is no way to predict the outcome of the coin toss ahead of time? the best, thus we can do is to predict that the coin will come up with heads or tails, and our prediction will be correct with the probability 1/2. Such a coin toss has one bit of entropy since there are two possible outcomes that occur with equal probability, and learning the actual outcome contains one bit of information. Contrarily, a coin toss with a coin that has two heads and no tails has zero entropy since the coin will always come up heads, and the outcome can be predicted perfectly.

In previous subsection, we have discussed the fundamental concept of entropy. This subsection will illustrate the information in terms of bits which can be represented by the K-sparse signal x. In other words, we are interested in determining how large the entropy of the K-sparse signal x is. In general, K-sparse signal x has K nonzero entries. For example, given a signal vector $y_{M\times 1}$, we have to compute how much information in terms of bits which $y_{M\times 1}$ will represent. In order to answer this question, we shall divide the case into two exclusive ones. To simplify the answer, let denote D be an $M \times N$ Fourier transform matrix or dictionary of atoms with prime N. Thus, we obtain $y_{M\times 1} = D_{M\times N}x$. If the map is one-to-one correspondent, which means $M \geq 2K$, the entropy of x is the entropy of $y_{M\times 1}$.

Lemma 2.9.1 *Let D be an $M \times N$ Fourier transform matrix with prime N, where $M \geq 2K$. Let x be a K-sparse signal. Then, the entropy of y given D is $H(x)$, i.e., $H(y|D) = H(Dx|D) = H(x)$. If $M < 2K$, then $H(y|D) = H(Dx|D) \leq H(x)$.*

$$\begin{aligned} H(x) &= H(t = (t_1, \ldots, t_K), s = (s_1, \ldots, s_K)) \\ &= H(t) + H(s|t) \\ &= H(t) + H(s) \end{aligned} \tag{2.54}$$

Suppose that the supporting set of size K is uniformly randomly distributed, the entropy of $H(t_1, \ldots, t_K)$ can be written as

$$H(t_1, \ldots, t_K) = \log \binom{N}{K}. \tag{2.55}$$

Applying the Stirling's approximation for the factorial function, we can obtain

$$\log_2\left(\frac{1}{N+1}\right) + NH\left(\frac{K}{N}\right) \leq \log_2\binom{N}{k} \leq NH\binom{N}{k}. \tag{2.56}$$

When N is large, one can derive $\log_2\binom{N}{k} \cong NH\left(\frac{K}{N}\right)$. On the other hand, when K is small compared to N, the entropy function $H\left(\frac{K}{N}\right) = \frac{K}{N}\log_2\frac{N}{K} + \left(\frac{N-K}{N}\right)\log_2\left(\frac{N}{N-K}\right)$ can be approximated with the first term only, which means $H\left(\frac{K}{N}\right) \approx \frac{1}{N}K\log_2\frac{N}{K}$. Thus, we can obtain when $K \ll N$, that

$$NH\left(\frac{K}{N}\right) \approx K\log_2\left(\frac{N}{K}\right). \tag{2.57}$$

In conclusion, if $M \geq 2K$, any compression map from x to $y = Dx$ is one-to-one correspondent. Therefore, the entropy of y is also the same as the entropy of x.

2.9.3 Mutual Information

Mutual information of two variables X and Y can be defined as

$$I(X; Y) = \sum_{y\in Y}\sum_{x\in X} p(x, y)\log\frac{p(x, y)}{p(x)p(y)} \tag{2.58}$$

where $p(x, y)$ is the joint probability distribution function of X and Y, and $p(x)$ and $p(y)$ are marginal probability distribution functions of X and Y, respectively. Obviously, the mutual information measures the mutual independence of variables, i.e., it measures how much information the variables share each other with the most common unit of the measurement bits. Mutual information, in information theory, can reduce the uncertainty of one variable given knowledge of another. From Eq. (2.58), one can see that if the two variable X and Y are completely independent, then $p(x, y) = p(x)p(y)$. Therefore,

$$\log\left(\frac{p(x, y)}{p(x)p(y)}\right) = \log 1 = 0 \tag{2.59}$$

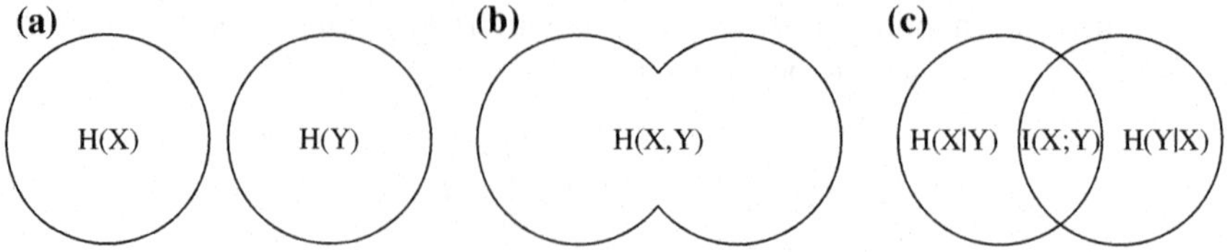

Fig. 2.6 The relationship between entropy and mutual information **a** Marginal entropies. **b** Join entropy. **c** Mutual information

which means X and Y do not share any information at all. The mutual information can be equivalently written as

$$\begin{aligned} I(X;Y) &= H(X) - H(X|Y) \\ &= H(Y) - H(Y|X) \\ &= H(X) + H(Y) - H(X|Y) \\ &= H(X,Y) - H(X|Y) - H(Y|X) \end{aligned} \tag{2.60}$$

where $H(X)$ and $H(Y)$ are the marginal entropies, and $H(X, Y)$ is the joint entropies of X and Y as shown in Fig. 2.6. If $H(X)$ is considered as a measure of uncertainty of variable, then $H(X|Y)$ is a measure of what Y does not say about X.

In communication channel, input X getting through transmission medium will produce output Y. In the perfect transmission, i.e., if the channel is noiseless, the input is equal the to output, namely $X = Y$. However, in real-world channels, the transmission medium is noisy, an input X is converted to an output Y with probability $P(Y|X)$.

Given a communication channel, for example, one can transmit any messages s from a set of M possible messages by performing following three steps.

(1) Assign a string $x = (x_1, x_2, \ldots, x_n)$ of length n to each message s. Each $x(s)$ is called *codeword*. The processing of generating from a set of message to a set of codeword is called encoding.
(2) Transmit the corresponding string $x(s)$ over the channel which yield output y with the same length n.
(3) Use output y to reconstruct the transmitted message x by using a deterministic function named *decoding*. The decoding then maps each y to one symbol s'.

Remarkably, first the number of transmitted messages is much less than the number of possible messages. Then, each message x_i is randomly and independently selected from a distribution, denoted as $P(X)$. Therefore, when one designs a communication channel, only M and $P(X)$ can be controlled. Thus, in general, one adjusts $P(X)$ to make the number of message M large, and simultaneously keeps the error, rate, i.e., the rate which messages are decoded incorrectly, small. The conditional distribution $P(Y|X)$ is a physical property of the channel itself, so it is not under the control of designer.

Fano's inequality has been widely used in lowering bounds of probability of transmission error through a communication channel. It is famous for linking the transmission error probability of a noisy communication channel to a standard information theoretic quantities including entropy and mutual information.

Let X and Y be the random variables representing the input and output, respectively, with the joint probability $P(x, y)$. Let e be the occurrence of error, i.e., that $X \neq \tilde{X}$, where $\tilde{X} = f(X)$ a noise approximate version of X. Fano's inequality is defined as

$$H(X|Y) \leq H(e) + P(e) \log(|\chi| - 1) \tag{2.61}$$

where χ is denoted as the support of X,

$$H(X|Y) = -\sum_{i,j} P(x_i, y_j) \log P(x_i|y_j) \tag{2.62}$$

is the conditional entropy,

$$P(e) = P(X \neq \tilde{X}) \tag{2.63}$$

is the probability of the communication error, and

$$H(e) = -P(e) \log P(e) - (1 - P(e)) \log(1 - P(e)) \tag{2.64}$$

is the corresponding binary entropy.

The inequality of Eq. (2.61) can be applied to lower bound the probability of support set recovery error. By making use of a bound $H(e) \leq 1$ and Fano's inequality, the decision error probability can be lower bounded as follows:

$$P(e) \geq \frac{H(X|Y) - 1}{\log|\chi| - 1} \tag{2.65}$$

Suppose $M \geq 2K$, then the map is one-to-one correspondent from X to Y. Therefore, $H(X|Y) = 0$ for $M \geq 2K$.

2.10 Sparse Convex Optimization

2.10.1 Introduction to Convex Optimization

If we want to know what is the convex *optimization problem*, first we need to know what is the *convex set*.

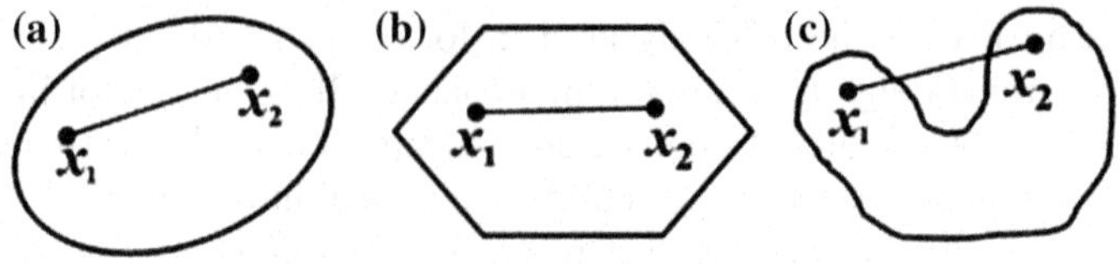

Fig. 2.7 Some examples about convex/nonconvex sets, where **a** and **b** are convex sets, and **c** is nonconvex set

Definition 2.10.1 (*Convex Set*) D is a set of $\mathbb{R}^N$. If any two points $\boldsymbol{x}_1, \boldsymbol{x}_2 \in D$ and $\lambda \in [0, 1]$ have the property as follows:

$$\lambda \boldsymbol{x}_1 + (1 - \lambda)\boldsymbol{x}_2 \in D.$$

We can call that this set D is a convex set, and $\lambda \boldsymbol{x}_1 + (1 - \lambda)\boldsymbol{x}_2$ is the convex combination of $\boldsymbol{x}_1$ and $\boldsymbol{x}_2$.

There are some examples, which are shown in Fig. 2.7 about the convex set in 2D space. We can note that if the set D is convex, and any two points $\boldsymbol{x}_1, \boldsymbol{x}_2 \in D$, we can get the segment which connect these two points also contained in set D.

After we have known what is the convex set, we need to know another important property of the convex optimization.

Definition 2.10.2 (*Convex Function*) The set $D \subset \mathbb{R}^N$ is a nonempty convex set, if $\forall \boldsymbol{x}_1, \boldsymbol{x}_2 \in D$ and $\forall \alpha \in (0, 1)$ the following equation satisfied

$$f(\alpha \boldsymbol{x}_1 + (1 - \alpha)\boldsymbol{x}_2) \leq \alpha f(\boldsymbol{x}_1) + (1 - \alpha) f(\boldsymbol{x}_2),$$

we call the function $f(\boldsymbol{x})$ is the *convex function* in set D. If $' \leq'$ is replaced by $' <'$ in the above equation, we call the function $f(\boldsymbol{x})$ is *strictly convex function.*

From the definition of the convex function, we can see that the linear interpolation of two points on the convex function is not smaller than the function value. This can be seen from the Fig. 2.8 which is a scalar convex function.

There are some theorems about the convex function

Fig. 2.8 The scaler convex function

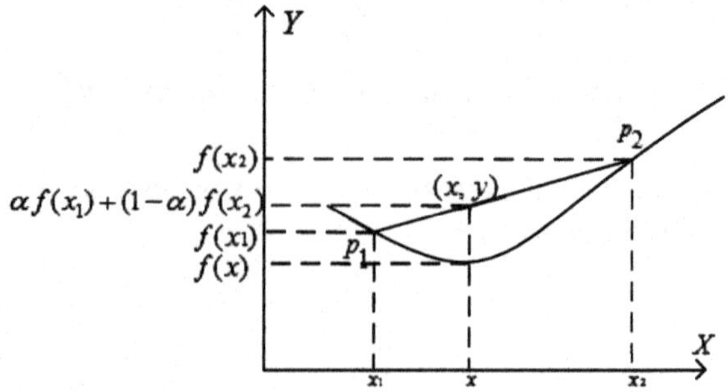

Theorem 2.10.1 *If f_1, f_2 are convex functions in convex set D, and λ is a real number, we can get λf_1 and $f_1 + f_2$ are also convex functions.*

Theorem 2.10.2 *The set D is a convex set in $\mathbb{R}^N$, f is a convex function in set D, so f is continuous in set D.*

Theorem 2.10.3 *The set D is a nonempty convex set, f is a convex function in set D, we can get the following conclusions:*

(1) The set $D_\alpha = \{\boldsymbol{x} | \boldsymbol{x} \in D, f(\boldsymbol{x}) \leq \alpha\}$ is convex.
(2) The local minimal points of f in D is also the global minimal points of f, and the set of local minimal points is convex.

Theorem 2.10.4 *The set D is the nonempty open convex set, $f(\boldsymbol{x})$ is a differentiable function in set D. The $f(\boldsymbol{x})$ is the convex function if and only if $\forall \boldsymbol{x}, \boldsymbol{y} \in D$,*

$$f(\boldsymbol{y}) \geq f(\boldsymbol{x}) + (\boldsymbol{y} - \boldsymbol{x})^T \nabla f(\boldsymbol{x}).$$

The theorems above tell us how to judge a function is convex function. The following definition defines the *convex optimization problem* by the convex function

Definition 2.10.3 (*Convex Optimization Problem*) For the optimization problem

$$\min f(\boldsymbol{x}) = f(x_1, x_2, \ldots, x_N),\ \boldsymbol{x} \in \mathbb{R}^N, \text{s.t. } g_j(\boldsymbol{x}) \leq 0, \quad j = 1, 2, \ldots, m \tag{2.66}$$

if the object function $f(\boldsymbol{x})$ and the constraint function $g_j(\boldsymbol{x})$ for $j = 1, 2, \ldots, m$ are convex function, we call this optimization problem is a convex optimization problem.

There are some properties about the convex optimization problem, before we present these properties, we need to know the definition of *feasible region*.

Definition 2.10.4 (*Feasible Region*) The feasible region of a optimization problem is the set of points that satisfy the constraint condition of this optimization problem.

Theorem 2.10.5 *The feasible region of the convex optimization problem $D = \{\boldsymbol{x} | g_j(\boldsymbol{x}) \leq 0, j = 1, 2, \ldots, m\}$ is convex.*

Theorem 2.10.6 *If give a point $\boldsymbol{x}_k$, then we can get the convex set*

$$S = \{\boldsymbol{x} | \boldsymbol{x} \in D, f(\boldsymbol{x}) \leq f(\boldsymbol{x}_k)\}$$

By the Theorem 2.10.6, we can imagine that if the object function is a function of two variables, the contour line of this function is the form of convex nested circles.

Theorem 2.10.7 *Any local optimal solution of the convex optimization problem is the global optimal solution.*

Theorem 2.10.8 *If the object function of the convex optimization problem $f(\boldsymbol{x})$ is the strictly convex function, the global optimal solution must be the only solution.*

2.10.2 Gradient, Subgradient, Accelerated Gradient

1. Gradient Descent

Gradient descent method is the first-order optimization algorithm. It is also called the *steepest descent*. The core of the gradient descent method is using the gradient descent direction iteratively at a fixed step to search for the local minimum of the object function.

The multivariable object function is differentiable in a neighborhood of a point $\boldsymbol{a}$, by the property of the gradient, and then the negative gradient direction $-\nabla F(\boldsymbol{a})$ is the decreasing fastest direction from $\boldsymbol{a}$. We can get that if

$$\boldsymbol{b} = \boldsymbol{a} - \gamma \nabla F(\boldsymbol{a}) \tag{2.67}$$

for γ small enough, then $F(\boldsymbol{a}) \geq F(\boldsymbol{b})$. Using this property, we start from a point $\boldsymbol{x}_0$ and have

$$\boldsymbol{x}_{n+1} = \boldsymbol{x}_n - \gamma_n \nabla F(\boldsymbol{x}_n), \quad n \geq 0. \tag{2.68}$$

Further more, we can get

$$F(\boldsymbol{x}_0) \geq F(\boldsymbol{x}_1) \geq F(\boldsymbol{x}_2) \geq \ldots, \tag{2.69}$$

thus the sequence $\{\boldsymbol{x}_n\}$ can converge to the local minimum. The *step size* γ can be changed at every iteration. If F satisfy certain assumption, we can particularly choose the γ. This can guarantee to convergence to a local minimum, which is illustrated in Fig. 2.9.

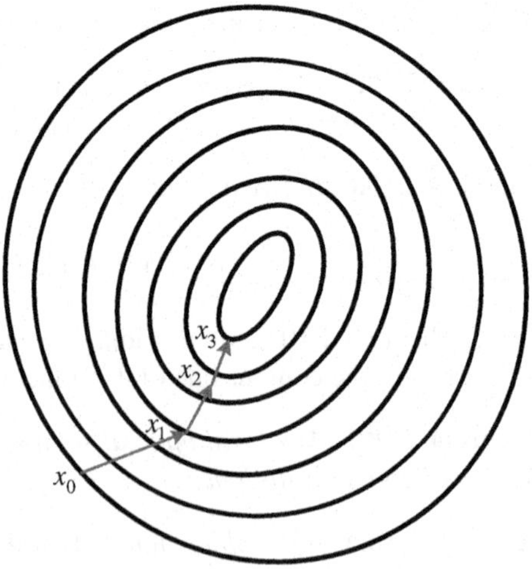

Fig. 2.9 Gradient descent with a constant step size γ

For example, the linear squares problem is used to minimize the following object function

$$F(\boldsymbol{x}_0) = \|A\boldsymbol{x} - \boldsymbol{y}\|_{\ell_2}^2. \tag{2.70}$$

This object function is smooth at every point, and we can compute its gradient as follows:

$$\nabla F(\boldsymbol{x}) = 2A^T(A\boldsymbol{x} - \boldsymbol{y}). \tag{2.71}$$

Using Eq. 2.71, we can iteratively find the points until the process convergence.

2. Subgradient Methods

In gradient descent or conjugate gradient methods, we need to compute the gradient of the object function. However, in case the object function is nonsmooth, we cannot use the gradient methods to solve optimization problem. We can see one model of the sparse representation problem,

$$\arg\min_{\boldsymbol{x}} = \|A\boldsymbol{x} - \boldsymbol{y}\|_{\ell_2}^2 + \lambda\|\boldsymbol{x}\|_{\ell_1}. \tag{2.72}$$

Because the ℓ_1-norm regularization term is nonsmooth, we cannot use the gradient methods. However, we can use the *subgradient methods*.

The *subgradient method* is a algorithm which can be used for minimization of the nondifferentiable convex function. There are some properties of subgradient method as follows [4]:

(1) The subgradient method applies directly to nondifferentiable F;
(2) The step lengths are not chosen by the line search as the ordinary gradient method. In the most common cases, the step lengths are fixed in advance;
(3) The subgradient method is not a descent method; the function value can increase.

The subgradient method is the first-order algorithm, and then it is much slower than the interior-point methods (or Newton's method in unconstrained case). Thus its performance depends on the scale and condition of the problem. However, subgradient method has its own advantages over the interior-point method and Newton methods.

(1) It can be applied to wider range of problems than interior-point methods and Newton methods;
(2) The memory requirement can be much smaller than interior-point methods and Newton methods, it can be used in extremely large scale problems;
(3) It can be combined with primal or dual decomposition technique to develop a distributed algorithm consequently.

Now, We introduce the concept of subgradient.

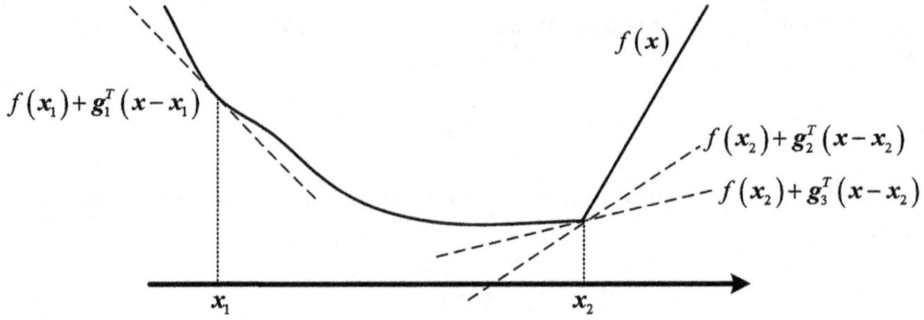

Fig. 2.10 The example of subgradient

Definition 2.10.5 (*Subgradient*) $\boldsymbol{g}$ is a subgradient of f (not necessarily convex) at point $\boldsymbol{x}$, if the following inequality is satisfied

$$f(\boldsymbol{y}) \geq f(\boldsymbol{x}) + \boldsymbol{g}^T(\boldsymbol{y} - \boldsymbol{x}), \forall \boldsymbol{y}. \tag{2.73}$$

One example of subgradient is illustrated in Fig. 2.10.

In the Fig. 2.10, $\boldsymbol{g}_2$, $\boldsymbol{g}_3$ are subgradients at $\boldsymbol{x}_2$, and $\boldsymbol{g}_1$ is a subgradient at $\boldsymbol{x}_1$. Note that some points have more than one subgradient. There are some further properties of subgradient:

(1) If f is convex, it has at least one subgradient at every point in domain of definition of f;
(2) If f is convex and differentiable, $\nabla f(\boldsymbol{x})$ is a subgradient of f at $\boldsymbol{x}$.

After giving the definition of *subgradient*, we shall give the definition of *subdifferential*.

Definition 2.10.6 (*Subdifferential*) The set of all subgradients of f at $\boldsymbol{x}$ is called the subdifferential of f at point $\boldsymbol{x}$, which can be noted as $\partial f(\boldsymbol{x})$.

From the definition of subdifferential, we can see that the subdifferential is a set. It also has some properties as follows:

(1) $\partial f(\boldsymbol{x})$ is a closed convex set;
(2) If f is convex and finite near the point $\boldsymbol{x}$, $\partial f(\boldsymbol{x})$ is nonempty;
(3) $\partial f(\boldsymbol{x}) = \{\nabla f(\boldsymbol{x})\}$, if f is differentiable at $\boldsymbol{x}$;
(4) if $\partial f(\boldsymbol{x}) = \{\boldsymbol{g}\}$, then f is differentiable at point $\boldsymbol{x}$ and $\boldsymbol{g} = \nabla f(\boldsymbol{x})$.

We need to note that in many applications, we do not need to calculate $\partial f(\boldsymbol{x})$, but only need to find one $g \in \partial f(\boldsymbol{x})$. We can use concepts subgradient and subdifferential to solve the ℓ_1-norm optimization convex problem [21], which will be used in Sect. 5.2.1.

Now, we shall briefly review how to use gradient and subgradient method to solve the LASSO problem. By the subgradient method, we can easily get the unique solution of

$$\arg\min_{\boldsymbol{x}} \frac{1}{2}\|\boldsymbol{x} - \boldsymbol{y}\|_{\ell_2}^2 + \lambda\|\boldsymbol{x}\|_{\ell_1} \tag{2.74}$$

for any $\boldsymbol{y} \in \mathbb{R}^D$, we have

$$x_i = S_\lambda(y_i), \tag{2.75}$$

where $S_\lambda(\cdot)$ is the *shrinkage operator* which is defined as

$$S_\lambda(y) = \operatorname{sgn}(y)\max\{|y| - \lambda, 0\}. \tag{2.76}$$

But for the LASSO problem Eq. (2.72), all elements of $\boldsymbol{x}$ are related by the matrix A. So, we cannot use the solution of Eq. (2.74) directly, but we can approximate the original object function by first-order Taylor expansion of $f(\boldsymbol{x}) = \|A\boldsymbol{x} - \boldsymbol{y}\|_{\ell_2}^2$ at the preceding point $\boldsymbol{x}_{k-1}$ and alternate the original LASSO problem as

$$\begin{aligned}\boldsymbol{x}_k = \arg\min_{\boldsymbol{x}} \Big\{ & f(\boldsymbol{x}_{k-1}) + \langle \boldsymbol{x} - \boldsymbol{x}_{k-1}, \nabla f(\boldsymbol{x}_{k-1})\rangle \\ & + \frac{1}{2t_k}\|\boldsymbol{x} - \boldsymbol{x}_{k-1}\|_{\ell_2}^2 + \lambda\|\boldsymbol{x}_1\|_{\ell_1}\Big\}. \end{aligned} \tag{2.77}$$

After ignoring the constant term, we can write the above equation as

$$\boldsymbol{x}_k = \arg\min_{\boldsymbol{x}} \left\{ \frac{1}{2t_k}\|\boldsymbol{x} - (\boldsymbol{x}_{k-1} - t_k \nabla f(\boldsymbol{x}_{k-1}))\|_{\ell_2}^2 + \lambda\|\boldsymbol{x}_1\|_{\ell_1}\right\}. \tag{2.78}$$

Then, we can use the solution of Eq. (2.74) to get the solution as

$$\boldsymbol{x}_k = \arg\min_{\boldsymbol{x}} S_{\lambda t_k}(\boldsymbol{x}_{k-1} - t_k \nabla f(\boldsymbol{x}_{k-1})). \tag{2.79}$$

This is a fixed-point way to get the optimal solution, and it has two steps: (1) Using the gradient descent method to get the intermediate point; (2) Using the *shrinkage operator* to get $\boldsymbol{x}_k$. The process above is the *Iterative Shrinkage-Thresholding Algorithm* (ISTA) [12].

3. Accelerated Gradient

Even though the ISTA algorithm is very simple and adequate for the large scale problem, it converges very slowly. Toward this end, A. Beck et al. proposed a *Fast Iterative Shrinkage-Thresholding Algorithm* (FISTA) which has a higher convergence rate $O(1/k^2)$ by using the *Accelerate Gradient Descent* (AGD) method as compared with ISTA is $O(1/k)$.

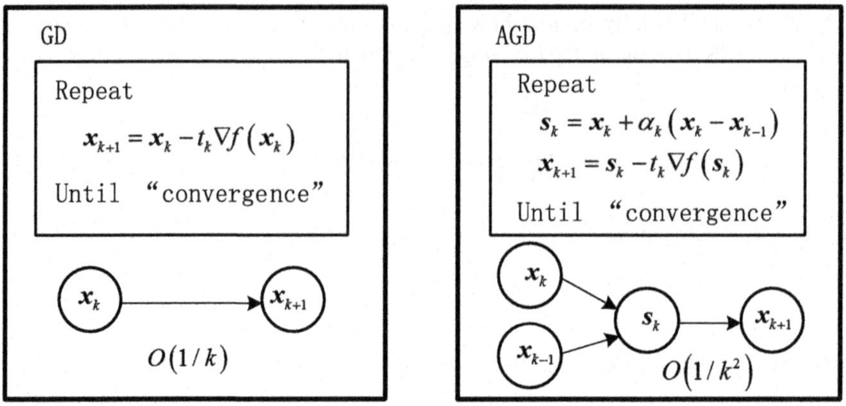

Fig. 2.11 The comparison between GD and AGD methods

The core idea of FISTA is using an accelerated gradient descent to replace the gradient descent step. The comparison of both gradient descent and accelerated gradient descent methods is illustrated in Fig. 2.11.

From Fig. 2.11, we can see that AGD method is using an intermediate variable $\boldsymbol{s}_k$ to get the final update $\boldsymbol{x}_{k+1}$. Using the AGD to replace the first step of ISTA, we can get the FISTA algorithm in sparse representation [3].

2.10.3 Augmented Lagrangian Method

Augmented Lagrangian methods are a certain class of algorithms to solve the constraint optimization problems. The core idea of the augmented Lagrangian methods is using the approximate unconstraint optimization problem to replace the constraint optimization problem. The difference between penalty methods and augmented Lagrangian methods is the augmented Lagrangian method that adds an additional term to the common penalty method's unconstraint object function. This difference can be seen from the following example.

We consider the optimization problem as follows:

$$\begin{aligned} &\arg\min_{\boldsymbol{x}} \quad f(\boldsymbol{x}) \\ &\text{s.t.} \quad g_i(\boldsymbol{x}) = 0, \quad i = 1, 2, \ldots, q. \end{aligned} \tag{2.80}$$

We only consider the equality constraints for simplicity. By the penalty method, we can approximate the original constraint problem by a unconstraint problem as follows:

$$L(\boldsymbol{x}, \boldsymbol{\lambda}) = f(\boldsymbol{x}) + \sum_{i=1}^{q} \lambda_i g_i(\boldsymbol{x}). \tag{2.81}$$

We can also use the augmented Lagrangian method to approximate the original constraint problem as follows:

$$L_\rho(\boldsymbol{x}, \boldsymbol{\lambda}) = f(\boldsymbol{x}) + \sum_{i=1}^{q} \lambda_i g_i(\boldsymbol{x}) + \frac{\rho}{2} \sum_{i=1}^{q} g_i(\boldsymbol{x})^2. \tag{2.82}$$

From both approximate replacement by penalty method and augmented Lagrangian method of the original constraint optimization, we can find the augmented Lagrangian method adds an additional term $\frac{\rho}{2}\sum_{i=1}^{q} g_i(\boldsymbol{x})^2$, which is used for punishing the violations of the equality constraints $g_i(\boldsymbol{x})$. It has been proved that when ρ is large enough, the solution of unconstraint problem of augmented Lagrangian can coincides with the constrained solution of the original problem. The iterations of the algorithm end when the gradient $\rho g_i(\boldsymbol{x}) \Delta g_i(\boldsymbol{x}) = \boldsymbol{0}$. The whole algorithm of the augmented Lagrangian method is alternately updating $\boldsymbol{x}$ and $\boldsymbol{\lambda}$.

(1) Find the unconstraint minimum

$$\boldsymbol{x}^{(t+1)} = \arg\min_{\boldsymbol{x}} L_\rho(\boldsymbol{x}, \boldsymbol{\lambda}). \tag{2.83}$$

(2) Update the multiplier vector $\boldsymbol{\lambda}$

$$\lambda_i^{(t+1)} = \lambda_i^{(t)} + \rho g_i(\boldsymbol{x}^{(t)}), \quad i = 1, \ldots, q \tag{2.84}$$

Using the augmented Lagrangian method, we solve the ℓ_1-norm convex optimization problem [20, 32]. Considering about the Basis Pursuit (BP) problem

Table 2.1 The Augmented Lagrangian algorithm flowchart

Input:	sensing matrix A, measurements $\boldsymbol{y}$, and parameter ρ
Initialization:	parameter vector $\boldsymbol{\lambda}$ with large value
while	(!stop criterion)
	Update the $\boldsymbol{x}$ as a LASSO problem
	$\boldsymbol{x}^{(t+1)} = \arg\min_{\boldsymbol{x}} \|\boldsymbol{x}\|_{\ell_1} + \langle \boldsymbol{\lambda}^{(t)}, A\boldsymbol{x} - \boldsymbol{y}\rangle + \frac{\rho}{2}\|A\boldsymbol{x} - \boldsymbol{y}\|_{\ell_2}^2$
	Update the parameter vector $\boldsymbol{\lambda}$
	$\boldsymbol{\lambda}^{(t+1)} = \boldsymbol{\lambda}^{(t)} + \rho(A\boldsymbol{x}^{(t+1)} - \boldsymbol{y})$
end while	
Output:	Coefficients $\boldsymbol{x}$

$$\begin{aligned} \arg\min_{x} \quad & \|x\|_{\ell_1}, \\ \text{s.t.} \quad & Ax = y \end{aligned} \tag{2.85}$$

The algorithm flow chart of ALM is shown in Table 2.1.

References

1. Achlioptas, D.: Database-friendly random projections: Johnson-Lindenstrauss with binary coins. J. Comput. Syst. Sci. **66**(4), 671–687 (2003)
2. Baraniuk, R., Davenport, M., DeVore, R., Wakin, M.: A simple proof of the restricted isometry property for random matrices. Constr. Approx. **28**(3), 253–263 (2008)
3. Beck, A., Teboulle, M.: A fast iterative shrinkage-thresholding algorithm for linear inverse problems. SIAM J. Imaging Sci. **2**(1), 183–202 (2009)
4. Boyd, S., Xiao, L., Mutapcic, A.: Subgradient Methods. Lecture, Stanford University, Autumn Quarter **54**(1), 48–61 (2003)
5. Candes, E.J.: The restricted isometry property and its implications for compressed sensing. Comptes Rendus Mathematique **346**(9), 589–592 (2008)
6. Candes, E.J., Romberg, J.K., Tao, T.: Stable signal recovery from incomplete and inaccurate measurements. Commun. Pure Appl. Math. **59**(8), 1207–1223 (2006)
7. Candes, E.J., Tao, T.: Decoding by linear programming. IEEE Trans. Inf. Theory **51**(12), 4203–4215 (2005)
8. Candes, E.J., Tao, T.: Near-optimal signal recovery from random projections: universal encoding strategies? IEEE Trans. Inf. Theory **52**(12), 5406–5425 (2006)
9. Chen, S.S., Donoho, D.L., Saunders, M.A.: Atomic decomposition by basis pursuit. SIAM J. Sci. Comput. **20**(1), 33–61 (1998)
10. Cohen, A., Dahmen, W., DeVore, R.: Instance optimal decoding by thresholding in compressed sensing. Technical Report DTIC Document (2008)
11. Cohen, A., Dahmen, W., DeVore, R.: Compressed sensing and best k-term approximation. J. Am. Math. Soc. **22**(1), 211–231 (2009)
12. Daubechies, I., Defrise, M., De Mol, C.: An iterative thresholding algorithm for linear inverse problems with a sparsity constraint. Commun. Pure Appl. Math. **57**(11), 1413–1457 (2004)
13. Davenport, M.A.: Random observations on random observations: Sparse signal acquisition and processing. Ph.D. thesis. Citeseer (2010)
14. Davenport, M.A., Duarte, M.F., Eldar, Y.C., Kutyniok, G.: Introduction to compressed sensing 93 (2011)
15. Donoho, D.L., Elad, M.: Optimally sparse representation in general (nonorthogonal) dictionaries via ℓ_1-minimization. Proc. Natl. Acad. Sci. **100**(5), 2197–2202 (2003)
16. Donoho, D.L., Huo, X.: Uncertainty principles and ideal atomic decomposition. IEEE Trans. Inf. Theory **47**(7), 2845–2862 (2001)
17. Donoho, D.L., Stark, P.B.: Uncertainty principles and signal recovery. SIAM J. Appl. Math. **49**(3), 906–931 (1989)
18. Elad, M.: Sparse and Redundant Representations: From Theory to Applications in Signal and Image Processing. Springer, New York (2010)
19. Eldar, Y.C., Kutyniok, G.: Compressed Sensing: Theory and Applications. Cambridge University Press, Cambridge (2012)
20. Goldstein, T., Osher, S.: The split Bregman method for ℓ_1-regularized problems. SIAM J. Imaging Sci. **2**(2), 323–343 (2009)
21. Hale, E.T., Yin, W., Zhang, Y.: Fixed-point continuation for ℓ_1-minimization: methodology and convergence. SIAM J. Optim. **19**(3), 1107–1130 (2008)

22. Haupt, J., Nowak, R.: Signal reconstruction from noisy random projections. IEEE Trans. Inf. Theory **52**(9), 4036–4048 (2006)
23. Johnson, W.B., Lindenstrauss, J.: Extensions of Lipschitz mappings into a Hilbert space. Contemp. Math. **26**(189–206), 1 (1984)
24. Lee, H.N.: Introduction to Compressed Sensing. Lecture Notes. Springer (2011)
25. Li, P., Hastie, T.J., Church, K.W.: Very sparse random projections. In: ACM SIGKDD International Conference on Knowledge Discovery and Data Mining (2006)
26. Muthukrishnan, S.: Data Streams: Algorithms and Applications. Now Publishers Inc. (2005)
27. Needell, D., Tropp, J.A.: CoSaMP: iterative signal recovery from incomplete and inaccurate samples. Commun. ACM **53**(12), 93–100 (2010)
28. Shannon, C.E.: Communication in the presence of noise. IEEE Proc. IRE **37**(1), 10–21 (1949)
29. Sharon, Y., Wright, J., Ma, Y.: Computation and relaxation of conditions for equivalence between ℓ_1 and ℓ_0 minimization. IEEE Trans. Inf. Theory **5** (2007)
30. Wang, H., Nie, F., Huang, H.: Multi-view clustering and feature learning via structured sparsity. In: ICML (2013)
31. Yanning Shen, J.F., Li, H.: Exact reconstruction analysis of log-sum minimization for compressed sensing. IEEE Signal Process. Lett. **20**(12), 1223–1226 (2013)
32. Yin, W., Osher, S., Goldfarb, D., Darbon, J.: Bregman iterative algorithms for ℓ_1-minimization with applications to compressed sensing. SIAM J. Imaging Sci. **1**(1), 143–168 (2008)
33. Zhang, K., Zhang, L., Yang, M.H.: Real-time compressive tracking. In: ECCV. Springer (2012)
34. Zhou Zhou, K.L., Fang, J.: Bayesian compressive sensing using normal product priors. IEEE Signal Process. Lett. **22**(5), 583–587 (2015)

Part II
Sparse Representation, Modeling and Learning

Chapter 3
Sparse Recovery Approaches

3.1 Introduction

Sparse structures are well suited for image/video interpretation, visualization, computation, classification, and analysis. Sparse representation is to either represent or approximate a feature vector with a linear combination of small portion of an overcomplete dictionary. Usually, the dictionary is a set of atoms whose number is more than the dimension of the feature space. Hence, the feature vector can be combined by multiple ways.

Suppose we have a dictionary matrix $A \in \mathbb{R}^{D \times N}$ with $D \ll N$ and any $\boldsymbol{y} \in \mathbb{R}^D$, and define the overdetermined linear system of equations

$$\boldsymbol{y} = A\boldsymbol{x}. \tag{3.1}$$

This system has infinitely many solutions, and we need to regularize the linear system to obtain a well-defined solution. By introducing a cost function, we define a general optimization

$$\arg\min_{\boldsymbol{x}} \parallel \boldsymbol{x} \parallel_{\ell_p}, \quad \text{s.t.} \quad A\boldsymbol{x} = \boldsymbol{y}, \tag{3.2}$$

where $\boldsymbol{x} \in \mathbb{R}^N$ is the decomposition coefficient vector. If we select $p = 2$, the strictly convex function $\parallel \boldsymbol{x} \parallel_p$ guarantees a unique solution. Consequently, Eq. (3.2) has a unique solution, $\hat{\boldsymbol{x}}$—the so-called minimum ℓ_2-norm solution explicitly by

$$\hat{\boldsymbol{x}} = (A^T A)^{-1} A^T \boldsymbol{y}. \tag{3.3}$$

This searching algorithm in Eq. (3.2) with $p = 2$ is also known as Method of Frames (MOF). Geometrically, the collection of all solutions to Eq. (3.2) is an affine subspace in $\mathbb{R}^N$. The MOF selects the elements of this subspace closest to the origin. Note that the MOF is not of sufficient sparsity. That is, if there is a very sparse

H. Cheng, *Sparse Representation, Modeling and Learning in Visual Recognition*,
Advances in Computer Vision and Pattern Recognition,
DOI 10.1007/978-1-4471-6714-3_3

solution in terms of the dictionary A, then the $\hat{\boldsymbol{x}}$ found by the MOF is likely to be much less sparse.

In this book, we consider another simple and intuitive regularization constraints-sparsity. This constraint leads to the fewest nonzero coefficients $\hat{\boldsymbol{x}}$. In this case, Eq. (3.2) with $p = 0$ is the fundamental sparse representation of $\boldsymbol{y}$ over A. The searching for a sparse solution can lead to a tractable problem. The literature describes a huge number of approaches to obtain the sparse solutions. These approaches fall into three rough categories: convex relaxation, greedy pursuits, and combinational approaches. The convex relaxation approaches include Basis Pursuit (BP) [13], interior point approaches [10, 31], projected gradient methods [23], and iterative thresholding [15]. The greedy pursuit [29] approaches include Orthogonal Matching Pursuit (OMP) [40, 47], stagewise Orthogonal Matching Pursuit (stOMP) [19], and Regularized Orthogonal Matching Pursuit (ROMP) [35, 36]. The combinational approaches include Fourier sampling algorithms [26, 27], Compressive Sampling Matching Pursuit (CoSaMP) [34], and Sparse Bayesian Learning [30, 49]. More specifically, ℓ_1-norm minimization is widely used in seeking sparsest solutions, thanks to the new compressive sensing theory, the ℓ_0–ℓ_1 equivalence theorem. There are five representative approaches, gradient projection, homotopy, iterative shrinkage–thresholding, proximal gradient, and alternating direction [51].

Convex relaxation and Greedy approaches are introduced in Sects. 3.2 and 3.3. Section 3.4 provides the basic definition of Sparse Bayesian Learning (SBL) and its variants. Moreover, a ℓ_0 gradient minimazation is used to approximate real ℓ_0 solution in Sect. 3.5. Finally, we introduce the sparse feature projection approach in Sect. 3.6.

3.2 Convex Relaxation

3.2.1 Linear Programming Solutions

1. Introduction

Basis Pursuit (BP) is a basic algorithm for decomposing a signal into superposition of dictionary elements, which has the smallest ℓ_1-norm of coefficients among all such decompositions. Compared with both MOF and MP, BP algorithms have better sparsity and superresolution [13]. Formally, BP can be written as

$$\hat{x} = \arg\min_{\boldsymbol{x}} \|\boldsymbol{x}\|_{\ell_1}, \quad \text{s.t.} \quad A\boldsymbol{x} = \boldsymbol{y}. \tag{3.4}$$

We would like to point out that the solution of Eq. (3.4) is similar to Eq. (3.2) but simply replacing the ℓ_p norm with ℓ_1 norm in Eq. (3.2). However, this has important consequences. MOF leads to a quadratic optimization problem with linear equality constraints and so involves essentially just the solution of a system of linear equations. However, BP requires solving a convex, nonquadratic optimization problem.

2. The Connection between ℓ_1-norm Minimization and LP

Regarding the solutions, there are two different versions of linear programming, LP1 and LP2 algorithms.

The LP1 Algorithm [13, 17]: We can formulate the ℓ_1-norm minimization problem into an LP problem in the following way:

$$\begin{aligned} &\arg\min_{\boldsymbol{u}} \ \ \boldsymbol{c}^T \boldsymbol{u}, \\ &\text{s.t.} \ \ \boldsymbol{y} = B\boldsymbol{u}, \end{aligned} \tag{3.5}$$

where $\mathbf{1} = [1, \ldots, 1]^T$, $B = [A, -A]$, $u = [\boldsymbol{x}_+^T, \boldsymbol{x}_-^T]^T \in \mathbb{R}^M$, $M = 2N$, $\boldsymbol{x}_+ = \max\{\boldsymbol{x}, 0\}$, $\boldsymbol{x}_- = \max\{-\boldsymbol{x}, 0\}$. Equation (3.4) can be converted into a standard linear programming problem by introducing variables x_i^+ and x_i^-, and setting $x_i = x_i^+ - x_i^-$ and $|x_i| = x_i^+ + x_i^-$, $1 \le i \le N$. In addition, we add constraints $x_i^+ \ge 0$ and $x_i^- \ge 0$. The resulting linear programming problem can then be solved with a linear programming solver such as a simplex algorithm [25]. By doing so, we build the connection between Eqs. (3.4) and (3.5). The LP1 algorithm is also known as Basis Pursuit, and its implementation can be referred to Appendix C.

The LP2 Algorithm: Given $\|\boldsymbol{x}\|_{\ell_1} = |x_1| + \cdots + |x_N|$, we have

$$\arg\min_{\boldsymbol{x}} \ \ |x_1| + \cdots + |x_N|, \ \ \text{s.t.} \ \ A\boldsymbol{x} = \boldsymbol{y}. \tag{3.6}$$

Equation (3.6) is not a linear programming problem since $\|\boldsymbol{x}\|_{\ell_1}$ is nonlinear. Now we add a new variable $\boldsymbol{t} = \{t_1, t_2, \ldots, t_N\}$ to remove the nonlinearities.

$$\begin{aligned} &\arg\min_{\boldsymbol{t}} \ \ \sum_{n=1}^{N} t_n, \\ &\text{s.t.} \ \ |x_n| \le t_n, \quad n = 1, 2, \ldots, N \\ &\qquad A\boldsymbol{x} = \boldsymbol{y}. \end{aligned} \tag{3.7}$$

Therefore, we have

$$\begin{aligned} &\arg\min_{\boldsymbol{t}} \ \ \sum_{n=1}^{N} t_n, \\ &\text{s.t.} \ \ -t_n \le x_n \le t_n, \quad n = 1, \ldots, N, \\ &\qquad A\boldsymbol{x} = \boldsymbol{y}. \end{aligned} \tag{3.8}$$

We simplify Eq. (3.8) as

$$
\begin{aligned}
\arg\min_{\boldsymbol{t}} \quad & \mathbf{1}^T \boldsymbol{t}, \\
\text{s.t.} \quad & \boldsymbol{I}\boldsymbol{x} - \boldsymbol{I}\boldsymbol{t} \leq \mathbf{0}, \\
& \boldsymbol{I}\boldsymbol{x} + \boldsymbol{I}\boldsymbol{t} \geq \mathbf{0}, \\
& \boldsymbol{A}\boldsymbol{x} = \boldsymbol{y},
\end{aligned} \tag{3.9}
$$

where $\mathbf{1} = [1, 1, \ldots, 1]^T$, and I is an identity matrix. Right now, both the objective function and constraints are linear. Thus, we transfer a ℓ_1-norm minimization problem Eq. (3.4) into a linear programming problem. We would like to point out that the dual form provides computational advantages instead of the primal problem especially for large scale cases. For details refer to Appendix A.3.

LP via interior point methods: The simplex method works around the boundary of this simplex by jumping from one vertex to an adjacent vertex, where the objective is better. Instead, the interior point method starts from an interior of the simplex until the interior point method converges. Moreover, great advances in interior point methods for convex optimization have been made since the work by Nesterov et al. [37]. Following the notation in [7], we introduced the primal–dual algorithm for linear programming. The standard linear programming is [9]

$$
\begin{aligned}
\arg\min_{\boldsymbol{x}} \quad & \boldsymbol{c}_0^T \boldsymbol{x}, \\
\text{s.t.} \quad & \boldsymbol{A}\boldsymbol{x} = \boldsymbol{y}, \\
& f_i(\boldsymbol{x}) \leq 0,
\end{aligned} \tag{3.10}
$$

where $\boldsymbol{x} \in \mathbb{R}^N$, $\boldsymbol{y} \in \mathbb{R}^D$, A is a $D \times N$ matrix, $f_i(x) = \boldsymbol{c}_i^T x + d_i$, $(i = 1, 2, \ldots, m)$ is a linear function, $\boldsymbol{c}_i \in \mathbb{R}^N$, $d_i \in \mathbb{R}$.

The Kavush–Kuhn–Ticker conditions are satisfied:

$$
\begin{cases}
\boldsymbol{c}_0 + A^T \boldsymbol{\nu}^* + \sum_i \lambda_i^* \boldsymbol{c}_i = \mathbf{0}, \\
\lambda_i^* f_i(x^*) = 0, \ i = 1, 2, \ldots, m, \\
A\boldsymbol{x}^* - \boldsymbol{y} = \mathbf{0}, \\
f_i(x^*) \leq 0, \ i = 1, 2, \ldots, m,
\end{cases} \tag{3.11}
$$

where $\boldsymbol{\nu}^* \in \mathbb{R}^D$ is a dual vector, $\boldsymbol{\lambda}^* \in \mathbb{R}^m$ is a Lagrange multiplier vector, and $\boldsymbol{\lambda}^* \geq \mathbf{0}$.

Basically, the primal–dual algorithm finds the optimal $\boldsymbol{x}^*$ by applying Newton's method to a sequence of modified version of KKT conditions. The solution procedure is the standard Newton method as follows. The system is linearized and solved at an interior point $(\boldsymbol{x}^t, \boldsymbol{\nu}^t, \boldsymbol{\lambda}^t)$. Furthermore, the new point $(\boldsymbol{x}^{t+1}, \boldsymbol{\nu}^{t+1}, \boldsymbol{\lambda}^{t+1})$ must be modified so that it remains in the interior.

In practice, we would like to relax the following conditions:

$$\begin{cases} \lambda_i f_i(x^*) = 0 & \Rightarrow \lambda_i f_i(x^*) = -y\tau^t, \tau^t > 0, \\ \lambda_i \geq 0 & \Rightarrow \lambda_i > 0, i = 1, 2, \ldots, m, \\ f_i(x^*) \leq 0 & \Rightarrow f_i(x^*) < 0, i = 1, 2, \ldots, m. \end{cases} \tag{3.12}$$

Substituting Eq. (3.12) into Eq. (3.11), we have

$$\begin{cases} \boldsymbol{r}_d = \boldsymbol{c}_0 + A^T \boldsymbol{v} + \sum_i \lambda_i \boldsymbol{c}_i, \\ \boldsymbol{r}_c = -\Lambda \boldsymbol{f} - \frac{1}{\tau}\mathbf{1}, \\ \boldsymbol{r}_p = A\boldsymbol{x} - \boldsymbol{y}, \end{cases} \tag{3.13}$$

where Λ is a diagonal matrix with $\Lambda_{ii} = \lambda_i$ and $\boldsymbol{f} = (f_1(x), f_2(x), \ldots f_m(x))^T$. Thus we combine Eq. (3.13) as a single residual function $\boldsymbol{r}(\boldsymbol{x}, \boldsymbol{\lambda}, \boldsymbol{v}) = [\boldsymbol{r}_d, \boldsymbol{r}_c, \boldsymbol{r}_p]^T$, and seek the optimal point $(\boldsymbol{x}^*, \boldsymbol{\lambda}^*, \boldsymbol{v}^*)$, such that $\boldsymbol{r}(\boldsymbol{x}^*, \boldsymbol{\lambda}^*, \boldsymbol{v}^*) = \mathbf{0}$. Since Eq. (3.12) is nonlinear, we use the Newton's method to solve this equation.

We use the first-order Taylor expansion to $r(\boldsymbol{x}, \boldsymbol{\lambda}, \boldsymbol{v})$ around the point $(\boldsymbol{x}, \boldsymbol{\lambda}, \boldsymbol{v})$ such that

$$\boldsymbol{r}(\boldsymbol{x} + \Delta\boldsymbol{x}, \boldsymbol{v} + \Delta\boldsymbol{v}, \boldsymbol{\lambda} + \Delta\boldsymbol{\lambda}) \approx r(\boldsymbol{x}, \boldsymbol{\lambda}, \boldsymbol{v}) + J(\boldsymbol{x}, \boldsymbol{\lambda}, \boldsymbol{v}) \begin{bmatrix} \Delta\boldsymbol{x} \\ \Delta\boldsymbol{\lambda} \\ \Delta\boldsymbol{v} \end{bmatrix}, \tag{3.14}$$

where the $J(\boldsymbol{x}, \boldsymbol{\lambda}, \boldsymbol{v})$ is the Jacobian of $\boldsymbol{r}$.

The Newton's method aims to seek that the residual at the next point is zero, i.e., $\boldsymbol{r}(\boldsymbol{x} + \Delta\boldsymbol{x}, \boldsymbol{v} + \Delta\boldsymbol{v}, \boldsymbol{\lambda} + \Delta\boldsymbol{\lambda}) = \mathbf{0}$. Thus, we have

$$J(\boldsymbol{x}, \boldsymbol{\lambda}, \boldsymbol{v}) \begin{bmatrix} \Delta\boldsymbol{x} \\ \Delta\boldsymbol{\lambda} \\ \Delta\boldsymbol{v} \end{bmatrix} = -\boldsymbol{r}(\boldsymbol{x}, \boldsymbol{\lambda}, \boldsymbol{v}). \tag{3.15}$$

Furthermore, we rewrite Eq. (3.15) as

$$\begin{bmatrix} 0 & C^T & A^T \\ -\Lambda C & -F & 0 \\ A & 0 & 0 \end{bmatrix} \begin{bmatrix} \Delta\boldsymbol{x} \\ \Delta\boldsymbol{\lambda} \\ \Delta\boldsymbol{v} \end{bmatrix} = - \begin{bmatrix} \boldsymbol{c}_0 + A^T\boldsymbol{v} + \sum_{i=0}^m \lambda_i \boldsymbol{c}_i \\ -\Lambda\boldsymbol{f} - \frac{1}{\tau}\mathbf{1} \\ A\boldsymbol{x} - \boldsymbol{y} \end{bmatrix}, \tag{3.16}$$

where $C = [\boldsymbol{c}_1, \boldsymbol{c}_2, \ldots, \boldsymbol{c}_m]^T \in \mathbb{R}^{m \times N}$, $F = \text{diag}(f_1(x), f_2(x), \ldots, f_m(x))$.

The second equation in Eq. (3.16) can be written as:

$$\Delta\boldsymbol{\lambda} = -F^{-1}(\Lambda C \Delta\boldsymbol{x} + \Lambda\boldsymbol{f} + \frac{1}{\tau}\mathbf{1}). \tag{3.17}$$

Submitting Eq. (3.17) into the first equation of Eq. (3.16), we have

$$-C^T F^{-1} \Lambda C \Delta \boldsymbol{x} + A^T \Delta \boldsymbol{v} = -\left(\boldsymbol{c}_0 + \sum_{i=0}^{m} \lambda_i \boldsymbol{c}_i + A^T \boldsymbol{v} \right) + C^T F^{-1} \Lambda \boldsymbol{f} + C^T F^{-1} \frac{1}{\tau} \mathbf{1}, \tag{3.18}$$

where

$$C^T F^{-1} \Lambda \boldsymbol{f} = C^T \Lambda F^{-1} \boldsymbol{f} = C^T \Lambda \mathbf{1} = \sum_{i=0}^{m} \lambda_i \boldsymbol{c}_i,$$
$$C^T F^{-1} \frac{1}{\tau} \mathbf{1} = \frac{1}{\tau} C^T \boldsymbol{f}^{-1}, \ \boldsymbol{f}^{-1} = (f_1^{-1}(\boldsymbol{x}), f_2^{-1}(\boldsymbol{x}), \ldots, f_n^{-1}(\boldsymbol{x}))^T. \tag{3.19}$$

Thus we rewrite the first equation and the third equation of the Eq. (3.16) as

$$\begin{bmatrix} -C^T F^{-1} \Lambda C & A^T \\ A & 0 \end{bmatrix} \begin{bmatrix} \Delta \boldsymbol{x} \\ \Delta \boldsymbol{v} \end{bmatrix} = \begin{bmatrix} -\boldsymbol{c}_0 + (1/\tau) C^T \boldsymbol{f}^{-1} - A^T \boldsymbol{v} \\ \boldsymbol{y} - A\boldsymbol{x} \end{bmatrix}. \tag{3.20}$$

Thus, we can obtain $(\Delta \boldsymbol{x}, \Delta \boldsymbol{v})$ by solving Eq. (3.20) and then obtain $\Delta \boldsymbol{\lambda}$ from Eq. (3.17). Finally, we have a step direction $(\Delta \boldsymbol{x}, \Delta \boldsymbol{\lambda}, \Delta \boldsymbol{v})$. Here, we choose the step length $0 < s \leq 1$ to satisfy two criterions:

(1) Interior point: $x + s\Delta x$ and $\lambda + s\Delta\lambda$ are in the interior, i.e., $f_i(\boldsymbol{x} + s\Delta \boldsymbol{x}) < \mathbf{0}$, and $\boldsymbol{\lambda} + s\Delta\boldsymbol{\lambda} > \mathbf{0}, \forall i$.

(2) Decreasing residual:

$$\|\boldsymbol{r}_\tau(\boldsymbol{x} + s\Delta \boldsymbol{x}, \boldsymbol{\lambda} + s\Delta\boldsymbol{\lambda}, \boldsymbol{v} + s\Delta \boldsymbol{v})\|_{\ell_2} \leq (1 - \alpha s) \cdot \|\boldsymbol{r}_\tau(\boldsymbol{x}, \boldsymbol{\lambda}, \boldsymbol{v})\|_{\ell_2}, \tag{3.21}$$

where α is a user-specified parameter, usually $\alpha = 0.01$.

3.2.2 Second-Order Cone Programs with Log-Barrier Method

In this section, we introduce Second-Order Cone Programs (SOCPs) with log-barrier methods. In sparse regularization, we have

$$\hat{\boldsymbol{x}} = \arg\min_{\boldsymbol{x}} \quad \|\boldsymbol{x}\|_{\ell_1}, \quad \text{s.t.} \quad \|A\boldsymbol{x} - \boldsymbol{y}\|_{\ell_2} \leq \varepsilon. \tag{3.22}$$

Candes et al. [11] proved that there exists a sufficiently sparse $\boldsymbol{x}_0$ such that $\boldsymbol{y} = A\boldsymbol{x}_0 + \boldsymbol{e}$, $\|\boldsymbol{e}\|_{\ell_2} \leq \varepsilon$, then the solution $\hat{\boldsymbol{x}}$ of Eq. (3.22) will be closed to $\boldsymbol{x}_0$ where ε is a user-specified parameter.

As we know, the implementation of the primal–dual technique for solving SOCP is not straightforward as in the LP case. This section will introduce the SOCP using a log-barrier method, and Eq. (3.22) can be reformulated as SOCP as

$$\widehat{\boldsymbol{x}} = \arg\min_{(\boldsymbol{x},\boldsymbol{u})} \quad \mathbf{1}^T \boldsymbol{u},$$
$$\text{s.t.} \quad \begin{cases} \boldsymbol{x} - \boldsymbol{u} \leq \mathbf{0}, \\ -\boldsymbol{x} - \boldsymbol{u} \leq \mathbf{0}, \\ \frac{1}{2}(\|A\boldsymbol{x} - \boldsymbol{y}\|_{\ell_2}^2 - \varepsilon^2) \leq \mathbf{0}, \end{cases} \tag{3.23}$$

where $\mathbf{1} = [1, 1, \ldots, 1]^T$. Without loss of generality, we still use $\boldsymbol{x}$ to replace $[\boldsymbol{x}; \boldsymbol{u}]$

For better solving Eq. (3.23), we rewrite it in more general form as

$$\begin{aligned} &\arg\min_{\boldsymbol{x}} \quad f_0(\boldsymbol{x}), \\ &\quad \text{s.t.} \quad f_i(\boldsymbol{x}) \leq 0, i = 1, 2, \ldots, m, \\ &\qquad\quad f_j(\boldsymbol{x}) = 0, j = m+1, \ldots, m+n. \end{aligned} \tag{3.24}$$

We first formulate Eq. (3.24) using the logarithmic barrier functions as

$$\begin{aligned} &\arg\min_{\boldsymbol{x}} \quad f_0(\boldsymbol{x}) + \lambda_t \sum_{i=1}^{m} -\lg(-f_i(\boldsymbol{x})), \\ &\text{s.t.} \quad f_j(\boldsymbol{x}) = 0, \ \ j = m+1, m+2, \ldots, m+n, \end{aligned} \tag{3.25}$$

where $\lambda_t > 0$ is a Lagrange multiplier $\lambda_t < \lambda_{t-1}$, t is the iteration index. Here we move the inequality constraints into the objective function except the equality constraints. Similar to Lagrange methods, a logarithmic-type displeasure function is used to approximate Eq. (3.24). Since $f_i(\boldsymbol{x})$ is non-positive, $-f_i(\boldsymbol{x})$ is positive within the feasible set. Moreover, $-f_i(\boldsymbol{x})$ is approaching zero, when x approaches the boundary of feasible set. Furthermore, $\lg(-f_i(\boldsymbol{x}))$ becomes smaller in magnitude within the feasible set, and approaches negative infinitely near the boundary. Finally, increasing λ_t in each iteration will play a role of a 'wall' near the boundary of the feasible set.

In the iterative Newton's method, each iteration proceeds by using quadratic approximations as

$$f_0(\boldsymbol{x} + \Delta\boldsymbol{x}) \approx f_0(\boldsymbol{x}) + \boldsymbol{g}_x^T \Delta\boldsymbol{x} + \frac{1}{2}\Delta\boldsymbol{x}^T H_x \Delta\boldsymbol{x} = q(\boldsymbol{x} + \Delta\boldsymbol{x}), \tag{3.26}$$

where

$$\text{(Gradient)} \quad \boldsymbol{g}_x = \boldsymbol{c} + \lambda \sum_i \frac{1}{f_i(\boldsymbol{x})} \nabla f_i(\boldsymbol{x}), \tag{3.27}$$

and

$$\text{(Hessian Matrix)} \quad H_x = \lambda \sum_i \frac{1}{f_i(\boldsymbol{x})^2} \nabla f_i(\boldsymbol{x}) (\nabla f_i(\boldsymbol{x}))^T - \lambda \sum_i \frac{1}{+f_i(\boldsymbol{x})} \nabla^2 f_i(\boldsymbol{x}). \tag{3.28}$$

Given that $\boldsymbol{x}$ is feasible, i.e., $A\boldsymbol{x} - \boldsymbol{y} = 0$. Now, we try to calculate the step $\Delta\boldsymbol{x}$ by using the following equation

$$\arg\min_{\Delta x} q(\Delta\boldsymbol{x}), \quad \text{s.t. } [A, 0]\Delta\boldsymbol{x} = 0. \tag{3.29}$$

Then its Lagrangian equation is

$$L(\Delta\boldsymbol{x}, \lambda) = q(\Delta\boldsymbol{x}) + \lambda([A, 0]\Delta\boldsymbol{x})^T, \tag{3.30}$$

where λ is the Lagrange multipliers. According to KKT conditions, we have

$$\begin{cases} \frac{\partial L}{\partial \Delta x} & = \boldsymbol{g}_x + H_z\Delta\boldsymbol{x} + \lambda[A, 0]^T, \\ \frac{\partial L}{\partial \lambda} & = [A, 0]\Delta\boldsymbol{x}. \end{cases} \tag{3.31}$$

We rewrite Eq. (3.31) as

$$\begin{bmatrix} H_x & (A, 0)^T \\ (A, 0) & 0 \end{bmatrix} \begin{bmatrix} \Delta\boldsymbol{x} \\ \boldsymbol{\lambda} \end{bmatrix} = \begin{bmatrix} -\boldsymbol{g}_x \\ \boldsymbol{0} \end{bmatrix}. \tag{3.32}$$

From this equation, we can obtain $\Delta\boldsymbol{x}$. Then we calculate $\boldsymbol{x}_{t+1}$ as

$$\boldsymbol{x}_{t+1} = \boldsymbol{x}_t + q_{step}\Delta\boldsymbol{x}, \tag{3.33}$$

where q_{step} is set semi-heuristically.

3.2.3 ℓ_1-Homotopy Methods

1. Introduction

Traditionally, recovering sparse solutions is treated as a combination optimization problem. Thus, it could fail in many big data applications due to extremely high computational complexity. For example, Basis Pursuit algorithms using linear programming involve the solution of $N \times N$ linear systems, and also repeat it many times thus costing order $O(N^3)$ flops, where N is the number of feature vectors in dictionary A.

Toward this end, Osborne et al. proposed the ℓ_1-Homotopy method for solving a noisy overdetermined ℓ_l penalized least squares problem [38, 39]. Donoho et al. extended it to solve an underdetermined problem using the ℓ_1-norm minimization [18]. The Homotopy was defined as a deformation between two functions. Moreover, ℓ_1-Homotopy methods assume that its objective functions are obtained from the ℓ_2-norm constraints to ℓ_1-norm constraints by a Homotopy mapping parameterized by λ. Traditionally, we could search the sparse solution from a dense one to the sparse one by using iterations steps. Instead, the Homotopy method works from the 'sparsest' solution, $x = 0$, and successively updates the sparse solution by adding or removing elements from current active set. Thus, the Homotopy methods work well for Big Data as long as it has a sparse setting.

Furthermore, the Homotopy method has the following superior properties.

- Efficiency: It is an efficient method especially for Big Data ℓ_1-norm minimization problems. As Donoho et al. mentioned in [18], it runs as fast as the OMP-LARS, since it starts at the sparest solution and approaches the sparse solution.
- K-iteration steps: We assume the signal $\boldsymbol{x}$ is K-sparse, and obtain the K-sparse solution in K-iteration steps. It works like OMP.
- An unified framework: The Homopoty methods unified the ℓ_1-norm minimization problem using an unconstrained ℓ_1 penalized least square problem with a Lagrange multiplier. Moreover, it bridges ℓ_1 minimization and OMP-LARS.

2. The Definition of ℓ_1-Homotopy Method

Definition 3.2.1 (*Homotopy*) In topology, the deformation between two continuous functions from one topological space to another is called homotopy.

Definition 3.2.2 (*ℓ_1-Homotopy*) In ℓ_1-norm minimization, the regularization parameter λ yields the trade-off between the data item and sparse item. The transforms by varying λ from one solution space to another space are called ℓ_1-Hommotopy.

Definition 3.2.3 (*K-step Solution Property* [18]) An algorithm $\mathscr{A}$ has the K-step solution property at a given problem instance $(A, \boldsymbol{y})$ drawn from a problem suite $S(E, V; D, N, K)$ if, when applied to the data $(A, \boldsymbol{y})$, the algorithm terminates after at most K step with the correct solution.

The $S(E, V; D, N, K)$ is a collection of problems defined by three components: (a) an ensemble E of matrices A of size $D \times N$; (b) an ensemble V of N-vectors $\boldsymbol{x}$ with at most K nonzeros; (c) an induced ensemble of left-hand sides $\boldsymbol{y} = A\boldsymbol{x}$.

Tibshirani proposed the Least Absolute Shrinkage and Selection Operator (LASSO) [44] as

$$\arg\min_{\boldsymbol{x}} \| \boldsymbol{y} - A\boldsymbol{x} \|_{\ell_2}^2, \quad \text{s.t. } \| \boldsymbol{x} \|_{\ell_1} \leq e, \tag{3.34}$$

where e is a user-specific parameter. In this equation, a least square data fit is subject to an ℓ_1-norm constraint on the coefficients. In [44], Eq. (3.34) is an overdetermined linear system.

Now, we can reformulate Eq. (3.34) into an constrained optimization problem

$$\arg\min_{\boldsymbol{x}} \|\boldsymbol{y} - A\boldsymbol{x}\|_{\ell_2}^2 + \lambda \|\boldsymbol{x}\|_{\ell_1}, \tag{3.35}$$

where λ is a Homotopy parameter, usually λ should be set in accordance with the noise level. When λ takes an approximate value, Eqs. (3.34) and (3.35) are equivalent. In other words, ℓ_1-Homotopy methods are more general forms of ℓ_1-norm minimization problem, and its special cases include BP, LASSO, LARS, and OMP. ℓ_1-Homotopy

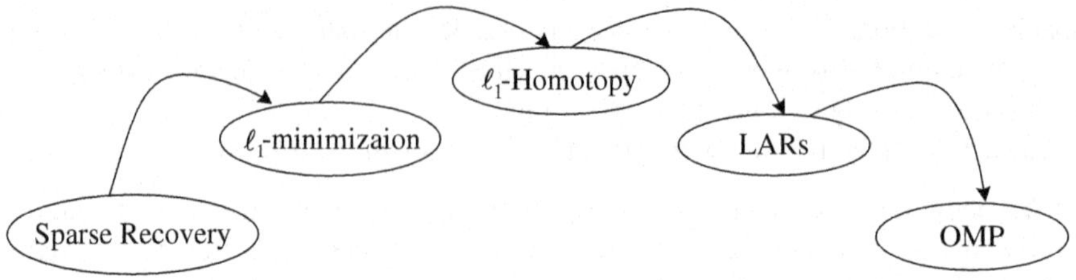

Fig. 3.1 The relationship among sparse recovering, ℓ_1 minimization, ℓ_1-Homotopy and OMP [18]

transformations provide a principle to handle ℓ_1-norm minimization problems by tracing the path of solutions as the Homotopy parameter varies [18].

The relationship among various sparse representation is shown in Fig. 3.1. ℓ_1-Homotopy provides an unified yet fast solution of ℓ_1-Norm minimization problems by using at most K-step interaction. Both LARs and GMP are the special cases of ℓ_1-Homotopy. First of all, LARs is a simplification of the Hmotopy algorithm by removing the condition for sign argument of the current solution and the residual correlation [18]. Second, OMP and LARs are similar in algorithm structure. However, OMP solves a least squares at each iteration, while LARS solves a linearly penalized least squares problems. Finally, note that ℓ_1-Homotopy allows us to remove terms from the active set, while both LARs and OMP allow to insert terms one by one into the active set but not removing any active terms.

Assume $\lambda \in (0, \infty)$ is a utility variable, and each λ corresponds to a solution $\boldsymbol{x}_\lambda$. In general, large λ put more emphasis on the ℓ_1-norm coefficients, while a small λ can more emphasis on the ℓ_2-norm data term. Hence, we can obtain a solution $\hat{\boldsymbol{x}}_\lambda : \lambda \in (0, \infty)$ path when λ varies, and $\hat{\boldsymbol{x}}_\lambda$ converges to the solution of Eq. (3.35). Similarly, LASSO algorithm can obtain a solution path $\hat{\boldsymbol{x}}_\lambda : \lambda \in (0, \infty)$, which follows the properties of the ℓ_l-Homotopy methods. Furthermore, Osborne et al. observed that the solution path is a polygonal, and characterized the changes in the solutions at vertices of the polygonal path [38]. More interestingly, vertices on this solution path correspond to subset models of solutions. Here, the active set is an involving set which is defined as the index set of nonzero elements of $\boldsymbol{x}$ at current iteration. The ℓ_1-Homotopy methods follow the solution path by mapping from one vertex to another vertex. It starts at $\hat{\boldsymbol{x}}_\lambda = 0$ for a large value of λ, and finally reaches the solutions related to vertices of the polygonal path by adding or removing elements from the active set. We define the objective function as

$$f_\lambda(\boldsymbol{x}) := \|\boldsymbol{y} - A\boldsymbol{x}\|_{\ell_2}^2 + \lambda\|\boldsymbol{x}\|_{\ell_1}. \tag{3.36}$$

As we know before, we can solve ℓ_1-norm minimization as λ is initialized as a large value and varied while converging to the solution. Here we will introduce the selection rules obtained from convex analysis.

According to convex analysis, a necessary condition for $\boldsymbol{x}_\lambda$ to be a minimizer of $f_\lambda(\boldsymbol{x})$ is that $0 \in \frac{\partial f_\lambda(\boldsymbol{x})}{\partial \boldsymbol{x}}|_{\boldsymbol{x}=\boldsymbol{x}_\lambda}$. We have

$$\left.\frac{\partial f_\lambda(\boldsymbol{x})}{\partial \boldsymbol{x}}\right|_{\boldsymbol{x}=\boldsymbol{x}_\lambda} = -A^T(\boldsymbol{y} - A\boldsymbol{x}_\lambda) + \lambda \partial \|\boldsymbol{x}_\lambda\|_{\ell_1}, \tag{3.37}$$

where

$$\left.\frac{\partial \|\boldsymbol{x}\|_1}{\partial \boldsymbol{x}}\right|_{\boldsymbol{x}=\boldsymbol{x}_\lambda} = \left\{ \boldsymbol{u} \in \mathbb{R}^N \middle| \begin{array}{ll} u_i = \text{sgn}(x_{\lambda,i}), & x_{\lambda,i} \neq 0 \\ u_i \in [-1, 1], & x_{\lambda,i} = 0 \end{array} \right\}, \tag{3.38}$$

where $x_{\lambda,i}$ is the ith element of the $\boldsymbol{x}_\lambda$. Let $S = \{i|x_{\lambda,i} \neq 0\}$ denote the support of $\boldsymbol{x}_\lambda$, and $C = A^T(\boldsymbol{y} - A\boldsymbol{x}_\lambda)$ the vector of residual correlations. Then we can rewrite Eq. (3.38) as the two conditions,

$$\begin{cases} \text{(sign agreement)} & C(i) = \lambda \cdot \text{sgn}(x_{\lambda,i}), \\ \text{(upper-bound)} & |C(i)| \leq \lambda. \end{cases} \tag{3.39}$$

Note that the two conditions Eq. (3.39) mean that residual correlations on the support of S must all have magnitude equal to λ, and the signs of the corresponding elements of $\boldsymbol{x}_\lambda$ should match the signs of residual correlations, and conversely, residual to λ. The Homotopy method strictly follows the two conditions by tracing out the optimal solution path $\boldsymbol{x}_\lambda$. Since the path $\boldsymbol{x}_\lambda$ is a piecewise linear path with a discrete number of vertices, we can make the operation successful.

The ℓ_1-Homotopy method flow is shown in Fig. 3.2. This implementation consists of initialization, updating direction, determining the step size, and updating the active set. The algorithm works in an iterative manner. In iteration t, the ℓ_1-Homotopy first calculates an update direction by solving

$$A_I^T A_I d_t(I) = \text{sgn}\ C_t(I), \quad d_t(I) = 0. \tag{3.40}$$

This update direction guarantees that all the magnitudes of residual correlations on the active set decline equally. Afterwards, the algorithm calculates the step size to the next breakpoint.

Along the Homotopy path, there are two cases of constraint violations. The first case is that a nonactive element of c_t would increase in magnitude beyond λ, violating the upper bound in Eq. (3.39). This first occurs when

$$s_t^+ = \min_{i \in I^c} \left\{ \frac{\lambda - C_t(i)}{1 - \boldsymbol{a}_i^T \boldsymbol{v}_t}, \frac{\lambda + C_t(i)}{1 + \boldsymbol{a}_i^T \boldsymbol{v}_t} \right\}, \tag{3.41}$$

where $\boldsymbol{v}_t = A_I d_t(I)$, and the minimum is taken only over positive arguments. The second case is when an active coordinate crosses zero, violating the sign agreement in Eq. (3.39). This occurs first when

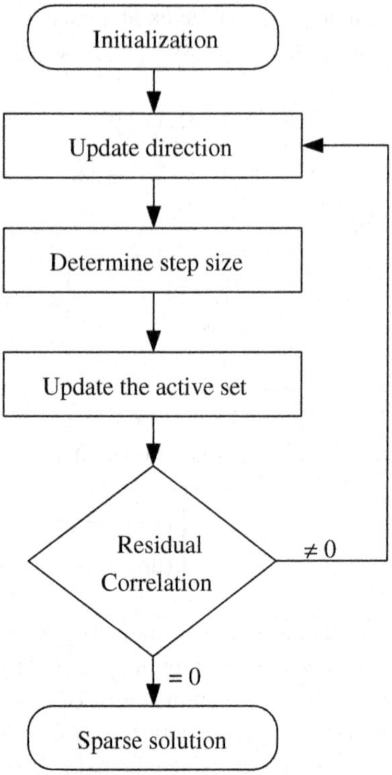

Fig. 3.2 The flow chart of ℓ_1-Homotopy method

$$s_t^- = \min_{i \in I} \left\{ \frac{-\boldsymbol{x}_t(i)}{d_t(i)} \right\}, \tag{3.42}$$

where the minimum is taken only over positive arguments. Therefore, the step size is calculated by

$$s_t = \min\{s_t^+, s_t^-\}. \tag{3.43}$$

Furthermore, we update the active set by either appending I with i^+, or removing i^-

$$\boldsymbol{x}_t = \boldsymbol{x}_{t-1} + s_t \boldsymbol{d}_t. \tag{3.44}$$

The ℓ_1-Homotopy terminates when $\|C_t\|_\infty = 0$.

3.2.4 Elastic Net

In this section, we introduce another regularization and variable selection algorithms proposed by Zou and Hastie [53]. Elastic Net (EN), similar to LASSO algorithm can obtain sparse solutions. Moreover, the EN algorithms encourage a grouping effect. More interestingly, it can work for High Dimension Low Sample Size (HDLSS) issues [21, 32].

Let A be the model Matrix, and y be the response. We can assume

$$\sum_{i=1}^{N} x_i = 0, \sum_{i=1}^{N} a_{ij} = 0, \sum_{i=1}^{N} a_{ij}^2 = 1, j = 1, \ldots, D. \tag{3.45}$$

Now, the Naive Elastic Net (NEN) criterion is defined as follows [33].

$$f(\lambda_1, \lambda_2, \boldsymbol{x}) = \|y - A\boldsymbol{x}\|_{\ell_2}^2 + \lambda_2 \|\boldsymbol{x}\|_{\ell_2}^2 + \lambda_1 \|\boldsymbol{x}\|_{\ell_1}, \tag{3.46}$$

where λ_1 and λ_2 are nonnegative Lagrange multipliers. Hence from Eq. (3.46), we can estimate $\boldsymbol{x}$ as follows:

$$\hat{\boldsymbol{x}} = \arg\min_{\boldsymbol{x}} f(\lambda_1, \lambda_2, \boldsymbol{x}). \tag{3.47}$$

Note that Eq. (3.46) is a penalized least squares method. Let $\alpha = \frac{\lambda_2}{\lambda_1 + \lambda_2}$, and the EN can be rewritten as the following optimization problem

$$\hat{\boldsymbol{x}} = \arg\min_{\boldsymbol{x}} \|\boldsymbol{y} - \boldsymbol{x}\|_{\ell_2}^2, \text{ s.t. } (1 - \alpha)\|\boldsymbol{x}\|_{\ell_1} + \alpha\|\boldsymbol{x}\|_{\ell_2}^2 \leq e, \tag{3.48}$$

where e is a user-specified constant. $(1-\alpha)\|\boldsymbol{x}\|_1 + \alpha\|\boldsymbol{x}\|_2^2$ is the Elastic Net penalty, which is a convex combination of the LASSO and ridge penalty. When $\alpha = 0$, the NEN reduces to the LASSO algorithm; When $\alpha = 1$, it reduces to a ridge regression. For the NEN algorithm, $\alpha \in (0, 1)$, it is a strictly convex problem combining the properties of both LASSO and ridge regression as shown in Fig. 3.3. In [3], Zou et al. proved that NEN is an equivalent LASSO problem on augmented data. The sample size in the augmented data is $N + D$ and A has rank D. That is, even we have very small sample size, the NEN can work well. This property overcomes the limitations of the LASSO. Moreover, Zou et al. also introduced the grouping effect of the NEN.

3.3 Greedy Algorithms

3.3.1 MP and OMP

The most well-known greedy algorithms are MP and OMP, and OMP is an extension of MP. Let us consider our fundamental sparse coding problem as

$$\arg\min_{\boldsymbol{x}} \|\boldsymbol{y} - A\boldsymbol{x}\|_{\ell_2}, \quad s.t \ \|\boldsymbol{x}\|_{\ell_0} \leq K, \tag{3.49}$$

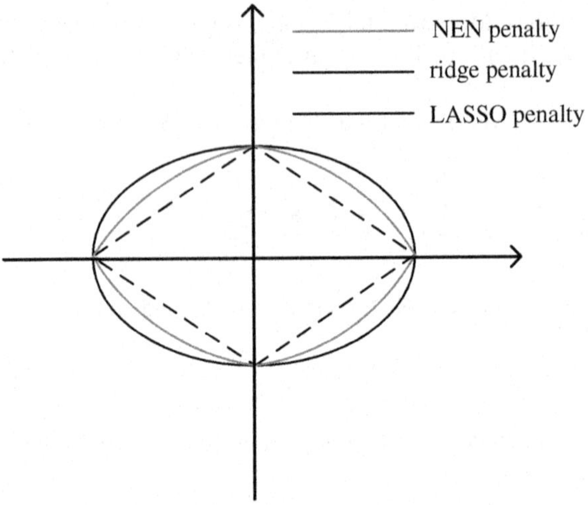

Fig. 3.3 Different penalty functions correspond to different sparse recovery approaches, NEN, ridge regression, and LASSO

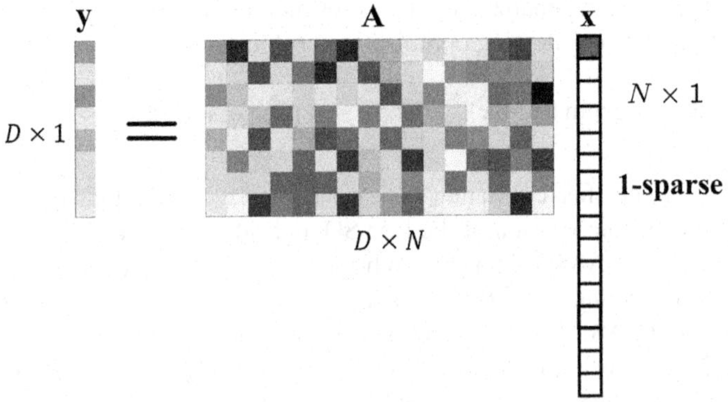

Fig. 3.4 K-sparse signal recovery problem ($K = 1$)

where $A = [A_1, A_2, \ldots, A_N]$, in two different cases, i.e., $K = 1$ and general K as followings.

1-sparse case: The MP/OMPs are stepwise toward selection algorithms. Assume that we have some problems with Eq. (3.49), $\arg\max_i \langle A_i, \boldsymbol{y} \rangle$ is the sparse solution of $\boldsymbol{x}$, shown in Fig. 3.4.

K-sparse case: Now we discuss how to extend 1-sparse problem to K-sparse problem. In matching pursuit, $\boldsymbol{x}$ is initialized as 0 and the residual $\boldsymbol{r} = \boldsymbol{y}$. Then, in each iteration, as 1-sparse signal recovery problem, we select the atom maximum with the residual $\boldsymbol{r}$. Afterwards, both the residual and the coefficients are updated. Finally, it will output the sparse solution if the residual does not change. Otherwise, it continues the iteration procedure. Figure 3.5 shows the iteration procedure of MP,

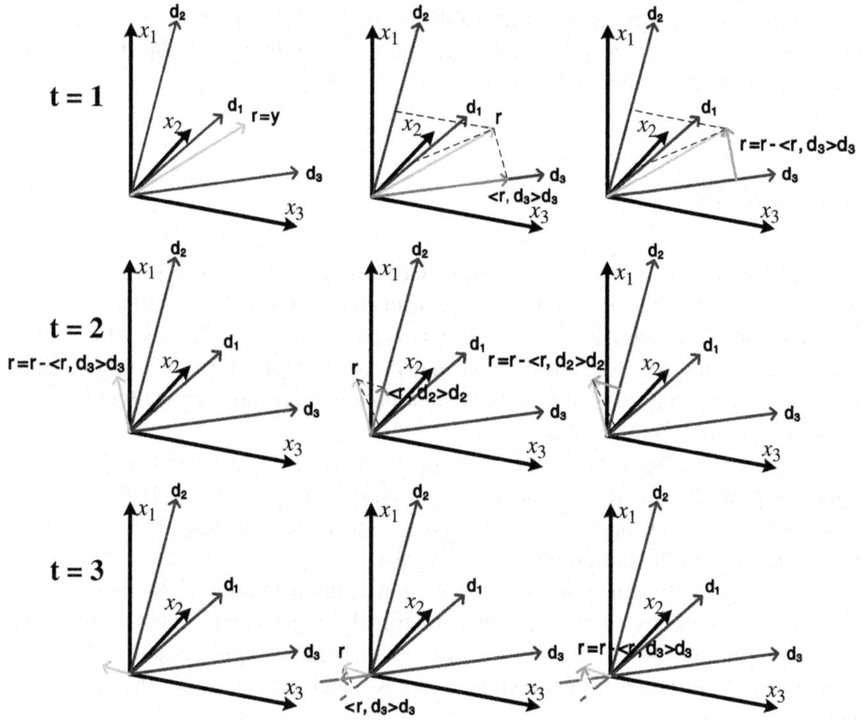

Fig. 3.5 The iteration procedure of MP

where the d_1, d_2, d_3 are the basis, $\boldsymbol{r}$ is the residual and $\boldsymbol{y}$ is the input signal for sparse representation. The purpose of every step is updating the residual.

The algorithm of MP is illustrated as Table 3.1. We would like to point out that OMP is very similar to MP except all the coefficients at time t are updated by calculating the orthogonal projection of the signal onto the set of atoms selected. A hierarchical Matching Pursuit was proposed for feature learning by Bo et al. [6].

Table 3.1 The MP algorithm flowchart

Input: Dictionary A, $\boldsymbol{y}$, and K

Initialization: Residuals $\boldsymbol{r} = \boldsymbol{y}$

while $(|\boldsymbol{x}| < K)$

Select the atom with maximum linear corelation with the residual:

$\hat{i} = \arg\max_i |A_{.i}^T \boldsymbol{r}|$;

Update the coefficients and the residual:

$\hat{x}_i = \hat{x}_i + A_{.i}^T \boldsymbol{r},$;

$\boldsymbol{r} = \boldsymbol{r} - A_{.i}^T \boldsymbol{r} A_{.i}$;

end while

Output: Coefficients $\boldsymbol{x}$.

We would like to point out that OMP is very similar to MP except all the coefficients at time t are updated by calculating the orthogonal projection of the signal onto the set of atoms selected.

3.3.2 CoSaMP

Compressive Sampling Matching Pursuit (CoSaMP) is one of core greedy pursuit since it guarantees efficiency and provides strict error bounds. Thanks to incorporating ideas from the combinatorial algorithms [34]. CoSaMP is extremely efficient for practical problems due to requiring only matrix-vector multiplication with the sampling matrix. For compressible signals, the computational complexity is $O(D \log^2 D)$ (D is the input signal dimensions).

The basic task in sparse recovery is to locate the largest components in the target signal. Inspired by the RIP, if the sampling matrix A satisfied the RIP $\delta_{2s} \leq c$, the vector $A^T Ax$ can approach x. Moreover, the largest entries of $A^T Ax$ point approaches toward the largest entries of signal x.

Since $\boldsymbol{y} = A\boldsymbol{x}$, we can approximate $\boldsymbol{y}$ by applying the matrix A^T to the samples. The algorithm works by iteratively approximating the target signal, where the residual plays an important role in finding the sparse solution. Each approximation includes the residual. At iteration t, the updated samples which reflect the residual are used to construct an approximation for the residual. This allows us to identify the largest components in the residual. The signal estimation is used to approximate the signal by least squares on the support set. The iteration is repeated until the criterion is satisfied (Table 3.2).

(**Performance Guarantee**) Let us see how CoSaMP provides vigorous error bounds. Assume that

(1) the sampling matrix A has RIP(2s),
(2) $\boldsymbol{y} = A\boldsymbol{x} + \boldsymbol{e}$, $\boldsymbol{e}$ is arbitrary noise.

Theorem 3.3.1 (CoSaMP [36]) *Suppose that A is an $D \times N$ sample matrix with restricted isometry constant $\delta_2 K \leq C$. Let $Y = AX + e$ be a vector of sample of an arbitrary signal, contaminated with arbitrary noise. For a given precision parameter η, the CoSaMP produces an K-sparse approximation $\hat{\boldsymbol{x}}$ that satisfied*

$$||x - \hat{x}||_{\ell_2} \leq C \cdot max\{\eta, \frac{1}{\sqrt{K}}||x - x_{\frac{K}{2}}||_{\ell_1} + ||e||_{\ell_2}\}, \tag{3.50}$$

where $bmx_{K/2}$ is a best 2K-Sparse approximation to X.

Table 3.2 The CoSaMP algorithm flowchart [34]

Input: Dictionary A, noisy sample vector $\boldsymbol{y}$, and K
Initialization: Residuals $\boldsymbol{r} = \boldsymbol{y}$
while (!*convergence*)
Form signal proxy:
$\hat{\boldsymbol{y}} = A^T \boldsymbol{r}$;
Identify the supports:
$\Omega \leftarrow \mathrm{supp}(\hat{\boldsymbol{y}}_{2K})$;
$T \leftarrow \Omega \bigcup \mathrm{supp}(\boldsymbol{x})$;
Signal estimation by least square:
$\boldsymbol{x}|_T = (A)_T^{\dagger} \boldsymbol{y}$;
$\boldsymbol{x}|_T^c = \boldsymbol{0}$;
Update the residuals:
$\boldsymbol{r} = \boldsymbol{y} - A\boldsymbol{x}$
end while
Output: Coefficients $\boldsymbol{x}$.

3.3.3 Iterative Hard Thresholding Algorithm

Solving Eq. (3.49) is NP-hard in general. Toward this end, two strategies are used to obtain the approximate solution, greedy strategies and relaxation of the ℓ_0-Norm cost function. In Sect. 3.2, we replace the ℓ_0-Norm constraint by the ℓ_1-Norm constraint as BP [13] which has good performance but has high computational complexity. Thus, greedy strategies are more popular due to its fast iterative procedures, and are widely used in many applications. Among greedy algorithms, iterative threshold algorithm has drawn much attention [2, 4, 8, 15, 20]. We rewrite Eq. (3.49) into

$$\arg\min_{\boldsymbol{x}} \|\boldsymbol{y} - A\boldsymbol{x}\|_{\ell_2}^2 + \lambda \|\boldsymbol{x}\|_{\ell_0}. \tag{3.51}$$

Let us introduce a surrogate objective function [3, 32],

$$f_\lambda(\boldsymbol{x}, \boldsymbol{z}) = \|\boldsymbol{y} - A\boldsymbol{x}\|_{\ell_2}^2 + \lambda \|\boldsymbol{x}\|_{\ell_0} - \|A\boldsymbol{x} - A\boldsymbol{z}\|_{\ell_2}^2 + \|\boldsymbol{x} - \boldsymbol{z}\|_{\ell_2}^2. \tag{3.52}$$

Note that the local approximation to this non-convex problem (Eq. (3.51)) can be obtained based on the surrogate objective function. Therefore, we can optimize Eq. (3.52) instead of directly optimizing Eq. (3.51). Furthermore, we rewrite Eq. (3.52) as

$$\begin{aligned} f_\lambda(\boldsymbol{x}, \boldsymbol{z}) = \sum_j \Big(x_j^2 - 2x_j(z_j + A_{.j}^T \boldsymbol{y} - A_{.j}^T A\boldsymbol{z}) + \lambda |x_i|_0 \Big) \\ + \|\boldsymbol{y}\|_{\ell_2}^2 + \|\boldsymbol{z}\|_{\ell_2}^2 - \|A\boldsymbol{z}\|_{\ell_2}^2, \end{aligned} \tag{3.53}$$

where $A_{.j}$ is the jth column of A, $|x_i|_0 = 1$ if $x_i \neq 0$ and 0 otherwise. Considering two cases, $x_i = 0$ and $x_i \neq 0$. In the first case, the elementwise cost is 0. In the second case, the cost is

$$x_j^2 - 2x_j(z_j + A_{.j}^T \boldsymbol{y} - A_{.j}^T A\boldsymbol{z}) + \lambda. \tag{3.54}$$

Its minimum is achieved at $\hat{x}_j = z_j + A_{.j}^T \boldsymbol{y} - A_{.j}^T A\boldsymbol{z}$. Thus, we can see that the minimum of Eq. (3.52) is obtained at

$$\boldsymbol{x} = H_{\sqrt{\lambda}}(\boldsymbol{z} + A^T(\boldsymbol{y} - A\boldsymbol{z})). \tag{3.55}$$

The IHT algorithm is defined as

$$\boldsymbol{x}_{t+1} = H_{\sqrt{\lambda}}(\boldsymbol{x}_t + A^T(\boldsymbol{y} - A\boldsymbol{x}_t)), \tag{3.56}$$

where $H_{\sqrt{\lambda}}$ is the nonlinear projection which implements the elementwise hard thresholding.

Now we discuss an iterative algorithm for the K-sparse problem as

$$\arg\min_{\boldsymbol{x}} \|\boldsymbol{y} - A\boldsymbol{x}\|_{\ell_2}^2, \quad \text{s.t.} \quad \|\boldsymbol{y}\|_{\ell_0} \leq K, \tag{3.57}$$

and have the following iterative algorithm:

$$\boldsymbol{x}_{t+1} = H_K(\boldsymbol{x}_t + A^T(\boldsymbol{y} - A\boldsymbol{x}_t)), \tag{3.58}$$

where H_K is a nonlinear projection that sets all but the K largest elements of its arguments to zero. This is the K-sparse version of the IHT algorithm. Some implementation issues refer to [5].

3.4 Sparse Bayesian Learning

The Bayesian framework of compression sensing has the following amazing properties: (1) Measure of confidence and robustness error bars can be estimated along with estimating X, which measures the confidence of X. Meanwhile, the framework models the noise naturally and provides the estimate of noise variance. (2) The error bars provide a principle way to determine how many measurement are sufficient for CS signal reconstruction. Moreover, the measurements are optimized adaptively and not determined randomly. (3) In case noise is free, the global minimum of ℓ_1-norm optimization is not the sparest solution [16, 45]. Moreover, Sparse Bayesian Learning can provide better sparse solution. (4) SRL can handle some extreme cases, such as the columns of sensing matrix are correlated very much, while ℓ_1-norm optimization algorithm may fail. (5) In many practical applications, signals usually have some structures, which can be used to improve the performance of space recovery approach. Bayesian frameworks provide more flexibility to incorporate structure information [1].

We can represent features in sparse form by some linear basis A, implying that the signal can be represented by the combination of A's columns. From previous section, we can get the sparse coefficients by solving an object function based on ℓ_p regularization term (such as LASSO, Basis Pursuit). In this section, we employ a Bayesian formalism for estimating the underlying signal $\boldsymbol{x}$ based on $\boldsymbol{y}$.

3.4.1 Bayesian Viewpoint of Sparse Representation

1. Sparse Representation as Linear Regression Problem

As we mentioned before, the sparse representation problem can be described as :

$$\boldsymbol{y} = A\boldsymbol{x} + \boldsymbol{e} \ , \tag{3.59}$$

where $\boldsymbol{e}$ is the noise vector which is a zero-mean Gaussian distribution with unknown variance σ^2. Therefore, we have the Gaussian likelihood model

$$p(\boldsymbol{y}|\boldsymbol{x};\sigma^2) = (2\pi\sigma^2)^{-D/2} \exp\left(-\frac{1}{2\sigma^2}\|\boldsymbol{y} - A\boldsymbol{x}\|_2^2\right) \ . \tag{3.60}$$

Equation (3.60) formulates sparse representation problem into a linear regression problem with a constraint (prior) that $\boldsymbol{x}$ is sparse. Given A and Y, we can estimate $\boldsymbol{x}$ and σ^2. In a Bayesian analysis we seek a full posterior density function for $\boldsymbol{x}$ and σ^2.

2. Sparseness Prior and MAP Approximation

In a Bayesian formulation, we should model $\boldsymbol{x}$ as a sparse prior. A widely used sparseness prior is the Laplace density function [49]:

$$p(\boldsymbol{x}|\lambda) = (\lambda/2)^N \exp\left(-\lambda \sum_{i=1}^{N} |x_i|\right) \ . \tag{3.61}$$

Assume that the likelihood function follows Eq. (3.60), the solution in Eq. (3.59) corresponds to a Maximum A Posteriori (MAP) estimate for $\boldsymbol{x}$ using the prior in Eq. (3.61).

3.4.2 *Sparse Representation via Relevance Vector Machine*

1. Hierarchical Sparseness Prior

We discussed the formulation of estimation $\boldsymbol{x}$ as a MAP approximation to a Bayesian linear regression analysis in the previous section. However, we do not realize an estimate of the full posterior on $\boldsymbol{x}$ and σ^2. As we know, the Laplace prior is not conjugate to the Gaussian livelihood, and thus the Bayesian inference may not be implemented in closed form.

Toward this end, Sparse Bayesian learning has addressed this by combing with the Relevance Vector Machine [RVM] [37]. By constraint a hierarchical prior in the RVM is used to replace a Laplace prior on $\boldsymbol{x}$. The hierarchical prior is similar to the Laplace prior but follows conjugate-experimental analysis. Then we define a zero-mean Gaussian prior on $\boldsymbol{x}$ as

$$p(\boldsymbol{x}|\boldsymbol{\alpha}) = \prod_{i=1}^{N} \mathrm{N}(x_i|0, \alpha_i^{-1}) \, , \tag{3.62}$$

where α_i is the precision (inverse variance) of a Gaussian density function. Furthermore, a Gamma prior is considered over α:

$$p(\boldsymbol{\alpha}; a, b) = \prod_{i=1}^{N} \Gamma(\alpha_i|a, b) \, . \tag{3.63}$$

By marginalizing over the hyperparameters $\boldsymbol{\alpha}$, the overall prior on $\boldsymbol{x}$ is then evaluated as

$$p(\boldsymbol{x}|a, b) = \prod_{i=1}^{N} \int_0^{\infty} \mathrm{N}(x_i|0, \alpha_i^{-1})\Gamma(\alpha_i|a, b)d\alpha_i \, . \tag{3.64}$$

The density function $\Gamma(\alpha_i|a, b)$ is the conjugate prior for α_i, when x_i plays the role of observed data and $\mathrm{N}(x_i|0, \alpha_i^{-1})$ is a likelihood function. Consequently, the integral $\int_0^{\infty} \mathrm{N}(x_i|0, \alpha_i^{-1})\Gamma(\alpha_i|a, b)d\alpha_i$ can be evaluated analytically, and it corresponds to the Student-t distribution.With appropriate choice of a and b, the Student-t distribution is strongly peaked at $x_i = 0$, therefore, the prior in Eq. (3.64) favors most x_i being zero (i.e., it is a sparseness prior). Similarly, a Gamma prior $\Gamma(\alpha_0|c, d)$ is introduced in the inverse of the noise variance $\alpha_0 = 1/\sigma^2$.

Note that the Bayesian linear model considered in RVM is essentially one of the simplified models for Bayesian model selection. Although more accurate model may be desired, the main motivation for adopting the RVM is due to its highly efficient computation as discussed below.

2. Bayesian Sparse Representation via RVM

Assuming the hyperparameters $\boldsymbol{\alpha}$ and α_0 are known, given the y and A, the posterior for coefficients $\boldsymbol{x}$ can be expressed analytically as a multivariate Gaussian distribution with mean and covariance:

$$\begin{cases} \boldsymbol{\mu} & = \alpha_0 \Sigma A^T \boldsymbol{x} \\ \Sigma & = (\alpha_0 A^T A + \Lambda)^{-1} \end{cases}, \tag{3.65}$$

where $\Lambda = diag(\alpha_1, \alpha_2, \ldots, \alpha_M)$. In RVM, sparse recovering of $\boldsymbol{x}$ thus becomes the search for the hyperparameters $\boldsymbol{\alpha}$ and α_0. In the RVM, these hyperparameters are estimated from the data by performing over $\boldsymbol{x}$, the marginal likelihood for $\boldsymbol{\alpha}$ and α_0. $L(\boldsymbol{\alpha}, \alpha_0)$ can be formulated as

$$\begin{aligned} L(\boldsymbol{\alpha}, \alpha_0) &= \log p(\boldsymbol{y}|\boldsymbol{\alpha}, \alpha_0) = \log \int p(\boldsymbol{y}|\boldsymbol{x}, \alpha_0) p(\boldsymbol{x}|\boldsymbol{\alpha}) d\boldsymbol{x} \\ &= -\frac{1}{2}[N \log 2\pi + \log |C| + \boldsymbol{y}^T C^{-1} \boldsymbol{y}], \end{aligned} \tag{3.66}$$

with $C = \sigma^2 I + A \Lambda^{-1} A^T$. We use the type II ML approximation to estimate both $\boldsymbol{\alpha}$ and α_0 by maximizing Eq. (3.66). It can be implemented via the EM algorithm, and we have

$$\alpha_i^{new} = \frac{\gamma_i}{\mu_i^2}, \qquad i \in \{1, 2, \ldots, M\}, \tag{3.67}$$

where μ_i is the ith posterior mean of coefficients $\boldsymbol{x}$ from Eq. (3.65) and $\gamma_i \triangleq 1 - \alpha_i \Sigma_{ii}$, with Σ_{ii} the ith diagonal element of the posterior weight covariance matrix from Eq. (3.65). For the noise variance $\sigma^2 = 1/\alpha_0$, differentiation leads to the reestimate:

$$\alpha_0^{new} = \frac{K - \sum_i \gamma_i}{\|\boldsymbol{y} - A\boldsymbol{\mu}\|_2^2}. \tag{3.68}$$

Note that $\boldsymbol{\alpha}^{new}$ and α_0^{new} are functions of μ and Σ, while μ and Σ are functions of $\boldsymbol{\alpha}$ and α_0. This suggests an iterative algorithm, which iterates between Eqs. (3.65), (3.67) and (3.68), until the convergence criterion has been satisfied. In this process, it is observed that many of the α_i tend to infinity for those x_i that have insignificant amplitudes for representation of $\boldsymbol{y}$; only a relatively small set of x_i, for which the corresponding α_i remains relatively small, contribute for representation of $\boldsymbol{y}$, and the level of sparseness is determined automatically. It is also important to note that, as a result of the estimation type II ML of Eq. (3.66), the point estimates (rather than the posterior densities) of $\boldsymbol{\alpha}$ and α_0 are sought. Therefore, there is no need to set *a, b, c* and *d* on the Gamma hyperpriors. This is equivalent to setting *a, b, c* and *d* to zero, and thus uniform hyperpriors on $\boldsymbol{\alpha}$ and α_0 have been invoked. From the previous section discussion, it is useful to have a measure of uncertainty in the coefficients $\boldsymbol{x}$, since $\boldsymbol{x}$ is drawn from a multivariate Gaussian distribution with mean and covariance defined in Eq. (3.65), so this is one of the properties that the Bayesian SR framework can get, while the ℓ_1 based framework does not possess.

3.4.3 Sparse Bayesian Learning

In the previous section, Sparse Bayesian Learning (SBL) comes from the RVM [45] as shown in Eqs. (3.62) and (3.63). In this formulation, it is assumed that the prior of the coefficients $\boldsymbol{x}$ is a zero-mean Gaussian distribution on each element of coefficients. And the precision α_i of a Gaussian density function satisfies the Gamma distribution. So it can get the analytically Student-t distribution. With appropriate choice of a and b, the Student-t distribution is strongly peaked about at $x_i = 0$ to satisfy the sparsity. In this section, we shall give a simple formulation to describe SBL algorithm. Instead of giving the parameter's prior distribution, the SBL algorithm can estimate the parameters directly from the data.

1. Model Prior Formulation

The parametric form of the SBL coefficients prior is given by [49]

$$p(\boldsymbol{x}; \boldsymbol{\gamma}) = \prod_{i=1}^{N} (2\pi\gamma_i)^{-\frac{1}{2}} \exp(-\frac{x_i^2}{2\gamma_i}) , \tag{3.69}$$

where $\boldsymbol{\gamma} = [\gamma_1, \ldots, \gamma_N]^T$ is a vector of N hyperparameters, which models the prior variance of $\boldsymbol{x}$. These hyperparameters can be estimated from the data by marginalizing over the coefficients and the performing ML optimization. The likelihood which has been mentioned in the Eq. (3.60) marginalizing p.d.f is given by

$$p(\boldsymbol{y}; \boldsymbol{\gamma}, \sigma^2) = (2\pi)^{-\frac{D}{2}} |\Sigma_y|^{\frac{1}{2}} \exp\left(-\frac{1}{2}\boldsymbol{y}^T \Sigma_y^{-1} \boldsymbol{y}\right) , \tag{3.70}$$

where $\Sigma_y \triangleq \sigma^2 I + A\Gamma A^T$, and $\Gamma \triangleq \text{diag}(\boldsymbol{\gamma})$. This procedure is referred to as evidence maximization or type II maximum likelihood [12].

For fixed values of the hyperparameters governing the prior, the posterior density of the coefficients is Gaussian,

$$p(\boldsymbol{x}|\boldsymbol{y}; \boldsymbol{\gamma}, \sigma_2) = N(\boldsymbol{\mu}, \Sigma_x) , \tag{3.71}$$

with

$$\begin{cases} \boldsymbol{\mu} &= \sigma^{-2} \Sigma_x A^T \boldsymbol{y} \\ \Sigma_x &= (\sigma^{-2} A^T A + \Gamma^{-1})^{-1} \end{cases} , \tag{3.72}$$

2. Hyperparameter Learning

After obtaining the posterior of coefficients, from the Eq. (3.72) we can estimate the hyperparameter of $\boldsymbol{\gamma}$ and σ^2. By getting the marginalized p.d.f (3.70), the optimal hyperparameters correspond to maximum marginalized p.d.f. we minimize the effective SBL cost function [49]

$$\begin{aligned} L(\boldsymbol{\gamma}, \sigma^2) &\triangleq -2 \log \int p(\boldsymbol{y}|\boldsymbol{x}, \sigma^2) p(\boldsymbol{x}; \boldsymbol{\gamma}) d\boldsymbol{x} \\ &= -2 \log p(\boldsymbol{y}; \boldsymbol{\gamma}, \sigma^2) \equiv \log |\Sigma_y| + \boldsymbol{x}^T \Sigma_y^{-1} \boldsymbol{x}. \end{aligned} \tag{3.73}$$

Treating the unknown coefficients as hidden variable, we can minimize this expression over $\boldsymbol{x}$ and σ^2 using a simple EM algorithm for covariance estimation. For E-step, this requires computation of the coefficients posterior using Eq. (3.72), while the M-step is expressed via the updated rule.

$$\begin{aligned} &E_{\boldsymbol{x}|\boldsymbol{y},\boldsymbol{\gamma},\sigma^2}[-\log p(\boldsymbol{y}, \boldsymbol{x}; \boldsymbol{\gamma}, \sigma^2)] \\ &= E_{\boldsymbol{x}|\boldsymbol{y},\boldsymbol{\gamma},\sigma^2}[-\log p(\boldsymbol{y}|\boldsymbol{x}; \sigma^2)] + E_{\boldsymbol{x}|\boldsymbol{y},\boldsymbol{\gamma},\sigma^2}[-\log p(\boldsymbol{x}|\boldsymbol{\gamma})]. \end{aligned} \tag{3.74}$$

From the second term of the right side of the Eq. (3.74), by the EM algorithm, we can get the optimal hyperparameter $\boldsymbol{\gamma}$, as

$$\gamma_i = (\Sigma_x)_{i,i} + \mu_i^2. \tag{3.75}$$

From the first term of the right side of the equation by the EM algorithm, we can have

$$(\sigma^2)^{(t+1)} = \frac{\|\boldsymbol{y} - A\boldsymbol{\mu}\|_2^2 + (\sigma^2)^{(t)} \sum_{i=1}^N [1 - (\gamma_i^{(t)})^{-1} (\Sigma_x)_{i,i}]}{D}. \tag{3.76}$$

Interestingly, upon convergence, we find that many of the γ_i's are driven to zero. In other words, if $\gamma_i = 0$, then $p(x_i; \gamma_i = 0) = \delta(x_i)$, which will dominate the likelihood term and force the posterior probability to satisfy

$$\text{Prob}(x_i = 0|\boldsymbol{y}; \gamma_i = 0, \sigma^2) = 1. \tag{3.77}$$

Additionally, in noiseless environments, we may want to allow $\sigma^2 \to 0$. Using straightforward results from linear algebra, we can get the expression for $\boldsymbol{\mu}$ and Σ_x:

$$\boldsymbol{\mu} = \Gamma^{1/2} (A\Gamma^{1/2})^{\dagger} \boldsymbol{y}, \tag{3.78}$$

$$\Sigma_x = [I - \Gamma^{1/2} (A\Gamma^{1/2})^{\dagger} A]\Gamma, \tag{3.79}$$

where $(.)^{\dagger}$ denotes the Moore–Penrose pseudoinverse. In this formulation, it is very transparent how the sparsity profile of $\boldsymbol{\gamma}$ dictates $\boldsymbol{\mu}$ [49].

3.5 ℓ_0-Norm Gradient Minimization

In this section, we shall introduce ℓ_0-gradient minimization to solve the sparse recovery problem. By contrast, it uses a sparse gradient counting scheme in an optimization framework, where a new strategy is used to guarantee the fixed discrete number of intensity changes among spatial neighboring elements (i.e., pixels). Mathematically, it is equivalent to ℓ_0-norm for sparsity pursuit. The ℓ_0 gradient minimization can globally control how many nonzero gradient resulting in approximating prominent structures [50].

3.5.1 *Counting Gradient Difference*

1. 1D Case

The ℓ_0 regularization term on gradient of the 1D signal can be defined as:

$$c(\boldsymbol{f}) = \#\{p \mid |f_p - f_{p+1}| \neq 0\}, \tag{3.80}$$

where p and $p+1$ index neighboring elements in result $\boldsymbol{f}$. $|f_p - f_{p+1}|$ is a gradient in the form of forward difference. #{} is the counting operator which output the number of p satisfy the constraint $|f_p - f_{p+1}| \neq 0$, which means the ℓ_0-norm of the gradient of $\boldsymbol{f}$. The result of the 1D signal smoothing via Eq. (3.83) is intuitively shown in Fig. 3.6. In Fig. 3.6c, we can see the result with $k = 6$ by minimizing Eq. (3.84) by exhaustive search. The result of the ℓ_0 method flattens details and sharpens main edges. The overall shape is also in line with the original one because intensity change must arise along significant edges to reduce as much as possible the total energy. The first term of the Eq. (3.83) is used to constrain that many pixels do not drastically change their color, and by the constraint of ℓ_0-norm, many low-amplitude structures can be primarily removed. We also can use the general formulation Eq. (3.84) to smooth the signal and the results are illustrated in Fig. 3.7. We can see from the Fig. 3.7 that the number of nonzero gradients is monotone with respect to $1/\lambda$.

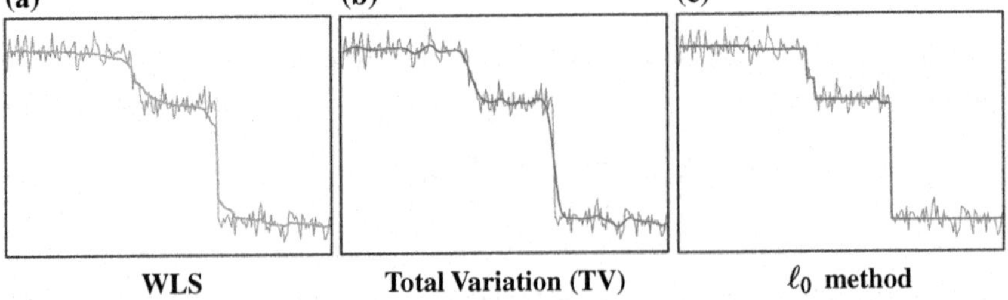

Fig. 3.6 Signal obtained from an image scanline, containing both details and sharp edges: **a** Result of WLS optimization [22]; **b** Result of TV smoothing [42]; **c** L0 smoothing result [50]

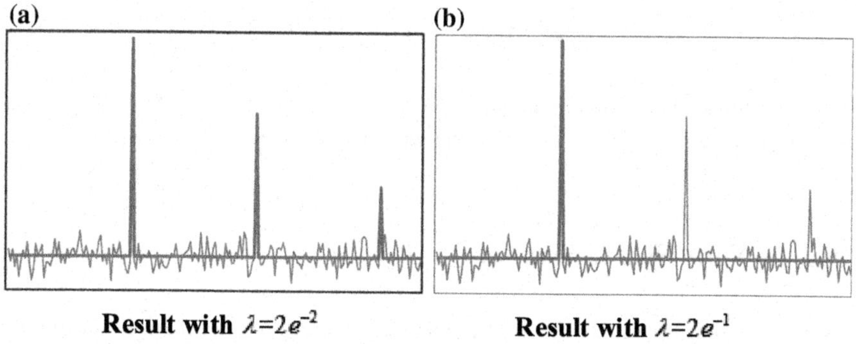

Fig. 3.7 1D signal with spike-edges in different scales. **a** Result of solving the Eq. (3.84) with $\lambda = 2e^{-2}$. **b** Result of solving the Eq. (3.84) with $\lambda = 2e^{-1}$ [50]

2. 2D Case

After introducing the 1D signal smoothing method via ℓ_0-norm minimization, this part we shall introduce how to use the ℓ_0-norm minimization method for 2D signal smoothing especially for image smoothing. The input signal is denoted as I, the result of smoothing is denoted as S and the gradient of position p is denoted as $\nabla S_p = (\partial_x S_p, \partial_y S_p)^T$, which is calculated as difference between neighboring position along the x and y directions. The ℓ_0-norm regularization term of the method is expressed as

$$C(S) = \#\{p||\partial_x S_p| + |\partial_y S_p| \neq 0\}. \tag{3.81}$$

It is used to count p whose magnitude $|\partial_x S_p| + |\partial_y S_p|$ is not zero. The fidelity term can be replaced by $\|S - I\|_F^2$ naturally. The 2D signal smoothing problem can be formulated as

$$\operatorname*{argmin}_S \|S - I\|_F^2 + \lambda C(S). \tag{3.82}$$

3.5.2 ℓ_0-Norm Sparse Optimization Problems

We denote the input discrete signal by $\boldsymbol{g}$ and the result after smoothing by $\boldsymbol{f}$. The general formulation of the ℓ_0 gradient minimization method can be defined as:

$$\operatorname*{argmin}_{\boldsymbol{f}} \|\boldsymbol{f} - \boldsymbol{g}\|_{\ell_2}^2 \quad \text{s.t.} \quad c(\boldsymbol{f}) = K, \tag{3.83}$$

where $c(\boldsymbol{f}) = K$ indicates the nonzero number of the gradient. We can change the formulation of the object function Eq. (3.83) to a general form as

$$\operatorname*{argmin}_{f} \|\boldsymbol{f} - \boldsymbol{g}\|_{\ell_2}^2 + \lambda c(\boldsymbol{f}), \tag{3.84}$$

where λ is the trade-off parameter. A large λ makes the result have few edges. The number of nonzero gradients is monotone with respect to $1/\lambda$.

3.5.3 ℓ_0-Norm Sparse Solution

It is obvious that Eq. (3.82) involves a discrete counting metric, then, it is difficult to solve because the two terms model, respectively, the pixelwise difference and global discontinuity statistically. The traditional methods such as gradient decent or other discrete optimization methods are not suitable. It uses a special alternating optimization strategy with half-quadratic splitting by introducing auxiliary variables to expand the original terms and update them iteratively [50]. In the optimization process, both of the optimization subproblem have the closed-form solution.

We can introduce auxiliary variables h_p and v_p which are corresponding to $\partial_x S_p$ and $\partial_y S_p$ respectively, and the objective function can be rewritten as

$$\operatorname*{argmin}_{S,\boldsymbol{h},\boldsymbol{v}} \left\{ \sum_p \left[(S_p - I_p)^2 + \beta((\partial_x S_p - h_p)^2 + (\partial_y S_p - v_p)^2) \right] + \lambda C(\boldsymbol{h}, \boldsymbol{v}) \right\}, \tag{3.85}$$

where $C(\boldsymbol{h}, \boldsymbol{v}) = \#\{p||h_p| + |v_p| \neq 0\}$ and β is an automatically adapting parameter to trade-off the similarity between variables $(\boldsymbol{h}, \boldsymbol{v})$ and their corresponding gradient.

Subproblem 1: Computing S

The S estimation subproblem corresponds to minimizing

$$\operatorname*{argmin}_{S} \left\{ \sum_p \left[(S_p - I_p)^2 + \beta((\partial_x S_p - h_p)^2 + (\partial_y S_p - v_p)^2) \right] \right\}. \tag{3.86}$$

We can diagonalize derivative operators after Fast Fourier Transform (FFT) for speedup and yields the solution as

$$S = \mathscr{F}^{-1} \left(\frac{\mathscr{F}(I) + \beta(\mathscr{F}(\partial_x)^* \mathscr{F}(\boldsymbol{h}) + \mathscr{F}(\partial_y)^* \mathscr{F}(\boldsymbol{v}))}{\mathscr{F}(1) + (\mathscr{F}(\partial_x)^* \mathscr{F}(\partial_x) + \mathscr{F}(\partial_y)^* \mathscr{F}(\partial_y))} \right), \tag{3.87}$$

where $\mathscr{F}$ is the FFT operator and $\mathscr{F}()^*$ denotes the complex conjugate. $\mathscr{F}(1)$ is the Fourier Transform of the delta function. The plus, multiplication, and division are all componentwise operators. Compared to minimizing directly Eq. (3.86), which involves very large matrix inversion, computation in the Fourier domain is much faster due to the simple componentwise division [50].

Table 3.3 The ℓ_0 gradient minimization algorithm [50]

Input: image I, smoothing weight λ, parameter β_0, β_{max} and rate κ
Initialization: $S \leftarrow I$, $\beta \leftarrow \beta_0$, $t \leftarrow 0$
repeat
 With $S^{(t)}$, solve for $h_p^{(t)}$ and $v_p^{(t)}$ in Eq. (3.90)
 With $\boldsymbol{h}^{(t)}$ and $\boldsymbol{v}^{(t)}$, solve for $S^{(t+1)}$ with Eq. (3.87)
 $\beta \leftarrow \kappa\beta, t++$
until $\beta \geq \beta_{max}$
Output: result image S.

Subproblem 2: Computing $(\boldsymbol{h}, \boldsymbol{v})$

The $(\boldsymbol{h}, \boldsymbol{v})$ estimation subproblem corresponds to minimizing

$$\underset{\boldsymbol{h},\boldsymbol{v}}{\operatorname{argmin}} \left\{ \sum_p \left[(\partial_x S_p - h_p)^2 + (\partial_y S_p - v_p)^2 \right] + \frac{\lambda}{\beta} C(\boldsymbol{h}, \boldsymbol{v}) \right\}, \tag{3.88}$$

where $C(\boldsymbol{h}, \boldsymbol{v})$ returns the number of nonzero elements in $|\boldsymbol{h}|+|\boldsymbol{v}|$. The h_p and v_p can be efficiently estimated by individually process. The objective function to estimate $(\boldsymbol{h}, \boldsymbol{v})$ can be rewritten as

$$\sum_p \underset{h_p, v_p}{\operatorname{argmin}} \left\{ (\partial_x S_p - h_p)^2 + (\partial_y S_p - v_p)^2 + \frac{\lambda}{\beta} H(|h_p| + |v_p|) \right\}, \tag{3.89}$$

where $H(|h_p| + |v_p|)$ is a binary function returning 1 if $|h_p| + |v_p| \neq 0$ and 0 otherwise. So, the solution for each pixel p is

$$(h_p, v_p) = \begin{cases} (0, 0) & (\partial_x S_p)^2 + (\partial_y S_p)^2 \leq \lambda/\beta \\ (\partial_x S_p, \partial_y S_p) & \text{otherwise} \end{cases}. \tag{3.90}$$

Parameter β can monotonically increase in every iteration from β_0, it is multiplied by κ each time until reaching the β_{max}. This scheme accelerates convergence. The ℓ_0 Gradient Minimization algorithm is concluded in Table 3.3.

3.5.4 Applications

1. Image Smoothing

For color image, we need to consider the gradient magnitudes in RGB. So, the $|\partial S_p|$ is defined as the sum of gradient magnitudes in RGB. The performance of this method is very impressive comparing with other smoothing method. We show

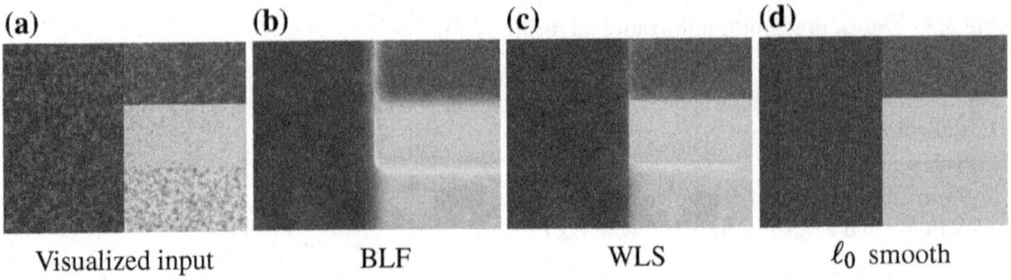

Fig. 3.8 Noisy image created by Farbman et al. [22]. **a** Color visualized noisy input. **b** Bilateral filtering (BLF) [46]. **c** Result of WLS optimization [22]. **d** ℓ_0 smoothing method [50]

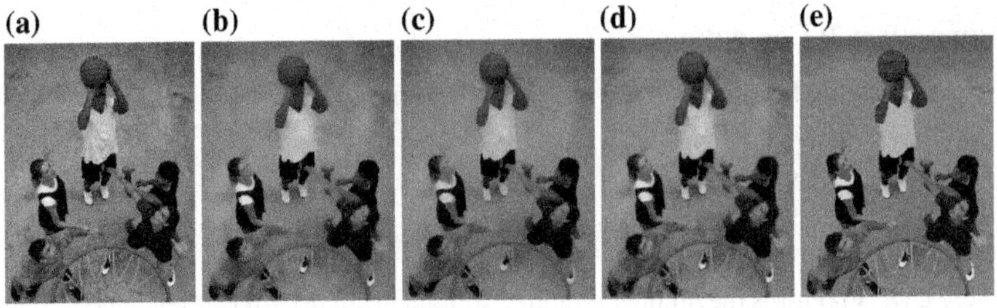

Fig. 3.9 The smooth results and comparison [50]. **a** Input. **b** BLF. **c** WLS. **d** TV. **e** ℓ_0 method

the performance in a toy problem which is created by Farbman et al. [22] and was illustrated in Fig. 3.8.

The example of image smoothing via ℓ_0 gradient minimization algorithm is illustrated in Fig. 3.9.

2. Edge Extraction

Using the ℓ_0-norm gradient minimization method, we can remove the statistically insignificant details by global optimization, meanwhile enhance the significant edges. The example of edge extraction is shown in Fig. 3.10.

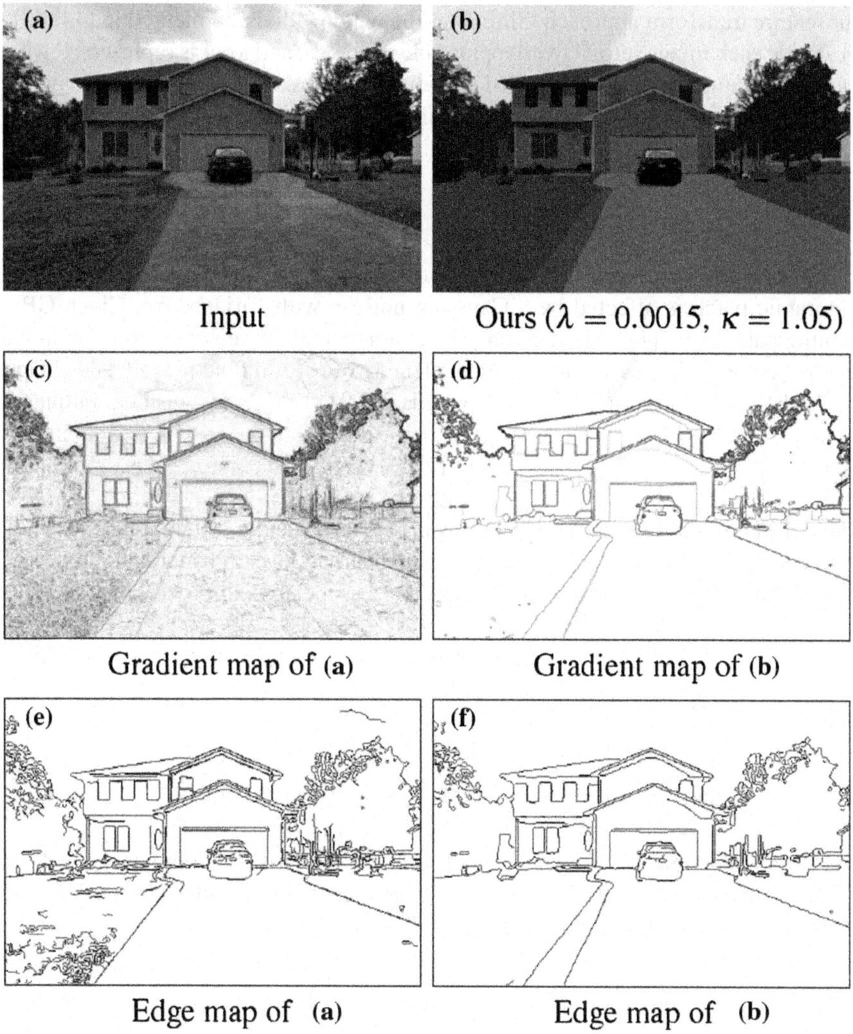

Fig. 3.10 Edge enhancement and extraction. The ℓ_0 gradient minimization method suppresses low-amplitude details and enhances high-contrast edges. The combined effect is to remove textures and sharpen main edges even if their gradient magnitudes are not significant locally [50]

3.6 The Sparse Feature Projection Approach

3.6.1 Gaussian Process Regression for Feature Transforms

Gabor features have been successfully applied to object representation in various computer vision tasks, such as texture segmentation and recognition [48], face recognition [52], and vehicle detection [14, 43]. We use Gabor features to validate our feature transform approach. Similar to the window division method in [14, 43], we divide each image into D overlapping sub-windows, and a car is represented with statistical features, mean μ, standard deviation σ, and skewness κ, from a convolution between a sub-window and a Gabor filter [43]. Therefore, we obtain a feature vector as follows:

$$f = [\mu_1, \sigma_1, \kappa_1, \mu_2, \sigma_2, \kappa_2, \ldots, \mu_D, \sigma_D, \kappa_D]. \tag{3.91}$$

We assume that a transformed feature vector $\hat{f}$ from a feature vector of a panoramic patch is affected by a Gaussian noise ε with variance σ^2. Given GPR training pairs, $\mathbf{S} = \{F_a, \hat{F}_e\}$, we can predict a new feature vector $\hat{f}_*$ from an input feature vector f_*. Let us define a nonlinear feature transform function $\mathscr{T}[\cdot]$ that maps the N-dimensional input f obtained from Eq. (3.91) to a N-dimensional output $\hat{f}$ by

$$\hat{f} = \mathscr{T}[f] = w^{\mathrm{T}}\phi(f), \tag{3.92}$$

where T denotes matrix transpose. In this paper, we consider different patches with different feature distortions from different interest windows in panoramic images.

Now consider a transformed feature vector $\hat{f}$ as a Gaussian Process (Fig. 3.11)

$$p(\hat{f}|\mu(f), k(f_p, f_q)) \sim \mathscr{GP}(\mu(f), k(f_p, f_q)), \tag{3.93}$$

where

$$\begin{cases} \mu(f) = \mathrm{E}[\hat{f}] = \mathrm{E}[\mathscr{T}[f]] \\ k(f_p, f_q) = k_{pq} = \mathrm{E}[(f_p - \mu(f_p))(f_q - \mu(f_q))] \end{cases}. \tag{3.94}$$

The kernel function k_{pq} provides evidence how correlated two outputs $\hat{f}_p$ and $\hat{f}_q$ are. In this paper, the squared exponential covariance function with isotropic distance measure we use has the following form [41]

$$k_{pq} = \sigma_f^2 \exp\left(-\frac{1}{2\ell^2}\|f_p - f_q\|^2\right) + \sigma_n^2\delta_{pq}, \tag{3.95}$$

where $\{\sigma_f^2, \ell, \sigma_n\}$ are hyperparameters of GPR. For simplicity of the notation, we absorb the variance σ^2 of observation of $\hat{f}$ into the hyperparameters, $\Theta = \{\sigma_f^2, \ell, \sigma_n, \sigma^2\}$. We will determine Θ from training pairs $\mathbf{S}$ by maximizing the marginal likelihood, the detail refers to [41].

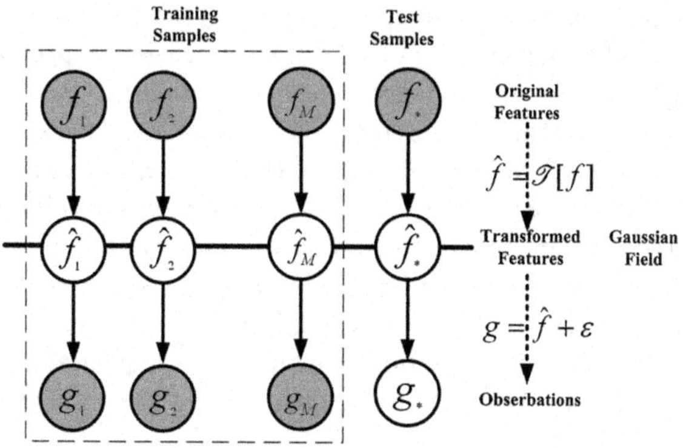

Fig. 3.11 The graphical model for feature transforms using GPR: each *circle* in this figure represents a random variable, and each *gray circle* is an observed variable while each *open circle* is a latent variable

Given a test feature vector f_*, we transform it to obtain $\hat{f}_*$ according to the mapping relationship implicitly in GPR training pairs $\mathbf{S}$ and the covariance function in Eq. (3.95). The mean $\mu(f_*)$ and variance $\mathrm{cov}_{\hat{f}_*}$ of feature vector $\hat{f}_*$ can be written as

$$\begin{cases} u_{\hat{f}_*} = \mathbf{k}_*^{\mathrm{T}}[\mathbf{K} + \sigma^2\mathbf{I}]^{-1}\hat{F}_e, \\ \mathrm{cov}_{\hat{f}_*} \triangleq k(f_*, f_*) - \mathbf{k}_*^{\mathrm{T}}[\mathbf{K} + \sigma^2\mathbf{I}]^{-1}\mathbf{k}_*, \end{cases} \tag{3.96}$$

where

$$\mathbf{k}_* = \mathbf{k}(x_*) = [k(f_*, f_1), k(f_*, f_2), \ldots, k(f_*, f_M)]^{\mathrm{T}}$$

and

$$\mathbf{K} = \mathbf{K}(F_a, F_a) = [k(f_p, f_q)]_{p \times q}.$$

3.6.2 Sparse Projection of Input Feature Vectors

The problem with high-dimensional data is that for many input feature vectors, their covariances with GPR training feature vectors are usually quite small, thus the result of a Gaussian process regression tends to fall outside of the distribution of Gaussian processes, thus affecting the subsequent classification performance. To address this problem, we propose to project an input feature vector f_* to the convex hull spanned by the GPR training vectors F_a with a sparseness constraint, that is,

$$\arg\min_{\alpha} \|F_a\alpha^{\mathrm{T}} - f_*\|_2^2 - \lambda\|\alpha\|_2^2, \qquad \text{s.t.} \begin{cases} \alpha_1 + \cdots + \alpha_N = 1 \\ \alpha_1, \ldots, \alpha_N \geq 0 \end{cases}, \tag{3.97}$$

where $\alpha = [\alpha_1, \ldots, \alpha_N]^{\mathrm{T}}$ are the unknown coefficients. The term $\|\alpha\|_2^2$ is the sparseness term which measures the sparseness of the coefficients. We would like to point out that similar sparseness terms have been used in face recognition work [28]. This term penalizes solutions which have many nonzero coefficients. The rational behind the sparseness constraint is that the feature vectors are usually defined over a number of subregions in the high-dimensional space where each subregion can be better approximated with a linear space. In Eq. (3.97), λ is a user-specified weighting parameter that balances the projection error and the sparseness penalty. One extreme case is when λ is equal to zero. In this case, the sparseness constraint has no effect and the system projects f_* to the convex hull of all the feature vectors in F_a. The other extreme is when λ approaches infinity. In this case, the system degenerates to the Nearest Neighbor Feature Projection (NNFP) scheme, that is, the projection of f_* is the one in F_a that has smallest distance to f_*.

The objective function in Eq. (3.97) is a quadratic programming problem which can be solved by an existing quadratic programming solver[1] [24].

References

1. Baraniuk, R.G., Cevher, V., Duarte, M.F., Hegde, C.: Model-based compressive sensing. IEEE Trans. Inf. Theory **56**(4), 1982–2001 (2010)
2. Blumensath, T., Davies, M.E.: Gradient pursuits. IEEE Trans. Signal Process. **56**(6), 2370–2382 (2008)
3. Blumensath, T., Davies, M.E.: Iterative thresholding for sparse approximations. J. Fourier Anal. Appl. **14**(5–6), 629–654 (2008)
4. Blumensath, T., Davies, M.E.: Iterative hard thresholding for compressed sensing. Appl. Comput. Harmon. Anal. **27**(3), 265–274 (2009)
5. Blumensath, T., Davies, M.E., et al.: How to use the iterative hard thresholding algorithm. In: Signal Processing with Adaptive Sparse Structured Representations (2009)
6. Bo, L., Ren, X., Fox, D.: Multipath sparse coding using hierarchical matching pursuit. In: IEEE CVPR (2013)
7. Boyd, S., Vandenberghe, L.: Convex Optimization. Cambridge University Press, Cambridge (2004)
8. Bredies, K., Lorenz, D.A.: Iterated hard shrinkage for minimization problems with sparsity constraints. SIAM J. Sci. Comput. **30**(2), 657–683 (2008)
9. Candes, E., Romberg, J.: l1-magic: Recovery of sparse signals via convex programming. http://www.acm.caltech.edu/l1magic/downloads/l1magic.pdf**4** (2005)
10. Candès, E.J., Romberg, J., Tao, T.: Robust uncertainty principles: exact signal reconstruction from highly incomplete frequency information. IEEE Trans. Inf. Theory **52**(2), 489–509 (2006)
11. Candes, E.J., Romberg, J.K., Tao, T.: Stable signal recovery from incomplete and inaccurate measurements. Commun. Pure Appl. Math. **59**(8), 1207–1223 (2006)
12. Chen, S., Gunn, S.R., Harris, C.J.: The relevance vector machine technique for channel equalization application. IEEE Trans. Neural Netw. **12**(6), 1529–1532 (2001)
13. Chen, S.S., Donoho, D.L., Saunders, M.A.: Atomic decomposition by basis pursuit. SIAM J. Sci. Comput. **20**(1), 33–61 (1998)
14. Cheng, H., Zheng, N., Sun, C., Wetering, H.: Boosted Gabor features applied to vehicle detection. In: IEEE ICPR (2006)
15. Daubechies, I., Defrise, M., De Mol, C.: An iterative thresholding algorithm for linear inverse problems with a sparsity constraint. Commun. Pure Appl. Math. **57**(11), 1413–1457 (2004)
16. Donoho, D.L., Elad, M.: Optimally sparse representation in general (nonorthogonal) dictionaries via l1 minimization. Proc. Natl. Acad. Sci. **100**(5), 2197–2202 (2003)
17. Donoho, D.L., Huo, X.: Uncertainty principles and ideal atomic decomposition. IEEE Trans. Inf. Theory **47**(7), 2845–2862 (2001)

[1]http://www-fp.mcs.anl.gov/otc/Guide/SoftwareGuide/Blurbs/bqpd.html.

18. Donoho, D.L., Tsaig, Y.: Fast Solution of l1-Norm Minimization Problems When the Solution May Be Sparse. Department of Statistics, Stanford University (2006)
19. Donoho, D.L., Tsaig, Y., Drori, I., Starck, J.L.: Sparse solution of underdetermined systems of linear equations by stagewise orthogonal matching pursuit. IEEE Trans. Inf. Theory **58**(2), 1094–1121 (2012)
20. Elad, M., Matalon, B., Zibulevsky, M.: Coordinate and subspace optimization methods for linear least squares with non-quadratic regularization. Appl. Comput. Harmon. Anal. **23**(3), 346–367 (2007)
21. Eldar, Y.C., Kutyniok, G.: Compressed Sensing: Theory and Applications. Cambridge University Press, Cambridge (2012)
22. Farbman, Z., Fattal, R., Lischinski, D., Szeliski, R.: Edge-preserving decompositions for multi-scale tone and detail manipulation. In: ACM Transactions on Graphics (2008)
23. Figueiredo, M.A., Nowak, R.D., Wright, S.J.: Gradient projection for sparse reconstruction: application to compressed sensing and other inverse problems. IEEE J. Sel. Top. Signal Process. **1**(4), 586–597 (2007)
24. Fletcher, R.: Practical Methods of Optimization, 2nd edn. Wiley, Chichester (2004)
25. Gale, D.: Linear programming and the simplex method. Not. AMS **54**(3), 364–369 (2007)
26. Gilbert, A.C., Guha, S., Indyk, P., Muthukrishnan, S., Strauss, M.: Near-optimal sparse Fourier representations via sampling. In: ACM Symposium on Theory of Computing (2002)
27. Gilbert, A.C., Muthukrishnan, S., Strauss, M.: Improved time bounds for near-optimal sparse Fourier representations. In: Optics & Photonics (2005)
28. Hoyer, P.O.: Non-negative matrix factorization with sparseness constraints. J. Mach. Learn. Res. **5**, 1457–1469 (2004)
29. Huang, H., Makur, A.: Backtracking-based matching pursuit method for sparse signal reconstruction. IEEE Signal Process. Lett. **18**(7), 391–394 (2011)
30. Ji, S., Xue, Y., Carin, L.: Bayesian compressive sensing. IEEE Trans. Signal Process. **56**(6), 2346–2356 (2008)
31. Koh, K., Kim, S.J., Boyd, S.: An interior-point method for large-scale? 1-regularized logistic regression. J. Mach. Learn. Res. **1**(4), 606–617 (2007)
32. Lange, K., Hunter, D.R., Yang, I.: Optimization transfer using surrogate objective functions. J. Comput. Graph. Stat. **9**(1), 1–20 (2000)
33. Li, Q., Lin, N.: The bayesian elastic net. Bayesian Anal. **5**(1), 151–170 (2010)
34. Needell, D., Tropp, J.A.: Cosamp: Iterative signal recovery from incomplete and inaccurate samples. Appl. Comput. Harmon. Anal. **26**(3), 301–321 (2009)
35. Needell, D., Vershynin, R.: Uniform uncertainty principle and signal recovery via regularized orthogonal matching pursuit. Found. Comput. Math. **9**(3), 317–334 (2009)
36. Needell, D., Vershynin, R.: Signal recovery from incomplete and inaccurate measurements via regularized orthogonal matching pursuit. IEEE Sel. Top. Signal Process. **4**(2), 310–316 (2010)
37. Nesterov, Y., Nemirovskii, A.S., Ye, Y.: Interior-point polynomial algorithms in convex programming. SIAM **13**, 405 (1994)
38. Osborne, M.R., Presnell, B., Turlach, B.A.: A new approach to variable selection in least squares problems. IMA J. Numer. Anal. **20**(3), 389–403 (2000)
39. Osborne, M.R., Presnell, B., Turlach, B.A.: On the Lasso and its dual. J. Comput. Graph. Stat. **9**(2), 319–337 (2000)
40. Pati, Y.C., Rezaiifar, R., Krishnaprasad, P.: Orthogonal matching pursuit: Recursive function approximation with applications to wavelet decomposition. In: IEEE Asilomar Conference on Signals, Systems and Computers (1993)
41. Rasmussen, C.E., Williams, C.K.I.: Gaussian Processes for Machine Learning. The MIT Press, Cambridge. http://www.gaussianprocess.org/gpml/ (2006)
42. Rudin, L.I., Osher, S., Fatemi, E.: Nonlinear total variation based noise removal algorithms. Phys. D: Nonlinear Phenom. **60**(1), 259–268 (1992)
43. Sun, C., Bebis, G., Miller, R.: On-road vehicle detection using evolutionary Gabor filter optimization. IEEE Trans. Intell. Transp. Syst. **6**(2), 125–137 (2005)

44. Tibshirani, R.: Regression shrinkage and selection via the lasso. J. R. Stat. Soc. **58**(1), 267–288 (1996)
45. Tipping, M.E.: Sparse bayesian learning and the relevance vector machine. J. Mach. Learn. Res. **1**, 211–244 (2001)
46. Tomasi, C., Manduchi, R.: Bilateral filtering for gray and color images. In: IEEE ICCV (1998)
47. Tropp, J.A., Gilbert, A.C.: Signal recovery from random measurements via orthogonal matching pursuit. IEEE Trans. Inf. Theory **53**(12), 4655–4666 (2007)
48. Weldon, T.P., Higgins, W.E., Dunn, D.F.: Efficient Gabor filter design for texture segmentation. Pattern Recognit. **29**(12), 2005–2015 (1996)
49. Wipf, D.P., Rao, B.D.: Sparse Bayesian learning for basis selection. IEEE Trans. Signal Process. **52**(8), 2153–2164 (2004)
50. Xu, L., Lu, C., Xu, Y., Jia, J.: Image smoothing via l 0 gradient minimization. ACM Trans. Graph. **30**(6), 174 (2011)
51. Yang, A.Y., Sastry, S.S., Ganesh, A., Ma, Y.: Fast ℓ_1-minimization algorithms and an application in robust face recognition: a review. In: IEEE ICIP (2010)
52. Yu, S., Shan, S., Chen, X., Gao, W.: Hierarchical ensemble of global and local classifiers for face recognition. In: IEEE CVPR (2007)
53. Zou, H., Hastie, T.: Regularization and variable selection via the elastic net. J. R. Stat. Soc. **67**(2), 301–320 (2005)

Chapter 4
Robust Sparse Representation, Modeling and Learning

4.1 Introduction

Traditional statistical techniques implicitly assume that more than half the data obeys the parametric models. This assumption is not suitable in many practical data. Thus, it could be a failure to cope well with deviations from a standard distribution. In robust statistical approaches, breakdown point is used to define the robustness, where the smallest fraction of outliers in a data set can result in poor performance. Toward this end, robust statistical approaches indeed consider these deviations, thus yielding higher accuracy of inference during the procedure of estimating the parameters of the models. Robust statistics can provide the theoretical justification on using the robust approaches. Since the 1960s, many robust approaches have been developed to be less sensitive to outliers.

There are many robust techniques in computer vision [23], such as Hough transform [14], RANSAC algorithms [3], least median of squares (LMedS). As we know, many computer vision data cannot meet the breakdown point assumption. Thus, traditional statistical techniques cannot work well in this case. Moreover, feature vectors from computer vision tasks are really more challenging than those in statistics. In other words, we can directly use the robust statistical techniques for most computer vision tasks [23].

Sparse representation and learning are commonly used in image/video feature learning [5]. One major research effort of sparse coding is to improve its robustness [20, 36]. Toward this end, two major strategies have been proposed to handle this issue. One is to modify the sparsity constraint. Yang et al. proposed a new strategy, Robust Sparse Coding (RSC), by modeling the sparse coding as an M-estimator regression problem [36]. Similarly, Wang et al. proposed a Robust Elastic Net (REN) approach by replacing ℓ_2-norm in elastic net equation using a robust function [5, 15], where distribution-induced weight function is used to leverage the importance of different points. Another one is to combine transfer learning and sparse coding techniques to construct robust sparse coding, called Transfer Sparse Coding (TSC) for classifying cross-distribution images [20].

H. Cheng, *Sparse Representation, Modeling and Learning in Visual Recognition*,
Advances in Computer Vision and Pattern Recognition,
DOI 10.1007/978-1-4471-6714-3_4

4.2 Robust Statistics

The complexities of the data/features in computer vision is more than what we imagine, and the robust estimators are the simple steps in complex vision tasks. There exists a big gap between computer vision and statistics. Consequently, Hough transform and RANSAC were developed in the computer vision community and not in the statistics community. However, the robust framework in statistics still plays a fundamental role in image/video understanding. Moreover, P. Meer et al. pointed out that almost all of the robust approaches are residual-based [23]. Thus, how to define the proper residuals according to specific tasks is critical in vision tasks. Once we define the residuals, we have to model the invariance properties of residuals with respect to scales. Usually, both computer vision and M-estimators treat scales as unknown.

4.2.1 Connection Between MLE and Residuals

First of all, we have the probabilistic formulation in a 2D situation as follows:

$$p(\boldsymbol{X}_i|\Theta) \propto \exp\left\{-\frac{(ax_i + by_i + c)^2}{2\sigma^2}\right\}, \tag{4.1}$$

where $\boldsymbol{X}_i = (x_i, y_i)$, $\Theta = (a, b, c)$, σ is the parameter. Then, we can get

$$\begin{aligned} L(\boldsymbol{X}|\Theta) &= \log P(\boldsymbol{X}_i|\Theta) \\ &= \log\left(\prod_i p(\boldsymbol{X}_i|\Theta)\right) \propto -\sum_i \frac{(ax_i + by_i + c)^2}{2\sigma^2}. \end{aligned} \tag{4.2}$$

Equations (4.1) and (4.2) build a connection between least squares estimation and maximum likelihood estimation. By defining $d(\boldsymbol{X}_i|\Theta) = |ax_i + by_i + c|$, we can rewrite Eq. (4.2) as

$$L(\boldsymbol{X}|\Theta) = -\sum_i \frac{d^2(\boldsymbol{X}_i|\Theta)}{2\sigma^2}. \tag{4.3}$$

Equation (4.3) assumes that all the data obeys *Gaussian distribution*. However, features/data in computer vision violate this assumption. In other words, there exist many outliers. The quadratic functions of residuals increase too quickly, and outliers contribute as much to likelihood as all inliers.

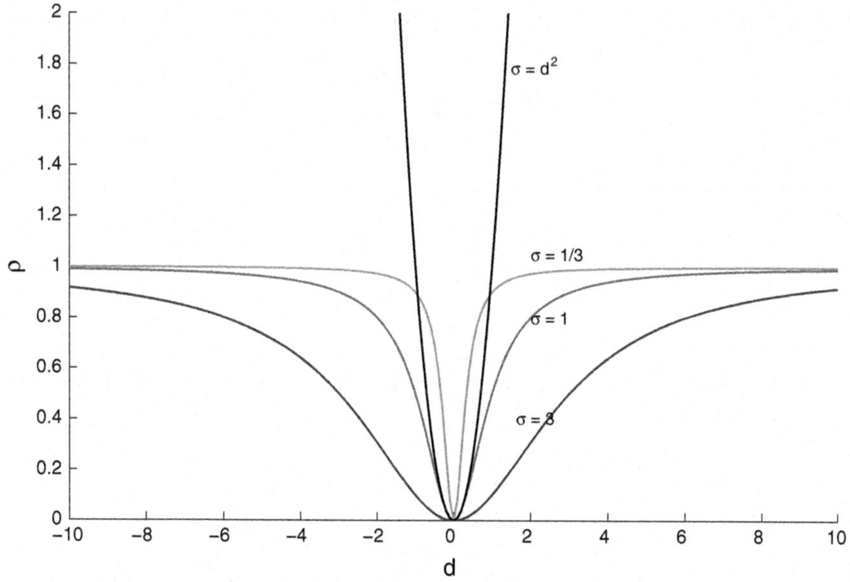

Fig. 4.1 An example of the M-estimator object function $\rho = \frac{d^2}{\sigma^2+d^2}$

4.2.2 M-Estimators

Most of the location estimators we consider are *M-estimators*. The name derived from 'MLE-like' estimator. *M-estimator* is to replace $\rho(d) = d^2$ with trimmed distance functions which are less sensitive to outliers, then parameter σ controls the sensitivity of outliers. The σ is smaller, the outliers are more downweighted. The relationship between ρ-function with σ is shown in Fig. 4.1. The algorithm flowchart is defined in Table 4.1.

In M-estimators, we define the objective function $\sum_i \rho(d(\boldsymbol{X}_i, \Theta); \sigma)$, where a common choice is $\rho(d, \sigma) = \frac{d^2}{\sigma^2+d^2}$. The mean corresponds to $\rho(d) = d^2$, and the

Table 4.1 The algorithm flowchart of M-estimator

Given points $(X_1, X_2, \ldots, X_N)$ and initial estimate of the parameter Θ_0.
Repeat:

$$\sigma_t = 1.4826 \operatorname*{median}_i d(X_i, \Theta_t); \tag{4.7}$$

$$\Theta_{t+1} = \arg\min_{\Theta} \sum_i \rho(d(X_i, \Theta_t)) \tag{4.8}$$

median corresponds to $\rho(d) = |d|$. We define $\psi(d) = \rho'(d)$ if ρ has a derivative. The function

$$\psi(d) = \begin{cases} d, & |d| < c \\ 0, & \text{otherwise} \end{cases}$$

corresponds to *metric trimming* and large outliers have no influence at all. The function

$$\psi(d) = \begin{cases} -2c, & d < -c \\ d, & |d| < c \\ 2c, & d > c \end{cases}$$

is known as *metric Winsorizing* and brings in extreme observations to $\mu \pm c$. The corresponding $\rho(d)$ is

$$\rho(d) = \begin{cases} d^2, & \text{if } |d| < c \\ c(2|d| - c), & \text{otherwise} \end{cases}$$

and corresponds to a density with a Gaussian center and double-exponential tails. We can note that $\rho(d)$ increases at an accelerating rate when d in the range of $|d| < c$, while for absolute error when d is out of the range $|d| < c$. This estimator is due to Huber. Note that its limit as $c \to 0$ is the median, and as $c \to \infty$ the limit is the mean. The value $c = 1.345$ gives 95 % efficiency at the normal.

Tukey's *biweight* can be defined as

$$\psi(d) = d\left[1 - \left(\frac{d}{R}\right)^2\right]_+^2,$$

where $[]_+$ denotes the positive part of $1 - (\frac{d}{R})^2$. This implements 'soft' trimming. The value $R = 4.685$ gives 95 % efficiency at normal.

Hampel's ψ has several linear pieces,

$$\psi(d) = \text{sgn}(d) \begin{cases} |d| & 0 < |d| < a \\ a & a < |d| < b \\ a(c - |d|)/(c - b) & b < |d| < c \\ 0 & c < |d| \end{cases},$$

for example, with $a = 2.2$, $b = 3.7$, $c = 5.9$ which is illustrated in Fig. 4.2.

Figure 4.2 illustrates these functions, Tukey biweight, trimmed mean, Huber ,and Hampel. There is a scaling problem with the last four choices, since they depend on a scale factor (c, R or s). We can apply the estimator to rescale the results, that is,

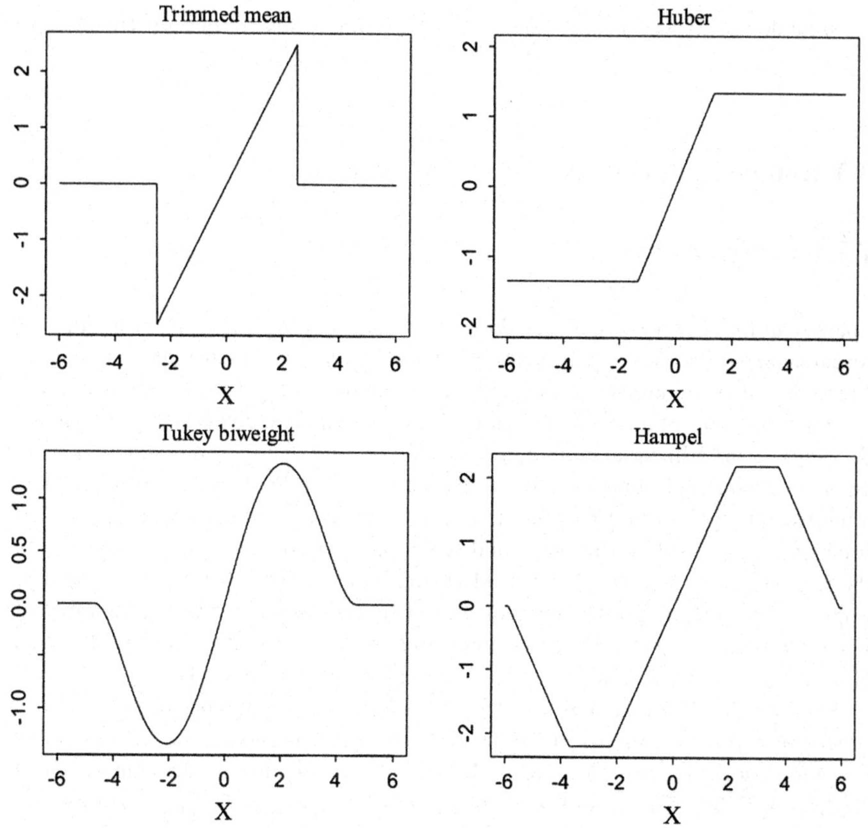

Fig. 4.2 The ψ-function for four common M-estimators [30]

$$\min_{\mu} \sum_i \rho\left(\frac{y_i - \mu}{s}\right) \tag{4.4}$$

for a scale factor s, for example the MAD estimator. Alternatively, we can estimate s in a similar way. The MLE for density $s^{-1} f((x - \mu)/s)$ gives rise to the equation

$$\sum_i \psi\left(\frac{y_i - \mu}{s}\right)\left(\frac{y_i - \mu}{s}\right) = n, \tag{4.5}$$

which is not resistant (and is biased at the normal). We modify this to

$$\sum_i \chi\left(\frac{y_i - \mu}{s}\right) = (n - 1)\gamma, \tag{4.6}$$

for bounded χ, where γ is chosen for consistency at the normal distribution, so $\gamma = E_\chi(N)$.

4.3 Robust Sparse PCA

4.3.1 Introduction

Sparse learning-based dimension reduction approaches have drawn much attention of researchers worldwide recently, since it can reduce not only dimensionality of feature spaces but also the number of explicitly used feature vectors [37, 40]. As we know, principal component analysis (PCA), whose each principal component (PC) can be decomposed as a linear combination of all the original features, are widely used in data processing and dimensionality reduction [17, 34]. PCA can be formulated as a regression-type optimization problem, and then we can obtain sparse loadings by imposing least absolute shrinkage and selection operator (LASSO) constraints on the regression coefficients [17, 40]. Moreover, convex optimization is also used to improve interpretation of the standard PCA [8]. Traditionally, when the number of feature dimensions is larger than the number of observation vectors, we have to select all of the feature vectors and thus it cannot reduce their dimensions.

Suppose the data matrix is $\mathbf{X} \in \mathbb{R}^{n \times p}$, where n is the number of observations or samples, p is the number of features or variable dimensions. The singular value decomposition (SVD) of $\mathbf{X}$ is $\mathbf{X} = \mathbf{U}\boldsymbol{\Sigma}\mathbf{V}^T$, or the eigenvalue decomposition of $\mathbf{X}^T\mathbf{X} = \mathbf{V}\boldsymbol{\Sigma}^2\mathbf{V}^T$. The PCs of $\mathbf{X}$ are defined as $\mathbf{P} = \mathbf{X}\mathbf{V}_k = \mathrm{U}_k\boldsymbol{\Sigma}_k$, which capture the maximum variability of $\mathbf{X}$ and guarantees minimal information loss, where $\mathbf{V}_k \in \mathbb{R}^{p \times k}$ is called as principal loading matrix or projecting matrix. Since the entries of $\mathbf{V}_k$ usually are dense, the PCs of PCA are the linear combination of all the observations. Thus, the PCA is not the real feature extraction approach. Then, Tibshirani proposed a sparse regression algorithm: LASSO. Following this expression, the $\mathbf{V}$ is sparse and its nonzero entries correspond to the main features of the $\mathbf{X}$.

As the oldest single-layer feature extraction algorithm, principal component analysis (PCA) [17, 34] combines the probabilistic, auto-encoder and manifold views of feature learning. Its main idea is to find a projection matrix (a.k.a. loading matrix) that maximizes the variance of a sample set. The PCA can be formulated as a ℓ_2-norm regression type optimization problem. Thus the general PCA can work well under Gaussian assumptions. However, the real samples could be corrupted or occluded thus resulting in high noises, which may violate the Gaussian assumptions. In order to alleviate this problem, ℓ_1-norm PCA approaches are formulated by using maximum likelihood estimation (MLE) to the given samples, where the error between projection space and the original sample is assumed to follow a Laplacian distribution instead of a Gaussian distribution [2, 11, 18]. But in practice, this may not work very well, especially when there are corruptions, occlusions, and noises [36]. In this case, the outliers have a very large influence on the ℓ_1-norm residual. Hence, robust statistics have been developed for handling those issues, such as M-estimators [25], [9] were proposed to replace the ℓ_2/ℓ_1-norm. In [9], the authors perform a gradient descent approach with local quadratic approximation to solve the M-estimators problem. It is an efficient and robust approach for feature learning, and we will compare it with our approach in the following, so we named it as "FRPCA".

Even though the ℓ_1-norm-based PCA and other robust PCA can handle the outliers to some degree, most of these approaches need to assume that the observation samples are large enough, namely the sample set is nonsingular matrix. However, such as in scene monitoring, we only have limited observation numbers which is much less than the number of features. We named it as High Dimension, Low Sample Size (HDLSS) problem. In this case, the traditional eigen-decomposition-based PCA methods cannot give the proper solutions. Feature learning from HDLSS data is challenging for visual representation [7, 16, 26, 27, 32, 39, 40].

It would be interesting to discover sparse principal components, i.e., sets of sparse vectors spanning a low-dimensional space that explains most of the variance present in the data. In this case, sparse principal component analysis (SPCA) provides a direct way to reduce the number of feature vectors for feature representation and learning [40]. Accordingly, various SPCA approaches have been developed [8, 9, 12, 22, 27], where the residual follows Gaussian/Laplacian distribution. However, there are some outliers in the sample data in practice. In this case, the ℓ_2-norm cannot give the right solution, as shown in Fig. 4.3b. The outliers have a very large influence on ℓ_2-norm because the residual $\mathbf{e}$ is squared. Consequently, $y = \|\mathbf{e}\|_2^2$ is increased sharply when its value is increasing, shown in Fig. 4.3a. Furthermore, some strategies using ℓ_1-norm are used to handle this issue in PCA [2, 11, 18, 19, 24, 25]. Indeed, in some cases, the ℓ_1-norm performs better than ℓ_2-norm, as shown in Fig. 4.3b. Unfortunately, ℓ_1-norm cannot model the outlier problem explicitly. From Fig. 4.3c, we can see when the outlier lies in x-axis, the ℓ_1-norm fails to obtain the right solution. In this case, robust PCA using ρ functions could handle these outliers very well.

Obviously, when $n > p$ and $\mathbf{X}$ is a column full rank matrix, the PCA and LASSO have unique solutions. However, in many scenarios, the observations are limited and the feature dimensions are much more than observation numbers. For example, in

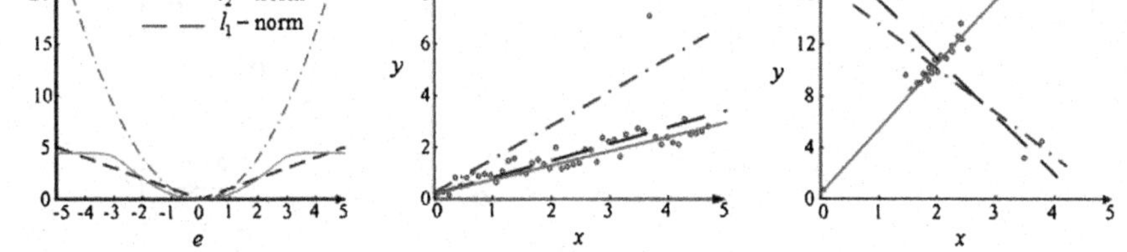

Fig. 4.3 An illustration for various PCA approaches: **a** Different residual functions, ℓ_1-norm, ℓ_2-norm, and the ρ-function; **b** Toy data 1; **c** Toy data 2 (best viewed in color)

background modeling, it usually has $p > n$. In this case, both standard PCA and LASSO do not have unique solutions. They select at most n features that seems to be a limiting feature selection. On the other hand, if a group of features correlated to each other, the PCA and LASSO only randomly select one of them. That will lose some performance on feature extracting. To solve the $p > n$ problem and give the group selection, Zou et al. proposed the EN algorithm [39] and a new sparse PCA (SPCA) approach [40]. Moreover, Zhou et al. extend the EN on the sparse manifold learning [37].

There are other robust PCA or SPCA that were proposed [1, 10, 29] to solve the outlier problem. Candes et al. also gave solutions on robust PCA [4] using Augmented Lagrangian Method on low-rank matrix decomposition. Croux et al. used grid algorithm to compute the sparse and robust principal components [6]. Yang et al. induced a robust sparse coding for face recognition [36], where an iteratively reweighted sparse coding approach was used. Feature learning from HDLSS data is challenging for visual representation [7, 16, 26, 27, 32, 39, 40].

The Elastic Net (EN) approach [39] is proposed to solve these problems. Afterwards, the sparse principal component Analysis (SPCA) [40] was proposed by formulating PCA as the EN regression optimization problem, which can generate modified principal components (PCs) with sparse loadings and has the HDLSS asymptotic property [26]. However, since SPCA and EN approaches are based on ℓ_2-norm, they are sensitive to outliers. Figure 4.4 illustrates the performance of PCA and its variants on a toy data with outliers. The toy data are some points of a line, but there are several points far away from their correct coordinates. The PCA, ℓ_1-PCA [19], SPCA, FRPCA [9] and the proposed Robust Elastic Net (REN) feature learning approaches are used to find the loading vector of this line. It is shown that the ℓ_1-norm estimator performs better than ℓ_2-norm based PCA and SPCA. The M-estimator-based FRPCA and the proposed REN get the best performance. However, the residual error of FRPCA is much bigger than that of REN, which will be shown in our experiments

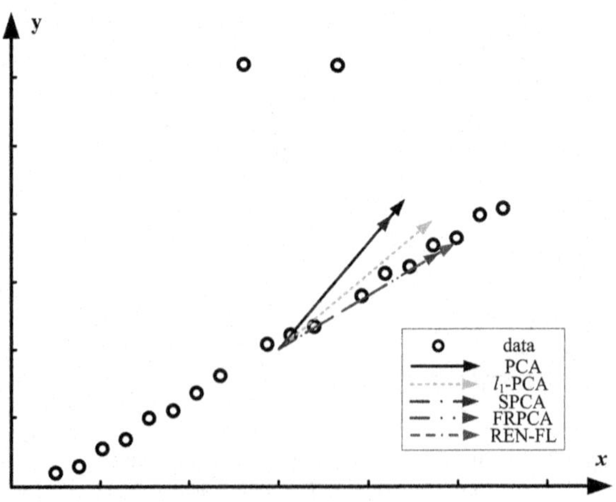

Fig. 4.4 A toy data with outliers. The 'o' denotes the original data; the *lines with arrow* denote the first loading vector yielded by PCA, ℓ_1-PCA, SPCA, FRPCA, and the proposed REN, respectively

in Sect. 4.3.4. It is also noted that, as the HDLSS problem cannot be expressed in 2D space clearly, we just illustrate the robustness of our proposed approach in Fig. 4.4.

When the observations are either corrupted or occluded by noise, some robust feature learning and sparse coding approaches are used to solve the outliers. Fernando et al. proposed a fast M-estimation-based approach using gradient iteration algorithm [29]. Wang et al. proposed a kernel-based feature extraction algorithm to handle nonlinear classification problem [31]. But neither of these solutions are sparse. Candes et al. gave the solutions on robust sparse PCA using low-rank matrix decomposition [4], but assumed that there are enough images for the same class. Croux et al. used grid algorithm to compute the sparse and robust principal components [6]. Wright et al. induced a Sparse Representation Coding (SRC) for robust face recognition [35]. As extensions of SRC, Yang et al. induced a iteratively Reweighted Sparse Coding (RSC) algorithm [36], Tang et al. presented a greedy regression algorithm to deal with single-image superresolution problem [28], Lu et al. presented a locality weighted SRC algorithm [21]. Usually, in most of these sparse approaches, the training samples are noise free and use PCA to extract the principal features.

Most of the previous sparse PCA and robust PCA could have failed when the data consisted of outlier or the number of sampling was much less than the number of feature dimensions. In the following sections, we discuss the robust elastic net approach to solve these problems.

4.3.2 PCA

Let us first briefly review regression-type optimization framework of PCA. The PCs of data matrix $\mathbf{X}$ is $\mathbf{P} = \mathbf{X}V_k^T$, where $\mathbf{X} = \mathbf{U}\mathbf{D}\mathbf{V}^T$, $\mathbf{V}_k$ is called loading matrix or projecting matrix. Usually $k \ll p$, and thus dimensionality reduction is achieved. Furthermore, the uncorrelated PCs capture the maximum variability of $\mathbf{X}$, which guarantees minimal information loss. In regression-type optimization frameworks, PCA can be formulated as an LARS-EN problem [40]. The sparse solution of jth component $P_{\cdot j}$ can be solved by

$$\hat{\beta}_{opt} = \arg\min_{\beta_j} \|P_{\cdot j} - \mathbf{X}\boldsymbol{\beta}_j\|_2^2 + \lambda_1 \|\boldsymbol{\beta}_j\|_2^2 + \gamma_1 \|\boldsymbol{\beta}_j\|_1, \tag{4.9}$$

where both λ_1 and γ_1 are nonnegative Lagrange multipliers. Afterwards, we can obtain $\hat{V}_{\cdot j} = \hat{\boldsymbol{\beta}}_{opt}/\|\hat{\boldsymbol{\beta}}_{opt}\|_2$.

Equation (4.9) is a convex combination of the ridge penalty and ℓ_1-norm penalty. The ridge penalty is used to ensure the reconstruction of PCs, while the ℓ_1-norm penalty is used to ensure the sparsity of loadings. Larger γ_1 encourages a sparser $\hat{\beta}$. Given a fixed λ_1 and γ_1, optimizing Eq. (4.9) we can efficiently obtain $\hat{\beta}_{opt}$ using the LARS-EN algorithm [38].

Now we discuss PCA with noise. Assume data matrix $\mathbf{X} = \mathbf{S} + \mathbf{N}$, where $\mathbf{S}$ is original data matrix, and $\mathbf{N}$ is noise matrix. The noise-free PCs of $\mathbf{S} = \overline{\mathbf{U}}\,\overline{\mathbf{D}}\,\overline{\mathbf{V}}^T$

are $\overline{\mathbf{P}} = \mathbf{S}\overline{\mathbf{V}}_k$, where $\overline{\mathbf{V}}_k = [\alpha_1, \ldots, \alpha_k]$. Then the jth principal component $\overline{P}_{\cdot j} = \mathbf{S}\alpha_j = \mathbf{X}\alpha_j - \mathbf{N}\alpha_j$.

Similarly, we can estimate optimal PCs from observation matrix, $P_{\cdot j} = \mathbf{X}\boldsymbol{\beta}_j$, where $\boldsymbol{\beta}_j$ is from the loading matrix $\mathbf{V}_k$ estimated from $\mathbf{X}$. Suppose the ideal PCs are estimated by $\mathbf{X}\boldsymbol{\alpha}_j$, and the actual PCs are estimated by $\mathbf{X}\boldsymbol{\beta}_j$, then the PCA optimization problem is formulated as

$$\arg\min_{\boldsymbol{\alpha}_j, \boldsymbol{\beta}_j} \|\mathbf{X}\boldsymbol{\alpha}_j - \mathbf{X}\boldsymbol{\beta}_j\|_2^2, \quad \text{s.t. } \|\boldsymbol{\alpha}_j\|_2^2 = 1, \ \|\boldsymbol{\beta}_j\|_2^2 = 1. \tag{4.10}$$

4.3.3 Robust Sparse Coding

As we know, the traditional sparse coding can be formulated as

$$\arg\min_{\boldsymbol{x}} \|\boldsymbol{x}\|_{\ell_1} \quad \text{s.t.} \quad \|\boldsymbol{y} - A\boldsymbol{x}\|_{\ell_2}^2 \leq \varepsilon. \tag{4.11}$$

Equation (4.11) is widely used in various applications. However, there are many issues in this equation. First of all, ℓ_1-norm constraint $\|\boldsymbol{x}\|_{\ell_1}$ may not be good enough to represent the sparsity of features/data. Second, $\|\boldsymbol{y} - A\boldsymbol{x}\|_{\ell_2}$ is sensitive to outliers, especially in complex image/video data. Thus, much effort has been made to modify the sparsity constraint.

Given dictionary $A = [A_1; A_2; \ldots; A_N]$, we define the coding residuals $\boldsymbol{e} = \boldsymbol{y} - A\boldsymbol{x} = [e_1; e_2; \ldots; e_N]^T$. Thus, we have $e_i = A_i\boldsymbol{x}$. Assume $\{e_i\}_{i=1}^N$ are *i.i.d.* according to *p.d.f.* $p_\theta(e_i)$. Then, we have

$$L_\theta(e_1; e_2; \ldots; e_N) = \prod_{i=1}^{N} p_\theta(e_i). \tag{4.12}$$

The MLE of $\boldsymbol{x}$ is equivalent to maximize Eq. (4.12), or minimize the objective function

$$-\ln L_\theta = \sum_{i=1}^{N} \rho_\theta(e_i), \quad \rho_\theta(e_i) = -\ln p_\theta(e_i). \tag{4.13}$$

Upon this, Yang et al. proposed Robust Sparse Coding (RSC) as

$$\arg\min_{x} \sum_{i=1}^{N} \rho_\theta(y_i - A_i\boldsymbol{x}), \quad \text{s.t.} \quad \|\boldsymbol{x}\|_{\ell_1} \leq \varepsilon. \tag{4.14}$$

Actually, the proposed RSC in Eq. (4.14) is a more general sparse coding strategy, a sparsity-constrained MLE problem.

The key issue is to determine the ρ-function, ρ_θ. Iterative reweighted sparse coding strategy was proposed to solve Eq. (4.14) by approximating $F_\theta(\boldsymbol{e})$

$$F_\theta(\boldsymbol{e}) = \sum_{i=1}^{N} \rho_\theta(\boldsymbol{e}_i) \approx F_\theta(\boldsymbol{e}_0) + (\boldsymbol{e} - \boldsymbol{e}_0)^T F'_\theta(\boldsymbol{e}_0) + R_i(\boldsymbol{e}) = \widetilde{F}(\boldsymbol{e}). \tag{4.15}$$

Solving Eq. (4.15) by letting $\widetilde{F}(\mathbf{0}) = 0$, we let

$$W_{ii} = \omega_\theta(e_{0,i}) = \rho'_\theta(e_{0,i})/e_{0,i}. \tag{4.16}$$

Finally, we can select the logistic function as the weighting function

$$\omega_\theta(e_i) = \exp(a\delta - ae_i^2)/(1 + \exp(a\delta - ae_i^2)). \tag{4.17}$$

Furthermore, we have

$$\rho_\theta(e_i) = -\frac{1}{2a}(\ln(1 + \exp(a\delta - ae_i^2)) - \ln(1 + \exp(a\delta))). \tag{4.18}$$

Finally, the RSC can be rewritten as

$$\arg\min_{\alpha} \| W^{\frac{1}{2}}(\boldsymbol{y} - A\boldsymbol{x})\|_{\ell_2}^2, \quad \text{s.t.} \quad \|\boldsymbol{x}\|_{\ell_1} \leq \varepsilon. \tag{4.19}$$

4.3.4 Robust SPCA

1. The Naive Elastic Net Approach

In this section, we first review the elastic net approach as described in [39]. We consider the linear regression model of the data set $\mathbf{X}$, and suppose $\mathbf{y} = [y_1, \ldots, y_n]^T$ is the response. Moreover, we assume that $\mathbf{y}$ is centered and $\mathbf{x}^{(i)}$ are standardized. The EN criterion is defined as follows:

$$\hat{\beta} = \arg\min_{\boldsymbol{\beta}} \|\mathbf{y} - \mathbf{X}\boldsymbol{\beta}\|_2^2 + \lambda_2\|\boldsymbol{\beta}\|_2^2 + \lambda_1\|\boldsymbol{\beta}\|_1, \tag{4.20}$$

where λ_1 and λ_2 are nonnegative Lagrangian constants. Equation (4.20) can be rewritten as

$$\hat{\boldsymbol{\beta}}^* = \arg\min_{\boldsymbol{\beta}^*} \|\tilde{\mathbf{y}} - \widetilde{\mathbf{X}}\boldsymbol{\beta}^*\|_2^2 + \lambda_1\|\boldsymbol{\beta}^*\|_1, \tag{4.21}$$

where $\tilde{\mathbf{y}} = [\mathbf{y}; \mathbf{0}] \in \mathbb{R}^{(n+p)}$, $\widetilde{\mathbf{X}} = \sqrt{1+\lambda_2}\left[\mathbf{X}; \sqrt{\lambda_2}\mathbf{I}\right] \in \mathbb{R}^{(n+p)\times p}$, $\boldsymbol{\beta}^* = \sqrt{1+\lambda_2}\boldsymbol{\beta}$. Equation (4.21) is equivalent to a LASSO optimization problem. However, the sample size in Eq. (4.21) is $n + p$ and $\widetilde{\mathbf{X}}$ has rank p, which means that the

EN approach can potentially select all p features in all situations. This important property overcomes the limitations of LASSO in $p > n$ scenario. It was proved that EN has the ability of selecting grouped features.

Furthermore, the EN approach used sparse principal components analysis in feature learning [40]. Suppose the principal loadings of $\mathbf{X}$ are $\mathbf{v}_j, (j = 1, 2, \ldots, k)$, and set $\mathbf{B} = [\beta_1, \ldots, \beta_k] \in \mathbb{R}^{p\times k}$. If $\mathbf{A}$ and $\mathbf{B}$ satisfy the following criterion:

$$(\hat{\mathbf{A}}, \hat{\mathbf{B}}) = \arg\min_{\mathbf{A},\mathbf{B}} \left\| \mathbf{X} - \mathbf{X}\mathbf{B}\mathbf{A}^T \right\|_2^2 + \lambda_2 \|\mathbf{B}\|_2^2 + \lambda_1 \|\mathbf{B}\|_1,$$
$$\text{s.t.} \quad \|\mathbf{A}\|_2^2 = \mathbf{I}, \tag{4.22}$$

then $\hat{\beta}_j \propto \mathbf{v}_j$, i.e., $\mathbf{B}$ is the sparse principal loading matrix of $\mathbf{X}$. If $\mathbf{A} = \mathbf{B}$, the minimization is formulated as the standard PCA under the orthogonal constraint. For flexibility in iterations, the loading matrix are set as $\mathbf{A}$ and $\mathbf{B}$. Equation (4.22) is ℓ_2-norm constrained residual expression, which is sensitive to outliers as mentioned in Sect. 4.3.1.

2. The Definition of the Robust Elastic Net

For better modeling feature representation, especially in occluded and noisy data, we propose an MLE to find the optimal solution. Suppose $\mathbf{x}^{(i)}$ is the ith object, then $\mathbf{X} = [\mathbf{x}^{(1)}; \mathbf{x}^{(2)}; \ldots; \mathbf{x}^{(n)}]$. We construct a regression type representation to get the optimal estimation of $\mathbf{X}$. Define the residual of each observation as $\varepsilon^{(i)} \triangleq [e_{i1}, \ldots, e_{ip}] = \mathbf{x}^{(i)} - \mathbf{x}^{(i)}\mathbf{B}\mathbf{A}^T$, and suppose its entries e_{ij} are independently identically distributed (*i.i.d.*) with probability density function $f(e_{ij})$. The properties of unknown function $f(e_{ij})$ can refer to [36]. Then the likelihood estimator is $\mathbf{L}(\varepsilon^{(i)}) = \prod_{j=1}^{p} f(e_{ij})$. Define $\rho(e_{ij}) = -\ln f(e_{ij})$ and the MLE aims to minimize the objective function

$$-\ln \mathbf{L}(\varepsilon^{(i)}) = \sum_{j=1}^{p} -\ln f(e_{ij}) \triangleq \sum_{j=1}^{p} \rho(e_{ij}). \tag{4.23}$$

For all observations, using the sparse constraint of $\mathbf{B}$ and orthonormal constraints of both $\mathbf{A}$ and $\mathbf{B}$, the Robust Elastic Net (REN) feature learning can be formulated as follows:

$$(\hat{\mathbf{A}}, \hat{\mathbf{B}}) = \arg\min_{\mathbf{A},\mathbf{B}} \sum_{i=1}^{n}\sum_{j=1}^{p} \rho(e_{ij}) + \lambda_2 \|\mathbf{B}\|_2^2 + \lambda_1 \|\mathbf{B}\|_1$$
$$= \arg\min_{\mathbf{A},\mathbf{B}} \sum_{i=1}^{n}\sum_{j=1}^{p} \rho(x_{ij} - \sum_{k=1}^{p} x_{ik}\xi_{kj}) + \lambda_2 \|\mathbf{B}\|_2^2 + \lambda_1 \|\mathbf{B}\|_1,$$
$$\text{s.t.} \quad \|\mathbf{A}\|_2^2 = \mathbf{I}, \tag{4.24}$$

where the ξ_{ij} is the element of $\mathbf{B}\mathbf{A}^T$. Equation (4.24) is a general sparse constrained MLE problem, it will be degenerated to the EN when the residual follows a Gaussian distribution. Usually, Eq. (4.24) can be formulated as an iteration scheme based on weighted ℓ_2-norm:

$$
\begin{aligned}
(\hat{\mathbf{A}}, \hat{\mathbf{B}}) &= \arg\min_{\mathbf{A},\mathbf{B}} \sum_{i=1}^{n} \left\| \boldsymbol{\Omega}_i^{1/2} \left(\mathbf{x}^{(i)} - \mathbf{x}^{(i)} \mathbf{B}\mathbf{A}^T \right) \right\|_2^2 + \lambda_2 \|\mathbf{B}\|_2^2 + \lambda_1 \|\mathbf{B}\|_1 \\
&= \arg\min_{\mathbf{A},\mathbf{B}} \left\| \mathbf{W}^{1/2} \circ (\mathbf{X} - \mathbf{X}\mathbf{B}\mathbf{A}^T) \right\|_2^2 + \lambda_2 \|\mathbf{B}\|_2^2 + \lambda_1 \|\mathbf{B}\|_1, \\
&\quad \text{s.t.} \quad \|\mathbf{A}\|_2^2 = \mathbf{I},
\end{aligned} \tag{4.25}
$$

and

$$
\mathbf{W} = \text{unrvec}\left[\text{diag}(\boldsymbol{\Omega}_1), \ldots, \text{diag}(\boldsymbol{\Omega}_i)\right] \in \mathbb{R}^{n \times p}, \tag{4.26}
$$

where unrvec$(\cdot)$ denotes vectorize a matrix by rows, '$\circ$' denotes Hadamard product, and $\text{diag}(\boldsymbol{\Omega}_i) = [\omega(e_{i1}), \ldots, \omega(e_{ip})]$, $\omega(e_{ij}) = \mathrm{d}\rho(e_{ij})/(e_{ij}\mathrm{d}e_{ij})$. Then Eq. (4.24) is formulated as a weighted EN regression.

We would like to point out that the weight matrix W is induced by the probability density function $f(e_{ij})$. The weight functions act as filters that limit the contribution of the outliers in the data. By contrast, the outliers have low weight values, thus improving the robustness of traditional elastic net approaches. Therefore, we shall introduce how to define weight function in the following section.

3. Choosing the Weight Function

For robustness, the weight matrix $\mathbf{W}$ should be a function of the residues, and its value can become very small when the residual exceeds a threshold. In other words, the corresponding ρ-function is a symmetric function with a unique minimum at residual zero, and the value will be fixed when the residual exceeds a threshold. There are numerous ρ-functions that have been used in computer vision, such as Geman-McClure and Lorentzian functions. Following with the setting in [36], we choose a logistic function as the weight function

$$
\omega(e_{ij}) = \exp(\mu\delta - \mu e_{ij}^2)/(1 + \exp(\mu\delta - \mu e_{ij}^2)), \tag{4.27}
$$

whose corresponding ρ-function is

$$
\rho(e_{ij}) = -\frac{1}{2\mu} \left(\ln(1 + \exp(\mu\delta - \mu e_{ij}^2)) - \ln(1 + \exp(\mu\delta)) \right), \tag{4.28}
$$

where μ and δ are positive scalars, μ controls the decreasing rate from 1 to 0, and δ controls the location of a demarcation point. Set $\psi = [e_{i1}^2, \ldots, e_{ip}^2]^T$, we can get ψ_a by sorting ψ in ascending order. Let $k = \mathit{floor}(\tau n)$, $\tau \in (0, 1]$, and then we set $\delta = \psi_a(k)$, and $\mu = c/\delta$. In the experiments, we set $\tau = 0.5$, $c = 10$. It means that, for the normalized residual e, if $e < 0.5$, its corresponding weight $\omega \approx 1$, if $e > 0.5$, its corresponding weight $\omega \approx 0$, and the bigger the c correspond the higher the decreasing rate. In other words, beyond some threshold δ, the outlier would be adaptively assigned with low weights to reduce their affects on the regression estimation, thus resulting in more robust feature extraction.

4. Validating the REN Feature Learning for HDLSS

As we know, EN-based approaches work very well in HDLSS problems. The proposed robust elastic net approach as Eq. (4.25) is different from the traditional EN approach as Eq. (4.20). We will validate that the REN can also handle the HDLSS problem as follows.

Suppose the jth column of $\mathbf{A}$ and $\mathbf{B}$ are α_j and β_j, respectively. We have the following theorem.

Theorem 4.3.1 *For any* $\lambda_2 > 0$*, let*

$$(\hat{\mathbf{A}}, \hat{\mathbf{B}}) = \arg\min_{\mathbf{A},\mathbf{B}} \|\mathbf{W}^{1/2} \circ (\mathbf{X} - \mathbf{X}\mathbf{B}\mathbf{A}^T)\|_2^2 + \lambda_2 \|\mathbf{B}\|_2^2, \quad \text{s.t.} \quad \|\mathbf{A}\|_2^2 = \mathbf{I}, \tag{4.29}$$

then $\hat{\boldsymbol{\beta}}_j \propto \mathbf{v}_j$, $j = 1, 2, \ldots, k$.

The proof of Theorem 4.3.1 is shown in Appendix D.1.

Suppose the $\mathbf{A}_\perp$ is the orthonormal matrix of $\mathbf{A}$, we have

$$\begin{aligned} \|\mathbf{X} - \mathbf{X}\mathbf{B}\mathbf{A}^T\|_2^2 &= \|\mathbf{X}\mathbf{A}_\perp\|_2^2 + \|\mathbf{X}\mathbf{A} - \mathbf{X}\mathbf{B}\|_2^2 \\ &= \|\mathbf{X}\mathbf{A}_\perp\|_2^2 + \sum_{j=1}^{k} \|\mathbf{X}\alpha_j - \mathbf{X}\beta_j\|_2^2. \end{aligned} \tag{4.30}$$

Given $\mathbf{A}$ and adding the LASSO penalty into the criterion Eq. (4.29), the optimization of $\mathbf{B}$ is formulated as

$$\hat{\mathbf{B}} = \arg\min_{\mathbf{B}} \sum_{j=1}^{k} \left\| \mathbf{W}^{1/2} \circ (\mathbf{X}\alpha_j - \mathbf{X}\beta_j) \right\|_2^2 + \lambda_2 \left\| \boldsymbol{\beta}_j \right\|_2^2 + \lambda_1 \|\boldsymbol{\beta}_j\|_1, \quad \text{s.t.} \ \|\mathbf{A}\|_2^2 = \mathbf{I}. \tag{4.31}$$

Equation (4.31) is similar to Eq. (4.20), with simple algebra operations; it can be transformed into a LASSO problem on column full rank sampling data. With the Theorem 4.3.1 and the weight matrix $\mathbf{W}$, the solution of Eq. (4.31) is corresponding to the loading of $\mathbf{X}$. Then it is proved that the REN can handle the HDLSS problem and can get the loading matrix with robustness.

5. The Iterative Solution

In this part of the section, we propose an iterative approach to solve the REN feature learning approach.

In order to initialize the weight matrix $\mathbf{W}$, we should first estimate the residual $\varepsilon^{(i)}$ of $\mathbf{x}^{(i)}$. Since $\varepsilon^{(i)} = \mathbf{x}^{(i)} - \mathbf{x}^{(i)}\mathbf{B}\mathbf{A}^T$, we initial $\mathbf{A} = \mathbf{B} = \mathbf{V}_k$.

Given **A**, with the Theorem 4.3.1 and Eq. (4.31), we can use the LARS-EN algorithm [40] to estimate the **B**.

On the other hand, if **B** is fixed, we have the following Theorem.

Theorem 4.3.2 *Let* $\mathbf{M}_{n\times p} = \mathbf{W}^{1/2} \circ \mathbf{X}$, $\mathbf{N}_{n\times k} = \mathbf{W}^{1/2} \circ \mathbf{XB}$. *Consider the constrained minimization problem*

$$\hat{\mathbf{A}} = \arg\min_{A} \|\mathbf{M} - \mathbf{N}\mathbf{A}^T\|_2^2, \quad \text{s.t.} \quad \|\mathbf{A}\|_2^2 = \mathbf{I}. \tag{4.32}$$

Suppose the SVD of $\mathbf{M}^T\mathbf{N} = \mathbf{U}_1\boldsymbol{\Sigma}_1\mathbf{V}_1^T$, *then* $\hat{\mathbf{A}} = \mathbf{U}_1\mathbf{V}_1^T$.

The proof of Theorem 4.3.2 is shown in Appendix D.2

According to Theorems 4.3.1 and 4.3.2, we compute the weight matrix **W**, sparse loading matrix **B** and **A** in turn. The convergence is achieved when the difference of **B** between adjacent iteration is small enough. We use the angle between $\mathbf{B}^{(n)}$ and $\mathbf{B}^{(n+1)}$ as criterion, where the $\mathbf{B}^{(n)}$ denotes the nth iteration of **B**. The iteration will stop if the following holds:

$$\angle(\mathbf{B}^{(n)}, \mathbf{B}^{(n+1)}) < \varepsilon, \tag{4.33}$$

where ε is a small positive scalar. The detail algorithm is summarized in Table 4.2.

Table 4.2 The proposed REN feature learning algorithm

Input: observation data matrix **X**
Output: $\hat{\mathbf{v}}_j$
Initialization: $\mathbf{X} = \mathbf{U}\boldsymbol{\Sigma}\mathbf{V}^T$, $\hat{\mathbf{A}} = \mathbf{V}_k$, $\hat{\mathbf{B}} = \hat{\mathbf{A}}$
start:
while $\hat{\mathbf{B}}$ does not converge

- Given fixed $\hat{\mathbf{A}}$, for $j = 1, \cdots, k$,
  - for $i = 1, \cdots, n$, compute residual

$$\varepsilon^{(i)} = [e_{i1}, \cdots, e_{ip}] = \mathbf{x}^{(i)} - \mathbf{x}^{(i)}\hat{\mathbf{B}}\hat{\mathbf{A}}^T,$$

  - Estimate weight matrix **W** with Eq. (4.27) and Eq. (4.26),
  - Let $\mathbf{M} = \mathbf{W}^{1/2} \circ \mathbf{X}$, solve the EN problem in Eqn. (4.31) as

$$\hat{\boldsymbol{\beta}}_j = \boldsymbol{\beta}_j^T(\mathbf{M}^T\mathbf{M} + \lambda_2)\boldsymbol{\beta}_j - 2\boldsymbol{\alpha}_j^T\mathbf{M}^T\mathbf{M}\boldsymbol{\beta}_j + \lambda_1\|\boldsymbol{\beta}\|_1. \tag{4.34}$$

- For fixed $\hat{\mathbf{B}} = [\hat{\boldsymbol{\beta}}_1, \cdots, \hat{\boldsymbol{\beta}}_k]$, $\mathbf{N} = \mathbf{W}^{1/2} \circ \mathbf{X}\hat{\mathbf{B}}$, compute the SVD of $\mathbf{M}^T\mathbf{N} = \mathbf{U}_1\mathbf{D}_1\mathbf{V}_1^T$, update $\hat{\mathbf{A}} = \mathbf{U}_1\mathbf{V}_1^T$.

end *while*
Normalization: $\hat{\mathbf{v}}_j = \hat{\boldsymbol{\beta}}_j/\|\hat{\boldsymbol{\beta}}_j\|_2, j = 1, \cdots, k$.

In background modeling or object reconstruction, with the feature loading matrix $\hat{\mathbf{V}}_k$ estimated by REN, the ith object is reconstructed as

$$\hat{\mathbf{x}}^{(i)} = \mathbf{x}^{(i)} \hat{\mathbf{V}}_k \hat{\mathbf{V}}_k^T. \tag{4.35}$$

6. Toy Problem and Analysis

We provide three different experiments to validate the proposed approach, e.g., toy data with outliers, face recognition, and background reconstruction. For better representation, we call the Robust Elastic Net Feature Learning approach as 'REN-FL', and the Robust Elastic Net Classifier as 'REN-C'.

Consider the following 2D toy data $\mathbf{X}$

$$\begin{aligned} \mathbf{X} &= \begin{bmatrix} \cdots x_i \cdots \\ \cdots y_i \cdots \end{bmatrix}^T \\ &= \begin{bmatrix} -2.5 & -2 & -1.5 & -1 & \mathbf{-0.5} & \mathbf{0} & 0.5 & 1 & 1.5 & 2 & 2.5 \\ -4.93 & -3.96 & -2.94 & -1.98 & \mathbf{5.32} & \mathbf{5.95} & 1.03 & 2.01 & 3.01 & 4.08 & 5.07 \end{bmatrix}^T, \end{aligned} \tag{4.36}$$

where $\{x_i\}_{i=1}^n$ are generated from -2.5 to 2.5 with similar intervals 0.5; $\{y_i\}_{i=1}^n$ are generated from -5 to 5 with similar intervals 1. The $\{y_i\}$ add the uniform distribution in $[0, 0.1]$, except the two points $x_i = -0.5$ and $x_i = 0$. Hence, the corresponding values y_i of the two points are much bigger than the others, which are outliers. If we discard the outliers, the loading vector or projection vector would be $\beta = [0.45, 0.9]^T$.

To this data, PCA, ℓ_1-PCA, SPCA, FRPCA and the proposed REN-FL are applied to estimate the loading vectors and the data points. The loading vectors are obtained as $\beta_{PCA} = [0.30, 0.95]^T$, $\beta_{\ell_1} = [0.33, 0.95]^T$, $\beta_{SPCA} = [0.30, 0.95]^T$, $\beta_{FRPCA} = [0.43, 0.9]^T$ and $\beta_{REN} = [0.42, 0.91]^T$, respectively (shown in Fig. 4.5a).

The estimated results are shown in Fig. 4.5d, and the average residual errors of PCA, ℓ_1-PCA, SPCA, FRPCA, and the proposed REN-FL are 1.47, 1.38, 1.47, 1.25 and 1.12, respectively.

Second, consider the following y-axis outliers toy data $\mathbf{Y}$

$$\begin{aligned} \mathbf{Y} &= \begin{bmatrix} \cdots x_i \cdots \\ \cdots y_i \cdots \end{bmatrix}^T \\ &= \begin{bmatrix} -2.5 & -2 & -1.5 & -1 & -0.5 & 0 & \mathbf{0.5} & 1 & \mathbf{1.5} & 2 & 2.5 \\ 0.06 & 0.14 & 0.22 & 0.24 & -0.15 & -0.18 & \mathbf{5.48} & -0.2 & \mathbf{5.39} & 0.02 & 0.18 \end{bmatrix}^T, \end{aligned} \tag{4.37}$$

where $\{x_i\}_{i=1}^n$ are generated from -2.5 to 2.5 with similar intervals 0.5; $\{y_i\}_{i=1}^n$ are following a uniform distribution on $[-0.25, 0.25]$. There are two outliers at $x_i = 0.5$ and $x_i = 1.5$, And the corresponding values of y_i are much bigger than others, called y-axis outliers. If we discard the outliers, the loading vector would be $\beta = [1, 0]^T$.

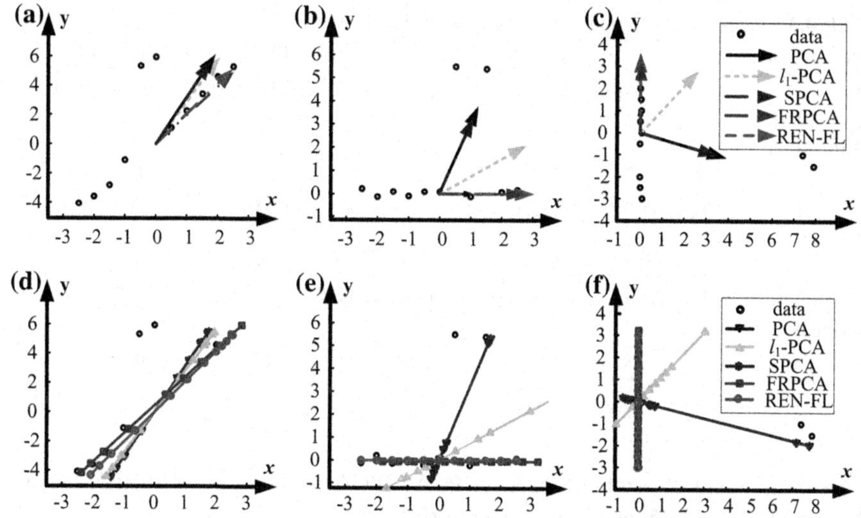

Fig. 4.5 A toy data with outliers. **a** Data with outliers and the projection vectors; **b** Data with y-outliers and the projection vectors; **c** Data with x-outliers and the projection vectors; **d** The estimated data line of (**a**); **e** The estimated data line of (**b**); **f** The estimated data line of (**c**). The '∘' points denotes the original data points; in (**a**–**c**), the *lines with arrows* denote the first corresponding loading vectors yielded by PCA, ℓ_1-PCA, SPCA, FRPCA and REN-FL, respectively. In (**d**–**f**), the *blue line* with '▽', the *pink line* with '△', the *green line* with '∗', the *brown line* with '□' and the *red line* with '∘' denote the estimated data lines by the PCA, ℓ_1-PCA, SPCA, FRPCA and REN-FL, respectively

To this data, PCA, ℓ_1-PCA, SPCA, FRPCA, and the proposed REN-FL are applied and the loading vectors are $\beta_{PCA} = [0.31, 0.95]^T$, $\beta_{\ell_1} = [0.81, 0.59]^T$, $\beta_{SPCA} = [0.31, 0.95]^T$, $\beta_{FRPCA} = [1, 0]^T$ and $\beta_{REN} = [1, 0.04]^T$, respectively (as shown in Fig. 4.5b). The estimated results are shown in Fig. 4.5e, and the average residual errors of PCA, ℓ_1-PCA, SPCA, FRPCA, and the proposed REN-FL are 2.09, 1.29, 2.09, 2.79 and 0.14, respectively.

Third, we also generate a x-axis outliers toy data $\mathbf{Z}$ as follows:

$$\mathbf{Z} = \begin{bmatrix} \cdots & x_i & \cdots \\ \cdots & y_i & \cdots \end{bmatrix}^T = \begin{bmatrix} -0.01 & -0.09 & -0.04 & \mathbf{7.9} & \mathbf{7.4} & -0.06 & 0.06 \\ -3 & -2 & -1 & \mathbf{0} & \mathbf{1} & 2 & 3 \end{bmatrix}^T, \quad (4.38)$$

where $\{y_i\}_{i=1}^n$ are generated from -3 to 3 with similar intervals 1; $\{x_i\}_{i=1}^n$ follow a uniform distribution on $[-0.1, 0.1]$. There are two outliers at $y_i = 0$ and $y_i = 1$. If we discard the outliers, the loading vector would be $\beta = [0, 1]^T$.

To the data $\mathbf{Z}$, PCA, ℓ_1-PCA, SPCA, FRPCA, and the proposed REN-FL are applied and the loading vectors are $\boldsymbol{\beta}_{PCA} = [0.97, 0.25]^T$, $\boldsymbol{\beta}_{\ell_1} = [0.69, 0.72]^T$, $\boldsymbol{\beta}_{SPCA} = [0.97, 0.25]^T$, $\boldsymbol{\beta}_{FRPCA} = [0, 1]^T$ and $\boldsymbol{\beta}_{REN} = [0.01, 1]^T$, respectively (shown as in Fig. 4.5c). The estimated results are shown in Fig. 4.5f, and

Table 4.3 The principal component vectors and the residual errors

Real vector	PCA	ℓ_1-PCA	SPCA	FRPCA	REN-FL
$\mathbf{X}$: $[0.45, 0.9]^T$ residual	$[0.30, 0.95]^T$	$[0.33, 0.95]^T$	$[0.30, 0.95]^T$	$[0.43, 0.9]^T$	$[0.42, 0.91]^T$
	1.47	1.38	1.47	1.25	**1.12**
$\mathbf{Y} : [1, 0]^T$ residual	$[0.31, 0.95]^T$	$[0.81, 0.59]^T$	$[0.31, 0.95]^T$	$\mathbf{[1, 0]}^T$	$[1, 0.04]^T$
	2.09	1.29	2.09	2.79	**0.14**
$\mathbf{Z} : [0, 1]^T$ residual	$[0.97, 0.25]^T$	$[0.69, 0.72]^T$	$[0.97, 0.25]^T$	$\mathbf{[0, 1]}^T$	$[0.01, 1]^T$
	2.54	1.81	2.54	3.25	**0.03**

the average residual errors of PCA, ℓ_1-PCA, SPCA and the proposed REN-FL are 2.54, 1.81, 2.54, 3.25, and 0.03, respectively.

The detail results are shown in Table 4.3. From this table, we can see that ℓ_2/ℓ_1-norm PCA were much influenced by the outliers while the proposed REN-FL suppressed the effect of the outlier efficiently.

From the three toy data, we would like to point out that, in general, the REN-FL approach can get almost the same performance as the FRPCA approach on loading vector estimation, but the REN-FL approach significantly outperforms the FRPCA approach in residual errors. In other words, the REN-FL approach has excellent performance on data reconstruction compared to the FRPCA approach.

4.3.5 Applications

1. Feature Learning and Classification

In object recognition and feature learning, the sparse representation approach [35] is formulated as:

$$\hat{\gamma} = \arg\min_{\gamma} \left\| \mathbf{y} - \mathbf{X}^T \gamma \right\|_2^2 + \lambda_1 \|\gamma\|_1, \tag{4.39}$$

where $\mathbf{y} \in \mathbb{R}^p$ is a new test sample belonging to the cth class, $\gamma \in \mathbb{R}^n$ is a coefficient vector whose entries are zero except those associated with the cth class.

Equation (4.39) is a convex optimization problem, which would be solved by the LASSO algorithm. The classifier will degenerate to a scaled version of nearest neighbor (NN) classifier when the training samples are correlated with each other within the same class. This is because the LASSO only selects a single training sample from the entire class. However, in object recognition, the testing object would be a combination of the same class. In other words, the solutions of Eq. (4.39) should have the ability of group selection. Furthermore, if the testing samples are corrupted, the criterion should be robust to outliers.

To solve these problems, similar to the above REN feature learning analysis, we use REN to carry out group selection and to eliminate the influence of the outlier images. Then the REN classifier is formulated as:

$$\hat{\gamma} = \arg\min_{\gamma} \left\| \boldsymbol{\Omega}^{1/2}(\mathbf{y} - \mathbf{X}^T\gamma) \right\|_2^2 + \lambda_2 \|\gamma\|_2^2 + \lambda_1 \|\gamma\|_1, \tag{4.40}$$

where the diagonal entries of $\boldsymbol{\Omega} \in \mathbb{R}^{p \times p}$ are $\omega(e_j)$, and $\mathbf{e} \triangleq [e_1, \cdots, e_p]^T = \mathbf{y} - \mathbf{X}^T\boldsymbol{\gamma}$.

Suppose the test sample $\mathbf{y}$ is approximated as $\hat{\mathbf{y}}_c = \mathbf{X}^T\hat{\gamma}_c$, there are several nonzero entries in $\hat{\boldsymbol{\gamma}}_c$ for the property of group selection. Then we can classify $\mathbf{y}$ based on these $\hat{\mathbf{y}}_c$ by assigning it to the class that minimizes the residual:

$$\hat{c} = \arg\min_{c} r_c(\mathbf{y}) \triangleq \|\mathbf{y} - \hat{\mathbf{y}}_c\|_2. \tag{4.41}$$

It is remarkable that Eq. (4.40) is just robust to testing sample with outliers. This is because the residuals are between the testing and training samples. If the training samples are noise-free, the weights of outliers in testing sample would be lower. But if the training samples are corrupted, even if testing sample is noise-free, the residuals would be big enough and treat the testing sample as "outliers". That would cause a wrong decision. To solve this problem, when the training samples are corrupted by outliers, the REN feature learning algorithm is used to extract principal features and eliminate the outliers in training samples. We first use the feature transformation operation $\mathbf{V}$ to project the image space to the feature space, and then apply it to Eq. (4.40) yielding

$$\hat{\boldsymbol{\gamma}} = \arg\min_{\gamma} \left\| \mathbf{V}^T \boldsymbol{\Omega}^{1/2}(\mathbf{y} - \mathbf{X}^T\gamma) \right\|_2^2 + \lambda_2 \|\boldsymbol{\gamma}\|_2^2 + \lambda_1 \|\boldsymbol{\gamma}\|_1. \tag{4.42}$$

Then the REN classifier is expressed in feature space as follows:

$$\hat{c} = \arg\min_{c} r_c(\mathbf{y}) \doteq \|\mathbf{V}^T\mathbf{y} - \mathbf{V}^T\hat{\mathbf{y}}_c\|_2. \tag{4.43}$$

The roles of $\mathbf{V}$ in Eqs. (4.42) and (4.43) are not only releasing feature dimension but also extracting the principal features.

2. Face Reconstruction and Recognition

In this section, we evaluate the proposed REN-FL and REN-C for two basic tasks, face reconstruction and recognition on the Extended Yale B data set. This face data set consists of about 2414 gray images of 38 individuals, each image with 192×168 pixels [13].

(1) Training and Testing Samples with Illumination Noise

The Extended Yale B database is cropped under 64 laboratory-controlled lighting conditions, which can be considered as illumination noise. In this experiment, we randomly select 10 % of the Extended Yale B images for training and the rest for testing, and the face images are resized to 51×58 pixels for the limitation of the computer memory. We use the standard PCA, ℓ_1-PCA, FRPCA and the proposed REN-FL to extract image features. The feature dimensions is set to 30.

Figure 4.6 shows the face reconstruction by those feature extraction approaches. The first column gives the testing images, the second–fifth columns are the reconstruction images by PCA, ℓ_1-PCA, FRPCA, and REN-FL, respectively. It is shown that the REN-FL gives the best reconstruction from the noise images feature extraction.

(2) Testing Samples are Block Occluded Randomly

A. Training samples are noise-free.

In this experiment, following the experimental setting in [35, 36], we choose Subsets 1 and 2 (719 images, normal lighting conditions) as training samples and Subsets 3 (455 moderate to more extreme lighting conditions) as testing samples. The images are resized to 84×96 pixels, and each pixel is regarded as a feature dimension which constitutes an 8, 064-dimensional input space. We simulate various levels of block occlusion, from 20–90 % of the testing samples are occluded by an unrelated image, whose size is 30 % of 84×96 pixels and located at a random position.

To these occluded images, the SRC [35], RSC [36], SPCA [40] and the proposed REN-C are used to recognize faces. The recognition rates are shown in Table 4.4, and

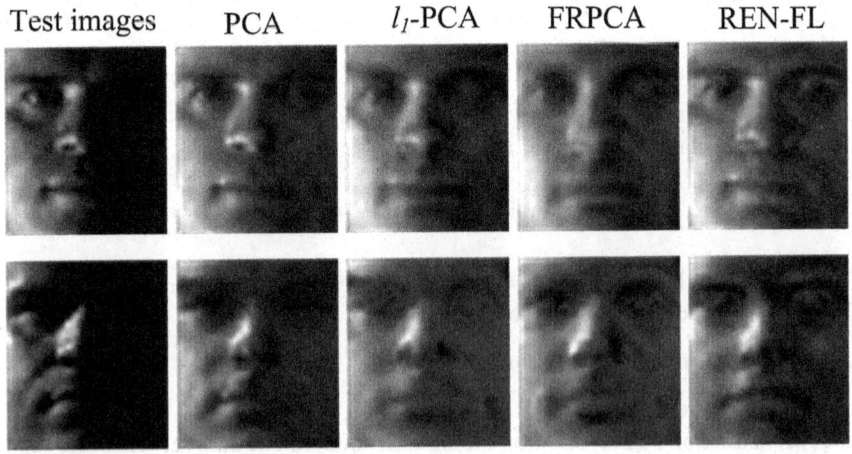

Fig. 4.6 Object reconstruction from the random illumination noise images with feature extraction. The first column gives the testing images. The second–fifth columns are the reconstruction images by PCA, ℓ_1-PCA, FRPCA, and REN-FL, respectively

Table 4.4 Object recognition rates with SRC, RSC, SPCA, and REN-C

Occlusion	20 %	30 %	40 %	50 %	60 %	70 %	80 %	90 %
SRC [35]	0.998	0.985	0.90	0.65	–	–	–	–
RSC	1	0.998	0.97	0.91	0.90	0.87	0.84	0.84
SPCA	1	1	0.98	0.95	0.89	0.87	0.85	0.82
REN-C	**1**	**1**	**1**	**1**	**0.99**	**0.98**	**0.98**	**0.97**

The training samples are noise-free, and 20–90 % of the testing samples are occluded by an unrelated image at random locations

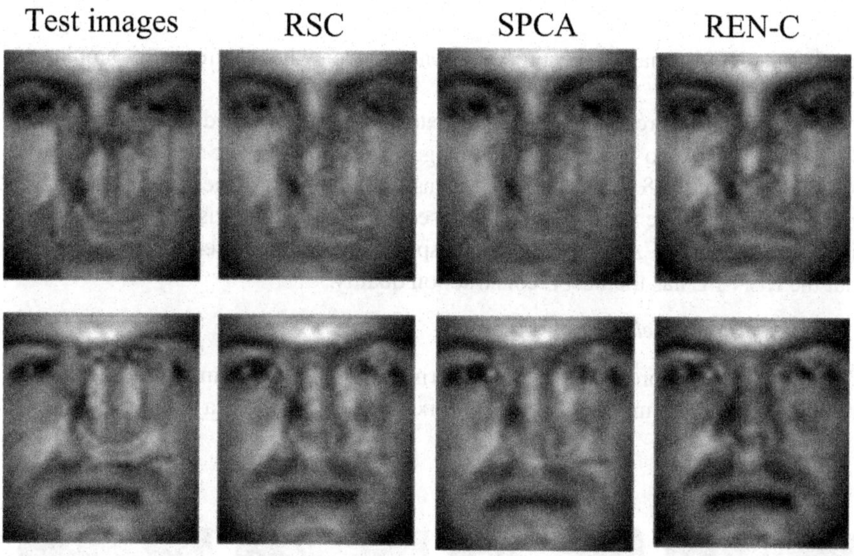

Fig. 4.7 Object reconstruction from the noise images, and the training samples are noise-free. The first column gives the testing images. The second–fourth columns are the reconstruction images by RSC, SPCA, and REN-C, respectively

Fig. 4.7 shows some reconstructed images by RSC, SPCA, and REN, respectively. It is shown that the REN has better performance on reconstruction.

B. HDLSS and training samples are occluded randomly.

In this experiment, we choose Subsets 1 (263 images) for training and Subsets 2 and 3 (911 images) for testing. The images are resized to 51×58 pixels, and the feature dimension is 2958, namely $p \gg n$. Among the training images, 30 % images of each individual training samples are randomly selected to occlude with an unrelated image, whose size is 30 % of 51×58 pixels and located at a random position. The 20–90 % of the testing samples are occluded by that unrelated image at random locations. To these occluded images, the SRC, RSC, and the proposed REN-C are used for recognition. Table 4.5 shows the experiment results, and we can

Table 4.5 Object recognition rates with SRC, RSC, SPCA, and REN-C

Occlusion	20 %	30 %	40 %	50 %	60 %	70 %	80 %	90 %
SRC	0.56	0.53	0.49	0.48	0.45	0.44	0.40	0.37
RSC	0.94	0.93	0.92	0.89	0.87	0.86	0.85	0.82
SPCA	0.95	0.93	0.93	0.91	0.90	0.89	0.89	0.85
REN-C	**0.96**	**0.96**	**0.95**	**0.95**	**0.92**	**0.91**	**0.90**	**0.90**

The 30 % training samples are occluded, and the 20–90 % of testing samples are occluded by an unrelated image at random locations

see that the REN-C has the best recognition rate even when the training samples are occluded.

Also, we use the proposed REN-FL to extract features first, and then used the RSC, SPCA and REN-C to reconstruct the images, respectively. The feature dimensions is set as 30. Figure 4.8 shows the face reconstruction by using these approaches. The first column gives the testing images, the second–fourth columns are reconstruction images by RSC, SPCA, and REN-FL, respectively. It can be seen from the results that the REN-FL has the best reconstruction quality.

3. Background Modeling

This application is presented by an experiment. In the experiment, the data set is a collection of 512 images (120×160 pixels) gathered from a static camera over

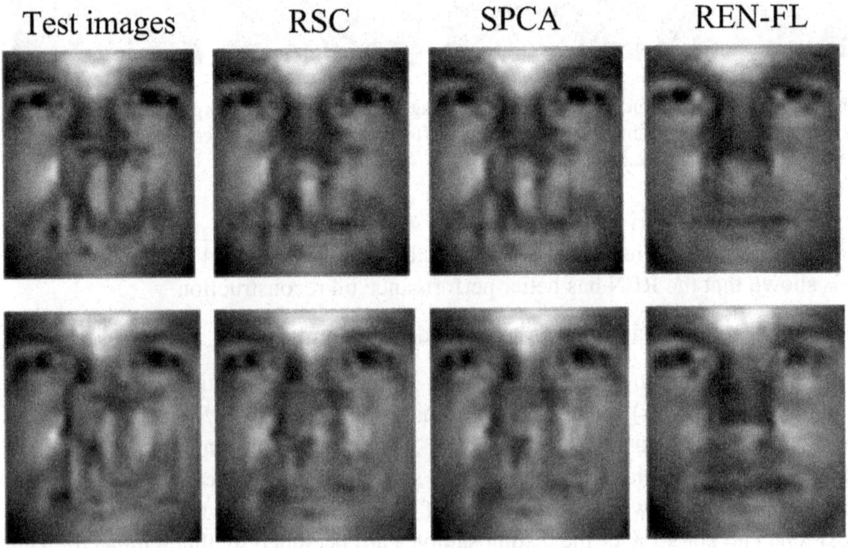

Fig. 4.8 Object reconstruction from the noise images with feature space. The first column gives the testing images. The second–fourth columns are reconstruction images by RSC, SPCA, and REN-FL, respectively

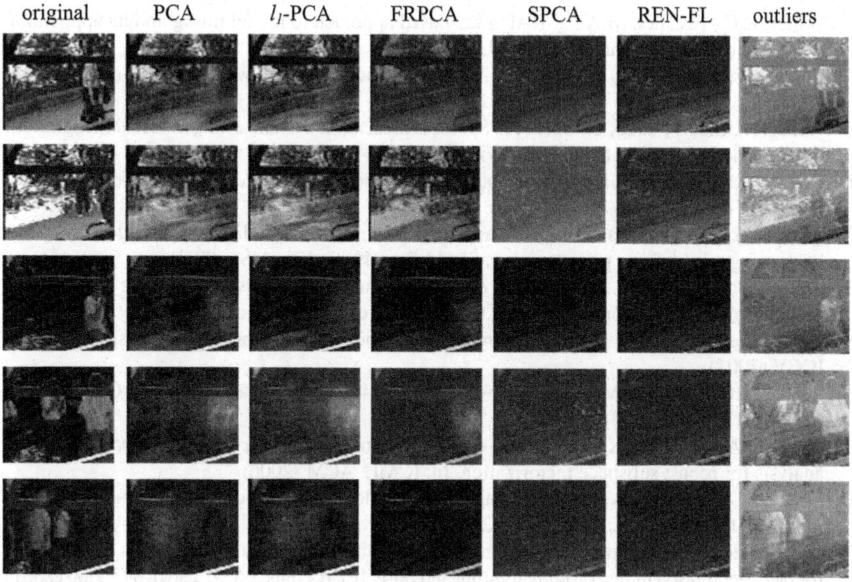

Fig. 4.9 Background reconstruction from the noise images with feature space. The first column gives the original images. The second–sixth columns are reconstructed images by PCA, ℓ_1-PCA, FRPCA, SPCA, REN-FL, and the outliers, respectively

2 days [33]. In addition to changes in the illumination of the static background, 45 % of the images contain people in various locations. While the people often pass through the view of the camera, they sometimes remain relatively still over several frames. Compared with the background, the changed illumination and people are considered as outliers. To this typical HDLSS problem, we applied the standard PCA, ℓ_1-PCA, FRPCA, SPCA, and the proposed REN-FL for the data set to reconstruct a background model. The feature dimension is set as 20.

Figure 4.9 shows the results of the background reconstruction using the standard PCA, ℓ_1-PCA, FRPCA, SPCA, and REN-FL, respectively. The last column gives the extracted outliers by REN-FL. We can see that the proposed REN-FL is able to well reconstruct the background since it can handle the illumination variations and the moving objects. Interestingly, even when image patches are corrupted very much by the outliers, the REN-FL still has excellent performance.

References

1. Aanæs, H., Fisker, R., Astrom, K., Carstensen, J.M.: Robust factorization. IEEE Trans. Pattern Anal Mach. Intell. **24**(9), 1215–1225 (2002)
2. Baccini, A., Besse, P., de Falguerolles, A.: An ℓ_1-norm PCA and a heuristic approach. In: Ordinal and Symbolic Data Analysis, pp. 359–368 (1996)

3. Bolles, R.C., Fischler, M.A.: A RANSAC-based approach to model fitting and its application to finding cylinders in range data. In: IJCAI (1981)
4. Candes, E., Li, X., Ma, Y., Wright, J.: Robust principal component analysis? (2009) Arxiv preprint
5. Cheng, H., Liu, Z., Yang, L., Chen, X.: Sparse representation and learning in visual recognition: theory and applications. Signal Process. **93**(6), 1408–1425 (2013)
6. Croux, C., Filzmoser, P., Fritz, H.: Robust sparse principal component analysis. Technometrics **55**(2), 202–214 (2013)
7. d'Aspremont, A., El Ghaoui, L., Jordan, M.I., Lanckriet, G.R.: A direct formulation for sparse PCA using semidefinite programming. SIAM Rev. **49**(3), 434–448 (2007)
8. d'Aspremont A., E.G.L.J.M.L.G.: A direct formulation for sparse PCA using semidefinite programming. In: Computer Science Division, University of California (2004)
9. De la Torre, F., Black, M.J.: Robust principal component analysis for computer vision. In: IEEE ICCV (2001)
10. De la Torre, F., Black, M.J.: A framework for robust subspace learning. Int. J. Comput. Vis. **54**(1–3), 117–142 (2003)
11. Ding, C., Zhou, D., He, X., Zha, H.: R 1-PCA: rotational invariant ℓ_1-norm principal component analysis for robust subspace factorization. In: ICML. ACM (2006)
12. Frieze, A., Kannan, R., Vempala, S.: Fast Monte-Carlo algorithms for finding low-rank approximations. J. ACM **51**(6), 1025–1041 (2004)
13. Georghiades, A., Belhumeur, P., Kriegman, D.: From few to many: illumination cone models for face recognition under variable lighting and pose. IEEE Trans. PAMI **23**(6), 643–660 (2001)
14. Hough, P.V.: Method and means for recognizing complex patterns. US Patent 3,069,654 (1962)
15. Huber, P.J.: Robust Statistics. Springer, Berlin (2011)
16. Jenatton, R., Obozinski, G., Bach, F.: Structured sparse principal component analysis. In: International Conference on Artificial Intelligence and Statistics (2010)
17. Jolliffe, I.: Principal Component Analysis. Wiley Online Library (2002)
18. Ke, Q., Kanade, T.: Robust L1 norm factorization in the presence of outliers and missing data by alternative convex programming. In: IEEE CVPR (2005)
19. Kwak, N.: Principal component analysis based on L1-norm maximization. IEEE Trans. Pattern Anal. Mach. Intell. **30**(9), 1672–1680 (2008)
20. Long, M., Ding, G., Wang, J., Sun, J., Guo, Y., Yu, P.S.: Transfer sparse coding for robust image representation. In: IEEE CVPR (2013)
21. Lu, C.Y., Min, H., Gui, J., Zhu, L., Lei, Y.K.: Face recognition via weighted sparse representation. J. Vis. Commun. Image Represent. **24**(2), 111–116 (2013)
22. Mackey, L.W.: Deflation methods for sparse PCA. In: Advances in Neural Information Processing Systems (2009)
23. Meer Guest Editor, P., Stewart Guest Editor, C.V., Tyler Guest Editor, D.E.: Robust computer vision: an interdisciplinary challenge. Comput. Vis. Image Underst. **78**(1), 1–7 (2000)
24. Meng D., Z.Q.X.Z.: Robust sparse principal component analysis. In: Preprint (2010)
25. Rousseeuw, P., Leroy, A., Wiley, J.: Robust Regression and Outlier Detection, 3 edn. Wiley Online Library (1987)
26. Shen, D., Shen, H., Marron, J.: Consistency of sparse PCA in high dimension, low sample size contexts. J. Multivar. Anal. **115**, 317–333 (2013)
27. Shen, H., Huang, J.Z.: Sparse principal component analysis via regularized low rank matrix approximation. J. Multivar. Anal. **99**(6), 1015–1034 (2008)
28. Tang, Y., Yuan, Y., Yan, P., Li, X.: Greedy regression in sparse coding space for single-image super-resolution. J. Vis. Commun. Image Represent. **24**(2), 148–159 (2013)
29. De la Torre, F., Black, M.J.: Robust principal component analysis for computer vision. In: IEEE ICCV (2001)
30. Venables, W.N., Ripley, B.D.: Modern Applied Statistics with S. Springer, New York (2002)
31. Wang, J., Fan, J., Li, H., Wu, D.: Kernel-based feature extraction under maximum margin criterion. J. Vis. Commun. Image Represent. **23**(1), 53–62 (2012)

32. Wang, J., Liu, Z., Chorowski, J., Chen, Z., Wu, Y.: Robust 3d action recognition with random occupancy patterns. In: ECCV. Springer (2012)
33. Wang, L., Cheng, H., Liu, Z., Zhu, C.: A robust elastic net approach for feature learning. J. Vis. Commun. Image Represent. **25**(2), 313–321 (2014)
34. Wold S., E.K.G.P.: Principal component analysis. Chemom. Intell. Lab. Syst. **2**, 37–52 (1987)
35. Wright, J., Yang, A., Ganesh, A., Sastry, S., Ma, Y.: Robust face recognition via sparse representation. IEEE Trans. PAMI **31**(2), 210–227 (2009)
36. Yang, M., Zhang, D., Yang, J.: Robust sparse coding for face recognition. In: IEEE CVPR (2011)
37. Zhou, T., Tao, D., Wu, X.: Manifold elastic net: a unified framework for sparse dimension reduction. Data Min. Knowl. Discov. **22**(3), 340–371 (2011)
38. Zou, H., Hastie, T.: Regression shrinkage and selection via the elastic net, with applications to microarrays. J. R. Stat. Soc.: Ser. B **67**, 301–320 (2003)
39. Zou, H., Hastie, T.: Regularization and variable selection via the elastic net. J. R. Stat. Soc. **67**(2), 301–320 (2005)
40. Zou, H., Hastie, T., Tibshirani, R.: Sparse principal component analysis. J. Comput. Graph. Stat. **15**(2), 265–286 (2006)

Chapter 5
Efficient Sparse Representation and Modeling

5.1 Introduction

5.1.1 Large-Scale Signal Representation and Modeling

Large-scale image classification and recognition become more and more popular [10, 13]. Also, sparse representation and modeling play an important role in visual recognition. Hence, it is critical to develop efficient coding for large-scale visual recognition.

In this chapter, large-scale sparse coding means that: (1) The number of overcomplete basis is greater than the feature dimensions. (2) The feature vectors lie in high dimensional spaces. In signal sparse representation, we divide signals into two categories, strictly sparse signals and approximately sparse signals. In the former case, $\|\boldsymbol{x}\|_{\ell_0} \leq K$. In the later case, $\boldsymbol{x}$ has $K \ll N$ dimensions with large magnitude, while the rest are not necessarily zero but small magnitude. Efficient sparse representation and modeling denotes the following two situations:

(1) Efficient Sparse Coding: Since learning large-scale and highly overcomplete representations are extremely expensive, such as BP and SBL, efficient sparse coding is to seek more efficient signal recovery algorithms by using feature-sign [21], iterative greedy rules [38, 41], and graphical models [3, 18]. Here, we assume that signals are strictly sparse, but not limited to this.

(2) Sparse Quantization: In visual recognition, we need to represent feature vectors and model objects. For either general signals or approximately K-Sparse signals, signals can be approximated by strictly K-Sparse signals, such as K-Highest sparse quantization [5, 6].

H. Cheng, *Sparse Representation, Modeling and Learning in Visual Recognition*,
Advances in Computer Vision and Pattern Recognition,
DOI 10.1007/978-1-4471-6714-3_5

5.1.2 The Computation Complexity of Different Sparse Recovery Algorithms

In sparse recovery algorithms, we try to calculate $\boldsymbol{x}$, given A and $\boldsymbol{y}$. Although, recovering $\boldsymbol{x}$ from $\boldsymbol{y} = A\boldsymbol{x} + \boldsymbol{\varepsilon}$ is an ill-posed inverse problem, the K-sparsity prior of $\boldsymbol{x}$ makes it enable to recover $\boldsymbol{x}$ when $D \ll N$. Recovering $\boldsymbol{x}$ essentially requires exhaustive searches over all subsets of columns of A, which is a NP-hard problem [15], finding C_K^N possible support sets.

As we mentioned in Chap. 2, thanks to the equivalence of the ℓ_0-norm and ℓ_1-norm sparse recovery algorithms, we reformulate ℓ_0-norm minimization problem into the ℓ_1-norm problem such as BP algorithms [7]. Chen et al. analyzed the main factors of computational complexity in BP algorithms, the dimensions of features, parameter settings, feature complexity, and BP formulation forms. The complexity of BP increases up quasilinearly as the dimensions of features since there are many invocations of conjugate gradient algorithms. The complexity of the primal-dual logarithmic barrier interior-point implementation depends on both the accuracies of the solution and the conjugate gradient solver. The sparity of features can speed the converges up. Different forms of BP formulations could greatly affect the complexity. Cheeman analyzed the optimization techniques for solving BP algorithms [7]. As we know, BP is to seek the best sparse representation of features by minimizing the ℓ_1-norm of x. The ℓ_1-norm optimization can be reformulated into a linear programming problem by adding the new variables. For coping with large-scale tasks, we can rewrite the LP problem into a dual linear program by using duality theory. By doing so, though BP greatly reduced the complexity, it is still impractical for many large-scale applications.

One popular way is to use iterative greedy algorithms, such as MP, OMP, CoSaMP, IHT, and subspace pursuit. OMP is a simple yet efficient way to recover sparse coefficients. The advantages of its computational complexity are from two aspects. First of all, OMP iteratively selects the vectors from the dictionary, which can recover the sparse coefficients with high probability. Second, the matrix decomposition can benefit the computational complexity of OMP. Moreover, different implementations of matrix decomposition have different numerical behaviors [26, 32]. Strum et al. summarized the complexities and memory requirements for different computation models of OMP [32].

In addition, H. Lee et al. proposed effective sparse coding algorithms by iteratively solving two convex optimization problems, ℓ_1-regularized least squares problem and ℓ_0-constrained least squares problem [3]. This resulted in a significant speed up for sparse recovery by feature-sign search algorithm. We shall introduce the details of feature-sign search algorithm in Sect. 5.2.2.

Moreover, D. Baron et al. performed optimal Bayesian inference using Belief Propagation, where the CS encoding matrix is represented as a graphical model [21]. Reducing the size of the graphical model with sparse encoding matrices, one can obtain a fast sparse coding algorithm, CS-BP.

Table 5.1 Computation complexity comparison

Algorithms	Implementation	Complexity
Ł$_0$-norm optimization	argmin $\|x\|_{\ell_0}$, s.t. $y = Ax$; $\boldsymbol{x}$ is K-sparse vector	$O(C_K^N)$
BP [7]	argmin $\|x\|_{\ell_1}$, s.t. $y = Ax$	$O(D^2 N^{\frac{3}{2}})$
OMP [39]	argmin $\|x\|_{\ell_0}$, s.t. $\|Ax - y\|_{\ell_2} \le \varepsilon$	$O(DN)$
CoSaMP [25]	Form proxy (DN); identification (N); support merger (K) LS estimation (KD); pruning (K); sample update (KD)	$O(N \lg N)$
CS-BP	Convolution: multiplication	$O(K \lg N)$
FSS [21]	Update active sets; feature-sign step; check the optimality conditions	$O(DN)$
SBL [43]	$P(x\|y, x) = N(x\|, \mu, \Sigma)$, type II maximum likelihood iterative procedure to estimate parameters	$O(ND^2)$
SSBL [38]	$P(x\|y, x) = N(x\|, \mu, \Sigma)$, type II maximum likelihood iterative procedure to estimate parameters	$O(DN)$

SBL has shown excellent performance compared to traditional convex optimization sparse coding algorithms.The SBL is to maximize a marginalized likelihood function with respect to hyper parameters in the model prior. M. Tipping et al. proposed an accelerated algorithm by a sequential addition and deletion of basis function [38].

In visual recognition, we may approximate signals in sparse ways. Hence, a K-Highest sparse quantization is used to represent patches [5] and classify objects [6]. Table 5.1 shows the complexity comparison among different sparse recovery algorithms.

5.2 The Feature-Sign Search Algorithms

5.2.1 Fixed-Point Continuations for ℓ_1-minimization

Consider the following minimization problem

$$\arg\min_{x} \ \Phi(\boldsymbol{x}) = \arg\min_{x} \ f(\boldsymbol{x}) + \lambda\|\boldsymbol{x}\|_{\ell_1} \tag{5.1}$$

where $\lambda > 0$, $f(\boldsymbol{x}) = \frac{1}{2}\|A\boldsymbol{x} - \boldsymbol{y}\|_{\ell_2}$ is differentiable and convex. In this equation, the objective function is the sum of two convex functions. As we know, the ℓ_1-norm item is not smooth, but it is not hard to reformulate it into a linear function and some linear constraints. However, the traditional approach has heavy computational burden especially for large-scale problems.

According to operator-splitting, we minimize $\Phi(\boldsymbol{x})$ by seeking a zero of the subdifferential $\partial\Phi(\boldsymbol{x})$ [15].

$$\begin{aligned}\partial\Phi(\boldsymbol{x}) = \partial(\Phi_1(\boldsymbol{x}) + \Phi_2(\boldsymbol{x})) = (\boldsymbol{x} + \tau\partial\Phi_1(\boldsymbol{x})) - (\boldsymbol{x} - \tau\partial\Phi_2(\boldsymbol{x})) \ni \mathbf{0}, \\ \Longleftrightarrow (I - \tau\partial\Phi_2)\boldsymbol{x} \in (I + \tau\partial\Phi_1)\boldsymbol{x}, \\ \Longleftrightarrow \boldsymbol{x} = (I + \tau\partial\Phi_1)^{-1}(I - \tau\partial\Phi_2)\boldsymbol{x},\end{aligned} \tag{5.2}$$

where $\tau > 0$.

Equation (5.2) can lead to the forward-backward splitting algorithm as

$$\boldsymbol{x}_{t+1} = (I + \tau\partial\Phi_1)^{-1}(I - \tau\partial\Phi_2)\boldsymbol{x}_t. \tag{5.3}$$

This is a fixed-point algorithm. For minimizing Eq. (5.1), $\partial\Phi_2(\boldsymbol{x}) = \lambda\nabla f$, and $(I + \tau\partial\Phi_1)^{-1}$ is component-wise shrinkage.

Now, we state some fundamental conditions and properties.

Lemma 5.2.1 (Shrinkage Operator, [15]) *The operator $s_v(\cdot)$ is component-wise non-expansive, i.e., for any $y^1, y^2 \in \mathbb{R}^D$,*

$$|s_v(y_i^1) - s_v(y_i^2)| \le |y_i^1 - y_i^2|, \forall i. \tag{5.4}$$

Thus, s_v is nonexpansive in any ℓ_p-norms, and if h is nonexpansive in a given norm, then $s_v \circ h$ is as well. The proof of this Lemma can be referred to [15].

In general, the shrinkage operator can be extended to sparse coding shrinkage method as follows [17]:

(1) Determining ω: Given a training set of x, we use sparse recovery approaches for calculating ω so that the component s_i in $s = \omega x$ has sparse distributions.
(2) Shrinking operator $g_i(\cdot)$: Given a test sample $\tilde{x}$, we have $y = \omega\tilde{x}$. Applying the shrinkage nonlinearity $g_i(\cdot)$ on each component $y_i : \hat{s}_i = g_i(y_i)$.
(3) Obtaining $\bar{x} : \bar{x} = \omega^T\hat{s}$.

Finally, we would like to point out two issues in the fixed-point continuations for ℓ_1-minimization. On the theoretical aspect, Hale et al. provided the convergency analysis and it is a global convergence [15]. On the computational aspect, the continuation strategy greatly reduced the number of iterations for a given λ.

Proposition 5.2.1 (Optimality as Fixed-Point Equation, [15]) *X^* is the set of optimal solution of Eq. (5.1). For any scalar $\tau > 0$, $\boldsymbol{x}^* \in X^*$ if and only if*

$$\boldsymbol{x}^* = sgn(\boldsymbol{x}^* - \tau g(\boldsymbol{x}^*)) \odot \max\{|\boldsymbol{x}^* - \tau g(\boldsymbol{x}^*)| - \frac{\tau}{\lambda}, 0\}. \tag{5.5}$$

where $g(\cdot) = \partial \nabla f$. *Equation (5.5) consists of two mappings:*

$$\begin{cases} h(\cdot) = I(\cdot) - \tau g(\cdot), \\ s_v(\cdot) = sgn(\cdot) \odot \max\{|\cdot| - v, 0\}, \end{cases} \quad (5.6)$$

where $\odot$ *denotes the component-wise product. Here,* $h(\cdot)$ *plays a role of gradient step, and* $s_v(\cdot)$ *reduces the magnitude of each nonzero component of the input by an amount less than or equal to* v*, thus, reducing the* ℓ_1*-norm.*

For solving Eq. (5.1), we naturally consider the fixed-point iterations

$$\boldsymbol{x}_{t+1} = s_v \circ h(\boldsymbol{x}_t), \quad \text{for } v = \frac{\tau}{\lambda}. \quad (5.7)$$

Hale et al. found that the connection between Eqs. (5.5) and (5.7)

$$s_v = (I + \tau\partial\Phi_1)^{-1}, \quad h = I - \tau\partial\Phi_2. \quad (5.8)$$

5.2.2 The Basic Feature-Sign Search Algorithm

The feature-sign search algorithm is a ℓ_1-regularized least squares algorithm [21]. The main idea is as follows: Assume that we know the signs (positive, zero or negative) of x_i at the optimal value, and we can replace each x_i with either x_i (if $x_i > 0$),-x_i (if x_i <0) or 0 (if x_i=0). Furthermore, we can reformulate Eq. (5.1) into a standard unconstrained Quadratic Programming [QP], where zero coefficients are ignored. Thus, we can solve Eq. (5.1) analytically and efficiently. However, the question is that we never know the signs of x until the solution is obtained. The efficient sparse recovery algorithm tries to guess the signs of each x_i. Given any sign guess, we can solve the resulting unconstrained QP refining the inconnected guess until the algorithm converges to the optimal sparse solution.

For solving Eq. (5.1), the feature-sign search algorithm maintains an active set of potentially nonzero coefficients and their signs, while the rest of other coefficients must be zero. The feature-sign search algorithm consists of three basic modules, updating active set and their signs, calculating a new x, and checking the optimal conditions. The flowchart of the feature-sign search algorithm can be checked in the Table 5.2.

Definition 5.2.2.1 Define an augmented optimization problem as the ℓ_1-norm minimization problem (Eq. (5.1)) with the augmented constraints that $\boldsymbol{x}$ is consistent with a given active set and sign vector.

Lemma 5.2.2.1 (Local Convergence, [21]) *In the following two cases, the feature-sign step is guaranteed to strictly reduce the objective:*
(1) If the augmented condition is satisfied, but the current $\boldsymbol{x}_c$ *is not optimal for the*

Table 5.2 The feature-sign search algorithm [21]

1 Initialize $x := \vec{0}$, $\theta := \vec{0}$, and *active set* := {}, where $\theta_i \in \{-1, 0, 1\}$ denotes $\text{sign}(x_i)$.

2 From zero coefficients of x, select $i = \arg\max_i \left|\frac{\partial \|y - Ax\|^2}{\partial x_i}\right|$.

Activate x_i (add i to the *active set*) only if it locally improves the objective, namely:

If $\frac{\partial \|y - Ax\|^2}{\partial x_i} > \gamma$, then set $\theta_i := -1$, *active set* := $\{i\} \cup$ *active set*

If $\frac{\partial \|y - Ax\|^2}{\partial x_i} < -\gamma$, then set $\theta_i := 1$, *active set* := $\{i\} \cup$ *active set*

3 Feature-sign step:

Let $\hat{A}$ be a submatrix of A that contains only the columns corresponding to the *active set*

Let $\hat{x}$ and $\hat{\theta}$ be subvectors of x and θ corresponding to the *active set*

Compute the analytical solution to the resulting unconstrained QP (minimization$_{\hat{x}} \|y - \hat{A}\hat{x}\|^2 + \gamma \hat{\theta}^T \hat{x}$):

$\hat{x}_{new} := (\hat{A}^T \hat{A})^{-1} \left(\hat{A}^T y - \gamma \frac{\hat{\theta}}{2}\right)$,

Perform a discrete line search on the closed line segment from $\hat{x}$ to $\hat{x}_{new}$:

Check the objective value at $\hat{x}_{new}$ and all points where any coefficient changes sign.

Update $\hat{x}$ (and the corresponding entries in x) to the point with the lowest objective value.

Remove zero coefficients of $\hat{x}$ from the *active set* and update $\theta := \text{sign}(x)$.

4 Check the optimality conditions:

(a) Optimality condition for nonzero coefficients: $\frac{\partial \|y - Ax\|^2}{\partial x_j} + \gamma\, \text{sign}(x_j) = 0, \forall x_j \neq 0$

If condition (a) is not satisfied, go to Step 3 (without any new activation); else check condition (b).

(b) Optimality condition for zero coefficients : $\left|\frac{\partial \|y - Ax\|^2}{\partial x_j}\right| \leq \gamma, \forall x_j = 0$

If condition (b) is not satisfied, go to Setp 2; otherwise return x as the solution.

augmented problem at the start of the step of calculating $\mathbf{x}$.
(2) If $\mathbf{x}_c$ *at the start of the step of updating the active set and their signs are optimal for the augmented optimization problem, but are not optimal for Eq. (5.1).*

Theorem 5.2.2.1 (Global Convergence, [21]) *The feature-sign search algorithm converges to a global optimum of the* ℓ_1*-norm minimization problem in a finite number of steps.*

The proof details of the theorem can be referred to [21].

5.2.3 The Subspace Shrinkage and Optimization Algorithm

Wen et al. proposed a subspace shrinkage and optimization algorithm for solving the ℓ_1-norm minimization problem [41]. This algorithm is divided into two iterative steps: subspace shrinkage phase and subspace optimization phase.

The Subspace Shrinkage Phase: As we mentioned before, the subspace shrinkage is defined as

$$s_v(x) = \text{sgn}(x) \odot \max\{|x| - v, 0\}. \tag{5.9}$$

Given a point $\boldsymbol{x}_t$, the iterative shrinkage procedure generates a new point

$$\boldsymbol{x}_{t+1} = S_v(\boldsymbol{x}_t - \lambda \boldsymbol{g}_t, \mu\lambda), \tag{5.10}$$

where μ is the length of step, and λ is defined in Eq. (5.1). More interestingly, Eq. (5.10) will yield the support and the signs of the optimal solution $\boldsymbol{x}^*$ of Eq. (5.1) in a finite number of iterations under suitable conditions. Through Eq. (5.10), we can obtain a solution of Eq. (5.1), but we need thousands of iterations to get a acceptable solution. So, after some iterations we can use the subspace optimization method to accelerate the process.

The Subspace Optimization Phase [41, 42]**:** A subspace optimization problem is formed by fixing the components in this working set to zero and approximating the $\|\boldsymbol{x}\|_{\ell_1}$ by using a smooth function. We can reformulate Eq. (5.1) as

$$\arg\min_{\boldsymbol{x}} \; f(\boldsymbol{x}) + \mu\xi, \;\; \text{s.t.} \; (\boldsymbol{x}, \xi) \in \Omega. \tag{5.11}$$

Its subspace optimization problem is

$$\arg\min_{x} \; \phi_a(x) = \arg\min_{x} \; \text{sign}(x^k_{I^k})^T x_{I^k} + f(x), \tag{5.12}$$

where the subscript I^k defines the nonzero coefficient positions in $\boldsymbol{x}$. We do not care about the zero coefficients.

5.3 Efficient Sparse Coding Using Graphical Models

5.3.1 Graphical Models of CS Encoding Matrix

Graph is one of popular models in many concrete problems, especially in probabilistic inference and learning [4]. A graph consists of nodes and links, where each node denotes a random variable, and the links represent probabilistic relations among those variables. Different structures by combing different nodes and links correspond to many graphical models, such as Bayesian Network and Markov Random Fields. For better inferencing and learning problems, expander graphs are sparse bipartite graphs that are connected very well, and are quantified by using vertex and edges. It has the following interesting properties [4]:

(1) The ratio between links and nodes is really sparse.
(2) Also it is robust for signal representation and modeling since it is highly well connected.

A factor graph is used to unify both undirected and directed graphical models. Factor graph models the relationship among large-scale variables by using a product of

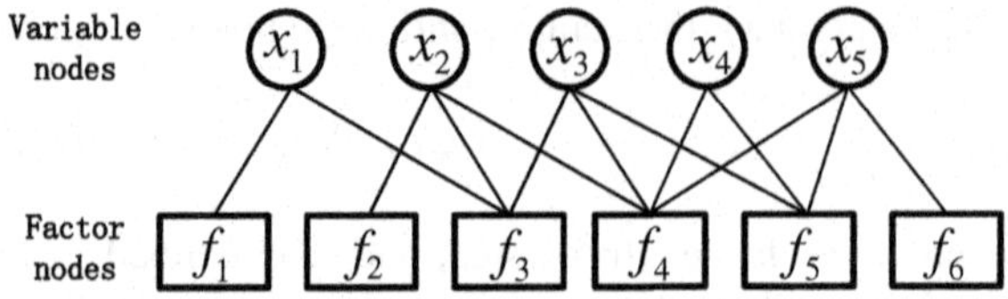

Fig. 5.1 The relationship between variable and factor nodes in a factor graph

factors. Define $X = [x_1, x_2, \ldots, x_N]^T$, we have the joint distribution of X as

$$p(X) = \prod_s f_s(\boldsymbol{X}_s), \tag{5.13}$$

where $\boldsymbol{X}_s$ is a subset of X. In factor graph, there exist two types of nodes: variable nodes and factor nodes. Moreover, those nodes are connected by links, shown in Fig. 5.1.

The joint distribution of Fig. 5.1 can be decomposed as

$$p(X) = f_1(x_1)f_2(x_2)f_3(x_1, x_2, x_3)f_4(x_2, x_3, x_4, x_5)f_5(x_3, x_4, x_5)f_6(x_5). \tag{5.14}$$

The factor graph provides a fundamental framework for efficient inference algorithms. Moreover, the sum-product algorithm is used to solve the problem of evaluating local marginal likelihoods over nodes. Belief propagation plays an important role in various computer vision tasks [11, 33], such as stereo vision [34], visual tracking [31], and BP is a special case of the sum-product algorithm. In fact, BP is used to get marginals

$$p(x) = \sum_{X \backslash \boldsymbol{x}} p(X), \tag{5.15}$$

and joint distribution is the product of

$$p(X) = \prod_{s \in N_e(x)} F_s(\boldsymbol{x}, \boldsymbol{X}_s), \tag{5.16}$$

where $N_e(x)$ is the set of neighbor factor nodes of x, and $\boldsymbol{X}_s$ is the set of all subvariables of the variable nodes x via factor node f_s, and $F_s(x, \boldsymbol{X}_s)$ is the product of all the factors in the graph associated with factor f_s, which is shown in Fig. 5.2.

Substituting Eq. (5.16) into Eq. (5.15), we have

$$p(x) = \prod_{s \in N_e(x)} \left[\sum_{X_s} F_s(x, X_s) \right] = \prod_{s \in N_e(x)} u_{f_s \to x}(x), \tag{5.17}$$

where $u_{f_s \to x}(x) \equiv \sum_{X_s} F_s(x, X_s)$, can be considered as messages from the factor node f_s to the variable node x.

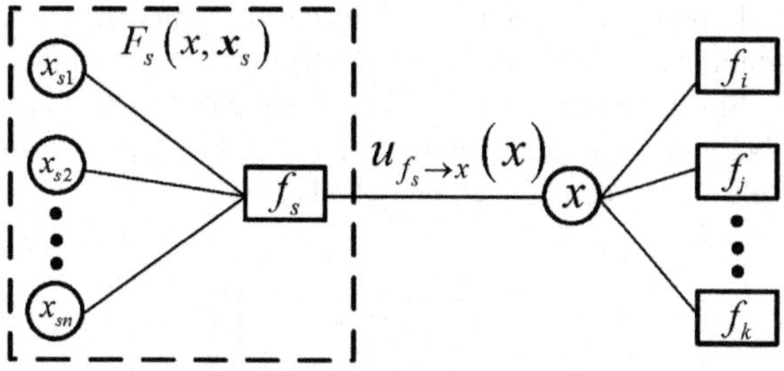

Fig. 5.2 A factor graph fragment for calculating $p(x)$

Similarly, we have

$$u_{x_m \to f_s}(x_m) = \prod_{\ell \in N_e(x_m) \backslash f_s} u_{f_\ell \to x_m}(x_m). \tag{5.18}$$

Note that: (1) From Eq. (5.17), $p(x)$ is obtained by the product of all the incoming messages arriving at node x; (2) From Eq. (5.18), we can take the product of the incoming messages along with all the other links for evaluating message from a variable node to an adjacent factor node.

5.3.2 Bayesian Compressive Sensing

For a K-sparse signal, we have

$$\boldsymbol{y} = \boldsymbol{A}\boldsymbol{x} + \xi = \boldsymbol{A}\boldsymbol{x}_s + \boldsymbol{A}\boldsymbol{x}_e + \xi = \boldsymbol{A}\boldsymbol{x}_s + \boldsymbol{\varepsilon}, \tag{5.19}$$

where $\boldsymbol{\varepsilon}$ is approximated as a zero-mean Gaussian noise $N(0, \sigma^2)$. Therefore, we have the likelihood model [19]

$$p(\boldsymbol{y}|\boldsymbol{x}_s, \sigma^2) = (2\pi\sigma^2)^{-K/2} \exp\left(-\frac{1}{2\sigma^2}\|\boldsymbol{y} - \boldsymbol{A}\boldsymbol{x}_s\|_{\ell_2}^2\right). \tag{5.20}$$

Equations (5.19) and (5.20) mean that we can formulate the compressed sensing problem into a linear regression problem given the prior that x_s is K-sparse.

The Laplace density function is a widely used sparsity prior as [12]

$$p(\boldsymbol{x}|\lambda) = \prod_i p(x_i|\lambda), \quad p(x_i|\lambda) = \frac{\lambda}{2} exp(-\lambda|x_i|), \tag{5.21}$$

where λ is a constant. In the Bayesian framework, we want to have a posterior density function. Moreover, the MAP solution using the Laplace prior in Eq. (5.21) is equivalent to the solution of $\hat{\boldsymbol{x}} = \arg\min_x \|\boldsymbol{y} - \boldsymbol{A}\boldsymbol{x}\|_{\ell_2}^2 + \lambda_1 \|\boldsymbol{x}\|_{\ell_1}$.

In relevance vector machine (RVM), a hierarchical prior has been used, and has similar properties as the Laplace prior but better conjugate exponential analysis [19].

Since the Laplace prior is not conjugated to the Gaussian likelihood, we may not obtain the analytical solution of $\boldsymbol{x}$ [14, 19], which is similar to hierarchical prior in Relevance Vector Machine (RVM) [37].

$$p(\boldsymbol{x}|\boldsymbol{\alpha}) = \prod_{i=1}^{N} N(x_i|0, \alpha_i^{-1}), \tag{5.22}$$

where α_i is the inverse-variance of a Gaussian density function. Moreover, α follows a Gamma prior

$$p(\alpha|a, b) = \prod_{i=1}^{N} \text{Gamma}(\alpha_i|a, b). \tag{5.23}$$

Therefor, we have

$$p(\boldsymbol{x}|a, b) = \prod_{i=1}^{N} \int_0^{\infty} N(x_i|0, \alpha_i^{-1})\text{Gamma}(\alpha_i|a, b). \tag{5.24}$$

Note that this equation can be solved analytically, and it corresponds to the student-t distribution [37]. We can obtain the sparse $\boldsymbol{x}$ by choosing appropriate a and b. Similarly, a Gamma prior $\text{Gamma}(\alpha_0|c, d)$ is introduced, where $\alpha_0 = 1/\sigma^2$. Figure 5.3 shows the graphical model of BCS.

Given $\boldsymbol{y}$ and A, $\boldsymbol{x}$ can be solved analytically as a multivariate Gaussian distribution with mean and covariance

$$\begin{cases} \boldsymbol{\mu} & = \alpha_0 \Sigma^T \boldsymbol{y}, \\ \Sigma & = (\alpha_0 A^T A + B)^{-1}. \end{cases} \tag{5.25}$$

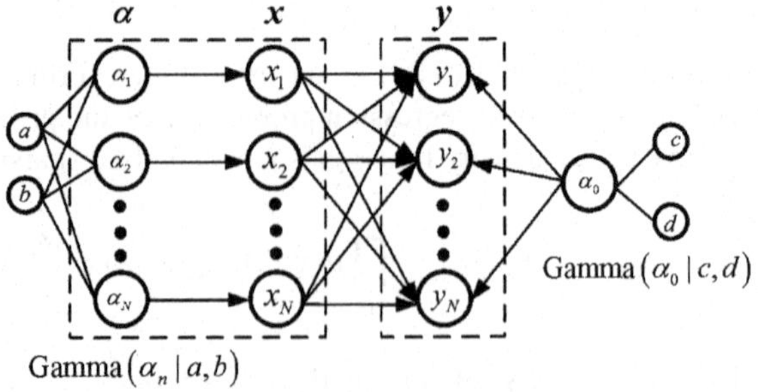

Fig. 5.3 The complete graphical model of the Bayesian compressive sensing framework

where $B = \text{diag}(\alpha_1, \alpha_2, \ldots, \alpha_N)$. Similar to RVM, we can use a type-II MLE to estimate the hyperparameters by

$$L(\alpha, \alpha_0) = \log p(\boldsymbol{y}|\boldsymbol{\alpha}, \alpha_0) = -\frac{1}{2}\left[K \log 2\pi + \log|C| + \boldsymbol{y}^T C^{-1} \boldsymbol{y}\right], \tag{5.26}$$

where $C = \sigma^2 I + AB^{-1}A^T$. By using EM algorithm, we have

$$\alpha_i^{new} = \gamma_i / u_i, \quad i = 1, 2, \ldots, N, \tag{5.27}$$

where u_i is the ith element of posterior mean from Eq. (5.25) and $\gamma_i = 1 - \alpha_i \Sigma_{ii}$, Σ_{ii} is the ith diagonal element of posterior covariance from Eq. (5.25). Considering the noise variance, we have

$$\alpha_0^{new} = \frac{N - \sum_i \gamma_i}{\|\boldsymbol{y} - A\boldsymbol{\mu}\|_{\ell_2}^2}. \tag{5.28}$$

From Eqs. (5.27) and (5.28), we can see that $\boldsymbol{\alpha}^{new}$ and α_0^{new} are functions of $\boldsymbol{\mu}$ and Σ; Similarly, $\boldsymbol{\mu}$ and Σ are functions of $\boldsymbol{\alpha}^{new}$ and α_0^{new}. Thus, we can use iteration algorithm to solve them until its convergence.

Bayesian compressive sensing provides a Bayesian framework for solving the inverse problem of compressive sensing. Moreover, Bayesian compressive sensing with one-bit quantized measurements has drawn much attention recently thanks to its potential benefits in signal acquisition. Unfortunately, it is prone to flip to their opposite states when there exists noise in signal processing. Li et al. proposed a robust one-bit Bayesian compressed sensing with sign-flip errors [22].

5.3.3 Bayesian Compressive Sensing Using Belief Propagation (CS-BP)

In Sect. 5.3.1, we know that a bipartite graph is used to represent A. Thus, we can use graphical models to inference the sparse coefficient x. Exact inference in graphical models is a NP-hard problem [9] since the number of loops in the graph from A is very large. However, the sparsity of A makes it possible to infer $\boldsymbol{x}$ approximately by using BP.

1. Two-state Gaussian Mixture Model as Sparsity Prior

As we discussed in Sect. 5.3.2, there are various sparsity priors, such as Laplace priors [12], hierarchical prior [19], and normal product priors [48]. Here, a two-state mixture model is used as a sparsity prior [3].

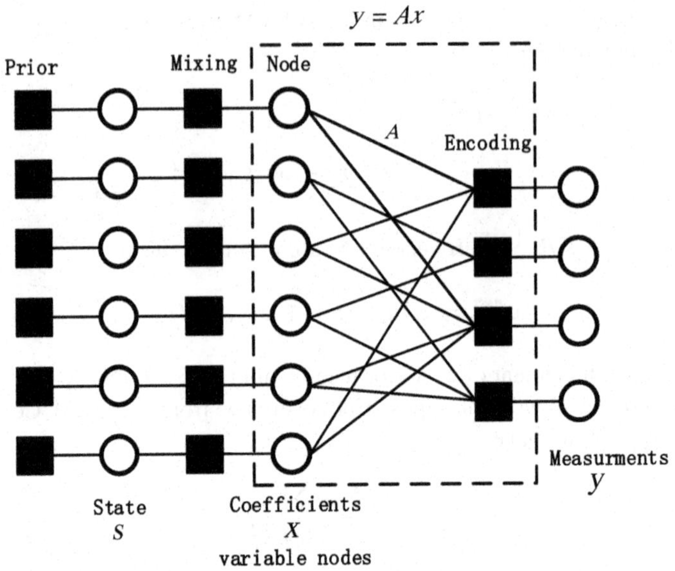

Fig. 5.4 Factor graph between variable nodes (*white circle*) and constraint nodes (*black square*) in CS-BP [3]

Define $X = [X_1, X_2, \cdots, X_N]^T$ as a random vector in $\mathbb{R}^N$, and $\boldsymbol{x} = [x_1, x_2, \cdots, x_N]$ is an instance of X. $S = [S_1, S_2, \ldots, S_N]^T$ is the random state vector associated with X. Thus we have (Fig. 5.4)

$$p(X_i|S_i = 1) \sim N(0, \sigma_1^2);\ \ p(X_i|S_i = 0) \sim N(0, \sigma_0^2), \tag{5.29}$$

where $\sigma_1^2 > \sigma_0^2$, $p(S_i = 1) = K/N$, and $p(S_i = 0) = 1 - K/N$. From the viewpoint of approximate signal models, long K-highest magnitude corresponds to zero-mean Gaussian distributions with high variance, while the rest $N - K$ magnitudes correspond to low variance. Therefore, the mixture model is represented by these parameters, σ_0^2, σ_1^2, and K/N. The two-Gaussian mixture mode can be seen in Fig. 5.5

2. Bayesian Inference Problem

Recovering the approximate sparse random signals can be formulated as a Bayesian inference problem as

$$\begin{aligned} \hat{x}_{MAP} &= \arg\max_{\boldsymbol{x}} p(X = \boldsymbol{x}) \\ \text{s.t.}\ \ \boldsymbol{y} &= A\boldsymbol{x} \end{aligned} \tag{5.30}$$

By contrast, $\boldsymbol{x}$ follows two-state Gaussian mixture model. As we know, exact inference in graphical models is NP-hard. However, CS-BP algorithms both reduce the

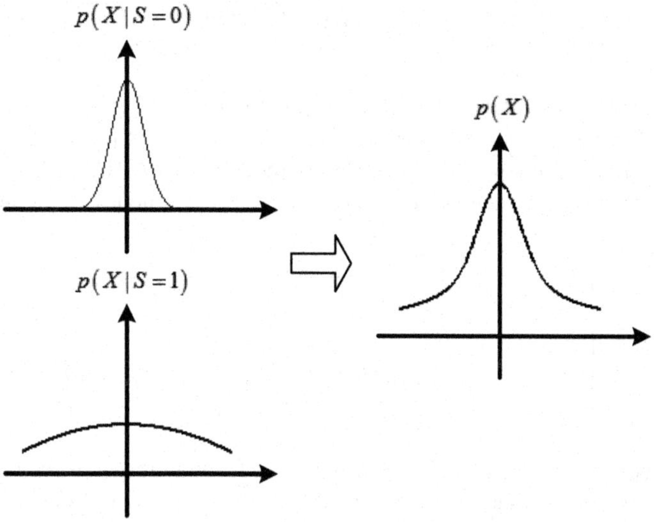

Fig. 5.5 Two-Gaussian mixture mode for sparse coefficients

number of loops and use efficient message-passing methods to estimate $\boldsymbol{x}$ approximately by using sparse A and BP algorithm.

Figure 5.4 shows the factor graph between variable nodes and factor nodes. In the figure, there are two types of nodes: variable nodes and factor nodes. The variables nodes consist of state variables, coefficient variables and signal variables. The factor nodes are prior constraint nodes, mixing constraint nodes, and encoding nodes. Moreover, prior constraint nodes follow the Bernoulli prior on state variables, mixing constraint nodes follow the conditional distribution on sparse coefficient variables given the state variables, and encoding constraint nodes follow the encoding matrix structure on signals. In Baron's CS-BP algorithm [3], sparse LDPC-like matrix A were used, where each element is restricted to $\{-1, 0, 1\}$. Though traditional dense matrix is capable of capturing the sparse signals better, it is hard to achieve fast encoding and decoding. By using sparse LDPC-like matrix, we can implement fast encoding and decoding by using sparse matrix multiplication. Furthermore, we model the sparse matrix A as a sparse bipartite graph. Then, the sparseness can reduce the number of loops in the graph structures, thus yielding fast message passing in Bayesian inference.

3. Passing Message

The core of CS-BP is to use an efficient, belief propagation method for Bayesian inference problems. We use a graphical model to model matrix A, where the marginal distributions of variable can be calculated in factor graph by passing message between variable nodes and constraint nodes.

$$p(v) = \prod_{u \in Ne(v)} \mu_{u \to v}(v). \tag{5.31}$$

Equation (5.31) is the fundamental marginal distribution, and various statistical characteristics can be obtained. Moreover, it is the basic equation for passing messages.

Now, we introduce how to solve sparse coefficients in MAP by passing messages. The messages sent between variable nodes and constraint nodes are in the form

$$\begin{cases} \mu_{v \to c} = \prod_{u \in Ne(v) \setminus \{c\}} \mu_{u \to v}(v) \\ \mu_{c \to v} = \sum_{\sim\{v\}} \left(\text{con}\,(Ne(c)) \prod_{\omega \in Ne(c) \setminus \{v\}} \mu_{\omega \to c}(\omega) \right) \end{cases}, \tag{5.32}$$

where $Ne(v)$ and $Ne(c)$ are sets of neighbors of v and c, respectively. con $(Ne(c))$ is the constraint on the set of variables nodes $Ne(c)$ and $\sim\{v\}$ is the set of neighbors of c excluding v.

For reducing computational complexity, we rewrite Eq. (5.32)

$$\begin{cases} \mu_{v \to c} = \dfrac{\prod_{u \in Ne(v)} \mu_{u \to v}(v)}{\mu_{c \to v}(v)} \\ \mu_{c \to v} = \sum_{\sim\{v\}} \left(\text{con}\,(Ne(c)) \dfrac{\prod_{\omega \in Ne(c)} \mu_{\omega \to c}(\omega)}{\mu_{v \to c}(v)} \right) \end{cases}. \tag{5.33}$$

Table 5.3 The CS-BP algorithm flowchart

Initialization: Initialize the iteration counter $t = 1$.
 -Set up data structures for factor graph messages $\mu_{v \to c}(v)$ and $\mu_{c \to v}(v)$.
 -Initialize messages $\mu_{v \to c}(v)$ from variable to constraint nodes with the signal prior.

Convolution:
 For each measurement $c = 1, \ldots, M$, which corresponds to constraint node c, compute $\mu_{c \to v}(v)$ via convolution Eqn.(5.18) for all neighboring variable nodes $N_e(c)$. If measurement noise is present, then convolve further with a noise prior.
 Apply damping methods such as message damping BP(MDBP) by weighting the new estimates from iteration t with estimates from previous iterations.

Multiplication:
 For each coefficient $v = 1, \ldots, N$, which corresponds to a variable node v, compute $\mu_{v \to c}(v)$ via multiplication (5.17) for all neighboring constraint nodes $n(v)$. Apply damping methods as needed. If the iteration counter has yet to reach its maximal value, then go to Convolution step.

Output:
 For each coefficient $v = 1, \ldots, N$, compute MMSE or MAP estimates (or alternative statistical characterizations) based on the marginal distribution $f(v)$ Eqn. 5.31.

The rational behind this is that in Eq. (5.33), the numerators are computed once and then used for all messages leaving the node being processed.

4. The Algorithm Flowchart

The algorithm flowchart of CS-BP is shown in Table 5.3

5.4 Efficient Sparse Bayesian Learning

5.4.1 Introduction

Sparse Bayesian Learning (SBL) has been drawn much attention in machine learning and computer vision community. Since it has many attractive properties: (1) The global minimum of ℓ_1-norm algorithm is always not the sparsest solution [43]. In this case, SBL has better performance; (2) ℓ_1-norm algorithms perform worse when the columns of sensing matrix are highly correlated. (3) SBL is equivalent to iterative weighted ℓ_1-norm minimization, where ℓ_1-norm optimization problem is just the first step of SBL. (4) It is more convenient for adding structure information to SBL frameworks [30].

SBL obtains sparse coefficients by using a type-II maximum likelihood to maximize the marginal likelihood in a batch way. Sequential SBL [38] has an "empty" initialization model, and sequentially "adds" basis function to increase the marginal likelihood. Similarly, we can increase the marginal likelihood by deleting function. By doing so, we can modify the sparse coefficients from an initial solution to an optimal solution.

5.4.2 Sequential Sparse Bayesian Models

In Sect. 3.5.1, we introduce how to formulate sparse representation as a linear regression. Also, sparse Bayesian learning can be used in classification, which refers to [38] without loss of generality. We will introduce sequential sparse Bayesian models in linear regression.

1. The Marginal Likelihood in linear regression

According to the generative model, we have

$$y = \hat{y} + \varepsilon = Ax + \varepsilon. \tag{5.34}$$

where A is the design matrix and x is the parameter vector. As seen in Sect. 3.5, SBL frameworks assume that the residuals obey the independent zero-mean Gaussian. First of all, we have the multivariate Gaussian likelihood

$$p(y|x,\sigma^2) = \frac{1}{(2\pi\sigma^2)^{\frac{D}{2}}} exp\left\{-\frac{||y-\hat{y}||_{\ell_2}{}^2}{2\sigma^2}\right\} \quad (5.35)$$

The prior is

$$P(x|\alpha) = \frac{1}{(2\pi)^{\frac{N}{2}}} \Pi_{n=1}^{N} \alpha_n^{\frac{1}{2}} exp\left(-\frac{\alpha_n x_n^2}{2}\right) \quad (5.36)$$

Thus, given α, we have

$$p(x|y,\alpha,\sigma^2) = p(y|x,\sigma^2)p(x|\alpha)|p(y|\alpha,\sigma^2) \quad (5.37)$$

Sparse Bayesian Learning is formulated as the local maximization s.t. α of the logarithm of the marginal likelihood $L(\alpha)$ [36].

$$L(\boldsymbol{\alpha}) = \log p(\mathbf{y}|\boldsymbol{\alpha},\sigma^2) = -\frac{1}{2}\left[D\log 2\pi + \log|C| + \mathbf{y}^T C^{-1}\mathbf{y}\right], \quad (5.38)$$

where

$$C = \sigma^2 I + A\Lambda^{-1}A^T, \quad (5.39)$$

and $\Lambda = diag(\boldsymbol{\alpha})$. The α_i is the precise of prior $p(x_i,\alpha_i)$, and σ^2 is the noise level of the likelihood which has been defined in Sect. 3.4.1.

2. Properties of the Marginal Likelihood

We can analyze the relation between every element of the $\boldsymbol{x}$, by decomposing the logarithm of marginal likelihood. From Eq. (5.39), we can easily rewrite it as

$$\begin{aligned} C &= \sigma^2 I + \sum_m \alpha_m^{-1} A_{.m} A_{.m}^T = \sigma^2 I + \sum_{m\neq i} \alpha_m^{-1} A_{.m} A_{.m}^T + \alpha_i^{-1} A_{.i} A_{.i}^T \\ &= C_{-i} + \alpha_i^{-1} A_{.i} A_{.i}^T. \end{aligned} \quad (5.40)$$

where C_{-i} is C without the contribution of ith column of A [36]. So, by the decomposition of C, the determinant and inverse of C can be expressed as

$$|C| = |C_{-i}||1 + \alpha_i^{-1} A_{.i}^T C_{-i}^{-1} A_{.i}|, \quad (5.41)$$

$$C^{-1} = C_{-i}^{-1} - \frac{C_{-i}^{-1} A_{.i} A_{.i}^T C_{-i}^{-1}}{\alpha_i + A_{.i}^T C_{-i}^{-1} A_{.i}}. \quad (5.42)$$

Substituting Eqs. (5.41) and (5.42) into Eq. (5.38) we get

$$\begin{aligned} L(\boldsymbol{\alpha}) = & -\frac{1}{2}\Bigg[D\log 2\pi + \log|C_{-i}| + \boldsymbol{y}^T C_{-i}^{-1}\boldsymbol{y} \\ & -\log\alpha_i + \log(\alpha_i + A_{.i}^T C_{-i}^{-1} A_{.i}) - \frac{(A_{.i}^T C_{-i}^{-1}\boldsymbol{y})^2}{\alpha_i + A_{.i}^T C_{-i}^{-1} A_{.i}}\Bigg] \\ = & L(\boldsymbol{\alpha}_{-i}) + \frac{1}{2}\left[\log\alpha_i - \log(\alpha_i + A_{.i}^T C_{-i}^{-1} A_{.i}) + \frac{(A_{.i}^T C_{-i}^{-1}\boldsymbol{y})^2}{\alpha_i + A_{.i}^T C_{-i}^{-1} A_{.i}}\right] \\ = & L(\boldsymbol{\alpha}_{-i}) + \ell(\alpha_i), \end{aligned} \tag{5.43}$$

where $\boldsymbol{\alpha}_{-i}$ is the hyperparameter vector $\boldsymbol{\alpha}$ without the ith element. So, we can note that $L(\boldsymbol{\alpha}_i)$ is the log marginal likelihood with α_i removed from the model, and we isolate a term $\ell(\alpha_i)$, which is related with α_i. With definition that

$$s_i \triangleq A_{.i}^T C_{-i} A_{.i}, \quad \text{and} \quad q_i \triangleq A_{.i}^T C_{-i}\boldsymbol{y}, \tag{5.44}$$

we can simplify the $\ell(\alpha_i)$ term as

$$\ell(\alpha_i) = \frac{1}{2}\left[\log\alpha_i - \log(\alpha_i + s_i) + \frac{q_i^2}{\alpha_i + s_i}\right]. \tag{5.45}$$

The q_i can be interpreted as the "quality" factor which measures how well $L(\boldsymbol{\alpha})$ increases by adding $A_{.i}$ into the model, and s_i can be interpreted as the "sparsity" factor which measures how much the $A_{.i}$ included serves to decrease the $L(\boldsymbol{\alpha})$ through "inflating" C [36]. We already have a simple expression about the log marginal likelihood. As we know, SBL learns the hyperparameters $\boldsymbol{\alpha}$ by maximizing the marginal likelihood which is equivalent to maximizing the log marginal likelihood. Next, we shall analyze under which condition we can get the maximum $L(\boldsymbol{\alpha})$.

From Eq. (5.45), we can easily get the first derivatives of $L(\alpha)$ as

$$\frac{\partial L(\boldsymbol{\alpha})}{\partial\alpha_i} = \frac{\partial\ell(\alpha_i)}{\partial\alpha_i} = \frac{\alpha_i^{-1}s_i^2 - (q_i^2 - s_i)}{2(\alpha_i + s_i)^2}. \tag{5.46}$$

We can get the stationary points by taking the $\frac{\partial L(\boldsymbol{\alpha})}{\partial\alpha_i} = 0$. Considering that the inverse variance $\alpha_i > 0$, we found that there are two kinds of stationary points which are $\alpha_i = +\infty$ and

$$\alpha_i = \frac{s_i^2}{q_i^2 - s_i}, \tag{5.47}$$

when $q_i^2 - s_i > 0$ as a consequence of $\alpha_i > 0$. If we want to know the properties of these stationary points, we need to consider about the second derivatives of $L(\alpha)$ which can be expressed as follows

$$\frac{\partial^2 L(\boldsymbol{\alpha})}{\partial^2 \alpha_i^2} = \frac{\partial^2 \ell(\boldsymbol{\alpha})}{\partial^2 \alpha_i^2} \tag{5.48}$$

$$= \frac{-\alpha_i^{-2} s_i^2 (\alpha_i + s_i)^2 - 2(\alpha_i + s_i)[\alpha_i^{-1} s_i^2 - (q_i^2 - s_i)]}{2(\alpha_i + s_i)^4}. \tag{5.49}$$

Now, we consider both the finite and infinite situations of the α_i stationary point.

(1) Finite α

Considering the finite α situation, by substituting Eq. (5.47) into Eq. (5.48), we can get

$$\left.\frac{\partial^2 L(\boldsymbol{\alpha})}{\partial^2 \alpha_i^2}\right|_{\alpha_i = \frac{s_i^2}{q_i^2 - s_i}} = \frac{-s_i^2}{2\alpha_i^2(\alpha_i + s_i)^2}. \tag{5.50}$$

So, if Eq. (5.50) is always negative, $\ell(\alpha_i)$ can get the maximum when $\alpha_i = \frac{s_i^2}{q_i^2 - s_i}$, which is in the situation of $q_i^2 - s_i > 0$.

(2) Infinite α

Substituting $\alpha = +\infty$ into Eq. (5.48), we can get the second derivation as zero. But, since $\alpha_i \to +\infty$ from Eq. (5.46), the sign gradient is given by the sign of $-(q_i^2 - s_i)$.

So, we can conclude that:

- If $q_i^2 - s_i > 0$, when $\alpha_i = +\infty$, the gradient is negative, and as α_i increases, $\ell(\alpha_i)$ will decrease. So, we must decrease α_i until it reaches $\alpha_i = \frac{s_i^2}{q_i^2 - s_i}$ to get the maximum of $\ell(\alpha_i)$. Also get that $\alpha_i = +\infty$ is a minimum of $\ell(\alpha_i)$.
- If $q_i^2 - s_i < 0$, conversely we can get $\ell(\alpha_i)$ can get its maximum at $\alpha_i = +\infty$.
- If $q_i^2 - s_i = 0$, both the stationary point situation coincide.

We can get these properties more intuitively from the Fig. 5.6.

3. Marginal Likelihood Maximization

By the properties we have mentioned above, we can desire the algorithm to efficiently maximize the $L(\boldsymbol{\alpha})$. We note that if we want to compute the s_i and q_i, we must to compute the corresponding C_{-i}^{-1}, which is not very efficient. So, we define the intermediate variable S_i and Q_m, which can make the computation of s_i and q_i more efficient. The definition of S_i and Q_i as

$$S_i \triangleq A_{.i}^T C^{-1} A_{.i}, \qquad Q_i \triangleq A_{.i}^T C^{-1} \mathbf{y} \tag{5.51}$$

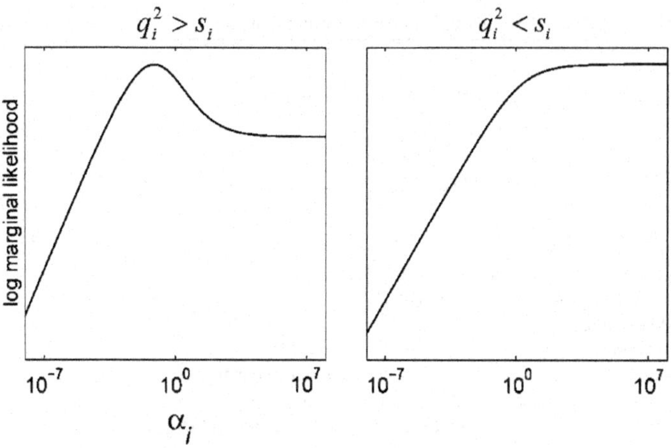

Fig. 5.6 The two situations of $\ell(\alpha_i)$ [36]

From Eq. (5.51), we can have

$$s_i = \frac{\alpha_i S_i}{\alpha_i - S_i}, \qquad q_i = \frac{\alpha_i Q_i}{\alpha_i - S_i}. \tag{5.52}$$

So, we can note that, when $\alpha_i = +\infty$, $s_i = S_i$ and $q_i = Q_i$. We can also decompose the C^{-1} to make the computation of S_i and Q_i more efficient.

$$S_i = A_{.i}^T B A_{.i} - A_{.i}^T B A_M \Sigma A_M^T B A_{.i} \tag{5.53}$$
$$Q_i = A_{.i}^T B \boldsymbol{y} - A_{.i}^T B A_M \Sigma A_M^T B \boldsymbol{y}. \tag{5.54}$$

Here, Σ is the covariance matrix of $\boldsymbol{x}$'s posterior distribution, which is defined in Eq. (3.65), $B = \sigma^{-2} I$ and A_M indicates the columns of A which have currently been included in the model. We need to note that Σ is also corresponding to the index which have currently been included in the model. So, in the process of maximizing the $L(\boldsymbol{\alpha})$, we can judge whether add $A_{.i}$ into model or delete $A_{.i}$ from the model by the following ways:

- If $A_{.i}$ is in the model ($\alpha_i < +\infty$) but $q_i^2 - s_i < 0$, then the $A_{.i}$ must be deleted (set $\alpha_i = +\infty$).
- If $A_{.i}$ is excluded from the model ($\alpha_i = +\infty$) but $q_i^2 - s_i > 0$, then the $A_{.i}$ must be added into the model (set $\alpha_i = \frac{s_i^2}{q_i^2 - s_i}$).

We can note that this is the greedy way to get the optimal solution of $L(\boldsymbol{\alpha})$.

Table 5.4 The flowchart of sequential sparse Bayesian learning [38]

Initialize:
A single basis vector $A_{.i}$,σ^2 and setting the α_i from Eqn. (5.47):

$$\alpha_i = \frac{\|A_{.i}\|^2}{(A_{.i}^T y)^2/\|A_{.i}\|_2^2 - \sigma^2}. \tag{5.55}$$

All other α_m set to zero.
Explicitly compute Σ and $\boldsymbol{\mu}$ (which are scalars initially),
along with initial values of s_m and q_m for all N bases $A_{.m}$.
Main while (!convergence)
Select a candidate basis vector A_i from the set of all N:
- If $q_i^2 - s_i > 0$ and $\alpha_i > 0$ (*i.e.* $A_{.i}$is in the model), **re-estimate** α_i.
- If $q_i^2 - s_i > 0$ and $\alpha_i = 0$ **add** $A_{.i}$ to the model with updated α_i.
- If $q_i^2 - s_i \leqslant 0$ and $\alpha_i > 0$ **delete** $A_{.i}$ form the model and set $\alpha_i = 0$.

Update Σ, $\boldsymbol{\mu}$ and all s_m and q_m.
End while
Output: $\boldsymbol{x} = \boldsymbol{\mu}, \quad \Sigma$.

5.4.3 The Algorithm Flowchart

We can use the greedy way to maximize the $L(\boldsymbol{\alpha})$ and define the sequential sparse Bayesian learning (SSBL) algorithm whose flowchart is shown in Table 5.4.

5.5 Sparse Quantization

5.5.1 Signal Sparse Approximation Problems

Signal approximation is to represent it using more elementary functions instead of using closed forms. Sparse approximation uses a sparse linear expression from an overcomplete dictionary to approximate signals/images. It is a very useful tool in many computer vision tasks, such as face recognition [44], label propagation [8], and feature coding [6].

Given dictionary $A \in \mathbb{R}^{D\times N}$, we represent $\boldsymbol{y}$ using K vectors of A as

$$\overline{\boldsymbol{y}} = \sum_{A_{.i}\in A,\ i\in\Lambda,\ |\Lambda|\le K} x_i A_{.i} \quad , \tag{5.56}$$

by minimizing

$$\|\boldsymbol{y} - \overline{\boldsymbol{y}}\|_{\ell_2}^2 = \sum_j (y_j - \overline{y}_j)^2, \tag{5.57}$$

where $\overline{y}_j$ is an approximation of y_j using A, and Λ is an index set. In practical applications, A could be either an orthogonal basis or a nonorthogonal basis, which induces different algorithms and problems [28].

5.5.2 *K*-Highest Sparse Quantization

1. Definitions

Definition 5.5.1 (*Quantization*) Quantization is a mapping of a vector $\mathbf{y}$ into its closest vector of the codebook $\{A_{.i}\}_{i=1}^{N}$ as

$$\hat{\mathbf{y}} = \arg\min_{\tilde{\mathbf{y}}\in\{A_{.i}\}} \|\tilde{\mathbf{y}} - \mathbf{y}\|_{\ell_2}^2. \tag{5.58}$$

Definition 5.5.2 (*Sparse Quantization*) Sparse quantization is a quantization in the code book $A \in \mathbb{R}_K^{D\times N}$, where $\mathbb{R}_K^{D\times N}$ denotes the space of $K-$sparse vectors in $\mathbb{R}^{D\times N}$. Moreover, the sparse quantization of $\mathbf{y}$ is

$$\hat{\mathbf{y}} = \arg\min_{\tilde{\mathbf{y}}\in\mathbb{R}_K^D} \|\tilde{\mathbf{y}} - \mathbf{y}\|_{\ell_2}^2. \tag{5.59}$$

Moreover, let $\mathbb{B}_K^D = \{0, 1\}_K^D$, binary sparse quantization is $\hat{\mathbf{y}} = \arg\min_{\tilde{\mathbf{y}}\in\mathbb{B}_K^D} \|\tilde{\mathbf{y}} - \mathbf{y}\|^2$. Boix et al. showed that sparse quantization can be obtained by a sorting algorithm [6] in the following proposition.

Proposition 5.5.1 *Binary sparse quantization can be obtained by*

$$\hat{y}_i = \begin{cases} 1, & \text{if } i \in K - \mathit{Highest}(\mathbf{y}) \\ 0, & \text{otherwise} \end{cases} \tag{5.60}$$

where $K-$Highest $(\mathbf{y})$ is the set of dimension including K highest values in the vector $\mathbf{y}$.

Definition 5.5.3 Let $\Phi(\mathbf{y})$ be the feature mapping based on dictionary A

$$\phi(\mathbf{y}) = \frac{1}{Z}[k(\mathbf{y}, A_{.1}), k(\mathbf{y}, A_{.2}), \ldots, k(\mathbf{y}, A_{.N})], \tag{5.61}$$

where $k(\cdot,\cdot) = \exp(-\beta d(\cdot,\cdot))$ is a kernel function; β is a constant which can be learned, $d(\cdot,\cdot)$ is a distance function, and Z is a normalization constant.

In visual recognition, feature extraction and encoding is an important step, in which vector quantization is a very popular algorithm. Moreover, vector quantization can be extended to the hard assignment. Boix et al. showed that hard assignment is a special sparse quantization as follows [6]:

Proposition 5.5.2 $\boldsymbol{\alpha}^* \in \mathbb{B}_K^N$ *denotes the result of hard assignment. Thus,* $\boldsymbol{\alpha}^*$ *can be obtained by using the sparse quantization of* $\phi(\mathbf{y})$ *as*

$$\boldsymbol{\alpha}^* = \arg\min_{\alpha \in \mathbb{B}_K^M} \|\boldsymbol{\alpha} - \phi(\mathbf{y})\|_{\ell_2}^2. \quad (5.62)$$

Let $\{-1, 0, 1\}_K^D = \mathbb{T}_K^D$, Propositions 5.5.1 can be easily extended as follows [5]:

Proposition 5.5.3 *Let* $\hat{\mathbf{y}}$ *be the quantization into* $\mathbb{T}_K^D$ *of* $\mathbf{y} \in \mathbb{R}^D$, *which is* $\hat{\mathbf{y}} = \arg\min_{\tilde{\mathbf{y}} \in \mathbb{T}_K^D} \|\tilde{\mathbf{y}} - \mathbf{y}\|_{\ell_2}^2$. *For* $\|\mathbf{y}\|_{\ell_2} \leq \|\mathbf{s}\|_{\ell_2}/\sqrt{K}$, *where* $\mathbf{s} \in \mathbb{T}_K^D$, $\hat{\mathbf{y}}$ *can be computed by*

$$\hat{y}_i = \begin{cases} sign(y_i), & if \ \ i \in K - Highest(|\mathbf{y}|) \\ 0, & otherwise \end{cases}, \quad (5.63)$$

where $|\mathbf{y}|$ *is the element-wise absolute value of* $\mathbf{y}$.

Figure 5.7 illustrates the error of input vector $\boldsymbol{x}$ which is quantified in $\mathbb{B}_2^3$, $\mathbb{T}_2^3$, and $\mathbb{R}_2^3$, respectively.

2. Efficient feature coding

Sparse quantization can be used in feature coding as it improves encoding efficiency and thanks to leveraging bitwise representation. A nested sparse quantization (NSQ) consists of two sequential steps: the outer one and the inner one [6]. In practice, the NSQ is equivalent to two optimization problems [6]:

$$\text{Inner SQ: } \hat{\mathbf{y}} = \arg\min_{\tilde{\mathbf{y}} \in \mathbb{B}_K^N} \|\tilde{\mathbf{y}} - Q(\mathbf{y})\|^2, \quad (5.64)$$

$$\text{Outer SQ: } \boldsymbol{\alpha} = \arg\min_{\tilde{\alpha} \in \mathbb{B}_{K'}^{N'}} \|\tilde{\boldsymbol{\alpha}} - \phi(\hat{\mathbf{y}})\|. \quad (5.65)$$

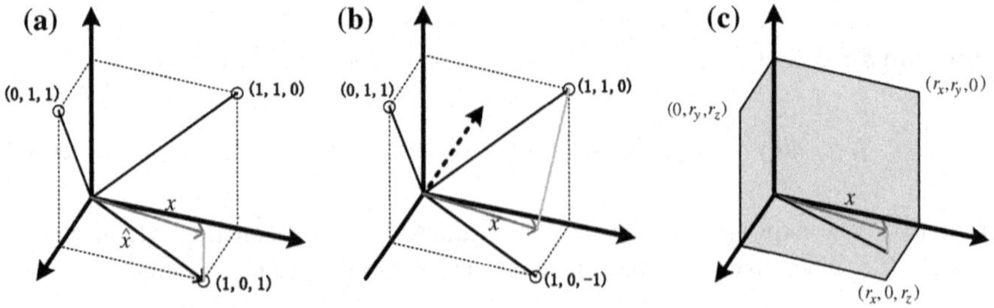

Fig. 5.7 The representation of $\mathbb{B}_2^3$, $\mathbb{T}_2^3$ and $\mathbb{R}_2^3$ space with the input vector $\boldsymbol{x}$ (*red line*) and the error (*green line*)

Table 5.5 The nested sparse quantization algorithm [6]

```
Input: y ∈ ℝ^D_+, A ∈ 𝔹^{D×N'}_{K'}
       ŷ ← Set K' highest values of y to 1 and the rest to 0
   for i = 1,...,N'
       φ_i(ŷ) = Σ_{j=1}^{D} (x̂_j ⊙ A_ij)
   end
Output: α ← Set K highest value of φ(x̂) to 1 and the rest to 0
```

The $Q(\boldsymbol{y})$ is a feature mapping that is similar to $\Phi(\boldsymbol{y})$ in Definition 5.5.3. More specifically, $Q(\boldsymbol{y}) = \boldsymbol{y}$. That is $Q(\boldsymbol{y})$ is a linear mapping in this case. Thus, we can use binary sparse quantization in Eq. (5.60) and then we have

$$\hat{\boldsymbol{y}} = \arg\min_{\tilde{\boldsymbol{y}} \in \mathbb{B}_K^N} \|\tilde{\boldsymbol{y}} - \boldsymbol{y}\|_{\ell_2}^2. \tag{5.66}$$

Alternatively, different $Q(\boldsymbol{x})$ may improve the performance of visual classification.

Combining Eqs. (5.64) and (5.65) can encode feature vectors, and then generate the global feature vectors of images given dictionary. Furthermore, we can use classifiers (e.g. SVM) to classify/recognize objects. The NSQ algorithm is summarized in Table 5.5. Note that the outer SQ is a mapping from a set of $\binom{N'}{K'}$ elements to $\binom{N}{K}$ possible outputs, where $\binom{N'}{K'} \gg \binom{N}{K}$.

We can note that the NSQ algorithm only can be used in the situation when input $\boldsymbol{y} \in \mathbb{R}_+^D$. But, sometimes, some elements of input vector $\boldsymbol{y}$ are negative, so, we can also generalize the NSQ algorithm to satisfy this situation by using the pace of $\mathbb{T}_K^D$. The generalized NSQ algorithm is summarized in Table 5.6.

We need to note that in the algorithm of Table 5.6, it does not need the code book, it considers all the elements in $\{\boldsymbol{b}_i\} = \bigcup_{0<p\leq D} \mathbb{T}_p^D$ and the final mapping only considers about the elements of the output of the loop, the rest of the other elements are zero which is defined as

Table 5.6 The generalized sparse quantization algorithm [5]

```
Input: y ∈ ℝ^D
   for a < p ≤ D
       β*_p = argmin_{β∈𝕋^D_p} ||β − y||_ℓ2
   end
Output: α = argmin_{α̃∈ℝ^Q} ||α̃ − φ̃(y, {β*_p})||_ℓ2
```

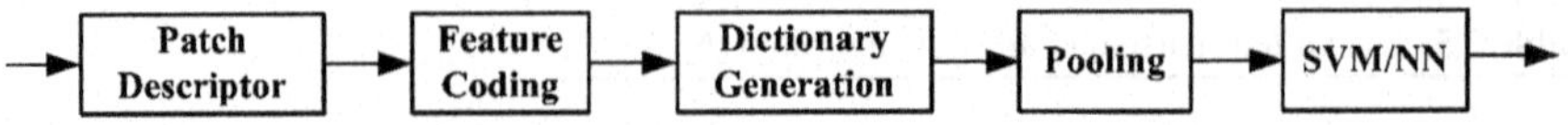

Fig. 5.8 The flowchart of SQ in visual recognition [6]

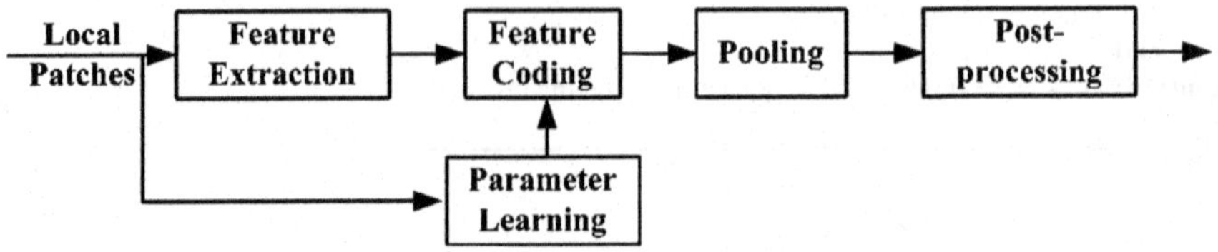

Fig. 5.9 The flowchart of SQ in local image description using SQ [5]

$$\tilde{\phi}_i(\boldsymbol{y}, \{\boldsymbol{\beta}_p^*\}) = \begin{cases} \phi_i(\boldsymbol{y}, \{\boldsymbol{\beta}_p^*\}) & \text{if } \boldsymbol{\beta}_p^* = \boldsymbol{b}_i \\ 0 & \text{otherwise} \end{cases}. \tag{5.67}$$

The more detail can be referred in [5].

3. Applications

Visual recognition: In general, visual recognition consists of patch descriptors, feature encoding, dictionary generation, pooling and classification. Typically, we can use histogram of oriented gradient extracted from patches on a regular grid at different scale, such as sift. Commonly used feature encoding strategies are hard assignment, locality-constrained linear coding (LLC) [40], and supper vector coding (SVC) [47]. Note that we use SQ to replace traditional feature encoding strategies. The dictionary A is typically generated using either unsupervised or supervised learning algorithms [24]. We use max-pooling in spatial pyramids that yields $\boldsymbol{x}$ binary vectors. Finally, either SVM or NNC can be used to recognize objects. The whole visual recognition algorithm flowchart is shown in Fig. 5.8.

Local Image description using SQ: Local image description plays a crucial role in visual recognition tasks. The patch description framework consists of three fundamental steps: extracting local features, encoding local features, and spatial pooling. The flowchart is illustrated in Fig. 5.9.

5.6 Hashed Sparse Representation

5.6.1 Hash Functions

Let us first give the definition of *hash function*.

Definition 5.6.1 (*Hash Function* [27]) **Hash functions** are mapping features of arbitrary size to fixed size, with slight differences in input features producing very big differences in output features. The output features are called hash values or hash codes.

Definition 5.6.2 (*Hashed Sparse Representation*) **Hashed Sparse Representation** is to find L subspaces which can be used to linearly represent y by L subdictionary A_j from A, where $A = [A_1, A_2, A_3, \dots, A_L]$.

If there are L allowable active sets of coefficients (the index of coefficients that allowed to be nonzero), and some hash function $g : \mathbb{R}^D \rightarrow \{1, \dots, L\}$ that map the input $\boldsymbol{y}$ to one of the L configurations, we can use this function to find the subspace of the input $\boldsymbol{y}$, and the sparse representation problem is equivalent to the *least-square* problem. The problem is how to find the hash function to map the input $\boldsymbol{y}$ to its linear expressing subspace? We will give the answer in the next subsection.

5.6.2 Structured Dictionary Learning

Considering N d-dimensional real vectors $Y = [y_1, y_2, y_3, \dots, y_N]$, N K-dimensional vectors $X = [x_1, x_2, x_3, \dots, x_N]$, and a $d \times K$ dictionary matrix A, we formulate the dictionary learning as

$$\underset{A,X}{\operatorname{argmin}} \sum_k \left(\frac{1}{2} \|\boldsymbol{y}_k - A\boldsymbol{x}_k\|_{\ell_2}^2 + \lambda \|\boldsymbol{x}_k\|_{\ell_1} \right), \tag{5.68}$$

where $\boldsymbol{X}$ are all the sparse representations of all the training data $\boldsymbol{Y}$. Sometimes only, the sparsity constraint cannot capture the data characteristics, so, it may add more regularization terms in the object function to describe the prior knowledge. If the data has both the sparsity and group structure, we can formulate the dictionary learning problem as

$$\underset{A,X}{\operatorname{argmin}} \sum_k \left(\frac{1}{2} \|\boldsymbol{y}_k - A\boldsymbol{x}_k\|_{\ell_2}^2 + \lambda_1 \sum_{g \in \mathcal{G}} \|\boldsymbol{x}_{[g]}\|_{\ell_2} + \lambda_2 \|\boldsymbol{x}_k\|_{\ell_1} \right), \tag{5.69}$$

where $\mathcal{G}$ is the group set, and $[g]$ is the corresponding index set of group g. So, we can generalize the dictionary problem as

$$\underset{A,X}{\operatorname{argmin}} \sum_k \left(\frac{1}{2} \|\boldsymbol{y}_k - A\boldsymbol{x}_k\|_{\ell_2}^2 + \beta(\boldsymbol{x}_k) \right), \tag{5.70}$$

where $\beta(\boldsymbol{x})$ is the structure regularization term, which combines the prior knowledge of the data. We can solve this problem in an alternate iteration way. First, compute the sparse representation of all the training data X^t by knowing the dictionary A^t. Second, updating the dictionary to get A^{t+1} by X^t. For the dictionary update stage, we need to solve the optimization problem as

Table 5.7 The structured dictionary learning algorithm

Input: The training data $\boldsymbol{Y}$, the parameter Θ_0;
Output: Dictionary A and sparse representation $\boldsymbol{X}$;
Initialize: A^0 by random sampling from the training data or K-means from the training data, t=0
While (not convergence)
Fix A^t update $\boldsymbol{X}^t$ by solving the convex optimization problem for every element in $\boldsymbol{Y}$

$$\underset{\boldsymbol{x}_k}{\operatorname{argmin}} \frac{1}{2}\|\boldsymbol{y}_k - A\boldsymbol{x}_k\|_{\ell_2}^2 + \beta(\boldsymbol{x}_k). \tag{5.72}$$

Fix X^t update A^{t+1} by solving the problem

$$\underset{A}{\operatorname{argmin}} \|\boldsymbol{Y} - A\boldsymbol{X}\|_F^2. \tag{5.73}$$

End while
Return: dictionary A and sparse code $\boldsymbol{X}$ of the training data $\boldsymbol{Y}$.

$$\underset{A}{\operatorname{argmin}} \|\boldsymbol{Y} - A\boldsymbol{X}\|_F^2. \tag{5.71}$$

We can solve it by K-SVD [29], coordinate descent method [23], and so on. The flowchart of the structured dictionary learning is illustrated in Table 5.7.

5.6.3 Hashing and Dictionary Learning

1. Structured dictionary learning

If we already have the L overlapping active groups $\{G_1, \ldots, G_L\}$. The dictionary A is combined by N column vectors. So, we can get $G_i \in \mathscr{P}(\{1, \ldots, N\})$, where $\mathscr{P}(\{1, \ldots, N\})$ are the subsets of $\{1, \ldots, N\}$. So, as the dictionary learning process which has been mentioned above, after initializing the dictionary, we need to compute the sparse coding of every training data. We denote $P_{G_i}\boldsymbol{y}$ as the project $\boldsymbol{y}$ on to the span of A_{G_i} for each i. The sparse coding process finds the best span of A_{G_i} to represent the data $\boldsymbol{y}$, which is formulated as

$$i = \arg \min_{\hat{i} \in \{1,\ldots,L\}} \|P_{G_{\hat{i}}}\boldsymbol{y} - \boldsymbol{y}\|_{\ell_2}^2. \tag{5.74}$$

So, we can get the coefficients corresponding to the index G_i as

$$\boldsymbol{x}_{G_i} = (A_{G_i}^T A_{G_i})^{-1} A_{G_i}^T \boldsymbol{y}, \tag{5.75}$$

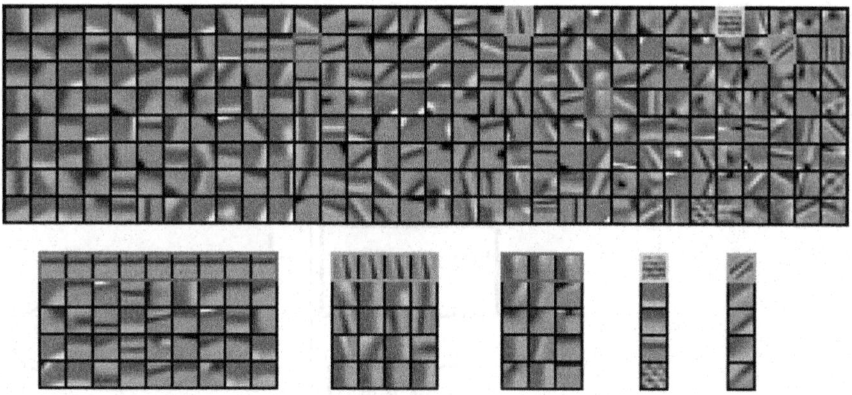

Fig. 5.10 The trained dictionary and groups [35]

and let the coefficients corresponding to index except G_i are all zeros. So, in this way we can compute all the sparse codes of the training set $\boldsymbol{Y}$. Then we can update the dictionary by convex problem

$$A^{new} = \arg\min_{A} \sum_{i} \|A\boldsymbol{x}_i - \boldsymbol{y}_i\|_{\ell_2}^2, \tag{5.76}$$

and repeat until its convergence. Although, we know how to learn the dictionary by knowing the group list, there are some questions. (1) How to group the data which is in the same group in the training data? (2) How to decide the group list? and (3) How to efficiently decide the group which the data belong to?

This dictionary (Fig. 5.10) is trained from 500,000 of 8×8 image patches. The dictionary has 256 elements, which is trained by K-SVD, and have trained 512 groups; each group has 5 dictionary elements in it [35]. The dictionary shown on top are ordered by popularity (the number of groups they belong to). Underneath, we show all the groups which contain the dictionary elements in color square. We can see the groups as "topics." Less popular elements can be seen as more special words.

Because we can save the group list and the corresponding pseudo-inverse matrix $(A_{G_i}^T A_{G_i})^{-1} A_{G_i}^T$ into the leaf node, the sparse coding computation complexity for every input vector only need $O(q + KD)$.

5.6.4 Flowchart of Algorithm

The flowchart of algorithm is illustrated in Fig. 5.11. We can see from the figure that after training, we do not need too many computation to get the sparse representation. We only need mapping the input to its group by searching from the retrieval tree and computing the matrix-vector product.

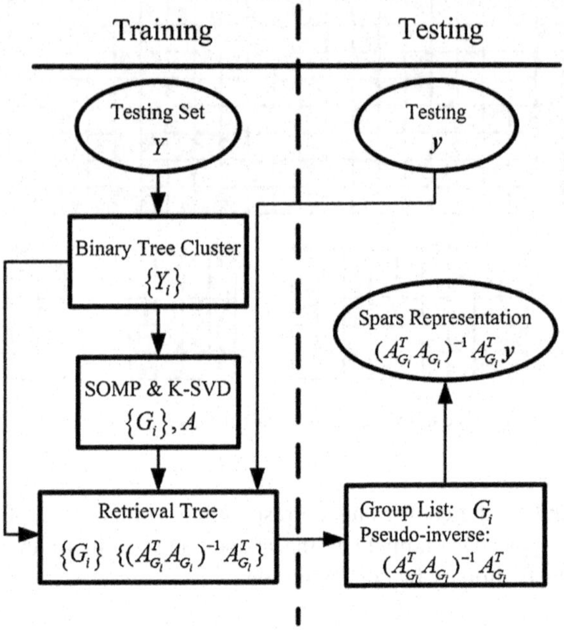

Fig. 5.11 The flowchart of hashed sparse representation

5.7 Compressive Feature

5.7.1 Generating Compressive

As shown in Fig. 2.3, each element v_i in low-dimensional feature $v \in \mathbb{R}^n$ is a linear combination of spatially distributed rectangle features. The way which the compressive features are computed is similar to the generalized Haar-like features [1]. By using the sparse measurement matrix to compress feature, we can alleviate the computational load of the Haar-like features. The compressive sensing theories ensure that the extracted features of our algorithm preserve almost all the information of the original image [46].

5.7.2 Applications

1. Visual Tracking

Zhang et al. used the compressed features in the real-time tracking problem, and get very good performance. As we know, $v \in \mathbb{R}^n$ is the low-dimensional representation of the original sample $z \in \mathbb{R}^m$ with $m \gg n$. With the assumption that v are independently distributed, we can model the tracking classifier with naive Bayes methods [20],

$$H(\mathbf{v}) = \log\left(\frac{\prod_{i=1}^{n} p(v_i|y=1)p(y=1)}{\prod_{i=1}^{n} p(v_i|y=0)p(y=0)}\right) = \sum_{i=1}^{n} \log\left(\frac{p(v_i|y=1)}{p(v_i|y=0)}\right), \quad (5.77)$$

where they assume uniform prior, $p(y=1) = p(y=0)$, and $y \in \{0, 1\}$ is a binary variable which represents the sample label. The conditional distribution of likelihood $p(v_i|y=1)$ and $p(v_i|y=0)$ in classifier $H(\mathbf{v})$ are assumed to obey the Gaussian distribution with parameters $(\mu_i^1, \sigma_i^1, \mu_i^0, \sigma_i^0)$ where

$$p(v_i|y=1) \sim N(\mu_i^1, \sigma_i^1), \qquad p(v_i|y=0) \sim N(\mu_i^0, \sigma_i^0). \quad (5.78)$$

The parameters in the Eq. (5.78) are updated as follows:

$$\mu_i^1 \leftarrow \lambda\mu_i^1 + (1+\lambda)\mu^1 \quad (5.79)$$

$$\sigma_i^1 \leftarrow \sqrt{\lambda(\sigma_i^1)^2 + (1-\lambda)(\sigma^1)^2 + \lambda(1-\lambda)(\mu_i^1 - \mu^1)^2}, \quad (5.80)$$

where λ is a learning rate parameter, $\mu^1 = \frac{1}{n_1}\sum_{k=1}^{n_1} v_i(k)$, $\sigma^1 = \sqrt{\frac{1}{n_1}\sum_{k=1}^{n_1}(v_i(k)-\mu^1)^2}$ and n_1 is the number of sample with index $y = 1$. The compressive tracking algorithm is summarized in Table 5.8.

2. Background Modeling

Yang et al. [45] used the compressive feature into background modeling and proposed Pixel-to-Model (P2M) method in crowed scenes background modeling. The whole framework of P2M background modeling method is illustrated in Fig. 5.12.

Table 5.8 Compressive tracking algorithm [46]

Input: t^{th} video frame

1) Sample a set of image patches, $A^{\gamma} = \{z| \|\mathbf{l}(z) - \mathbf{l}_{t-1}\| < \gamma\}$ where $\mathbf{l}_{t-1}$ is the tracking location at the $(t-1)^{th}$ frame, and extract the features with low dimensionality.
2) Use classifier H in Eqn. (5.77) to each feature vector $\mathbf{v}(z)$ and find the tracking location $\mathbf{l}_t$ with the maximal classifier response.
3) Sample two sets of image patches $A^{\alpha} = \{z| \|\mathbf{l}(z)\| < \alpha\}$ and $A^{\zeta,\beta} = \{z|\zeta < \|\mathbf{l}(z) - \mathbf{l}\| < \beta\}$ with $\alpha < \zeta < \beta$.
4) Extract the Features with these two sets of samples and update the classifier parameters according to Eqn. (5.79) and Eqn. (5.80)

Output: tracking location $\mathbf{l}_t$ and classifier parameters

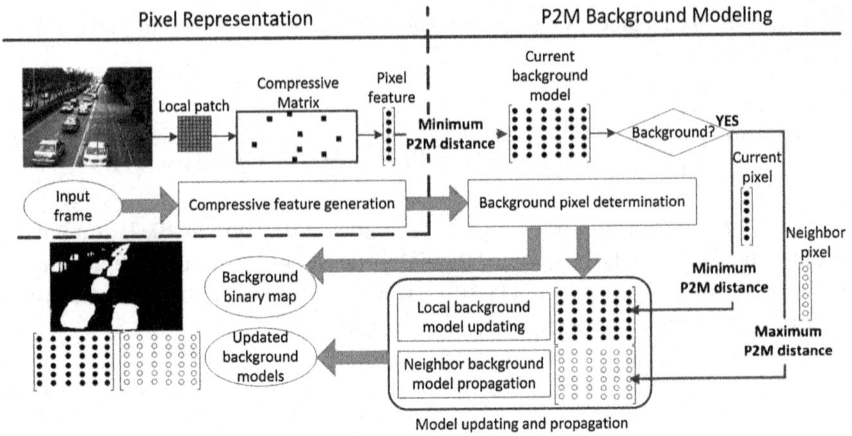

Fig. 5.12 The overview of proposed P2M background modeling framework [45]

In [45], the background model $M(x_i)$ of pixel x_i with index i is modeled by a collection of N context features $\{\boldsymbol{v}_k\}$ as

$$\boldsymbol{M}(x_i) = \{\boldsymbol{v}_1(x_i), \ldots, \boldsymbol{v}_k(x_i), \ldots, \boldsymbol{v}_N(x_i)\} \tag{5.81}$$

where each $\boldsymbol{v}_k$ is a Haar-like feature generated by projecting original surrounding patch $\boldsymbol{p}_k \in \mathbb{R}^m$ to a compressive low-dimensional space $\mathbb{R}^n$ as

$$\boldsymbol{v}_k = \boldsymbol{A}\boldsymbol{p}_k \tag{5.82}$$

Here we follow [46] and employ a sparse random matrix $\boldsymbol{A} \in \mathbb{R}^{n\times m}(n < m)$ for extracting the Haar-like feature from the surrounding patch $\boldsymbol{p}_k$ of pixel x_i (see the upper-left block of Fig. 5.12). The matrix $\boldsymbol{A}$ is pre-computed and will be kept fixed throughout the background modeling.

As illustrated in Fig. 5.13, each element v_{kl} of the generated feature is a local descriptor of the surrounding patch. Hence, the sample of each background model incorporates not only self pixel value but also context information. Note that the proposed model does not strictly constrain the similarity between neighboring pixels, which is not always reasonable for crowded scenes. Instead, we extend the pixel-wise values to region-level descriptors and allow the background pixel with dynamic contexts to better treat the uncertain dynamics of crowded scenes.

After pixel representation by compressive context feature with local descriptors, we need to determine whether current pixel x_i is a background pixel or not. Background subtraction can be considered as a classification problem and we want to determine x_i by classifying its current context feature with respect to the background model $\boldsymbol{M}(x_i)$. If x_i is classified as a background pixel, it will have a chance to update $\boldsymbol{M}(x_i)$. Moreover, it will also help updating the neighboring background

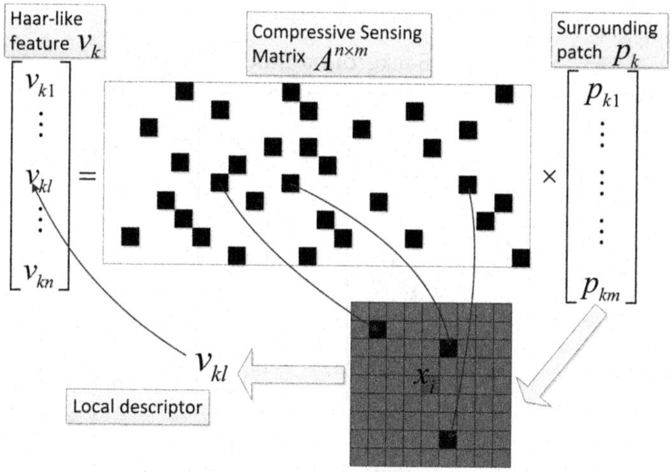

Fig. 5.13 The compressive pixel representation [45]

model $\boldsymbol{M}(x_j)$ to reconstruct the potential ghost hole in backgrounds (see right and bottom parts of Fig. 5.12).

Background Classification and Updating with Minimum P2M Distance

Previous works [2, 16] considered the similarity between one pixel value and each sample pixel value in the background model. Then if the number of matched sample pixels exceeds the threshold, it will be treated as a background pixel. They belong to pixel-to-pixel comparison approaches, which do not fully use the context information especially in crowded scenes, where the background pixel value may be not stable in color space. The generated local descriptors in Sect. 3 ensemble context information and are robust to environmental changes. The only problem is how to measure the similarity between the pixel and the background model. Inspired by the image-to-class nearest neighbor searching method, we propose the P2M distance calculated in terms of local descriptors to classify the pixel (see Fig. 5.14).

Let v_i denote the context feature of the determining pixel x_i, which is generated by Eq. (5.82). We define the minimum P2M distance between x_i and $\boldsymbol{M}(x_i)$ as

$$Min\_P2M(x_i, \boldsymbol{M}(x_i)) = \sum_{l=1}^{n} \min_{k\in\{1,2,\cdots,N\}} (v_{il} - v_{kl})^2 \tag{5.83}$$

where v_{il} and v_{kl} are the lth local descriptors in v_i and v_k, respectively.

Now, we can classify the pixel x_i by simply thresholding $Min\_P2M(x_i, \boldsymbol{M}(x_i))$. Then, we could update $\boldsymbol{M}(x_i)$ if x_i is a background pixel. We want to continuously populate the model to adapt to environmental changes. Hence, we assume that context descriptor v_{il} of background pixel x_i represents the most recent background information and can substitute its "nearest" counterpart as

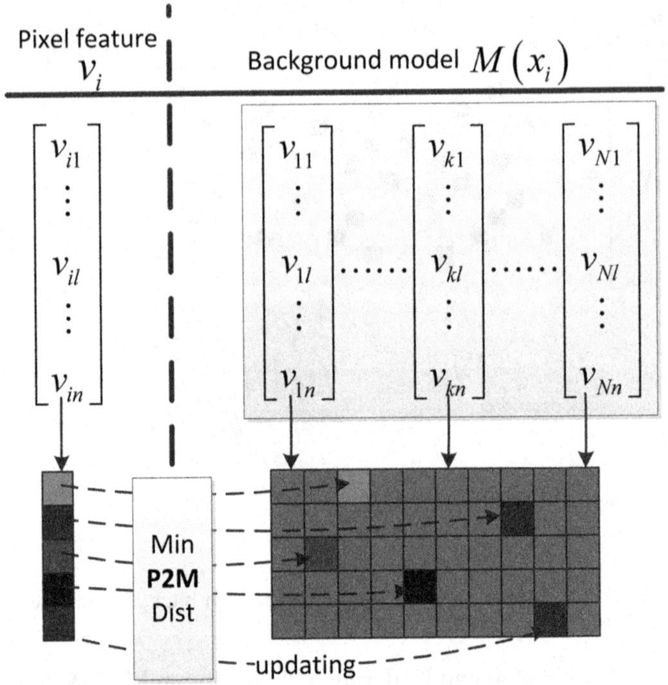

Fig. 5.14 Minimum P2M distance

$$v_{kl}^{new} = v_{il}, \; k = \underset{k \in \{1,2,\cdots,N\}}{\operatorname{argmin}} (v_{il} - v_{kl})^2 \tag{5.84}$$

where v_{kl}^{new} is the new descriptor updated by replacing the "nearest" descriptor v_{kl} in the background model $\boldsymbol{M}(x_i)$.

The classification and updating procedures are shown in Fig. 5.14. Instead of randomly replacing sample features which may erroneously remove valid information, model updating with minimum P2M distance can substitute the local descriptors in a smooth and fine way. It keeps our background model handling the newest context change with a smooth lifespan.

Background Propagation with Maximum P2M Distance

As mentioned in [2], it is reasonable to propagate the background information to the neighborhood since neighboring pixels are expected to have the similar properties. This propagation can help exploiting backgrounds uncovered by start moving foreground. We adopt this strategy to reconstruct the ghost holes caused by that motion phenomenon. Unlike [2] and [16] in which the chosen neighboring background model is updated in pixel-level, we update the neighboring background model according to the maximum P2M distance in the space of local descriptor. Similar to the minimum P2M distance in Eq. (5.83), the maximum P2M distance can be defined between the neighboring pixel x_j and its background model $\boldsymbol{M}(x_j)$ as

$$Max\_P2M(x_j, \boldsymbol{M}(x_j)) = \sum_{l=1}^{n} \max_{k\in\{1,2,\cdots,N\}} (v_{jl} - v_{kl})^2 \tag{5.85}$$

where x_j is the randomly chosen neighboring pixel of background pixel x_i. v_{kl} is the lth local descriptor in v_k of $\boldsymbol{M}(x_j)$.

The maximum P2M distance is the proper measure to speed up the updating of $\boldsymbol{M}(x_j)$. We can replace the potential "bad" descriptors which belong to the leaving objects by uncovered background descriptors as

$$v_{kl}^{new} = v_{jl},\ k = \underset{k\in\{1,2,\cdots,N\}}{\operatorname{argmax}} (v_{jl} - v_{kl})^2 \tag{5.86}$$

By doing so, we can achieve the fast reconstruction of ghost holes. Note that the erosion of foreground boundaries would be helpful since shadows around can be partially suppressed. The maximum P2M distance is illustrated in Fig. 5.15.

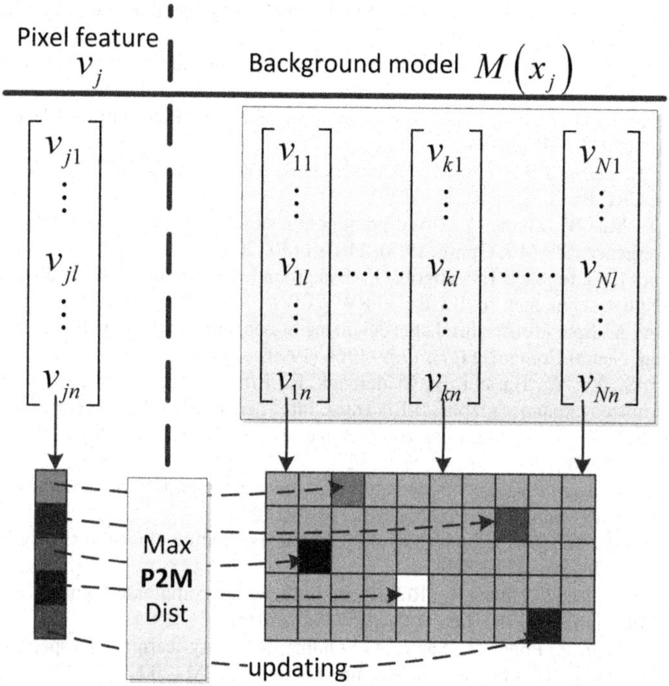

Fig. 5.15 Maximum P2M distance

References

1. Babenko, B., Yang, M.H., Belongie, S.: Robust object tracking with online multiple instance learning. IEEE Trans. Pattern Anal. Mach. Intell. **33**(8), 1619–1632 (2011)
2. Barnich, O., Van Droogenbroeck, M.: ViBe: a universal background subtraction algorithm for video sequences. IEEE TIP **20**(6), 1709–1724 (2011)
3. Baron, D., Sarvotham, S., Baraniuk, R.G.: Bayesian compressive sensing via belief propagation. IEEE Trans. Signal Process. **58**(1), 269–280 (2010)
4. Bishop, C.M., Nasrabadi, N.M.: Pattern Recognition and Machine Learning, vol. 1. Springer, New York (2006)
5. Boix, X., Gygli, M., Roig, G., Van Gool, L.: Sparse quantization for patch description. In: IEEE CVPR (2013)
6. Boix, X., Roig, G., Leistner, C., Van Gool, L.: Nested sparse quantization for efficient feature coding. In: ECCV. Springer, Berlin (2012)
7. Chen, S.S., Donoho, D.L., Saunders, M.A.: Atomic decomposition by basis pursuit. SIAM Rev. **43**(1), 129–159 (2001)
8. Cheng, H., Liu, Z., Yang, L.: Sparsity induced similarity measure for label propagation. In: IEEE ICCV (2009)
9. Cooper, G.F.: The computational complexity of probabilistic inference using bayesian belief networks. Artif. Intell. **42**(2), 393–405 (1990)
10. Deng, J., Dong, W., Socher, R., Li, L.J., Li, K., Fei-Fei, L.: Imagenet: a large-scale hierarchical image database. In: IEEE CVPR (2009)
11. Felzenszwalb, P.F., Huttenlocher, D.P.: Efficient belief propagation for early vision. Int. J. Comput. Vis. **70**(1), 41–54 (2006)
12. Figueiredo, M.: Adaptive sparseness using Jeffreys prior. In: Advances in Neural Information Processing Systems (2001)
13. Gao, T., Koller, D.: Discriminative learning of relaxed hierarchy for large-scale visual recognition. In: IEEE ICCV (2011)
14. Gelman, A., Carlin, J.B., Stern, H.S., Dunson, D.B., Vehtari, A., Rubin, D.B.: Bayesian Data Analysis. CRC Press, Boca Raton (2013)
15. Hale, E.T., Yin, W., Zhang, Y.: Fixed-point continuation for ℓ_1-minimization: methodology and convergence. SIAM J. Optim. **19**(3), 1107–1130 (2008)
16. Hofmann, M., Tiefenbacher, P., Rigoll, G.: Background segmentation with feedback: the pixel-based adaptive segmenter. In: IEEE CVPRW (2012)
17. Hyvärinen, A.: Sparse code shrinkage: denoising of nongaussian data by maximum likelihood estimation. Neural Comput. **11**(7), 1739–1768 (1999)
18. Jafarpour, S., Xu, W., Hassibi, B., Calderbank, R.: Efficient and robust compressed sensing using optimized expander graphs. IEEE Trans. Inf. Theory **55**(9), 4299–4308 (2009)
19. Ji, S., Xue, Y., Carin, L.: Bayesian compressive sensing. IEEE Trans. Signal Process. **56**(6), 2346–2356 (2008)
20. Jordan, A.: On discriminative vs. generative classifiers: a comparison of logistic regression and naive bayes. Adv. Neural Inf. Process. Syst. **14**, 841 (2002)
21. Lee, H., Battle, A., Raina, R., Ng, A.: Efficient sparse coding algorithms. Adv. Neural Inf. Process. Syst. **19**, 801–808 (2006)
22. Li, F., Fang, J., Li, H., Huang, L.: Robust one-bit bayesian compressed sensing with sign-flip errors. IEEE Signal Process. Lett. **22**(7), 857–861 (2015)
23. Mairal, J., Bach, F., Ponce, J., Sapiro, G.: Online dictionary learning for sparse coding. In: Annual International Conference on Machine Learning. ACM (2009)
24. Moosmann, F., Triggs, B., Jurie, F., et al.: Fast discriminative visual codebooks using randomized clustering forests. Adv. Neural Inf. Process. Syst. **19**, 985–992 (2007)
25. Needell, D., Tropp, J.A.: CoSaMP: iterative signal recovery from incomplete and inaccurate samples. Appl. Comput. Harmon. Anal. **26**(3), 301–321 (2009)

26. Pati, Y.C., Rezaiifar, R., Krishnaprasad, P.: Orthogonal matching pursuit: recursive function approximation with applications to wavelet decomposition. In: IEEE Conference on Signals, Systems and Computers (1993)
27. Rogaway, P., Shrimpton, T.: Cryptographic hash-function basics: definitions, implications, and separations for preimage resistance, second-preimage resistance, and collision resistance. In: Fast Software Encryption (2004)
28. Rubinstein, R., Bruckstein, A.M., Elad, M.: Dictionaries for sparse representation modeling. Proc. IEEE **98**(6), 1045–1057 (2010)
29. Rubinstein, R., Zibulevsky, M., Elad, M.: Efficient implementation of the K-SVD algorithm using batch orthogonal matching pursuit. CS Tech. **40**(8), 1–15 (2008)
30. Shen, Y., Duan, H., Fang, J., Li, H.: Pattern-coupled sparse bayesian learning for recovery of block-sparse signals. IEEE Trans. Signal Process. **63**(2), 360–372 (2015)
31. Sigal, L., Bhatia, S., Roth, S., Black, M.J., Isard, M.: Tracking loose-limbed people. In: IEEE CVPR (2004)
32. Sturm, B.L., Christensen, M.G.: Comparison of orthogonal matching pursuit implementations. In: Proceedings of Eusipco (2012)
33. Sudderth, E.B., Ihler, A.T., Isard, M., Freeman, W.T., Willsky, A.S.: Nonparametric belief propagation. Commun. ACM **53**(10), 95–103 (2010)
34. Sun, J., Zheng, N.N., Shum, H.Y.: Stereo matching using belief propagation. IEEE Trans. Pattern Anal. Mach. Intell. **25**(7), 787–800 (2003)
35. Szlam, A., Gregor, K., LeCun, Y.: Fast approximations to structured sparse coding and applications to object classification. In: ECCV. Springer, Berlin (2012)
36. Tipping, A., Faul, A.: Analysis of sparse bayesian learning. In: Proceedings of the Conference on Neural Information Processing Systems (2002)
37. Tipping, M.E.: Sparse Bayesian learning and the relevance vector machine. J. Mach. Learn. Res. **1**, 211–244 (2001)
38. Tipping, M.E., Faul, A.C., et al.: Fast marginal likelihood maximisation for sparse bayesian models. In: International Workshop on Artificial Intelligence and Statistics (2003)
39. Tropp, J.A., Gilbert, A.C.: Signal recovery from random measurements via orthogonal matching pursuit. IEEE Trans. Inf. Theory **53**(12), 4655–4666 (2007)
40. Wang, J., Yang, J., Yu, K., Lv, F., Huang, T., Gong, Y.: Locality-constrained linear coding for image classification. In: IEEE CVPR (2010)
41. Wen, Z., Yin, W., Goldfarb, D., Zhang, Y.: A fast algorithm for sparse reconstruction based on shrinkage, subspace optimization, and continuation. SIAM J. Sci. Comput. **32**(4), 1832–1857 (2010)
42. Wen, Z., Yin, W., Zhang, H., Goldfarb, D.: On the convergence of an active-set method for ℓ_1-minimization. Optim. Methods Softw. **27**(6), 1127–1146 (2012)
43. Wipf, D.P., Rao, B.D.: Sparse bayesian learning for basis selection. IEEE Trans. Signal Process. **52**(8), 2153–2164 (2004)
44. Wright, J., Yang, A.Y., Ganesh, A., Sastry, S.S., Ma, Y.: Robust face recognition via sparse representation. IEEE Trans. Pattern Anal. Mach. Intell. **31**(2), 210–227 (2009)
45. Yang, L., Cheng, H., Su, J., Chen, X.: Pixel-to-model background modeling in crowded scenes. In: IEEE International Conference on Multimedia and Expo (2014)
46. Zhang, K., Zhang, L., Yang, M.H.: Real-time compressive tracking. In: ECCV. Springer, Berlin (2012)
47. Zhou, X., Yu, K., Zhang, T., Huang, T.S.: Image classification using super-vector coding of local image descriptors. In: ECCV. Springer, Heidelberg (2010)
48. Zhou, Z., Liu, K., Fang, J.: Bayesian compressive sensing using normal product priors. IEEE Signal Process. Lett. **22**(5), 583–587 (2015)

Part III
Visual Recognition Applications

Chapter 6
Feature Representation and Learning

6.1 Introduction

Visual recognition is a significant challenge due to high variability of objects. A typical recognizing system consists of feature extraction, learning and object classification. Here, feature representation and learning play a really important role for achieving state-of-the-art recognition performance. Sparse representation is widely used in feature representation and learning [36, 51, 62]. There are many kinds of features for images/videos, such as global features (e.g., GIST [52]), patch-based features (e.g., Histogram of Gradient (HOG) [13], scale-invariant feature transformation (SIFT), and its variants [10, 37]).

In principal, feature representation can be considered as dimensionality reduction to remove irrelative noise and overcomplete features. There are three main techniques of feature representation and learning, i.e., feature extraction, dictionary learning, and feature learning. First of all, feature extraction is to transform raw features (e.g., pixel intensity) into new features with lower dimensions, such as principal component analysis (PCA), linear discriminant learning (LDA), singular value decomposition (SVD), and canonical correlation analysis (CCA). Moreover, feature learning is a set of techniques in machine learning that learns a mapping from original feature to another feature space. Feature learning could be either unsupervised or supervised, and may be implemented either separately or by combining with classifiers (e.g., SVM [76], SVM-RFE [16]). Feature representation and learning can be unified using sparse learning such as ℓ_1/ℓ_0 regularization [46]. Under this assumption, visual recognition follows a sparse decomposition with some dictionary; dictionary learning has recently drawn much attention in computer vision and signal processing.

H. Cheng, *Sparse Representation, Modeling and Learning in Visual Recognition*, Advances in Computer Vision and Pattern Recognition,
DOI 10.1007/978-1-4471-6714-3_6

6.2 Feature Extraction

The performance of Bag-of-Features (BoFs) approach is limited by the presence of uninformative features from the background or irrelevant objects. In [51], Naikal et al. proposed a method to select informative object features using Sparse PCA. In BoFs models, let $Y = [y_1, y_2, \ldots, y_n] \in \mathbb{R}^{D \times n}$ denote the training data matrix, where y_i is the histogram of training image i. Sparse Principal Component Analysis (SPCA) can obtain the first sparse eigenvector of $\Sigma_Y = \frac{1}{n} Y Y^T$ by optimizing the following objective function [78]

$$\hat{x} = \arg\min_{x} x^T \Sigma_A x, \text{ s.t. } \|x\|_{\ell_2} = 1, \|x\|_{\ell_1} \leq K. \tag{6.1}$$

The indices of the nonzero coefficients in $\hat{x}$ will be used in visual recognition, which are referred in [51]. Using Hotelling's deflation that eliminates the influence of the first sparse principal vector (PV), we can obtain the second sparse eigenvector $\hat{x}'$. In Naikal's experiments, the first two sparse PVs are sufficient for selecting informative features.

Although many recently developed feature representation models are powerful for visual recognition, some models are hard to train. Restricted Boltzmann Machines (RBMs) have good expressive power and can be used to build effective image representation. However, the training of RBMs is difficult. To address this problem, Sohn et al. [63] showed the connections between mixture models and RBMs and presented an efficient training algorithm for RBMs that utilized these connections. Moreover, they proposed the convolutional RBM which can capture larger spatial contexts and reduce the redundancy of feature representation. In addition, Wang et al. proposed RSPCA approach to solve the outlier problem by modeling the sparse coding as a sparsity-constrained weighted regression problem [67].

6.2.1 Feature Representation Using Sparse Coding

1. Histogram of Sparse Codes for Object Detection

Learning local image representations have drawn much attention in visual recognition. Therefore, many-hand engineered local descriptors have been developed, such as histogram of oriented gradients, scale-invariant feature transform. Moreover, sparse coding is a popular way to represent local images [6, 57]. We shall present a basic local image description using histogram sparse coding (Fig. 6.1).

Histograms of oriented gradients (HOG) are very effective and popular in visual object detection and recognition [13, 37]. In principal, HOG uses gradient orientations to represent local patches. By contrast, Histogram of Sparse Codes (HSC) resembles HOG, but it uses sparse coding and K-SVD techniques. Moreover, HSC consists of two basic molecules, dictionary learning and histogram generation.

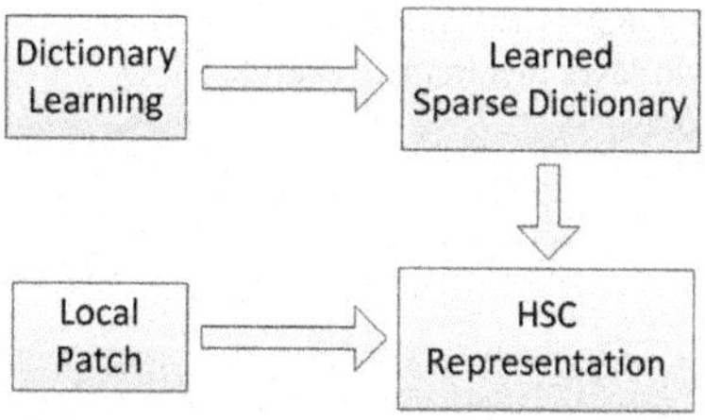

Fig. 6.1 The framework of generating histogram of sparse coding (HSC) representation

The dictionary is learned using K-SVD approach in an unsupervised manner. Afterward, per-pixel sparse codes are calculated in one patch using the learned dictionary, and histogram representation of the patch is used to aggregate the codes into the learned dictionary. Note that a new sparse coding strategy is used in HSC as

$$[|x_i|, \max\{x_i, 0\}, \max\{-x_i, 0\}],$$

where x_i is the sparse code of codeword i.

2. Convolutional Sparse Feature Coding

Learning multiple levels of feature representation in a hierarchical way is an important step in visual recognition systems. Traditional dictionary learning ignores the coded patch which works well with a dictionary in a convolutional fashion. kavukcuoglu et al. proposed feature learning techniques through convolutional filter banks [25]. By doing so, the redundancy of the image representation is greatly reduced. Furthermore, a fast approximation of the sparse code is used to improve the computational complexity due to patch-level inference.

Mathematically, the sparse coding of the image is formulated as

$$L(y, x, D) = \frac{1}{2}\|y - \sum_{m=1}^{M} D_m * x_m\|_{\ell_2}^2 + \|x\|_{\ell_1}, \tag{6.2}$$

where $\mathbf{D}_m$ is a 2D filter kernel, y is an image, x_m is a 2D feature map, '$*$' denotes the discrete convolution operator. Moreover, for faster approximation of the sparse code, a new optimization equation is used to improve its efficiency by

$$L(y, x, D, W) = \frac{1}{2}\|y - \sum_{m=1}^{M} D_m * x_m\|_{\ell_2}^2 + \sum_{m=1}^{M} \|x_m - f(W^m * y)\|_{\ell_2}^2 + \|x\|_{\ell_1}, \tag{6.3}$$

where $\mathbf{W}^m$ is an encoding convolution kernel, and f is a pointwise nonlinear function.

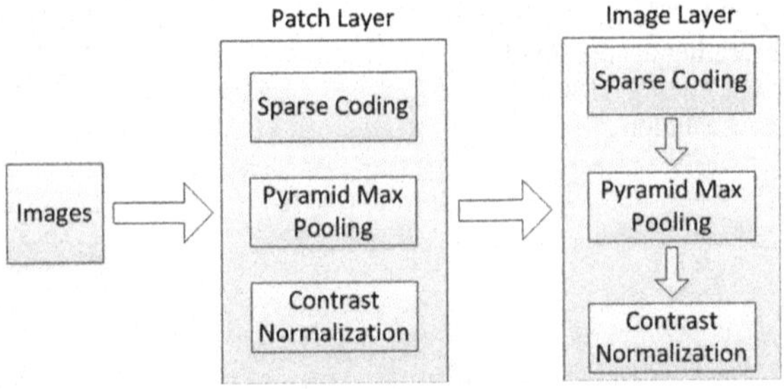

Fig. 6.2 The framework of two-layer hierarchical sparse coding

3. Hierarchical Sparse Coding

Hierarchy is a good strategy for feature representation, which is inspired by human brain [58]. Naturally, hierarchical sparse coding can work well in raw pixel levels [6, 73]. Bo et al. proposed a hierarchical matching pursuit for image classification [6], using orthogonal matching pursuit, shown in Fig. 6.2. This feature representation consists of three modules, e.g., batch orthogonal matching pursuit, spatial pyramid max pooling, and contrast normalization. First, K-SVD is used to learn the dictionary. Then the orthogonal matching pursuit (OMP) is used to compute sparse coefficients. Spatial pyramid max pooling plays an important role in generating histogram representations from sparse codes of raw pixels. Due to illumination variations and foreground-background contrast, large magnitude variation could result in recognition performance degradation. Hence, local contrast normalization is really essential for visual recognition.

Yu et al. proposed a hierarchical sparse coding to adopt the spatial neighborhood structure of the image [73]. The two-layer sparse coding models and the geometry layouts of local patches are shown in Fig. 6.2. The first layer works in single raw patches, while the second layer jointly works in the set of patches belonging to same group.

4. Sparse Code Gradient

Contour detection is a fundamental problem in visual recognition, where globalized probability of boundary (gPb) was originally designed for edge detection by combining local and global cues [44], and was applied in contour detection and image segmentation [3, 45]. Usually, brightness, color, and texture gradients are used in gPb. The gPb is written as

$$gPb(x, y, Q) = mPb + sPb. \tag{6.4}$$

Here mPb denotes multiscale oriented signal as

$$mPb(x, y, Q) = \sum_{i=1}^{P} \alpha_i G_i(x, y, Q), \tag{6.5}$$

where Q is orientation, (x, y) is pixel position, $G_i(.)$ is the ith local cue and α_i is the weight of the ith local cue.

sPb denotes the spectral term of boundaries as

$$sPb(x, y, Q) = \sum_{j=1}^{K} \frac{1}{\sqrt{\lambda_j}} sPb_{v_j}(x, y, Q), \tag{6.6}$$

where λ_j can be interpreted by generalized eigensystems as mass spring systems [44]; sPb_{v_j} is oriented signal w.r.t v_j. For better explaining sPb_{v_j}, affine matrix W, $(k+1)$ generalized eigenvectors $\{v_0, v_1, \ldots, v_k\}$, and the corresponding eigenvalues $\{\lambda_0, \lambda_1, \ldots, \lambda_k\}$ are introduced, similar to those in [60].

In general, gPb is built on a set of gradient features which are computed from local contrast of oriented disks by using chi-square distances of histograms. Those hard-designed gradient features are widely used in various computer vision tasks. Toward this end, a sparse coding gradient is used to replace the hard-designed probability boundary gradients. Then sparse coding gradient features are generated by pooling pixel-level sparse codes over multiscale half-disks for each orientation. The SCG features work very well in contour detection even for RGBD data [56].

6.2.2 Feature Coding and Pooling

In visual recognition tasks, after comprising a feature pooling step, feature coding is used to map local features into a more compact representation based on learned dictionaries. Feature Pooling is aggregating these compact representation together thus forming histogram representations, which collects different feature responses on different codewords. The generated histograms representation means image statistics, and different pooling function construct different image statistics [8]. The commonly used pooling functions are max pooling, average pooling, sum pooling, and others. Boureau et al. presented theoretical justification of feature pooling in visual recognition [8].

The standard sparse coding is written as [70]

$$\underset{U,A}{\text{argmin}} \sum_{m=1}^{M} ||y_m - Au_m||^2 + \lambda|u_m| \quad \text{s.t} \quad \|A_{.k}\| \leq 1, \forall k = 1, 2, \ldots, K, \tag{6.7}$$

where A is a dictionary learned from training samples. After learning A, feature coding is applied to optimize Eq. (6.7) w.r.t U only by using sparse recovery approaches as discussed in Chap. 2. Thus, U are the sparse codes of a local feature set Y. Feature pooling is formulated by

$$Z = F(U), \tag{6.8}$$

where $\mathscr{F}(.)$ is a pooling function on each column of $\mathbf{U}$. As a max pooling function, we have

$$z_j = \max\{|u_{1,j}|, |u_{2,j}|, \ldots, |u_{M,j}|\}, \tag{6.9}$$

where M is the number of local descriptors in one image. An average pooling function is formulated as

$$z_j = \frac{1}{M}\sum_{i=1}^{M} |u_{i,j}|. \tag{6.10}$$

6.2.3 Invariant Features

Most of the features extracted from above sections are designed to work well under controlled environment, where samples are usually captured from the frontal parallel viewpoint with normal poses. However, this assumption is not always true in our practical visual recognition. Therefore, exploring the feature invariance is very important and also attracting much interest of researchers. Note that feature here is highly related to sparse codes so we shall not distinguish feature invariance and sparsity invariance.

1. Scale and Translation Invariant Features: Both scale and translation/shift invariance are very useful property for feature representation since sample features may be shifted and misaligned. Let $Y = [y_1, y_2, \ldots, y_d] \in \mathbb{R}^{D \times n}$ denote image representation, where $\boldsymbol{y}_i$ is the ith local descriptor. Let $A \in \mathbb{R}^{D \times N}$ denote a dictionary. Hence, the sparse representation of a descriptor set are [71]

$$\hat{X} = \mathrm{argmin}_X \|Y - AX\|^2 + \gamma \|X\|_{\ell_1}. \tag{6.11}$$

Furthermore, the max pooling strategy is used to obtain a fixed-length *global pooling feature* as

$$\beta = \xi_{max}(\hat{X}). \tag{6.12}$$

As the authors mentioned that max pooling strategy is critical for the success of many sparse coding model [71]. The feature achieves a trade-off between translation invariance and the spatial information of the local image descriptors. We can combine sparse representation on different scales of spatial cell structures, resulting in a hierarchical model similar to spatial pyramid. Following notations of [71], the image can be modeled in R spatial scales. For each scale s, we divide the image into $2^{s-1} \times 2^{s-1}$ cells. The multiscale feature β is defined as

$$\beta = \bigcup_{s=1}^{R}[\beta^s] = \bigcup_{s=1}^{R}\left[\bigcup_{c=1}^{2^{s-1}} \beta_c^s\right]. \tag{6.13}$$

where β_c^s is feature for the cth spatial cell on the sth scale.

Moreover, Yang et al. [70] used sparse SPM to obtain discriminative features which worked well with a linear SVM. The extracted features were both scale and translation invariant. In [28], Krishnan et al. proposed the scale-invariant sparse representation. The key is the new scale-invariant ℓ_1/ℓ_2 regularizer that compensates for the attenuation of high frequencies, and therefore greatly stabilizes the kernel estimation process. Similarly, Yu et al. [73] proposed the use of two-layer sparse coding scheme at the pixel level. The first level encodes local patches. Codes are then passed to the second codebook, which jointly encodes signals from the region. The resulting hierarchical coding scheme is interpretable and shift-invariant. In [32], Li et al. proposed shift-invariant sparse representation for the modeling of actions. They approximated each time series by sparse linear combinations of shift-invariant sparse features. In these works, MoCap sequences were decomposed into the shift-invariant basis functions and their activations were used as the feature representation in action recognition.

2. Affine Invariant Features: Affine invariant image local features are basic requirements for many rigid object recognition, such as Affine Scale-Invariant Feature Transformation (ASIFT) [49]. However, as indicated by Kulkarni et al. [29], scale and translation invariant features generally work well for objects with similar poses or in cases where similar features for an object class can be generated by normalizing the pose. These features may not work well when sample images have a wide range of pose variations. Kulkarni et al. generated largely affine invariant features through learning a compact dictionary of features from affine-transformed input images. Their affine invariant features are called affine sparse codes and can make features of the same class clustered tightly around its mean. However, like many recognition algorithms, it also requires a large number of raw descriptors to form the high-dimensional features.

3. Expression-Insensitive Features: In sparsity-based face recognition, there is expression variation problem which tends to distort almost all the features of face samples and may compromise the sparse coding. To improve the robustness to expressions, Li et al. [33] designed a feature pooling and ranking scheme which first collects a large set of low level features via a training process, and then ranks them according to their sensitivities to expressions. By choosing higher ranked expression-insensitive features, this recognition algorithm achieves robustness to severe expressions and can be applied to 3D face recognition. Meanwhile, Nagesh et al. [50] used two feature images: one captures the holistic common features of the face, and the other captures the different expressions in all training samples. The expression changes are assumed sparse with respect to the whole image. Both algorithms [33, 50] showed superior performances compared to state-of-the-art face recognition approaches.

One of the classic problems in feature representation and learning is discriminative ability of features. SPCA is a useful way to extract features as well as to preserve the discriminative information. However, the discriminative information still cannot be fully preserved by the merit of PCA since the abandoned components may be discriminative parts (e.g., edges). How to represent features sparsely while preserving discriminative information is still an important challenge. Another important challenge is the invariance of the feature. Although scale, translation, affine, expression invariant features have been developed based on sparse representation, the viewpoint or pose changes still need to be handled.

6.3 Dictionary Learning

The goal of dictionary learning is to learn an effective dictionary from an overcomplete basis feature set specified for visual recognition. Inspired by the human brain strategy [53], sparse representation using only a few codewords of the dictionary has recently drawn more and more researchers in visual recognition [11, 12, 27, 40, 59]. This section shall introduce some of the latest approaches about dictionary learning, including online dictionary learning, discriminative dictionary learning, joints dictionary learning, supervised dictionary learning, and other tasks.

Following notations in [59], the sparse representation problem for dictionary learning can be formulated as

$$\underset{A,X}{\text{argmin}} \ \frac{1}{N}\sum_{n=1}^{N}(\frac{1}{2}\|y_n - Ax_n\|_2^2 + P(x_n, \lambda)), \tag{6.14}$$

where A is the "Dictionary" and X is the N sparsity vectors. $P(\beta_i, \lambda)$ is the penalty or regularization constraint of $\lambda\|x_i\|_{\ell_1}$ to produce sparse representation.

Generally, A, x can be alternatively optimized. When A is fixed, the problem is called sparse coding and the model with ℓ_1 is the equivalence of LASSO model. When X is fixed, we need to optimize A using the classical first-order projected stochastic gradient descent algorithm such as the Newton method. As we know, most existing approaches apply ℓ_0/ℓ_1 constraint in the sparse decomposition for dictionary learning. However, ℓ_1 penalty may cause overpenalization.

6.3.1 K-SVD

1. K-means algorithm for vector quantization problem

First, we shall introduce the K-means algorithm because the K-SVD is the generalization of K-means. The dictionary of VQ problem is trained by K-means algorithm. The dictionary or codebook is denoted as $A = [A_{.1}, A_{.2}, \ldots, A_{.N}]$, every column of the dictionary is called the codeword. When A is given, each signal is represented by its closest codeword. The problem can be formulated as

$$\underset{x}{\text{argmin}} \ \|y - Ax\|_{\ell_2}^2 \quad \text{s.t.} \quad x = e_j \text{ for some } j. \tag{6.15}$$

The formulation obtains coding vectors in which each of them has only one element with 1 and the other elements are zeros. This is the extreme situation of sparse coding which only allows one nonzero coding coefficient, and the coefficient is force to 1. Given the training data $\boldsymbol{Y} = \{\boldsymbol{y}_i\}_{i=1}^n$, the overall MSE is

$$E = \sum_{i=1}^{n} \|y_i - Ax_i\|_{\ell_2}^2 = \|Y - AX\|_F^2. \tag{6.16}$$

The training step in VQ problem is using the training data to find the optimal codebook A, which can be formulated as

$$\min_{A,X} \left\{ \|Y - AX\|_F^2 \right\} \quad \text{s.t.} \quad x_i = e_j \text{ for some } j. \tag{6.17}$$

The K-means algorithm is an iterative method which is used to train the codebook for VQ. There are two central steps: (1) when the dictionary is fixed, update the codes X; (2) when coding step is done, use the codes to update the codebook. The K-means algorithm is summarized in Table 6.1.

K-SVD for sparse representation

The sparse representation problem can be viewed as the generalization of the VQ, where the input is expressed by linear combination of the columns of the dictionary. The problem can be formulated as

$$\min_{A,X} \left\{ \|Y - AX\|_F^2 \right\} \quad \text{s.t.} \quad \forall i, \|x_i\|_{\ell_0} \le K. \tag{6.18}$$

Table 6.1 The K-means algorithm [1]

Input: The training data Y.
Output: The dictionary A, the codes X.
Initialize: $t = 1$; $A^{(0)} \in \mathbb{R}^{D\times M}$ is a random sample in $\boldsymbol{Y}$, $\|A^{\cdot j}\|_{\ell_2} = 1$.
While (!convergency)

- Sparse coding stage: Partition the training data Y into N sets
  $(R_1^{(t-1)}, R_2^{(t-1)}, \ldots, R_N^{(t-1)})$
  each holding the smple indices most similar to the column $A_{.k}^{(t-1)}$,
  $R_k^{(t-1)} = \left\{ i | \forall l \neq k \|y_i - A_{.k}^{(t-1)}\|_{\ell_2} < \|\boldsymbol{y}_i - A_{.l}^{(t-1)}\|_{\ell_2} \right\}.$
- Dictionary update stage: To update each column $j = 1, \cdots, N$ of $A^{(t-1)}$ by
  $A_{.j}^{(t)} = \frac{1}{|R_j^{(t-1)}|} \sum_{i\in R_j^{(t-1)}} \boldsymbol{y}_i$

$t = t + 1$.
End while

The K-SVD works in an iterative manner by alternating between sparse coding based on the current dictionary and dictionary based on the obtained sparse codes. These both steps jointly yield an accelerated convergence. The K-SVD is the fundamental dictionary learning algorithm, and was proposed by Aharon et al. [1]. Similar to K-means algorithm, the K-SVD obtains the updated dictionary by K singular value decomposition operations. The K-SVD algorithm is divided into two stages, sparse coding and codebook update.

The K-SVD algorithm solves Eq. (6.18) iteratively to obtain a dictionary using two stages. The sparse coding stage is used to compact the coefficient matrix by any pursuit approaches. In this stage, a K-sparse constraint is used. Now, we focus on considering about the dictionary updating stage. The problem is formulated as

$$\min_{A} \|Y - AX\|_F^2. \tag{6.19}$$

If we only consider one column of the dictionary such as $A_{.k}$ and the coefficients corresponding to it is the kth row of X, which is denoted as $X_{k.}$. The objective function can be reformulated as

$$\|Y - AX\|_F^2 = \| Y - \sum_{j=1}^{N} A_{.j} X_{j.} \|_F^2 \tag{6.20}$$

$$= \|(Y - \sum_{j \neq k} A_{.j} X_{j.}) - A_{.k} X_{k.}\|_F^2 \tag{6.21}$$

$$= \|E_k - A_{.k} X_{k.}\|_F^2, \tag{6.22}$$

where E_k is the error for all the n training data with kth atom is removed. We can simplify the Eq. (6.22) by only considering the y_i which uses the column $A_{.k}$. The index set is defined as follows

$$\omega_k = \{i | 1 \leq i \leq K, X_{k.}(i) \neq 0\}. \tag{6.23}$$

So, for computing error E_k, we only need to consider the E_k and $X_{k.}$ corresponding to the ω_k which is defined as E_k^R and $X_{k.}^R$. The core idea of K-SVD algorithm is using the principal direction corresponding to the largest eigenvalue of error E_k^R to update the kth column of dictionary. In this way, it can decrease the error in the next iteration. So, we can use SVD to decompose the error, $E_k^R = U \Delta V^T$. The first column of U is used to update the $A_{.k}$, and the first column of V multiplied by $\Delta(1, 1)$ is used to update $X_{k.}^R$. The algorithm flowchart is shown in Table 6.2.

The example dictionaries which are learned by K-SVD algorithm are illustrated in Fig. 6.3 [1].

Table 6.2 The flowchart of K-SVD [1]

Input: The training data $\boldsymbol{Y}$.
Output: The dictionary A, the codes $\boldsymbol{X}$.
Initialize: $t = 1$; $A^{(0)} \in \mathbb{R}^{D\times M}$ is a random matrix, $\|A^{\cdot j}\|_{\ell_2} = 1$.
While (!convergency)
- Sparse coding stage: To compact the coefficient vectors $\boldsymbol{x}_i$ for its corresponding $\boldsymbol{y}_i$ by using sparse recovery algorithms
  $\arg\min_x \|\boldsymbol{y}_i - A\boldsymbol{x}_i\|_{\ell_0}^2$, s.t. $\|\boldsymbol{x}_i\|_{\ell_0} \le K$.
- Dictionary update stage: To update each column $j = 1, \cdots, N$ of $A^{(t-1)}$ by
  - Compute the error matrix E_m by
    $E_m = Y - \sum_{j\neq m} A_{.j} X_{j.}$.
  - Generate $\bar{E_m}$ from E_m by choosing the corresponding columns of ω_m,
    where $\omega_m = \{i | 1 \le i \le n,\, X_{m.} \neq 0\}$.
  - Apply SVD on $\bar{E_m} = U\Delta V^T$, update by $A_{.m} = \boldsymbol{u}_1, X_{m.} = \Delta(1,1)\cdot V_{1.}$.

$t = t + 1$.
End while

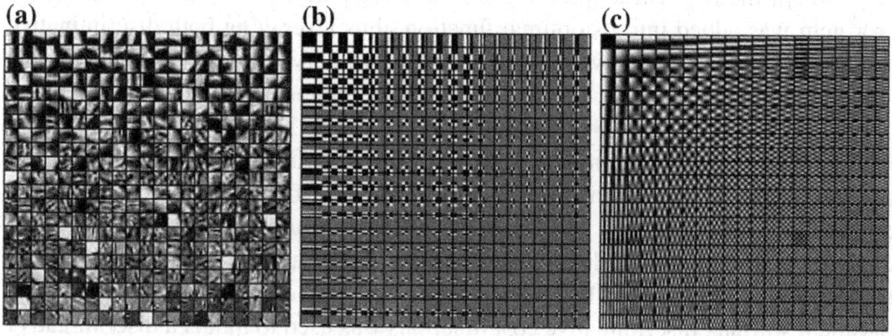

Fig. 6.3 The example of trained dictionaries which are obtained by K-SVD algorithm [1], **a** The learned dictionary. Its elements are sorted in an ascending order of their variance and stretched to maximal range for display purposes. **b** The overcomplete separable Haar dictionary and **c** the overcomplete DCT dictionary is used for comparison [1]

6.3.2 Discriminative Dictionary Learning

The traditional dictionary learning can be written as

$$\arg\min_{A.X} \; Rec(A, X) + Reg(X), \tag{6.24}$$

where $Rec(A, X)$ is the reconstruction error item. $Reg(X)$ is the regularization item, and also the sparsity constraint in sparse representation.

Furthermore, the discriminative dictionary learning is formulated as

$$\arg\min_{A,X} Rec(A, X) + Dis(A, X, B) + Reg(X), \tag{6.25}$$

where B is the set of training samples. Most of DDL approaches are formulated into Eq. (6.25), such as discriminative K-SVD (D-KSVD) [75], Label consistent K-SVD (LC-KSVD), Fisher discriminative, and DL (FDDL) [72].

In the early work of sparse representation-based visual recognition [69], the entire set of training samples were employed to construct the discriminative dictionary. A face image was classified by evaluating which led to the minimal reconstruction error. However, the dictionary used in it may not be effective enough to represent the query images due to the uncertain and noise information in the original training images. Besides, visual recognition applications favor the discriminative capability more than the native sparse reconstruction error. The original sample set contains a large number of atoms and may not fully exploit the hidden discriminative information.

To improve discriminative performance of original sparse representation, Zhang et al. proposed a discriminative K-SVD for dictionary learning in face recognition [75]. Except the reconstruction error item and regularization item, a classification error item was added into its optimal function, thus leveraging both discriminative power and representative power. The discriminative KSVD uses K-SVD to seek the globally optimal solution for all the parameters simultaneously.

Jiang et al. proposed a Label Consistent K-SVD (LC-KSVD) approach to learn a dictionary for sparse representation [20]. By contrast, a discriminative sparse coding was used to model discriminability in an optimization function, and can represent same class signals with very similar sparse representation.

Mairal et al. proposed to learn discriminative dictionary for local image analysis in sparse signal models [39]. In the procedure of learning discriminative dictionaries, classifical softmax discriminative cost functions was used to model a discriminative item. The previous DDL approaches we discussed basically follow Eq. (6.25). There are some DDL approaches working in somehow different ways. In [55], Ramirez et al. used the reconstruction error associated with each class as the discriminative information for classification. In this algorithm, an incoherence promoting term was added to the dictionary learning in order to make the dictionaries associated with different classes as independent as possible. The DDL highlights a clustering framework within the sparse modeling for dictionary learning.

Jiang et al. proposed the submodular dictionary learning where the objective function consists of the entropy rate of a random walk on a graph and a discriminative term [21]. Their dictionaries enforce features from the same class to have very similar sparse codes.

Yang et al. [72] employed the Fisher discriminative criterion to learn a structured dictionary, which explored the discrimination capability of sparse coding coefficients. The proposed dictionary learning model is expressed as

$$(A, X) = \arg\min_{(A,X)} r(A, Y, X) + \lambda_1 Reg(X) + \lambda_2 Dis(X), \tag{6.26}$$

where Y is the set of training samples which is represented by the coefficient matrix X over dictionary A. Apart from the sparsity term $Reg(X) = \|X\|_{\ell_1}$, the discriminative fidelity term $r(A, Y, X)$ and the discrimination constraint $Dis(X)$ are added to the dictionary learning. The model of Eq. (6.26) has shown the superiority to many state-of-the-art dictionary learning-based approaches in face recognition [72].

6.3.3 Online Dictionary Learning

1. Stochastic Approximation

Stochastic Approximation (SA) approach is widely used in online machine learning tasks [4, 5, 64]. Essentially, it solves a system of nonlinear equations. The classical SA approach can be written as

$$A_{t+1} = A_t + \alpha_t Y_t, \tag{6.27}$$

where α_t is the step-size, and Y_t is the measure of the system $h(A_t) + \omega_t$.

2. The classical dictionary learning techniques

Given training samples $Y = [y_1, y_2, \ldots, y_n] \in \mathbb{R}^{D\times n}$, the classical dictionary learning approaches are to optimize the empirical cost function as [2, 31, 53].

$$f_N(A) = \frac{1}{n}\sum_{i=1}^{n} L(y_i, A), \tag{6.28}$$

where $A \in \mathbb{R}^{D\times N}$ is the dictionary, and L is a loss function. Actually, dictionary learning is used to optimize Eq. (6.28) such that $f_N(A)$ should be very small if the dictionary A matches the Y very well.

In general, $n \gg D$, and $N \ll n$. Moreover, we represent each signal by only using a few columns of A in sparse representation. A commonly used loss function is the ℓ_1-sparse coding problem

$$\mathscr{L}(y, A) = \min_x \frac{1}{2}\|y - Ax\|_{\ell_2}^2 + \lambda\|x\|_{\ell_1} \tag{6.29}$$

where λ is a regularization parameter. In sparse representation, Eq. (6.29) is equivalent to BP and LASSO models. In Eq. (6.29), the larger λ yields a sparser solution for α. For obtaining, we shall minimize Eq. (6.29) w.r.t. A. However, the loss function $L(x, A)$ is non-convex. The classical dictionary learning approaches solve a joint optimization problem w.r.t. A and α by minimizing one while keeping the other one fixed [2, 31].

Table 6.3 Online dictionary learning

Initialize: $T = 1, A_0, C_0 = 0, B_0 = 0, \alpha$
For $t = 1$ to T do
Sample x_t from $p(x)$
Sparse coding: $\alpha_t = \text{argmin}_\alpha \frac{1}{2}\|x_t - A_{t-1}\alpha\|_{\ell_2}^2 + \lambda\|\alpha\|_{\ell_1}$.
$C_t \leftarrow C_{t-1} + \alpha_t\alpha_t^T$; $B_t \leftarrow B_{t-1} + x_t\alpha_t^T$;
Dictionary update: $A_t = \text{argmin}_A \frac{1}{t}\Sigma_{i=1}^t \frac{1}{2}\|x_i - A\alpha_i\|_{\ell_2}^2 + \lambda\|\alpha_i\|_{\ell_1}$.
End for
Return A_T

3. Online versions

In big data applications, classical batch optimization techniques are unsuitable for dictionary learning due to high speed and memory requirement. Hence, Aharon et al. proposed a first-order stochastic gradient descent with projection on the constraint set for dictionary learning [2]. Similarly, Mairal et al. proposed an iterative online algorithm by minimizing a quadratic surrogate function of the empirical cost over the set of constraints [43].

For the first-order stochastic gradient descent algorithm, the dictionary D can be updated by

$$A_t = \Pi_C[A_{t-1} - \alpha_t \nabla_A \ell(x_t, A_{t-1})], \tag{6.30}$$

where Π_C is the orthogonal projector; $\alpha_t = a/(t+b)$, a and b need to be selected in an application-dependent way. This algorithm was used in object recognition [24], factorization matrix [26], and image content representation [2].

For the second-order stochastic gradient descent algorithms, we can update the dictionary A by

$$A_t = A_{t-1} - \frac{1}{t}H^{-1}\nabla_A \ell(x_t, A_{t-1}), \tag{6.31}$$

where H^{-1} is the inverse of the Hessian matrix [7]. Here, Mairal et al. proposed an online dictionary learning approach [40, 43]. In principal, this dictionary learning can be considered as a variant of a second-order stochastic gradient descent algorithm by using a surrogate function.

The algorithm flowchart of online dictionary learning is shown in Table 6.3.

6.3.4 Supervised Dictionary Learning

From a theoretical point of view, supervised and unsupervised dictionary learning differ only whether labeled training data are used as input in a function formulation. Various general dictionary learning approaches have been proposed, such as k-means [61], mean shift [23] and manifold learning [22]. However, in these cases, the learned dictionaries may not be optimal for specific classifying tasks. Recently studies have been aimed at supervised dictionary learning using sparse signal model.

In [38], Mairal et al. proposed a novel sparse representation for signal belonging to different classes in terms of a shared dictionary and multiple class-decision functions. Compared with the earlier work in supervised methods, this model allows some features to be shared among multiple classes. Hence, the learned supervised dictionary can use more information for classification tasks. First, let us define softmax discriminative cost function as

$$\hat{S}_c(y, A, Q) = \arg\min_{x} \; S_c(x, y, A, Q), \tag{6.32}$$

where $S_c(x, y, A, Q) = \ell_c(g_i(y, x, Q)_{i=1}^{c}) + \lambda_0 \|y - Ax\|_{\ell_2}^2 + \lambda_1 \|x\|_{\ell_1}$, and $g_i(y, x, Q)$ is the ith decision function. Equation (6.32) combines classification/discriminative and classical reconstruction terms. Thus, the solution of Eq. (6.32) will lead to directive classification. Note that earlier supervised dictionary learning yields one dictionary per class [39].

By contrast, this model shares some features among multiple classes. Furthermore, the supervised dictionary learning (SDL) is defined as [38]

$$\underset{A,Q}{\text{argmin}} \sum_{i=1}^{C} \sum_{j \in T_i} \hat{S}_i(y_j, A, Q) + \lambda_2 \|Q\|_{\ell_2}^2, \text{ s.t. } \|d_i\|_{\ell_2} \le 1, \tag{6.33}$$

where T_i is the ith set of training data, $i = 1, 2, \ldots, C$.

6.3.5 Joint Dictionary Learning and Other Tasks

Sometimes, sparse dictionary learning problem is combined with other tasks and jointly optimized. For example, Pham et al. proposed a method to jointly construct the overcomplete dictionary and find the optimal classifier parameters [54]. Mairal et al. combined self-similarity generation with dictionary learning in a unified sparse representation framework. This task was achieved by jointly decomposing groups of similar signals on subsets of the learned dictionary. Similarly, Dong et al. [14] also shared the idea that dictionary learning and structural clustering can be unified and proposed a clustering-based sparse representation. The core idea is to regularize dictionary learning by local sparsity constraints, while to regularize structural clustering via nonlocal sparsity and incorporate them into a unified variational framework. In [14], Yang et al. learned dictionaries for sparse modeling in coupled feature spaces. The learning algorithm is formulated as a generic bilevel optimization problem which constrained relationships between two signal spaces. To handle heavy occlusions and pose variations in visual tracking, Zhang et al. [74] proposed a multitask sparse representation method for robust object tracking where the particle representations are jointly learned.

6.3.6 Applications—Image/Video Restoration

In sparse image models, it is assumed that natural images follow a decomposition over a learned dictionary. Moreover, a K-SVD algorithm was used in image/video denoising [7, 41, 42].

First, image degraded models can be modeled as additive ones by

$$\tilde{y} = y_0 + \xi, \ \ \xi \text{is a white gaussian noise.} \tag{6.34}$$

Thus, image denoising can be formulated as an energy minimization problem [15]

$$\{\hat{x}_{ij}, \hat{A}, \hat{y}_0\} = \underset{A, x_{i,j}, y}{\text{argmin}} \ \lambda \|y - \tilde{y}\|_{\ell_2}^2 + \sum_{i,j} \mu_{i,j} \|x_{i,j}\|_{\ell_0} + \sum_{i,j} \|Ax_{i,j} - R_{i,j} y\|_{\ell_2}^2, \tag{6.35}$$

where $R_{i,j}$ is an extraction operator that can extract $\sqrt{d} \times \sqrt{d}$ patch of coordinate $[i, j]$ from the image, d is the number of dimension of code words. In Eq. (6.35), the first term is reconstructive error between y and $\tilde{y}$, the second term is sparsity one and the third term is reconstructive error from learned dictionary that ensures decomposition consistency.

Simply, the gray-scale denoising algorithm can be directly used in color images by concatenating each color channel. Alternatively, a new parameter was introduced to learn the correlation between the color channels in [41, 42]. Moreover, video denoising algorithms based on K-SVD had been developed in [41]. Here, temporal correlation in videos was used to increase denoising performance.

6.4 Feature Learning

6.4.1 Dimensionality Reduction

Principal Component Analysis (PCA) is a useful technique for dimension reduction. The core of PCA is orthogonal transformation which is called Karhunen-Loève (K-L) transformation. The K-L transformation is used to get rid off the correlation of the original data space, which turns the original space to the orthogonal space. We consider about a data set of observation $\{x_n\}, n = 1, \ldots, N$. The data's covariance matrix can be defined as

$$S = \frac{1}{N} \sum_{n=1}^{N} (x_n - \bar{x})(x_n - \bar{x})^T, \tag{6.36}$$

where $\bar{x}$ is the mean of the data which can be defined as follows

$$\bar{x} = \frac{1}{N}\sum_{n=1}^{N} x_n. \tag{6.37}$$

If every dimension of the data has the correlation that means the data is redundant, and vice versa. So, we want to get rid off the correlation that means the covariance matrix is a diagonal matrix. By the matrix theory, we can get rid off the correlation by the following step:

(1) Solve the equation

$$|\lambda I - S| = 0 \tag{6.38}$$

to get all the eigenvalue $\lambda_1, \lambda_2, \ldots, \lambda_D$;

(2) Then we can get the eigenvector u_i which corresponds to the eigenvalue above by solving the following equation

$$Su_i = \lambda_i u_i; \tag{6.39}$$

(3) We need to normalize all the eigenvectors to make them $u_i^T u_i = 1$;

(4) We can get the orthogonal matrix A by combining all the eigenvectors as column

$$A = [u_1, u_2, \ldots, u_D]; \tag{6.40}$$

(5) Set $y = A^T(x - \overline{x})$ to get the K-L transformation for the data $\{x_n\}$.

We can easily get that the covariance matrix of y is

$$C_y = A^T SA = \text{diag}(\lambda_1, \lambda_2, \ldots, \lambda_D), \tag{6.41}$$

which is a diagonal matrix, so, we remove the correlation of dimension. We also shall get

$$x = Ay = [u_1, u_2, \ldots, u_D]y, \tag{6.42}$$

it can be seen as the K-L expansion of x. If we want to reduce the dimension of x, we can abandon some y_i to approximate the x. We assume that only keeping M dimension of y with $M < D$, we can get the approximation of x as

$$\hat{x} = y_1 u_1 + y_2 u_2 + \cdots + y_M u_M = \sum_{i=1}^{M} y_i u_i. \tag{6.43}$$

We want to use M dimension to approximate the D dimension data with the error as small as possible. We want to minimize the error which can be formulated as

$$\operatorname{argmin} \varepsilon = E\{[x - \hat{x}]^T [x - \hat{x}]\}. \tag{6.44}$$

The $E\{[x - \hat{x}]^T [x - \hat{x}]\}$ is the mean square error. So, we can derive the Eq. (6.44) as follows

$$\varepsilon = E\left\{\left[\sum_{i=M+1}^{D} y_i u_i\right]^T \left[\sum_{i=M+1}^{D} y_i u_i\right]\right\} \tag{6.45}$$

Since the eigenvectors are mutually orthogonal, so we can get

$$\varepsilon = E\left\{\sum_{i=M+1}^{D} y_i^2\right\} = E\left\{\sum_{i=M+1}^{D} [(x - \overline{x})^T u_i]^2\right\} \tag{6.46}$$

$$= E\left\{\sum_{i=M+1}^{D} u_i^T (x - \overline{x})(x - \overline{x})^T u_i\right\} \tag{6.47}$$

$$= \sum_{i=M+1}^{D} u_i^T E\{(x - \overline{x})(x - \overline{x})^T\} u_i \tag{6.48}$$

$$= \sum_{i=M+1}^{D} \boldsymbol{u}_i^T S u_i \tag{6.49}$$

$$= \sum_{i=M+1}^{D} \lambda_i. \tag{6.50}$$

From the Eq. (6.50), we know that if we want to minimize error, we need to abandon the elements of y corresponding to the $D - M$ smallest eigenvalues, which is equivalent to choose the elements of y corresponding to the M largest eigenvalues.

PCA is based on these theories as mentioned above. It uses the eigenvectors which corresponds to the M largest eigenvalues to compress the data. So, it gives the compressed data with the minimum mean square error.

6.4.2 Sparse Support Vector Machines

In many visual recognition, features are sparse, and various feature learning approaches via Support Vector Machine (SVM) have been proposed. To obtain a sparser decision rule for SVM, two categories of sparse SVM were proposed, ℓ_1-norm SVM [9, 65, 76] and ℓ_0-norm SVM [65].

In a standard two-class classifying problem, given a set of training data (x_1, y_1), $(x_2, y_2), \ldots, (x_n, y_n)$, ($x_i \in \mathbb{R}^D$ is a feature and $y_i \in \{1, -1\}$ is a class label), Traditional Support Vector Machine (SVM) can be formulated as [76]

$$\underset{\beta_0, \beta}{\operatorname{argmin}} \sum_{i=1}^{n} \left[1 - y_i \left(\beta_0 + \sum_{j=1}^{q} \beta_j h_j(x_i) \right) \right]_+ + \lambda \|\beta\|_{\ell_2}^2, \tag{6.51}$$

where $h_j(.)$ is a basis function. So we can define $f(x)$ a regression function as follows

$$f(x) = \beta_0 + \sum_{j=1}^{q} \beta_j h_j(x). \tag{6.52}$$

To obtain $\hat{\beta}_0$ and $\hat{\beta}$, we classify x by $\operatorname{sgn}[\hat{f}(x)]$.

By substituting the ℓ_2-norm term, we consider the ℓ_1-norm SVM problem

$$\underset{\beta_0, \beta}{\arg\min} \sum_{i=1}^{n} \left[1 - y_i \left(\beta_0 + \sum_{j=1}^{q} \beta_j h_j(x_i) \right) \right]_+ + \lambda \|\beta\|_{\ell_1}, \tag{6.53}$$

Similarly, we can obtain ℓ_0-norm SVM by substituting $\lambda \|\beta\|_{\ell_1}$ with $\lambda \|\beta\|_{\ell_0}$.

6.4.3 Recursive Feature Elimination

The recursive feature elimination (RFE) strategy iteratively removes less important features according to certain weights [16]. SVM-RFE is an application of RFE taking into account the weight of support vector [16, 66].

Mathematically, a linear classifier can be defined as

$$f(x) = w^T x + b, \tag{6.54}$$

with

$$w = \sum_k \alpha_k y_k x_k, \quad \text{and} \quad b = y_k - w^T x_k. \tag{6.55}$$

From Eq. (6.55), we can see that w is a linear combination of training samples. Here, most α_k are zero, and nonzero α_k correspond to support vectors. In SVM-RFE, α_k is used for evaluating features.

The SVM-RFE algorithm flowchart is as follows.

Table 6.4 The SVM-RFE algorithm flowchart

Input:	Training Samples $(x_1, y_1), (x_2, y_2), \cdots, (x_n, y_n)$
Initialize:	Subset of active features $s = [1, 2, \cdots, m]$
	Ranking List: $r = [\,]$
while	$(s! = [\,])$
	Compute the feature weights by using SVM:
	$\alpha = \text{SVM-train}(\mathbf{X}, \mathbf{Y})$;
	$w = \sum_k \alpha_k y_k x_k$;
	$c_i = w_i^2, \forall i.$
	Update Feature List:
	$f = \text{argmin}(c)$;
	$r = [s(f), r]$;
	$s = s(1 : f-1, f+1 : length(s))$.
end while	
Output:	Feature ranked list r.

Due to the natural sensitivity of SVM to noises, the basic SVM-RFE works not very well in extreme conditions. Tapia et al. proposed sparse and stable feature selection with consensus SVM-RFE [66] (Table 6.4).

6.4.4 Minimum Squared Error (MSE) Criterions

Let us first introduce the feature learning algorithm based on the minimum squared error (MSE) criterion, and then discuss Sparse MSE (SMSE) criterion [34].

A linear discriminant function is written as

$$f(x) = \sum_{i=1}^{d} w_i x_i + w_0 = y^T a, \tag{6.56}$$

where $y = [1, x_1, x_2, \ldots, x_d]^T, a = [w_0, w_1, w_2, \ldots, w_d]^T$. Thus, we obtain a canonical hyperplane defined as follows

$$\mathbf{Y}a = b, \tag{6.57}$$

where $Y = [y_1, y_2, \ldots, y_n]^T$(margin vector), $y_i^T a = b_i$. It is impractical to obtain the exact solution of Eq. (6.57) due to the overdetermined problem, so we can use classical relaxation to solve Eq. (6.57) by minimizing the MSE criterion.

$$\arg\min_a \|Ya - b\|_{\ell_2}^2 = \text{argmin}_a \sum_{i=1}^{n} (y_i^T a - b_i)^2, \tag{6.58}$$

For better selection of features, a sparsity regularization term is added into the MSE criterion. Feature learning is formulated into Sparse MSE criterion as follows

$$\arg\min_{a} \|Ya - b\|_{\ell_2}^2 + \lambda\|a\|_{\ell_0}. \tag{6.59}$$

As discussed in Chap. 2, we can approximate the solution of Eq. (6.59) by transforming Eq. (6.59) into a ℓ_0-norm version. Therefore, a relaxed version of MSE can be used to approximate Eq. (6.59).

6.4.5 Elastic Net Criterions

The naive Elastic Net Criterion is defined as [77]

$$L(\lambda_1, \lambda_2, \beta) = \|y - \mathbf{A}x\|_{\ell_2}^2 + \lambda\|x\|_{\ell_2}^2 + \lambda\|x\|_{\ell_1}. \tag{6.60}$$

Equation (6.60) can be considered as a Penalized Least Squares Criterion. Furthermore, a Robust Elastic Net Criterion (REN) is defined as [68]

$$L(\lambda_1, \lambda_2, \beta) = \rho(\|y - Ax\|_{\ell_2}^2) + \lambda\|x\|_{\ell_2}^2 + \lambda\|x\|_{\ell_1}, \tag{6.61}$$

where $\rho(.)$ is a cost function. Choosing proper $\rho(.)$ functions can obtain good feature learning algorithm especially for outliers in visual recognition and back ground modeling [68].

6.4.6 Sparse Linear Discriminant Analysis

Fisher linear discriminant analysis can be written as

$$J(w) = \frac{w^T S_B w}{w^T \mathbf{S}_w w}, \tag{6.62}$$

where

$$\mathbf{S}_B = (u_1 - u_0)(u_1 - u_0)^T, S_w = (\Sigma_1 - \Sigma_0), \tag{6.63}$$

Fisher linear discriminant analysis can be formulated as a generalized eigenvalue decomposition. Hence, solving FLDA is equivalent to maximize the Reyleigh quotient which is the core of many problems in machine learning. Eq. (6.62) can be rewritten as Lagrange multipliers

$$L = w^T S_B w - \lambda(w^T S_w w - K). \tag{6.64}$$

Finally, Eq. (6.65) can be solved by a generalized eigenvalue problem,

$$\hat{w} = \frac{u_1 - u_0}{\Sigma_1 + \Sigma_0}. \tag{6.65}$$

The Sparse LDA (SLDA) is obtained by adding a cardinality constraint on w as follows

$$\arg\max_w \frac{w^T \mathbf{S}_B w}{w^T \mathbf{S}_w w}, \qquad \text{s.t. card}(w) = k, \tag{6.66}$$

where $\text{card}(w) = \|w\|_{\ell_0}$. When $S_w = I$, SLDA is transformed into SPCA. As we know, Eq. (6.66) is non-convex and NP-hard, Moghaddam et al. derived a generalized inclusion principal for variational eigenvalue bounds [47, 48].

6.4.7 Saliency Feature Mapping Using Sparse Coding

Visual saliency is an important feature for object recognition in computer vision [17–19], which was inspired by human vision systems. Saliency detection is to find some image region which is significant from the rest by calculating saliency feature mapping. The commonly used features are colors, textures, orientation, edges, etc. Han et al. proposed an object-oriented visual saliency detection using sparse coding [17], where sparse representations are obtained by learning on a large amount of eye-fixation patches. Lang et al. proposed a saliency detection approach by using low-rank representation and sparse coding representation [30].

1. The Framework of Saliency Detection

Figure 6.4 shows the general frameworks of saliency detection by using sparse coding. Regrading sparse coding, we have to calculate the features of testing images and training images, and generate the basis functions. Following that, saliency mapping is generated by using sparse coding coefficients even other feature structures.

In saliency detection, we divide the testing image into nonoverlapping patches, and then the image is represented as $X = [x_1, x_2, \ldots, x_N] \in R_N$. The goal of saliency detection is to find a function $S(x_i)$ to measure the saliency value of x_i.

2. Some Sparse Coding Strategies

(1) Multitask Sparsity Pursuit In MTSP, the image was modeled as

$$X = XZ_0 + E_0. \tag{6.67}$$

(2) Object-Oriented Saliency Detection

Han et al. proposed saliency detection consists of three modules, ICA-based image sparse representation, saliency modeling, and saliency map. First, ICA is used to find

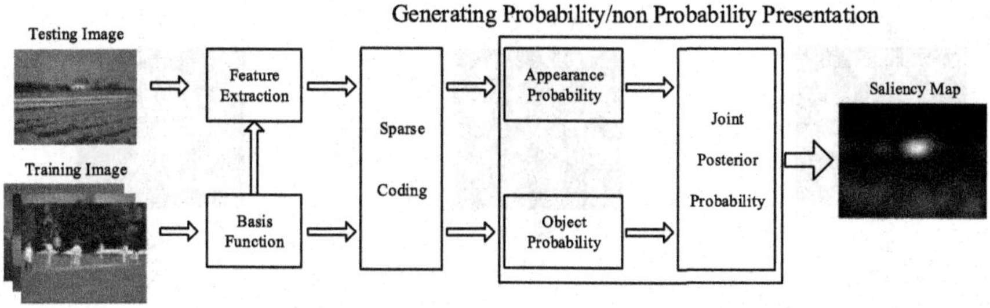

Fig. 6.4 The general framework of saliency detection by using sparse coding

a set of basis functions since it has many good properties to represent images. Second, we can model saliency by using appearance and objects. For example, the appearance variety probability is represented by GMM, and the object likelihood is inferred by using GMM components. Finally, different case can be merged to generate saliency map. Consider about one kind of feature

$$X = XZ_0 + E_0, \tag{6.68}$$

where XZ_0 denotes the nonsalient part (background), which can be represented by itself and E_0 denotes the salient part. The strong correlation of background patches suggest that the Z_0 must have low-rank property. On the other hand, the salient part only have a small part of image, so, the salient must have the sparsity property. Thus, it can be formulated as a low-rank representation problem [35]:

$$\begin{aligned} \underset{Z_0, E_0}{\operatorname{argmin}} \quad & \|Z_0\|_* + \lambda \|E_0\|_{\ell_{2,1}} \\ \text{s.t.} \quad & X = XZ_0 + E_0, \end{aligned} \tag{6.69}$$

where $\|\cdot\|_*$ denotes the nuclear norm, $\|\cdot\|_{\ell_{2,1}}$ denotes the sum of ℓ_2-norms of the columns of matrix which is defined as

$$\|E_0\|_{\ell_{2,1}} = \sum_i \sqrt{\sum_j (E_0(j,i))^2}, \tag{6.70}$$

where $E_0(j,i)$ denotes the (j,i)th entry of E_0. The $\ell_{2,1}$-norm encourage the column sparsity, which is suitable for saliency detection. The mapping function $S(P_i)$ can be formulated as

$$S(P_i) = \|E_0^*(:,i)\|_{\ell_2}, \tag{6.71}$$

where E_0^* denotes the the optimal solution of E_0 in Eq. (6.69). One example is illustrated in Fig. 6.5.

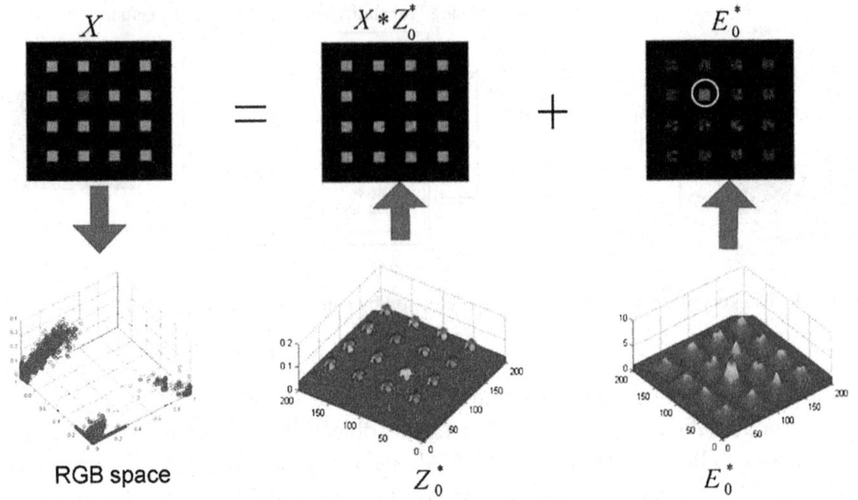

Fig. 6.5 The toy problem example of low-rank constraint [30]

The low-rank representation model which is considered above can only process one type of features. C. Lang et al. [30] extended the LRR model and proposed the multitask sparsity pursuit (MTSP) model to confuse some types of feature for the saliency detection, which can be formulated as follows:

$$\begin{aligned} &\underset{\{Z_i\},\{E_i\}}{\operatorname{argmin}} \sum_{i=1}^{K} \|Z_i\|_* + \lambda \|E\|_{\ell_{2,1}} \\ &\text{s.t.} \quad X_i = X_i Z_i + E_i, i = 1, \ldots, K \end{aligned} \tag{6.72}$$

where $E = [E_1; E_2; \ldots; E_K]$ is formed by concatenating $E_1, E_2, \ldots, E_K$ along the column. This can be jointly considered about the K types of features. The magnitude of $E_1, E_2, \ldots, E_K$ are jointly consistent.

References

1. Aharon, M., Elad, M., Bruckstein, A.: K-SVD: an algorithm for designing overcomplete dictionaries for sparse representation. IEEE Trans. Signal Process. **54**(11), 4311–4322 (2006)
2. Aharon, M., Elad, M.: Sparse and redundant modeling of image content using an image-signature-dictionary. SIAM J. Imaging Sci. **1**(3), 228–247 (2008)
3. Arbelaez, P., Maire, M., Fowlkes, C., Malik, J.: Contour detection and hierarchical image segmentation. IEEE Trans. Pattern Anal. Mach. Intell. **33**(5), 898–916 (2011)
4. Bach, F., Moulines, E., et al.: Non-asymptotic analysis of stochastic approximation algorithms for machine learning. In: NIPS (2011)
5. Bach, F.: Stochastic gradient methods for machine learning (2014)

6. Bo, L., Ren, X., Fox, D.: Hierarchical matching pursuit for image classification: architecture and fast algorithms. In: NIPS, vol. 1, pp. 2115–2123 (2011)
7. Bottou, L., Bousquet, O.: The tradeoffs of large scale learning. In: NIPS, vol. 4 (2007)
8. Boureau, Y.L., Ponce, J., LeCun, Y.: A theoretical analysis of feature pooling in visual recognition. In: ICML (2010)
9. Chan, A.B., Vasconcelos, N., Lanckriet, G.R.: Direct convex relaxations of sparse SVM. In: ACM International Conference on Machine Learning (2007)
10. Cheng, H., Liu, Z., Zheng, N., Yang, L.: A deformable local image descriptor. In: IEEE CVPR (2008)
11. Chiang, C.K., Duan, C.H., Lai, S.H., Chang, S.F.: Learning component-level sparse representation using histogram information for image classification. In: IEEE ICCV (2011)
12. Cong, Y., Yuan, J., Liu, J.: Sparse reconstruction cost for abnormal event detection. In: IEEE CVPR (2011)
13. Dalal, N., Triggs, B.: Histograms of oriented gradients for human detection. In: IEEE CVPR (2005)
14. Dong, W., Li, X., Zhang, D., Shi, G.: Sparsity-based image denoising via dictionary learning and structural clustering. In: IEEE CVPR (2011)
15. Elad, M., Aharon, M.: Image denoising via learned dictionaries and sparse representation. In: IEEE CVPR (2006)
16. Guyon, I., Weston, J., Barnhill, S., Vapnik, V.: Gene selection for cancer classification using support vector machines. Mach. Learn. **46**(1–3), 389–422 (2002)
17. Han, J., He, S., Qian, X., Wang, D., Guo, L., Liu, T.: An object-oriented visual saliency detection framework based on sparse coding representations. IEEE Trans. Circuits Syst. Video Technol. **23**(12), 2009–2021 (2013)
18. Hou, X., Zhang, L.: Dynamic visual attention: searching for coding length increments. In: Advances in Neural Information Processing Systems (2009)
19. Hou, X., Zhang, L.: Saliency detection: a spectral residual approach. In: IEEE CVPR (2007)
20. Jiang, Z., Lin, Z., Davis, L.S.: Learning a discriminative dictionary for sparse coding via label consistent K-SVD. In: IEEE CVPR (2011)
21. Jiang, Z., Zhang, G., Davis, L.S.: Submodular dictionary learning for sparse coding. In: IEEE CVPR (2012)
22. Jiang, Y.G., Ngo, C.W.: Visual word proximity and linguistics for semantic video indexing and near-duplicate retrieval. Comput. Vis. Image Underst. **113**(3), 405–414 (2009)
23. Jurie, F., Triggs, B.: Creating efficient codebooks for visual recognition. In: IEEE ICCV (2005)
24. Kavukcuoglu, K., Ranzato, M., LeCun, Y.: Fast inference in sparse coding algorithms with applications to object recognition (2010) arXiv preprint
25. Kavukcuoglu, K., Sermanet, P., Boureau, Y.L., Gregor, K., Mathieu, M., LeCun, Y.: Learning convolutional feature hierarchies for visual recognition. In: NIPS, vol. 1 (2010)
26. Koren, Y., Bell, R., Volinsky, C.: Matrix factorization techniques for recommender systems. Computer **42**(8), 30–37 (2009)
27. Kreutz-Delgado, K., Murray, J.F., Rao, B.D., Engan, K., Lee, T.W., Sejnowski, T.J.: Dictionary learning algorithms for sparse representation. Neural Comput. **15**(2), 349–396 (2003)
28. Krishnan, D., Tay, T., Fergus, R.: Blind deconvolution using a normalized sparsity measure. In: IEEE CVPR (2011)
29. Kulkarni, N., Li, B.: Discriminative affine sparse codes for image classification. In: IEEE CVPR (2011)
30. Lang, C., Liu, G., Yu, J., Yan, S.: Saliency detection by multitask sparsity pursuit. IEEE Trans. Image Process. **21**(3), 1327–1338 (2012)
31. Lee, H., Battle, A., Raina, R., Ng, A.Y.: Efficient sparse coding algorithms. Adv. Neural Inf. Process. Syst. **19**, 801 (2007)
32. Li, Y., Fermuller, C., Aloimonos, Y., Ji, H.: Learning shift-invariant sparse representation of actions. In: IEEE CVPR (2010)
33. Li, X., Jia, T., Zhang, H.: Expression-insensitive 3d face recognition using sparse representation. In: IEEE CVPR (2009)

34. Liang, Y., Wang, L., Xiang, Y., Zou, B.: Feature selection via sparse approximation for face recognition (2011) arXiv preprint
35. Liu, G., Lin, Z., Yu, Y.: Robust subspace segmentation by low-rank representation. In: ICML (2010)
36. Liu, H., Yu, L.: Toward integrating feature selection algorithms for classification and clustering. IEEE Trans. Knowl. Data Eng. **17**(4), 491–502 (2005)
37. Lowe, D.G.: Distinctive image features from scale-invariant keypoints. Int. J. Comput. Vis. **60**(2), 91–110 (2004)
38. Mairal, J., Bach, F., Ponce, J., Sapiro, G., Zisserman, A., et al.: Supervised dictionary learning (2008)
39. Mairal, J., Bach, F., Ponce, J., Sapiro, G., Zisserman, A.: Discriminative learned dictionaries for local image analysis. In: IEEE CVPR (2008)
40. Mairal, J., Bach, F., Ponce, J., Sapiro, G.: Online dictionary learning for sparse coding. In: Annual International Conference on Machine Learning. ACM (2009)
41. Mairal, J., Sapiro, G., Elad, M.: Learning multiscale sparse representations for image and video restoration. Technical report, DTIC Document (2007)
42. Mairal, J., Elad, M., Sapiro, G.: Sparse representation for color image restoration. IEEE Trans. Image Process. **17**(1), 53–69 (2008)
43. Mairal, J., Bach, F., Ponce, J., Sapiro, G.: Online learning for matrix factorization and sparse coding. J. Mach. Learn. Res. **11**, 19–60 (2010)
44. Maire, M., Arbelaez, P., Fowlkes, C., Malik. J.: Using contours to detect and localize junctions in natural images. In: IEEE CVPR (2008)
45. Martin, D.R., Fowlkes, C.C., Malik, J.: Learning to detect natural image boundaries using local brightness, color, and texture cues. IEEE Trans. Pattern Anal. Mach. Intell. **26**(5), 530–549 (2004)
46. Masaeli, M., Dy, J.G., Fung, G.M.: From transformation-based dimensionality reduction to feature selection. In: ICML (2010)
47. Moghaddam, B., Weiss, Y., Avidan, S.: Fast pixel/part selection with sparse eigenvectors. In: IEEE ICCV (2007)
48. Moghaddam, B., Weiss, Y., Avidan, S.: Generalized spectral bounds for sparse LDA. In: International conference on Machine Learning. ACM (2006)
49. Morel, J.M., Yu, G.: ASIFT: a new framework for fully affine invariant image comparison. SIAM J. Imaging Sci. **2**(2), 438–469 (2009)
50. Nagesh, P., Li, B.: A compressive sensing approach for expression-invariant face recognition. In: IEEE CVPR (2009)
51. Naikal, N., Yang, A.Y., Sastry, S.S.: Informative feature selection for object recognition via sparse PCA. In: IEEE ICCV (2011)
52. Oliva, A., Torralba, A.: Building the gist of a scene: the role of global image features in recognition. Prog. Brain Res. **155**, 23–36 (2006)
53. Olshausen, B.A., Field, D.J.: Sparse coding with an overcomplete basis set: a strategy employed by v1? Vis. Res. **37**(23), 3311–3325 (1997)
54. Pham, D.S., Venkatesh, S.: Joint learning and dictionary construction for pattern recognition. In: IEEE CVPR (2008)
55. Ramirez, I., Sprechmann, P., Sapiro, G.: Classification and clustering via dictionary learning with structured incoherence and shared features. In: IEEE CVPR (2010)
56. Ren, X., Bo, L.: Discriminatively trained sparse code gradients for contour detection. In: NIPS, vol. 2, pp. 584–592 (2012)
57. Ren, X., Ramanan, D.: Histograms of sparse codes for object detection. In: IEEE CVPR (2013)
58. Riesenhuber, M., Poggio, T.: Hierarchical models of object recognition in cortex. Nat. Neurosci. **2**(11), 1019–1025 (1999)
59. Shi, J., Ren, X., Dai, G., Wang, J., Zhang, Z.: A non-convex relaxation approach to sparse dictionary learning. In: IEEE CVPR (2011)
60. Shi, J., Malik, J.: Normalized cuts and image segmentation. IEEE Trans. Pattern Anal. Mach. Intell. **22**(8), 888–905 (2000)

61. Sivic, J., Zisserman, A.: Video Google: a text retrieval approach to object matching in videos. In: IEEE ICCV (2003)
62. Sohn, K., Jung, D.Y., Lee, H., Hero, A.O.: Efficient learning of sparse, distributed, convolutional feature representations for object recognition. In: IEEE ICCV (2011)
63. Sohn, K., Zhou, G., Lee, H.: Jointly learning and selecting features via conditional point-wise mixture RBMs (2012)
64. Srebro, N., Tewari, A.: Stochastic optimization for machine learning. In: ICML (2010)
65. Tan, M., Wang, L., Tsang, I.W.: Learning sparse SVM for feature selection on very high dimensional datasets. In: International Conference on Machine Learning (2010)
66. Tapia, E., Bulacio, P., Angelone, L.: Sparse and stable gene selection with consensus SVM-RFE. Pattern Recognit. Lett. **33**(2), 164–172 (2012)
67. Wang, L., Cheng, H.: Robust sparse PCA via weighted elastic net. In: Pattern Recognition (2012)
68. Wang, L., Cheng, H., Liu, Z., Zhu, C.: A robust elastic net approach for feature learning. J. Vis. Commun. Image Represent. **25**(2), 313–321 (2014)
69. Wright, J., Yang, A.Y., Ganesh, A., Sastry, S.S., Ma, Y.: Robust face recognition via sparse representation. IEEE Trans. Pattern Anal. Mach. Intell. **31**(2), 210–227 (2009)
70. Yang, J., Yu, K., Gong, Y., Huang, T.: Linear spatial pyramid matching using sparse coding for image classification. In: IEEE CVPR (2009)
71. Yang, J., Yu, K., Huang, T.: Supervised translation-invariant sparse coding. In: IEEE CVPR (2010)
72. Yang, M., Zhang, D., Feng, X.: Fisher discrimination dictionary learning for sparse representation. In: IEEE ICCV (2011)
73. Yu, K., Lin, Y., Lafferty, J.: Learning image representations from the pixel level via hierarchical sparse coding. In: IEEE CVPR (2011)
74. Zhang, T., Ghanem, B., Liu, S., Ahuja, N.: Robust visual tracking via multi-task sparse learning. In: IEEE CVPR (2012)
75. Zhang, Q., Li, B.: Discriminative K-SVD for dictionary learning in face recognition. In: IEEE CVPR (2010)
76. Zhu, J., Rosset, S., Hastie, T., Tibshirani, R.: 1-norm support vector machines. In: NIPS (2003)
77. Zou, H., Hastie, T.: Regularization and variable selection via the elastic net. J. R. Stat. Soc. **67**(2), 301–320 (2005)
78. Zou, H., Hastie, T., Tibshirani, R.: Sparse principal component analysis. J. Comput. Graph. Stat. **15**(2), 265–286 (2006)

Chapter 7
Sparsity-Induced Similarity

7.1 Introduction

Sparse representation has been widely used in pattern recognition and machine learning [11, 19, 30, 46], computer vision [9, 48, 50, 62, 66, 76], multimedia signal processing [53], etc. Mathematically, solving sparse representation involves seeking the sparsest linear combination of basis functions from an overcomplete dictionary. The rationale behind this is the sparse connectivity among nodes in the human brain [45]. Hence, how to represent or reconstruct signals with sparse samples becomes an extremely important problem in machine learning and computer vision. In many real applications such as video and image processing, the data sets are usually large and high dimensional [47, 70]. Sparse representation has proved to be an effective technique for handling them [69, 70].

As we know, the similarity among features especially in high-dimensional features spaces plays an important role in unsupervised learning [43], semi-supervised learning [5, 29], and supervised learning [39, 55, 61]. One main drawback of most existing similarity measures such as the Euclidean distance and Gaussian Kernel Similarity measure is that the similarity measure completely ignores the class structure. In image classification and object recognition, people usually use high-dimensional feature vectors while assuming that the feature vectors for each class belong to a lower dimensional subspace. The subspace structure can be discovered when there is enough training data, and researchers have shown that the subspace representation is effective for image classification and object recognition. However, when there is little training data available, such as in semi-supervised training or unsupervised training, it is impossible to compute the subspace structure. Consequently, the similarity measure between feature points are usually based on pairwise Euclidean distance while the subspace structure is ignored. How to leverage the hidden subspace structure for similarity measure is a crucial issue in supervised/semi-supervised learning, which has not been addressed before.

H. Cheng, *Sparse Representation, Modeling and Learning in Visual Recognition*,
Advances in Computer Vision and Pattern Recognition,
DOI 10.1007/978-1-4471-6714-3_7

In this chapter, we introduce a new technique to compute similarities among the data points based on sparse decomposition in ℓ_1 norm sense. We call it *Sparsity-Induced Similarity measure (SIS)*. The main idea is that the sparse decomposition of a data point reflects its true neighborhood structure and provides a similarity measure between the data points and its neighbors. The proposed method does not need a separate phase to estimate the neighborhood patches before measuring similarities. In other words, we do not need to rely on the Euclidean distance to predetermine its k nearest neighbors. Our approach is loosely related to distance metric learning approaches which need more data though these approaches can explore local structures among data [64, 68]. In addition, Shakhnarovich [49] measured patch similarities using sparse overcomplete code coefficients. This technique requires training data to learn the basis vectors. In contrast, our technique does not require any training data for similarity measure.

We apply the proposed SIS to both label propagation and action recognition, and evaluate the proposed approach on some public data sets for label propagation and action recognition, respectively, for example, Cedar Buffolo binary Digits data set [31] which is commonly used for evaluating graph-based semi-supervised learning methods, UIUC car data set [1], ETH-80 object data set [36], scene-15 data set [26, 35, 44], which are commonly used data sets for object/scene recognition, the KTH action data set [34], and the Weizmann action data set [7]. The experimental results indicate that the proposed SIS measure significantly improves the performance of both label propagation and action recognition.

7.2 Sparsity-Induced Similarity

7.2.1 The Clustering Condition of Subspaces

In this section, we introduce clustering conditions of subspaces. In [23, 24], it was shown that when the subspaces are either independent or disjoint, the sparse solution works well. However, in this section, we shall relax this condition. By doing so, we can measure feature similarity even in both dependent and joint subspaces. In other words, this section provides theoretical guarantee for Sparse-Induced Similarity Measure applied in arbitrary high-dimensional nonlinear spaces.

Given a set of vectors $\mathbf{S} = \{\mathbf{f}_1, \ldots, \mathbf{f}_n\}$ in $\mathbb{R}^d$, we define Span ($\mathbf{S}$) to be the set of all the vectors which can be represented as linear combinations of the vectors in $\mathbf{S}$. Let $\mathbf{V}$ denote a subspace of $\mathbb{R}^d$.

Definition 7.1 $\mathbf{S}$ is called sparse complete for $\mathbf{V}$ if (1) $\mathbf{V} \subset$ Span($\mathbf{S}$) and (2) for any given $\mathbf{f} \in \mathbf{V}$, if $\mathbf{X} = (x_1, \ldots, x_n)$ is the optimal solution of

$$\operatorname{argmin} \|\mathbf{X}\|_{\ell 0}, \text{ s.t. } \mathbf{f} = \sum_{i=1}^{n} x_i \mathbf{f}_i, \tag{7.1}$$

then $x_i = 0$ for all i with $\mathbf{f}_i \not\subset \mathbf{V}$.

The first condition says that any vector in $\mathbf{V}$ can be represented as a linear combination of the vectors in $\mathbf{S}$. The second condition states that the sparsest representation of any vector in $\mathbf{V}$ can only be achieved when all the sparse basis vectors (those with nonzero coefficients) belong to $\mathbf{V}$.

Let $\mathbf{V}_1, \ldots, \mathbf{V}_m$ denote a set of subspaces of $\mathbb{R}^d$, and $\mathbf{S}_i = \mathbf{S} \bigcap \mathbf{V}_i$. Assume $\mathbf{S} = \bigcup_{i=1}^m \mathbf{S}_i$. Denote $\mathbf{V}_i^c = \text{Span}(\mathbf{S} \backslash \mathbf{S}_i)$, and $\mathbf{V}_i^o = \mathbf{V}_i \bigcap \mathbf{V}_i^c$. Note that we do not require $\mathbf{V}_i^o$ to be empty. In other words, there could be intersections between two subspaces.

Theorem 7.1 *If $\mathbf{V}_i = Span(\mathbf{S}_i)$, and $\mathbf{S}$ is sparse complete for $\mathbf{V}_i^o$ for all $i = 1, \ldots, n$, then $\mathbf{S}$ is sparse complete for $\mathbf{V}_i$ for all $i = 1, \ldots, n$.*

Proof Given $\mathbf{f} \in \mathbf{V}_i$, let $\mathbf{X}^* = (x_1^*, \ldots, x_n^*)$ denote the solution of the optimization Eq. (7.1). Denote $\mathbf{G} = \{j \mid x_j^* \neq 0 \text{ and } \mathbf{f}_j \in \mathbf{S}_i\}$, and $\mathbf{G}^c = \{j \mid x_j^* \neq 0 \text{ and } \mathbf{f}_j \notin \mathbf{S}_i\}$. Therefore, we have

$$\mathbf{f} = \sum_{j \in \mathbf{G}} x_j^* \mathbf{f}_j + \sum_{j \in \mathbf{G}^c} x_j^* \mathbf{f}_j. \tag{7.2}$$

We want to show that $\mathbf{G}^c$ is empty. Suppose, on the contrary, that $\mathbf{G}^c$ is not empty. Denote $\mathbf{g} = \sum_{j \in \mathbf{G}} x_j^* \mathbf{f}_j$ and $\mathbf{g}^c = \sum_{j \in \mathbf{G}^c} x_j^* \mathbf{f}_j$. Then $\mathbf{g} \in \mathbf{V}_i$, $\mathbf{g}^c \in \mathbf{V}_i^c$, and $\mathbf{f} = \mathbf{g} + \mathbf{g}^c$. Since $\mathbf{f} \in \mathbf{V}_i$ and $\mathbf{g} \in \mathbf{V}_i$, we have $\mathbf{g}^c = \mathbf{f} - \mathbf{g} \in \mathbf{V}_i$. Since $\mathbf{S}$ is sparse complete for $\mathbf{V}_i^o$, there must exist nonzero coefficients $\mathbf{Z} = (z_{p_1}, \ldots, z_{p_k})$ so that $\mathbf{g}^c = \sum_{j=1}^k z_{p_j} \mathbf{f}_{p_j}$, where $k <\mid \mathbf{G}^c \mid$ and $\mathbf{f}_{p_j} \in \mathbf{V}_i^o$ for all $j = 1, \ldots, k$. Therefore, we have

$$\mathbf{f} = \mathbf{g} + \mathbf{g}^c = \sum_{i \in \mathbf{G}} x_i^* \mathbf{f}_i + \sum_{j=1}^{k} z_{p_j} \mathbf{f}_{p_j}. \tag{7.3}$$

Since $k <\mid \mathbf{G}^c \mid$, Eq. (7.3) is a sparser representation than Eq. (7.2), which is a contradiction. Therefore, $\mathbf{G}^c$ must be empty.

The following Corollary was first proved by E. Elhamifar and R. Vidal [23–25, 57].

Corollary 7.1 *If $V_i = Span(S_i)$ and $V_i \bigcap V_j = \emptyset$ for all $i \neq j$, $1 \leq i \leq n$, $1 \leq j \leq n$, then $\mathbf{S}$ is sparse complete for all V_i, $1 \leq i \leq n$.*

Proof Since $\mathbf{V}_i \bigcap \mathbf{V}_j = \emptyset$ for all $i \neq j$, $\mathbf{V}_i^o = \mathbf{V}_i \bigcap \mathbf{V}_i^c = \emptyset$. Thus $\mathbf{V}_i^o$ is sparse complete. From Theorem 7.1, $\mathbf{S}$ is sparse complete for $\mathbf{V}_i$.

Corollary 7.2 *Let d_i^o denote the dimension of linear subspace V_i^o. Assume $V_i = Span(S_i)$ and $\mathbf{S}$ contains at least d_i^o independent vectors that belong to V_i^o, $1 \leq i \leq n$. If any vector $\boldsymbol{f} \in V_i^o$ cannot be represented as a linear combination of d_i^o vectors in $S \backslash V_i^o$, then $\mathbf{S}$ is sparse complete for V_i, $1 \leq i \leq n$.*

Proof Given $\mathbf{f} \in \mathbf{V}_i^o$, suppose $\mathbf{X}^* = (x_1^*, \ldots, x_n^*)$ is a solution of the optimization equation Eq. (7.1). Denote $\mathbf{G} = \{j \mid x_j^* \neq 0 \text{ and } \mathbf{f}_j \in \mathbf{V}_i^o\}$, and $\mathbf{H} = \{j \mid x_j^* \neq 0$ and $\mathbf{f}_j \notin \mathbf{V}_i^o\}$. Then

$$\mathbf{f} = \sum_{j \in \mathbf{G}} x_j^* \mathbf{f}_j + \sum_{j \in \mathbf{H}} x_j^* \mathbf{f}_j. \tag{7.4}$$

Denote $\mathbf{g} = \sum_{j \in \mathbf{G}} x_j^* \mathbf{f}_j$ and $\mathbf{h} = \sum_{j \in \mathbf{H}} x_j^* \mathbf{f}_j$. Then $\mathbf{f} = \mathbf{g} + \mathbf{h}$. That is, $\mathbf{f} - \mathbf{g} = \mathbf{h}$. We want to show that $\mathbf{h}$ must be zero. Suppose, on the contrary, that $\mathbf{h}$ is not zero. Since $\mathbf{h} = \mathbf{f} - \mathbf{g} \in \mathbf{V}_i^o$, there must be at least d_i^o terms in $\sum_{j \in \mathbf{H}} x_j^* \mathbf{f}_j$. Therefore, there are at least d_i^o nonzero coefficients in the representation of Eq. (7.4). On the other hand, since the dimension of $\mathbf{V}_i^o$ is d_i^o and $\mathbf{S}$ contains at least d_i^o independent vectors that belong to $\mathbf{V}_i^o$, $\mathbf{f}$ can be represented as a linear combination of d_i^o vectors in $\mathbf{S}$. Therefore, this is a sparse representation of Eq. (7.4), which is a contradiction.

7.2.2 The Sparse-Induced Similarity Measure

1. Sparse Representation Assumptions

We observe that subspace assumption is closely related to sparse representation assumption, and we propose sparse decomposition as a way to define the similarity measure which takes into consideration the subspace structure. In particular, our technique is based on the following sparse representation assumptions on the feature vectors in each class.

Linearity: Any feature vector in a class can be represented as a linear combination of some other feature vectors in the same class.

Sparsity: Given a feature vector, its sparsest representation is achieved when all the basis feature vectors belong to the same class as the feature vector.

The linearity assumption has been used extensively in various computer vision tasks [41, 66, 77]. Note that for a data set with sufficient amount of data (regardless of whether they are labeled or not), the linear representation of a feature vector is usually far from unique. For example, a feature vector may be represented as a linear combination of a number of feature vectors from a different class or from multiple classes. The sparsity assumption states that when a feature vector is represented as linear combination of feature vectors in a different class, the representation tends to be less sparse. The sparsity assumption is the base for many sparse sensing researches [66], and it was used in [63] for face recognition. In this chapter, we propose to use sparsity assumption as a way to obtain similarity measure that reflects the subspace structure of classes.

Note that if the sparsity assumption is strictly satisfied, the sparse decomposition will provide a simple method for unsupervised clustering. For each feature vector $\mathbf{V}$, we decompose it as a sparse linear combination of the feature vectors. The feature vectors that have nonzero coefficients in the decomposition will be in the same class of $\mathbf{V}$. After performing this decomposition for every feature vector $\mathbf{V}$, we will be able to group them into connected components, and it is guaranteed that the feature vectors in each connected components belong to the same class. Group sparsity properties have shown very powerful discriminative capability in feature extraction and classification [13, 42]. Especially, we can model group sparsity into our similarity measure.

In practice, the data are noisy so the sparsity assumption may not be strictly satisfied. In fact, a random noise vector in general has a long tail (i.e., many small nonzero coefficients) in their sparse decomposition. Therefore making binary decisions do not work well. S, we use the coefficients as soft similarity measures.

2. The Definition of Noise-Free SIS

More formally, we propose the *Sparse-Induced Similarity Measure*. Let $\mathbf{F} = \{\mathbf{f}_1, \mathbf{f}_2, \ldots, \mathbf{f}_k, \ldots, \mathbf{f}_N\}$ denote all the feature vectors of a data set, whether they are labeled or not, where $\mathbf{f}_k \in \mathbb{R}^D$ and $\|\mathbf{f}_k\|_2 = 1$. Define $\mathbf{G}_k = \{\mathbf{f}_1, \ldots, \mathbf{f}_{k-1}, \mathbf{f}_{k+1}, \ldots, \mathbf{f}_N\}$. Let $\mathbf{X} = (x_1, \ldots, x_{k-1}, x_{k+1}, \ldots, x_N)^T$ denote the coefficients of the sparse decomposition. Given $\mathbf{F} = \{\mathbf{f}_k, \mathbf{G}_k\}$, $\mathbf{X}$ is defined by the following optimization problem:

$$(\ell_0) : \text{argmin}_{\mathbf{X}} \|\mathbf{X}\|_{\ell_0}, \;\; \text{s.t. } \mathbf{G}_k\mathbf{X} = \mathbf{f}_k, \tag{7.5}$$

where $\|\mathbf{X}\|_{\ell_0}$ is the ℓ_0 norm of $\mathbf{X}$.

This decomposition is different from the common sparse decomposition, but the problem is that the basic vectors are not necessarily orthogonal. In fact, strictly speaking, vectors in G_k do not form a basis. But Donoho and Elad [20] showed that such nonorthogonal sparse decomposition problem can still be solved through ℓ_1 minimization. That is, $\mathbf{X}$ can be obtained by solving the following linear programming problem:

$$(\ell_1) : \text{argmin}_{\mathbf{X}} \|\mathbf{X}\|_{\ell_1}, \;\; \text{s.t. } \mathbf{G}_k\mathbf{X} = \mathbf{f}_k, \tag{7.6}$$

where $\|\mathbf{X}\|_{\ell_1}$ is the ℓ_1 norm of $\mathbf{X}$.

We can convert it into a standard linear programming problem by introducing variables x_i^+ and x_i^-, and setting $x_i = x_i^+ - x_i^-$ and $|x_i| = x_i^+ + x_i^-$, $1 \le i \le N, i \ne k$, In addition, we add constraints $x_i^+ \ge 0$ and $x_i^- \ge 0$. The resulting linear programming problem is then solved by a simplex algorithm [12].[1]

The similarity between $\mathbf{f}_k$ and $\mathbf{f}_i$, $1 \le i \le N, i \ne k$, is defined as

$$s_{ki} = \frac{\max\{x_i, 0\}}{\sum_{j=1, j \ne k}^{N} \max\{x_j, 0\}}. \tag{7.7}$$

After repeating this procedure for every $\mathbf{f}_k \in \mathbf{F}$, $k = 1, \ldots, N$, we obtain a matrix s_{ij}, $1 \le i, j \le N$. Note that this matrix is not necessarily symmetric. To ensure symmetry, the final similarity between $\mathbf{f}_i$ and $\mathbf{f}_j$ is defined as $w_{ij} = \frac{s_{ij}+s_{ji}}{2}$. We set $w_{ii} = 1$.

[1] www.l1-magic.org.

Prior to computing the SIS, we need to normalize all the feature vectors so that their norms become 1. Normalization is necessary otherwise the decomposition coefficients would be sensitive to the magnitudes of the feature vectors. However, if the feature vectors are already normalized (such as SIFT features), then the normalization step is not needed.

If the amount of data is large, it becomes expensive to solve the linear programming problem of Eq. (7.5) for each feature vector. It has been shown [12, 21] that for ℓ_1-norm-based signal reconstruction, the number of basis vectors required to recover a sparse signal is only a small fraction of the signal's dimension. However, it is impossible to know which vectors should be selected as basis vectors and there could exist large correlation among basis vectors. A heuristics that we use in our experiments is the following. Given a feature vector $\mathbf{f}_k$, we choose the first CD vectors that are closest to $\mathbf{f}_k$ in terms of Euclidean distance where D is the dimension of feature vector and C is a user-specified parameter which is set to 1.5 in our experiments.

3. Noise Sparsity-Induced Similarity

Although sparse representation-based approaches have shown to be effective for various learning tasks, there also remain challenges in the high-dimensional nonlinear feature spaces due to noise effects. As we know, the robustness of sparse representation can be introduced from various ways [25]. In this section, we consider robustness to random corruption.

So far, we assume $\mathbf{f}_k$ can be decomposed as a sparse linear combination of $\mathbf{G}_k$ exactly. However, since real-world feature vectors are always noisy, it may not be possible to decompose $\mathbf{f}_k$ exactly as a sparse linear combination of $\mathbf{G}_k$. Hence, Eq. (7.5) can be modified explicitly for small possibly dense noise

$$\mathbf{f}_k = \mathbf{G}_k\mathbf{X} + \eta \tag{7.8}$$

where $\eta \in \mathbb{R}^D$ is a noise term with bounded energy $\|\eta\|_2 < \varepsilon$. The sparse solution $\mathbf{X}_0$ can still be approximately recovered by solving the following ℓ_1-minimization problem:

$$(\ell_1^s) : \text{argmin}_{\mathbf{X}} \|\mathbf{X}\|_{\ell_1}, \ \text{s.t.} \ \|\mathbf{G}_k\mathbf{X} - \mathbf{f}_k\|_2 \leq \varepsilon. \tag{7.9}$$

This convex optimization problem can be efficiently solved via second-order cone programming [8, 14, 63].

7.2.3 *Nonnegative Sparsity-Induced Similarity*

To satisfy the linear constraints of sparse coding, negative coefficients are usually needed. In some situations, such as when we use max pooling to extract dictionary basis, and similarity measures [17, 27], negative coefficients are not desirable. The reason behind this is that negative components would cause information loss and degrade the classification performance [67, 75]. For better alleviating this problem, nonnegative sparse coding is widely used in computer vision tasks [28, 38, 75]. By doing so, the nonnegative sparse coding algorithm aims to find the sparsest solution of an underdetermined and nonnegative linear system.

In this section, we shall formulate the constraint into the optimization equation by merging Eqs. (7.7) and (7.6) thus resulting in nonnegative similarity measure s_{ki} as in Eq. (7.7). Inspired by [28], based on the $\ell_0 - \ell_1$ equivalence theory and Lagrange multiplier methods, we can rewrite Eq. (7.6) as

$$\text{argmin}_{\mathbf{X}} \|\mathbf{G}_k\mathbf{X} - \mathbf{f}_k\|_2 + \lambda\|\mathbf{X}\|_{\ell_1}, \text{ s. t. } \mathbf{X} \geq 0. \tag{7.10}$$

where λ is the Lagrange multiplier.

The optimal equation in Eq. (7.10) can be reformulated as the following quadratic program:

$$\text{argmin}_{\mathbf{X}} \left(\frac{\lambda}{2} - \mathbf{G}_k^T\mathbf{f}_k\right)^T \mathbf{X} + \frac{1}{2}\mathbf{X}^T\mathbf{G}_k^T\mathbf{G}_k\mathbf{X}, \text{ s. t. } \mathbf{X} \geq 0. \tag{7.11}$$

Equation (7.11) is convex since $\mathbf{G}_k^T\mathbf{G}_k$ is a positive semidefinite matrix.

We would like to point out that nonnegative sparse coefficients can be obtained directly by optimizing Eq. (7.11) instead of the post processing step in Eq. (7.7).

7.2.4 Some Basic Issues in SIS

1. Locality and Sparsity

As some researchers observed that locality is more essential than sparsity, so locality must lead to sparsity but not necessarily vice versa [59, 70]. In other words, sparsity-induced similarity measure works well only when sparse coding is local. Consequently, we can select only a small fraction of basis vectors to compute sparse coefficients. By doing so, we can guarantee that the proposed sparsity-induced similarity measure is local.

2. Group Sparsity and SIS

As mentioned earlier, locality can improve sparse coding. Recently, group sparsity in feature spaces has been shown to be effective in classification task based on sparse representation [13, 42]. The rationale behind this is all the training samples corresponding to the same class have nonzero values in sparse coefficients. Actually, this case corresponds to a supervised learning problem, where class information can be used in sparse coding. However, for both unsupervised learning and semi-supervised learning, it is insufficient to model group sparsity. Hence, in some specific domains, e.g., supervised learning, we can incorporate group information into our SIS. For more general cases, we do not have group information. This is the reason why we do not model group information in our sparse coding.

3. Image and Local Descriptor Similarity Measure

The Structural SIMilarity (SSIM) index [60] is used to access the similarity between two images, and to improve traditional measure approaches like peak signal-to-noise ratio (PSNR). Here, the PSNR approaches estimate perceived errors while the SSIM approaches consider image degradation as perceived change in structural information. As we know, both PSNR and SSIM approaches do not encode the human vision system, thus failing to improve perceptual quality metric. We would like to point out that the proposed SIS could be suitable to assess the similarity between two images based on their extracted feature vectors since the human vision implicitly includes sparsity coding. In this section, we mainly focus on local descriptor/patch similarity measure, such as Scale Invariant Feature Transform (SIFT) [40], Spatio-Temporal Interest Points [34] (STIP).

4. Different Similarity Measures

Many different applications share a lot of similarities, e.g., geodesic distance, commute time, and diffusion time. These distances are all proven to be very robust graph-based similarities for supervised and semi-supervised learning [18]. The key difference between our technique and the technique reflected in [63] is the problem domain where the technology has been applied. Our technique addresses how to determine the similarity of two feature vectors without using any labels, while [63] addresses how to determine the distance between a feature vector and a class assuming there are sufficient labeled samples available for each class. One important implication is that our technique is useful for semi-supervised or unsupervised learning where [63] is not applicable. Moreover, the difference between the proposed SIS and the ℓ_1 graph proposed in [16, 65] is that the proposed technique can handle general similarity measure between two feature vectors while [16] mainly focuses on building the directed ℓ_1-graph, and its series of applications, such as data clustering, subspace learning, and semi-supervised learning are derived on the ℓ_1-graphs. By contrast, the proposed technique is capable of handling more general similarity measures, even in nongraph techniques. That is, graph similarity based on sparse coding is just a special case of the proposed technique.

7.2.5 A Toy Problem

Let us consider a toy problem to illustrate how sparsity representation can be used to improve similarity measure. Figure 7.1 shows a two-class classification problem. The points in each class belong to a linear subspace. Points $\mathbf{A}_1$, $\mathbf{A}_2$, $\mathbf{A}_3$, and $\mathbf{A}_4$ belong to class $\mathbf{A}$. Points $\mathbf{B}_1$, $\mathbf{B}_2$, $\mathbf{B}_3$, and $\mathbf{B}_4$ belong to class $\mathbf{B}$. Note that all the points are on the unit sphere as we assume they are normalized feature vectors. Figure 7.1 is obtained by projecting the $3D$ points to $2D$ XY plane for better visualization of the spatial relationship among the points. The coordinates of these points are

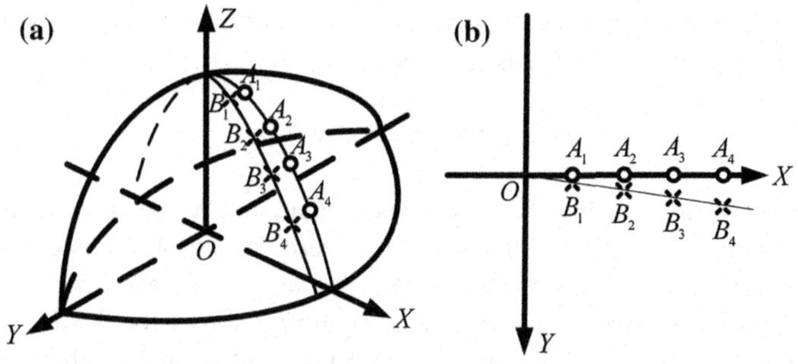

Fig. 7.1 An illustration of two-class classification problems: **a** 3D Case; **b** Points projection to 2D plane only for better illustration of spatial relationship among points

$$
\begin{aligned}
A_1 &= [0.1, 0, 0.9950], \; B_1 = [0.1, 0.025, 0.9947] \\
A_2 &= [0.2, 0, 0.9798], \; B_2 = [0.2, 0.050, 0.9785] \\
A_3 &= [0.3, 0, 0.9539], \; B_3 = [0.3, 0.075, 0.9510] \\
A_4 &= [0.4, 0, 0.9165], \; B_4 = [0.4, 0.100, 0.9110].
\end{aligned} \tag{7.12}
$$

It can be easily verified that for each point $\mathbf{A}_i, i = 1, \ldots, 4$, its closest point is $\mathbf{B}_i$ according to the Euclidean distance. Similarly, the closest point of $\mathbf{B}_i$ is $\mathbf{A}_i$. Figure 7.2 shows the label propagation result obtained by computing similarities based on the Euclidean distance while $\mathbf{A}_4$ and $\mathbf{B}_1$ are used as the labeled data. We can see that $\mathbf{A}_1$ and $\mathbf{A}_2$ are incorrectly labeled and $\mathbf{B}_3$ and $\mathbf{B}_4$ are incorrectly labeled as in class $\mathbf{B}$.

On the other hand, let us represent point $\mathbf{A}_2$ as a sparse linear combination of the rest of the points. That is, we seek coefficients, $x_1, x_3, x_4, y_1, y_2, y_3, y_4$, so that

$$
\mathbf{A}_2 = \sum_{i=1, i \neq 2}^{4} x_i A_i + \sum_{j=1}^{4} y_j B_j, \tag{7.13}
$$

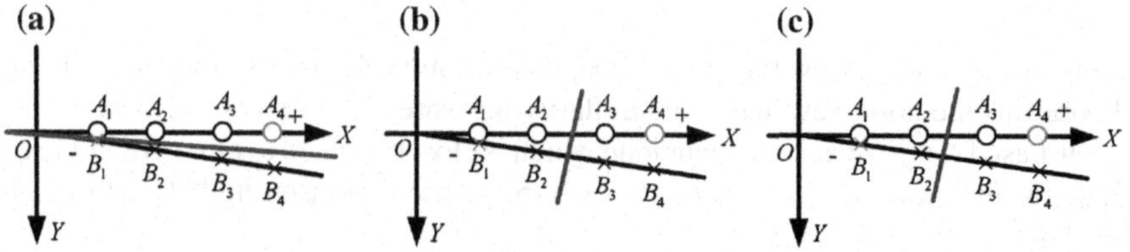

Fig. 7.2 Label propagation using three different similarity measures: **a** SIS; **b** Euclidean distance; **c** Linear neighbors in [58], where the number of nearest neighbors are 2. Here, *red dots* A_4 and B_1 are labeled data, and the *blue lines* are class boundaries (best viewed in color)

and the number of nonzero coefficients is the smallest. It can be verified that the sparsest decomposition is given as follows:

$$\mathbf{A}_2 = 0.5079\mathbf{A}_1 + 0.4974\mathbf{A}_3. \tag{7.14}$$

In this representation, $\mathbf{A}_1$ has the largest coefficient, and $\mathbf{A}_3$ has the second largest coefficient. The rest of the coefficients are all zero. Based on the coefficients, we conclude that $\mathbf{A}_2$ is most similar to $\mathbf{A}_1$ and $\mathbf{A}_3$. We can see that this similarity measure is more consistent with the class structure. Figure 7.2 shows the label propagation result obtained by using SIS measure and using $\mathbf{A}_4$ and $\mathbf{B}_1$ as the labeled data. We can see that all the points are correctly labeled.

Note that if we use linear decomposition without sparsity constraints, the resulting coefficients do not provide a good similarity measure. Again, let us consider $\mathbf{A}_2$ in the above example. Since there are multiple ways to represent $\mathbf{A}_2$ as a linear combination of the rest of the vectors, one possibility, as suggested by Wang and Zhang [58], is to choose a small number of nearest neighbors (in terms of Euclidean distance). If we choose the two-nearest neighbors of $\mathbf{A}_2$, which are $\mathbf{A}_1$ and $\mathbf{B}_2$, we obtain the following least-square solution:

$$\mathbf{A}_2 \approx 0.1361\mathbf{A}_1 + 0.8639\mathbf{B}_2. \tag{7.15}$$

According to this representation, $\mathbf{B}_2$ would be considered as the most similar to $\mathbf{A}_2$. Figure 7.2c shows the label propagation result obtained using Wang and Zhang's method for similarity measure. Again, $\mathbf{A}_4$ and $\mathbf{B}_1$ are used as the labeled data. We can see that the result is the same as that obtained by computing similarities based on Euclidean distance.

7.3 Application

7.3.1 Label Propagation

In this section, we review the label propagation framework as described in [79]. We choose this method to evaluate our similarity measure because it is a representative graph-based semi-supervised technique which is closely related to other graph-based methods, including random walk approach [52], spectral clustering [51], and graph cuts [74].

Label propagation is a way to propagate labels on a graph from labeled data to unlabeled data for different applications [33, 78, 79], for example, patch labelling [6], learning neighborhood structures [22], labeling of video sequences [2, 10], image annotation [3, 15, 32, 54]. The basic idea is, given a small number of labeled data, to propagate the labels through dense unlabeled regions and find more data with the similar properties as the labeled data, and use these selected unlabeled data to enhance a certain performance of a system. A straightforward solution is to compute pairwise similarities among all the data points, and then formulate the problem as a harmonic energy minimization problem [79] which has a closed-form solution. This technique is briefly summarized below.

Suppose there are K classes. Let $\mathbf{C} = \{1, 2, \ldots, K\}$ denote the set of class labels. Let $\mathbf{F}_l = [\mathbf{f}_1, \mathbf{f}_2, \ldots, \mathbf{f}_n]$ denote the labeled data. Let $\mathbf{F}_u = \left[\mathbf{f}_{n+1}, \mathbf{f}_{n+2}, \ldots, \mathbf{f}_{n+m}\right]$ denote the unlabeled data. Typically $n \ll m$. We use g_i to denote the label of $\mathbf{f}_i$, $i = 1, \ldots, n + m$. We assume $g_1, \ldots, g_n$ are known, and the task is to compute $g_{n+1}, \ldots, g_{n+m}$.

Consider a graph $\mathbf{G} = (\mathbf{V}, \mathbf{E})$ with nodes corresponding to $N = n + m$ feature vectors. There is an edge for every pair of the nodes. We assume there is an $N \times N$ symmetric weight matrix $\mathbf{W} = [w_{ij}]$ on the edges of the graph. The weight for each edge indicates the similarity between the two nodes that are adjacent to the edge. One commonly used similarity measure is the Gaussian Kernel Similarity- based weight matrix defined as

$$w_{ij} = \exp\left(-d_{\sigma^2}(\mathbf{f}_i, \mathbf{f}_j)\right) = \exp\left(-\frac{\|\mathbf{f}_i - \mathbf{f}_j\|}{\sigma^2}\right), \tag{7.16}$$

where σ is a hyperparameter. As pointed out in [58, 79], it is hard to determine the optimal value of σ, which causes the instability of label propagation process.

We propagate a label from a labeled feature to an unlabeled one through the edges between the two feature vectors. Larger edge weights mean that labels are easier to propagate. Here, we define a probabilistic transition matrix P_{ij}, which is the probability of transit from node i to j [78]

$$P_{ij} = \frac{w_{ij}}{\sum_{k=1}^{N} w_{ik}}. \tag{7.17}$$

Let $\mathbf{f} = (\mathbf{f}_L, \mathbf{f}_U)^T$ denote the labels of all feature vectors, where $\mathbf{f}_L$ are label matrix of labeled feature vectors, and $\mathbf{f}_U$ are unknown label matrix. Then, we divide matrix $\mathbf{P}$ into

$$\mathbf{P} = \begin{bmatrix} \mathbf{P}_{LL} & \mathbf{P}_{LU} \\ \mathbf{P}_{UL} & \mathbf{P}_{UU} \end{bmatrix}. \tag{7.18}$$

The label propagation algorithm is formulated as [78]

$$\mathbf{f}_U \leftarrow \mathbf{P}_{UU}\mathbf{f}_U + \mathbf{P}_{UL}Y_L \tag{7.19}$$

where $\mathbf{Y}_L$ is known as label matrix. The proof of the algorithm converges to a simple solution and can be referred to [78]

Let $\mathbf{D}$ denote a $N \times N$ diagonal matrix with $d_{ii} = \sum_j w_{ij}$. Denote $\mathbf{P} = \mathbf{D}^{-1}\mathbf{W}$. We split matrix $\mathbf{W}$ into 4 blocks

$$\mathbf{W} = \begin{bmatrix} \mathbf{W}_{nn} & \mathbf{W}_{nm} \\ \mathbf{W}_{mn} & \mathbf{W}_{mm} \end{bmatrix}, \tag{7.20}$$

where $\mathbf{W}_{nn}$ is the top left $n \times n$ submatrix of $\mathbf{W}$. We split $\mathbf{D}$ and $\mathbf{P}$ in the same way.

Denote $\mathbf{G}_n = (g_1, \ldots, g_n)^T$, $\mathbf{G}_m = (g_{n+1}, \ldots, g_{n+m})^T$, then $\mathbf{G}_m$ is computed by the following formula:

$$\mathbf{G}_m = (\mathbf{D}_{mm} - \mathbf{W}_{mm})^{-1}\mathbf{W}_{mn}\mathbf{G}_n = (\mathbf{I} - \mathbf{P}_{mm})^{-1}\mathbf{P}_{mn}\mathbf{G}_n. \tag{7.21}$$

The performance of such a graph-based label propagation technique relies on the weight matrix, i.e., the similarity measure between the nodes. Although there have been extensive studies on the label propagation techniques, little research has been reported on how to measure the similarities. The most commonly used similarity measure is the Gaussian Kernel Similarity-based measure Eq. (7.16) whose performance is sensitive to the parameter variance setting.

7.3.2 Human Activity Recognition

In this section, we further discuss the application of the proposed Sparsity-Induced Similarity measure on action recognition. Here, we represent an action as a space-time object and characterize it by a collection of Spatio-Temporal Interest Points (STIPs) [34] similar to that in [71–73]. Here, STIPs consist of Histogram of Gradient (HoG) and Histogram of Flow (HoF), which correspond to appearance features and motion features, respectively. Hence, each video clip consists of a collection of STIPs, $\nu = \{\mathbf{d}_k^\nu\}_{k=1}^{K_\nu}$. In the optimal NBNN (ONBNN) [4], a log-likelihood of a local descriptor $\mathbf{d}$ relative to class label c is defined as

$$\begin{aligned} -\log P(\mathbf{d}|c) &= -\log\left\{\frac{1}{Z_c}\exp\left(-\frac{\tau^c(\mathbf{d})}{2\sigma_c^2}\right)\right\} \\ &= \frac{\tau^c(\mathbf{d})}{2\sigma_c^2} + \log(Z^c), \end{aligned} \tag{7.22}$$

where $Z^c = |\chi^c|(2\pi)^{D/2}(\sigma^c)^D$ is a normalization factor obtained by normalizing the probability density function, and χ^c is the set of all STIPs from all training video clips within class c. Recall that $\tau^c(\mathbf{d})$ is the squared Euclidean distance of $\mathbf{d}$ to its nearest neighbor in χ^c. To our best knowledge, $\tau^c(\mathbf{d})$ in Eq. (7.22) is calculated by this Euclidean distance measure of feature vectors in almost all of I2CNN approaches.

For better capturing the structures of feature spaces, we use the proposed Sparsity-Induced Similarity Measure to calculate the distance between $\mathbf{d}$ and class

c in Naive Bayes-based Mutual Information Maximization (NBMIM) Classifiers, called **Sparse NBMIM (SNBMIM)**. Define $\mathbf{G}_k = \{\mathbf{F}^0, \mathbf{F}^1, \ldots, \mathbf{F}^c, \ldots, \mathbf{F}^{C-1}\}$ and $\mathbf{F}^c = \{\mathbf{f}_0^c, \mathbf{f}_1^c, \ldots, \mathbf{f}_{n_c}^c\}$, where n_c is the number of STIPs from training video clips within class c. Hence, given $\mathbf{f}_k = \mathbf{d}$, we can obtain nonnegative sparse coefficients $\mathbf{X} = \{\mathbf{X}^0, \mathbf{X}^1, \ldots, \mathbf{X}^c, \ldots, \mathbf{X}^{C-1}\}$ from Eq. (7.10), where $\mathbf{X}^c = \{x_0^c, x_1^c, \ldots, x_n^c, \ldots, x_{n_c}^c\}$. Therefore, we redefine the $\tau^c(\mathbf{d})$ using the nonnegative SIS between $\mathbf{d}$ and class c. In other words, we define $\tau^c(\mathbf{d})$ as a *max* pooling function on the nonnegative SIS

$$\tau^c(\mathbf{d}) = 1 - \frac{\max_{n\in[0,n_c]}\{x_n^c\}}{\max_c\left\{\max_{n\in[0,n_c]}\{x_n^c\}\right\}}. \tag{7.23}$$

According to naive Bayes formulation, we have class conditional likelihood of a video clip v

$$\begin{aligned} -\log P(v|c) &= \sum_{k=1}^{K_v}\left(\frac{\tau^c(\mathbf{d}_k^v)}{2\sigma_c^2} + \log(Z^c)\right) \\ &= \alpha_c \sum_{k=1}^{K_v} \tau^c(\mathbf{d}_k^v) + K_v\beta^c, \end{aligned} \tag{7.24}$$

where $\alpha_c = 1/(2\sigma_c^2)$ and $\beta^c = \log(Z^c)$. The final decision function is

$$\hat{c}_v = \operatorname{argmin}_c\left(\alpha_c \sum_{k=1}^{K_v} \tau^c(\mathbf{d}_k^v) + K_v\beta^c\right). \tag{7.25}$$

Inspired by [4], we learn the optimal α_c and β_c by minimizing a hinge loss of the proposed classifier. Moreover, minimizing the hinge loss can be recast as a linear programming, which is referred to [4] for details.

We would like to point out that the Sparse NBMIM is an application of the SIS to the human action recognition task. Moreover, we describe an adaptation of the NBMIM classifier [4], where the Sparse NBMIM uses the nonnegative SIS between a descriptor d and the class c instead of Euclidean distance. As we know, the NBMIM is a variant of NBNN and the NBNN kernel approach [56] is a kernelized version of the NBNN approach. Hence, we can naturally incorporate kernel tricks in our sparse NBMIM.

7.3.3 Visual Tracking

Sparse-induced similarity (SIS) has also been employed in visual tracking problems yielding a remarkable result. Liu et al. place SIS into the framework of particle filter to restore the tracker algorithm. In the framework [37], candidate feature vectors and identity matrices have been concatenated to produce the dictionary matrix A. Given the first frame r as a sparse linear combination of the candidate feature vectors, we obtain

$$\underset{x}{\operatorname{argmin}} ||x||_{l_1}, \quad \text{s.t } Ax = r, \quad r \geq 0, \tag{7.26}$$

where the coefficients of x show the relationship between the reference frame and the candidate frame, whether they are similar or not. Therefore, the similarity can be obtained as follows:

$$s_i = \frac{x_i}{\sum_{j=1, j \neq i}^{N} x_j}. \tag{7.27}$$

It has also been shown in [37] that the sparse representation gives good similarity measurement and effective distinguishing capability.

7.3.4 *Image Categorization*

In computer vision, the problem of image categorization is a very challenging task because of its computation complexity and laborious process. Inspired by SIS, Wang et al. proposed an approach that induced the undirected graph from the immediate output of SIS as co-linkage similarity. The weights of two features which express their similarity are symmetrized by

$$w_{ij} = \frac{s_{ij} + s_{ji}}{2}. \tag{7.28}$$

The resulted weights from Eq. (7.28) can form an undirected graph where the edge is assigned by the average of the two weights on both directions of the SIS. This may discard the structural information in edge direction, but co-linkage similarity symmetrically normalized both in-links and out-links of a directed graph in a balanced manner, so that effective mutual link reinforcement can be achieved.

7.3.5 *Spam Image Cluster*

Spam image problem is formulated as embedding the text content into graphical images to bypass traditional spam filters. Taking the advantage of SIS, Gao et al. proposed a nonnegative SIS for cluster analysis of the spam image [27]. They assumed that nonnegative linear combination of a small number of spam images in the same cluster can effectively represent the spam image.

Mathematically, let $X = [x_1, x_2, \ldots, x_{i-1}, x_{i+1}, \ldots, x_N]$ denote the feature vector of N images from a batch of e-mails in an e-mails server, the nonnegative SIS can be obtained as follows [27]:

$$\underset{a}{\text{argmin}} \frac{1}{2}||x_i - X_i.a||^2 + \frac{\beta}{2}||a||^2 + \lambda \sum_{j=1}^{n} a_j, \quad \text{s.t } \forall j = 1, \ldots, N, \; a_i \geq 0. \tag{7.29}$$

Equation (7.29) can be solved using a standard active set method as shown in [27].

References

1. Agarwal, S., Roth, D.: Learning a sparse representation for object detection. In: ECCV. Springer (2002)
2. Badrinarayanan, V., Galasso, F., Cipolla, R.: Label propagation in video sequences. In: IEEE CVPR (2010)
3. Bao, B., Ni, B., Mu, Y., Yan, S.: Efficient region-aware large graph construction towards scalable multi-label propagation. Pattern Recognit. **44**(3), 598–606 (2011)
4. Behmo, R., Marcombes, P., Dalalyan, A., Prinet, V.: Towards Optimal Naive Bayes Nearest Neighbor. Springer, Berlin (2010)
5. Bilenko, M., Basu, S., Mooney, R.: Integrating constraints and metric learning in semi-supervised clustering. In: ICML (2004)
6. Bishop, C.M., Ulusoy, I.: Object recognition via local patch labelling. In: Proceedings Workshop on Machine Learning (2005)
7. Blank, M., Gorelick, L., Shechtman, E., Irani, M., Basri, R.: Actions as space-time shapes. In: IEEE ICCV (2005)
8. Boyd, S., Vandenberghe, L.: Convex Optimization. Cambridge University Press, New York (2004)
9. Bruckstein, A., Donoho, D., Elad, M.: From sparse solutions of systems of equations to sparse modeling of signals and images. SIAM Rev. **51**(1), 34–81 (2009)
10. Budvytis, I., Badrinarayanan, V., Cipolla, R.: Label propagation in complex video sequences using semi-supervised learning. In: BMVC (2010)
11. Candes, E., Wakin, M.: An introduction to compressive sampling. IEEE Signal Process. Mag. **25**(2), 21–30 (2008)
12. Candes, E.J., Romberg, J., Tao, T.: Stable signal recovery from incomplete and inaccurate measurements. Commun. Pure Appl. Math. **59**(8), 1207–1223 (2008)
13. Chao, Y., Yeh, Y., Chen, Y., Lee, Y., Wang, Y.: Locality-constrained group sparse representation for robust face recognition. In: IEEE ICIP (2011)
14. Chen, S., Donoho, D., Saunders, M.: Atomic decomposition by basis pursuit. SIAM J. Sci. Comput. **20**(1), 33–61 (1999)
15. Chen, X., Mu, Y., Yan, S., Chua, T.: Efficient large-scale image annotation by probabilistic collaborative multi-label propagation. In: IEEE ICME (2010)
16. Cheng, B., Yang, J., Yan, S., Fu, Y., Huang, T.: Learning with ℓ_1-graph for image analysis. IEEE TIP **19**(4), 858–866 (2010)
17. Cheng, H., Liu, Z., Yang, J.: Sparsity induced similarity measure for label propagation. In: IEEE ICCV (2009)
18. Deng, Y., Dai, Q., Wang, R., Zhang, Z.: Commute time guided transformation for feature extraction. Comput. Vis. Image Underst. **116**, 473–483 (2012)

19. Donoho, D.: Compressed sensing. IEEE TIT **52**(4), 1289–1306 (2006)
20. Donoho, D.L., Elad, M.: Maximal sparsity representation via l1 minimization. Proc. Natl. Acad. Sci. **100**, 2197–2202 (2003)
21. Donoho, D.L., Tanner, J.: Counting faces of randomly-projected polytopes when the projection radically lowers dimension. J. Am. Math. Soc. **22**(1), 1–53 (2009)
22. Ebert, S., Fritz, M., Schiele, B.: Pick your neighborhood-improving labels and neighborhood structure for label propagation. In: Pattern Recognit. pp. 152–162 (2011)
23. Elhamifar, E., Vidal, R.: Sparse subspace clustering. In: IEEE CVPR (2009)
24. Elhamifar, E., Vidal, R.: Clustering disjoint subspaces via sparse representation. In: IEEE ICASSP (2010)
25. Elhamifar, E., Vidal, R.: Robust classification using structured sparse representation. In: IEEE CVPR (2011)
26. Feifei, L., Perona, P.: A Bayesian hierarchical model for learning natural scene categories. In: IEEE CVPR (2005)
27. Gao, Y., Choudhary, A., Hua, G.: A nonnegative sparsity induced similarity measure with application to cluster analysis of spam images. In: IEEE International Conference on Acoustics Speech and Signal Processing (2010)
28. He, R., Zheng, W., Hu, B., Kong, X.: Nonnegative sparse coding for discriminative semi-supervised learning. In: IEEE CVPR (2011)
29. Hoi, S., Liu, W., Chang, S.: Semi-supervised distance metric learning for collaborative image retrieval. In: IEEE CVPR (2008)
30. Huang, K., Aviyente, S.: Sparse representation for signal classification. In: NIPS (2006)
31. Hull, J.J.: A database for handwritten text recognition research. IEEE TPAMI **16**(5), 550–554 (1994)
32. Kang, F., Jin, R., Sukthankar, R.: Correlated label propagation with application to multi-label learning. In: IEEE CVPR (2006)
33. Kobayashi, T., Watanabe, K., Otsu, N.: Logistic label propagation. Pattern Recognit. Lett. **33**(5), 580–588 (2012)
34. Laptev, I.: On space-time interest points. IJCV **64**(2), 107–123 (2005)
35. Lazebnik, S., Schmid, C., Ponce, J.: Beyond bags of features: spatial pyramid matching for recognizing natural scene categories. In: IEEE CVPR (2006)
36. Leibe, B., Schiele, B.: Analyzing appearance and contour based methods for object categorization. In: IEEE CVPR (2003)
37. Liu, H., Sun, F.: Visual tracking using sparsity induced similarity. In: IEEE ICPR (2010)
38. Liu, Y., Wu, F., Zhang, Z., Zhuang, Y., Yan, S.: Sparse representation using nonnegative curds and whey. In: IEEE CVPR (2010)
39. Lowe, D.: Similarity metric learning for a variable-Kernel classifier. Neural Comput. **7**(1), 72–85 (1995)
40. Lowe, D.: Distinctive image features from scale-invariant keypoints. IJCV **60**(2), 91–110 (2004)
41. Mairal, J., Leordeanu, M., Bach, F., Hebert, M., Ponce, J.: Discriminative sparse image models for class-specific edge detection and image interpretation. In: ECCV. Springer (2008)
42. Majumdar, A., Ward, R.: Classification via group sparsity promoting regularization. In: IEEE ICASSP (2009)
43. Mitra, P., Murthy, C., Pal, S.: Unsupervised feature selection using feature similarity. IEEE Trans. Pattern Anal. Mach. Intell. **24**(3), 301–312 (2002)
44. Oliva, A., Torralba, A.: Modeling the shape of the scene: a holistic representation of the spatial envelope. IJCV **42**(3), 145–175 (2001)
45. Olshausen, B., Field, D.: Sparse coding with an overcomplete basis set: a strategy employed by v1? Vis. Res. **37**(23), 3311–3325 (1997)
46. Poggio, T., Girosi, F.: A sparse representation for function approximation. Neural Comput. **10**, 1445–1454 (1998)
47. Roweis, S., Saul, L.: Nonlinear dimensionality reduction by locally linear embedding. Science **290**(5500), 2323 (2000)

48. Sankaranarayanan, A., Turaga, P., Baraniuk, R., Chellappa, R.: Compressive acquisition of dynamic scenes. In: ECCV. Springer (2010)
49. Shakhnarovich, G.: Learning task-specific similarity. Ph.D thesis. MIT (2006)
50. Shen, X., Wu, Y.: Sparsity model for robust optical flow estimation at motion discontinuities. In: IEEE CVPR (2010)
51. Shi, J., Malik, J.: Normalized cuts and image segmentation. IEEE TPAMI **22**(8), 888–905 (2000)
52. Shi, J., Malik, J.: Partially labeled classification with Markov random walks. In: NIPS (2000)
53. Starck, J., Murtagh, F., Fadili, J.: Sparse Image and Signal Processing: Wavelets, Curvelets, Morphological Diversity. Cambridge University Press, Cambridge (2010)
54. Tang, J., Hong, R., Yan, S., Chua, T., Qi, G., Jain, R.: Image annotation by k NN-sparse graph-based label propagation over noisily tagged web images. ACM TIST **2**(2), 14 (2011)
55. Tsang, I., Kwok, J., Bay, C.: Distance metric learning with Kernels. In: ICANN (2003)
56. Tuytelaars, T., Fritz, M., Saenko, K., Darrell, T.: The NBNN Kernel. In: IEEE ICCV (2011)
57. Vidal, R.: Subspace clustering. IEEE Signal Process. Mag. **28**(2), 52–68 (2011)
58. Wang, F., Zhang, C.: Label propagation through linear neighborhoods. In: ICML (2007)
59. Wang, J., Yang, J., Yu, K., Lv, F., Huang, T., Gong, Y.: Locality-constrained linear coding for image classification. In: IEEE CVPR (2010)
60. Wang, Z., Bovik, A., Sheikh, H., Simoncelli, E.: Image quality assessment: from error visibility to structural similarity. IEEE TIP **13**(4), 600–612 (2004)
61. Weinberger, K., Blitzer, J., Saul, L.: Distance metric learning for large margin nearest neighbor classification. In: NIPS (2006)
62. Wright, J., Ma, Y., Mairal, J., Sapiro, G., Huang, T., Yan, S.: Sparse representation for computer vision and pattern recognition. Proc. IEEE **98**(6), 1031–1044 (2010)
63. Wright, J., Yang, A., Ganesh, A., Sastry, S., Ma, Y.: Robust face recognition via sparse representation. IEEE TPAMI **31**(2), 210–227 (2009)
64. Xing, E.P., Ng, A.Y., Jordan, M.I., Russell, S.: Distance metric learning, with application to clustering with side-information. In: NIPS (2002)
65. Yan, S., Wang, H.: Semi-supervised learning by sparse representation. In: SIAM International Conference on Data Mining, SDM (2009)
66. Yang, J., Wright, J., Ma, Y., Huang, T.: Image super-resolution as sparse representation of raw image patches. In: IEEE CVPR (2008)
67. Yang, J., Yu, K., Gong, Y., Huang, T.: Linear spatial pyramid matching using sparse coding for image classification. In: IEEE CVPR (2009)
68. Yang, L., Jin, R.: Distance Metric Learning: A Comprehensive Survey, vol. 2, pp. 1–51. Michigan State University (2006)
69. Yu, K., Zhang, T.: High dimensional nonlinear learning using local coordinate coding. In: IEEE ICML (2009)
70. Yu, K., Zhang, T., Gong, Y.: Nonlinear learning using local coordinate coding. In: NIPS (2009)
71. Yuan, J., Liu, Z., Wu, Y.: Discriminative subvolume search for efficient action detection. In: IEEE CVPR (2009)
72. Yuan, J., Liu, Z., Wu, Y.: Discriminative video pattern search for efficient action detection. IEEE TPAMI **33**(9), 1728–1743 (2011)
73. Yuan, J., Liu, Z., Wu, Y., Zhang, Z.: Speeding up spatio-temporal sliding-window search for efficient event detection in crowded videos. In: ACM International Workshop on Events in Multimedia (2009)
74. Zabih, R., Kolmogorov, V.: Spatially coherent clustering using graph cuts. In: IEEE CVPR (2004)
75. Zhang, C., Liu, J., Tian, Q., Xu, C., Lu, H., Ma, S.: Image classification by non-negative sparse coding, low-rank and sparse decomposition. In: IEEE CVPR (2011)
76. Zhang, L., Yang, M., Feng, X.: Sparse representation or collaborative representation: which helps face recognition? In: IEEE ICCV (2011)
77. Zhang, X., Liang, L., Tang, X., Shum, H.: L_1 regularized projection pursuit for additive model learning. In: IEEE CVPR (2008)

78. Zhu, X.: Semi-supervised learning with graphs. Ph.D. thesis, CMU-LTI-05-192. The School of Computer Science, Carnegie Mellon University, Pittsburgh, PA, (2002)
79. Zhu, X., Ghahramani, Z., Lafferty, J.: Semi-supervised learning using Gaussian fields and harmonic functions. In: ICML (2003)

Chapter 8
Sparse Representation and Learning-Based Classifiers

8.1 Introduction

Sparse Representation and Learning-based Classifiers (SRLC) are the results which combine pattern recognition and compressed sensing [21, 24]. Sparsity as a prior plays an important role in machine learning and computer vision. In different SRLCs, sparsity could be used in sample similarity [21, 24], histogram generation [12, 13, 20, 22], local feature similarity [7], and nearest neighbor classifiers [6, 14].

8.2 Sparse Representation-Based Classifiers (SRC)

8.2.1 *The SRC Algorithm and Its Invariants*

Similar to nearest neighbor classifiers [2, 8], SRC is a nonparameter learning approach proposed by Wright et al. [21]. The basic idea is that training samples form a training matrix as a dictionary and then the testing sample can be spanned by this dictionary sparsely. In other words, a testing sample is only related to few columns in this dictionary.

Let us introduce the basic formulation of SRC [21]. Given training matrix $A = [A_1, A_2, \ldots, A_N] \in \mathbb{R}^{D\times N}$, each testing sample can be linearly spanned by

$$y = Ax, \tag{8.1}$$

If the testing sample y belongs to the cth class, then

$$x = [0, \ldots, 0, x_{c,1}, x_{c,2}, \ldots, x_{c,n_c}, 0, \ldots, 0]^T, \tag{8.2}$$

H. Cheng, *Sparse Representation, Modeling and Learning in Visual Recognition*,
Advances in Computer Vision and Pattern Recognition,
DOI 10.1007/978-1-4471-6714-3_8

where $N = \sum_{c=1}^{C} x_c$. Furthermore, SRC is formulated as a minimizing ℓ_1-norm optimization problem

$$\text{(Basic SRC)} \quad \arg\min_{x} \|\boldsymbol{x}\|_{\ell_1}, \quad \text{s.t.} \quad \|y - A\boldsymbol{x}\|_{\ell_2} \leq \varepsilon. \tag{8.3}$$

Equation (8.3) is the robust version of SRC. In order to exploit the presumed sparsity in the problem, Wright et al. generated a random matrix $\Phi \in \mathbb{R}^{d \times D}$ (where $d \ll D$) and identified the vector $\boldsymbol{x}$ which minimizes the following ℓ_1-norm optimization problem [21]:

$$\ell_1\text{-norm optimization (Efficient SRC)} \quad \arg\min_{\boldsymbol{x} \in \mathbb{R}^N} \|\boldsymbol{x}\|_{\ell_1} \quad \text{s.t.} \quad \Phi \boldsymbol{y} = \Phi A \boldsymbol{x}, \tag{8.4}$$

or the related problem:

$$\arg\min_{\boldsymbol{x} \in \mathbb{R}^N} \|\boldsymbol{x}\|_{\ell_1} \quad \text{s.t.} \quad \|\Phi \boldsymbol{y} - \Phi A \boldsymbol{x}\|_{\ell_2} \leq \varepsilon, \tag{8.5}$$

for a given error tolerance $\varepsilon > 0$. Introducing the matrix Φ which significantly reduces the computational complexity (particularly when $d \ll D$) , yet the CS signal recovery theorem shows that when $d \geq O(\eta \log(N/\eta))$ the signal $\boldsymbol{x}$ can be exactly recovered (that is, it reaches the optimum of the original problem specified in Eq. (8.3)) with overwhelming probability at least $1 - e^{O(-d)}$. Shi et al. in [18] showed the connection between Hash Kernels and CS. In doing so they showed that it is possible to replace Φ with an implicit hash matrix $\mathbf{H}$ in order to reduce storage requirements and speed up face recognition with Orthogonal Matching Pursuit (OMP).

Zhang et al. proposed a Kernel Sparse Representation Classifier (KSRC) by introducing the kernel trick [24]. By doing so, the linear assumption is released by using nonlinear feature mapping in a Kernel feature space.

Given an arbitrary $\boldsymbol{y}$, a nonlinear mapping function Φ maps it into a high-dimensional kernel space,

$$\boldsymbol{y} \rightarrow \Phi(\boldsymbol{y}) = [\phi_1(\boldsymbol{y}), \phi_2(\boldsymbol{y}), \ldots, \phi_m(\boldsymbol{y})]^T. \tag{8.6}$$

Therefore, a testing sample is represented by the training matrix in kernel feature space by

$$\Phi(\boldsymbol{y}) = \sum_{i=1}^{N} x_i \Phi(\boldsymbol{a}_i) = \bar{A}\boldsymbol{x}, \tag{8.7}$$

where $\bar{A} = [\Phi(\boldsymbol{a}_1), \Phi(\boldsymbol{a}_2), \ldots, \Phi(\boldsymbol{a}_N)]$.

Thus, the kernel version of SRC is formulated by substituting Eq. (8.7) into Eq. (8.3).

Table 8.1 The algorithm flowchart of SRC

Step 1:	Input training samples $A = [A_1, A_2, \cdots, A_C] \in \mathbb{R}^{D\times N}$ for C classes. The query sample is $y \in \mathbb{R}^D$.
Step 2:	Normalize A so that each column has a unit ℓ_2 norm.
Step 3:	Solve the ℓ_1-minimization problem: $\hat{x} = \arg\min_x \|x\|_{\ell_1}$, s.t. $y = Ax$.
Step 4:	Compute the residuals $r_i(y) = \|y - A\delta_i(\hat{x})\|_{\ell_2}$ $(i = 1, \cdots, k)$, where δ_i denotes the characteristic function which selects the coefficients *w.r.t.* the *ith* class.
Step 5:	Output class$(y) = \arg\min_i r_i(y)$.

$$\text{(Kernel SRC)}\quad \arg\min_{x} \|\boldsymbol{x}\|_{\ell_1}, \quad \text{s.t.}\quad \Phi(\boldsymbol{y}) = \bar{A}\boldsymbol{x}. \tag{8.8}$$

Solving either Eq. (8.3) or Eq. (8.8), we can get the sparse coefficient of test sample $\boldsymbol{y}$. Solving Eq. (8.8) refers to [24]. Equation (8.3) can be transformed into a Second-Order Cone programming problem as mentioned in Chap. 3. The SRC algorithm flow chart is shown in Table 8.1.

8.2.2 Classification Error Analysis

Zhang et al. analyzed the classification error (SRC) especially for face recognition [23]. In many object recognition problems, i.e., face recognition, an important fact is that all the face images are somewhat similar, while some subjects may have very similar face images. This implies that dictionary A_i and dictionary A_j are not incoherent but can be highly correlated. Let $A_j = A_i + \Delta$. Using the NS classifier, for a query sample $\boldsymbol{y}$ from class i, we can calculate by least square method a vector $\boldsymbol{x}_i = \arg\min_x \|\boldsymbol{y} - A_i\boldsymbol{x}\|_{\ell_2}$. Let $\boldsymbol{e}_i = \boldsymbol{y} - A_i\boldsymbol{x}_i$. Similarly, if we represent $\boldsymbol{y}$ by class j, there is $\boldsymbol{x}_j = \arg\min_x \|\boldsymbol{y} - A_j\boldsymbol{x}\|_{\ell_2}$ and $\boldsymbol{e}_j = \boldsymbol{y} - A_j\boldsymbol{x}_j$. Suppose that $A_i, A_j \in \mathbb{R}^{D\times N}$, if δ is small such that [23]

$$\xi = \frac{\|\delta\|_F}{\|A_i\|_F} \le \frac{\sigma_n(A_i)}{\sigma_1(A_i)},$$

where $\sigma_1(A_i)$ and $\sigma_n(A_i)$ are the largest and smallest eigenvalues of A_i, respectively, then we have the following relationship between $\boldsymbol{e}_i$ and $\boldsymbol{e}_j$ [23]

$$\frac{\|\boldsymbol{e}_j - \boldsymbol{e}_i\|_{\ell_2}}{\|\boldsymbol{y}\|_{\ell_2}} \le \xi(1 + \kappa_2(A_i)) \min\{1, D - n\} + O(\xi^2), \tag{8.9}$$

where $\kappa_2(A_i)$ is the ℓ_2-norm conditional number of A_i.

From Eq. (8.9), we can clearly see that if δ is small, i.e., subject i and j look similar to each other, then the distance between $\boldsymbol{e}_i$ and $\boldsymbol{e}_j$ can be very small. This makes the classification very unstable because a small disturbance can lead to $\|\boldsymbol{e}_j\|_{\ell_2} < \|\boldsymbol{e}_i\|_{\ell_2}$, resulting in a wrong classification.

The above problem can be much alleviated by imposing some sparsity on $\boldsymbol{x}_i$ and $\boldsymbol{x}_j$. The reason is very simple. If $\boldsymbol{y}$ is from class i, it is more likely that we can use only a few samples (e.g., 5 or 6 samples) in A_i to represent $\boldsymbol{y}$ with good accuracy. In contrast, we may need more samples (e.g., 8 or 9 samples) in A_j to represent $\boldsymbol{y}$ with nearly the same accuracy. Under a certain sparsity constraint, the representation error of $\boldsymbol{y}$ by A_i will be visibly lower than that by A_j, making the classification of $\boldsymbol{y}$ easier. The sparse representation of $\boldsymbol{y}$ by A can be formulated as

$$\arg\min_{\boldsymbol{x}} \|\boldsymbol{y} - A\boldsymbol{x}\|_{\ell_2} \quad \text{s.t. } \|\boldsymbol{x}\|_{\ell_p} \leq \varepsilon, \tag{8.10}$$

where ε is a constant and p can be 0, 1, or any other eligible sparsity metric.

8.3 Sparse Coding-Based Spatial Pyramid Matching (ScSPM)

8.3.1 Assignment-Based Sparse Coding

Assignment-based Coding (AC) is one of most popular techniques in feature coding [3, 12, 13, 20, 22]. Given a feature, AC assigns it to one or multiple codewords. The fundamental problem is to calculate the distance between the feature and codewords.

Quantization is mapping a feature $\boldsymbol{y}$ into its closet vector of the codebook $A = \{\boldsymbol{a}_1, \boldsymbol{a}_2, \ldots, \boldsymbol{a}_m\}$. We have

$$\boldsymbol{y}^* = \arg\min_{\hat{\boldsymbol{y}} \in \{\boldsymbol{a}_i\}} = \|\hat{\boldsymbol{y}} - \boldsymbol{y}\|_{\ell_2}^2. \tag{8.11}$$

The goal of quantization is to reduce the cardinality of feature space, thus approximating the feature in the codebook space.

Vector quantization only chooses one codeword which is the closest to $\boldsymbol{y}$ using KNN. Thus we have

$$\arg\min_{\mathbf{U}} \sum_{n=1}^{N} \|\boldsymbol{y}_n - A\boldsymbol{u}_n\|_{\ell_2}^2 \tag{8.12}$$
$$\text{s.t. } Card(\boldsymbol{u}_n) = 1, |\boldsymbol{u}_n| = 1, \boldsymbol{u}_n \geq 0, \forall n.$$

In AC, Eq. (8.12) applies the learned dictionary A into a new feature set $Y = \{\boldsymbol{y}_n\}$. The dictionary A can be learned by

$$\arg\min_{A} \sum_{n=1}^{N} \arg\min_{k=1,2,\ldots,K} \|\boldsymbol{y}_n - \boldsymbol{a}_k\|_{\ell_2}^2. \tag{8.13}$$

Assignment-based Sparse Coding (ASC) can be formulated as

$$\arg\min_{\mathbf{U},\mathbf{A}} \sum_{n=1}^{N} \|\boldsymbol{y}_n - \mathbf{A}\boldsymbol{u}_n\|_{\ell_2} + \lambda\|\boldsymbol{u}_n\|_{\ell_1} \tag{8.14}$$

$$\text{s.t.}\|\boldsymbol{u}_n\| \le 1, \quad \forall n = 1, 2, \ldots, N. \tag{8.15}$$

Equation (8.14) can be solved by feature-sign search algorithm efficiently [16].

In usual, the dictionary is an overcomplete basis set. ASC consists of a training phase and a coding phase. The training phase of ASC is to solve Eq. (8.14) w.r.t. **U** and **A**. In the coding phase, we can optimize Eq. (8.14) w.r.t. **U** only. By contract, the advantages of ASC are as follows [22]. First of all, it is shown in many research that image features are sparse in principle. Second, sparse constraints provide more powerful representation since less nonzero items weight salient properties of images. Third, ASC emphasis is on lower reconstruction error and not the discriminative error.

8.3.2 The Spatial Pooling

According to Bag-of-features models, we can represent each image as a single feature vector by calculating the image statistics given a set of local descriptors in the following form

$$\mathscr{Z} = \mathscr{F}(\mathbf{U}), \tag{8.16}$$

where $\mathscr{F}(\cdot)$ is a pooling function defined on each column of **U**. Different pooling functions correspond to different image statistics. As we discussed in Sect. 6.2.2, the most commonly used pooling functions are averaging pooling functions and max pooling functions

$$\mathscr{Z} = \frac{1}{N}\sum_{n=1}^{N} \boldsymbol{u}_n, \tag{8.17}$$

$$\mathscr{Z}_j = \max\{|u_{j,1}|, |u_{j,2}|, \ldots, |u_{j,N}|\}. \tag{8.18}$$

Both pooling functions are widely used in biologically inspired models of image recognition [4]. In max pooling functions, only the maximum value within the reception field is propagated to the next layer, while average pooling functions work on the average value within the receptive field.

8.3.3 The Sparse Coding-Based Spatial Pyramid Matching

Bag-of-Features models in visual recognition are originally from Bag-of-words in document classification, where image features are treated as words [9]. Moreover, BoF models define vectors of occurrence counts of a set of local image features on a learned dictionary [17]. Furthermore, spatial pyramid matching approaches generate one histogram of each image by concatenating local histograms over different regions of different scales [15]. Traditional spatial pyramid matching approaches combining SPM kernels and SVMs had been successfully used in visual recognition. In this approach, the nonlinear SVMs have high computational complexity in both training and testing steps, and then it cannot handle more than thousands of training samples. Figure 8.1a shows the basic framework of the traditional SPM approach. It consists of four steps, extracting SIFTs. Assignment-based Coding, spatial pooling, and nonlinear classifiers.

The main difference between the traditional SPM approach and ScSPM is the global histogram generation of each image. The histogram generation of ScSPM is shown in Fig. 8.1. First of all, we extract SIFTs from one image. Second, sparse coding is used to get **U** given the learned dictionary A. This operation will go through each pyramid patch using multiscale max pooling functions. Thus, we have one histogram over each pyramid patch. Third, we concatenate all pyramid histograms, thus yielding one global histogram.

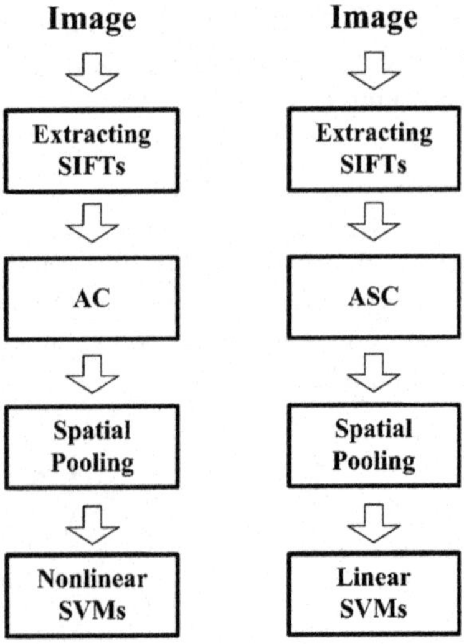

Fig. 8.1 Two different SPM approaches; **a** Traditional SPM; **b** ScSPM

8.4 Sparsity Coding-Based Nearest Neighbor Classifiers (ScNNC)

8.4.1 Sparse Coding-Based Naive Bayes Nearest Neighbor

Here, we represent an image as a collection of SIFTs, $\nu = \{\mathbf{d}_k^{\nu}\}_{k=1}^{K_\nu}$. In the optimal NBNN (ONBNN) [1], a log-likelihood of a local descriptor $\mathbf{d}$ relative to class label c is defined as

$$\begin{aligned} -\log P(\mathbf{d}|c) &= -\log\left\{\frac{1}{Z_c}\exp\left(-\frac{\tau^c(\mathbf{d})}{2\sigma_c^2}\right)\right\} \\ &= \frac{\tau^c(\mathbf{d})}{2\sigma_c^2} + \log(Z^c), \end{aligned} \tag{8.19}$$

where $Z^c = |\chi^c|(2\pi)^{D/2}(\sigma^c)^D$ is a normalization factor obtained by normalizing the probability density function, and χ^c is the set of all SIFT points from all training video clips within class c. Recall that $\tau^c(\mathbf{d})$ is the squared Euclidean distance of $\mathbf{d}$ to its nearest neighbor in χ^c. To our best knowledge, $\tau^c(\mathbf{d})$ in Eq. (7.22) is calculated by Euclidean distance measure of feature vectors in almost all of I2CNN approaches.

For better capturing the structures of feature spaces, we use the proposed Sparsity-Induced Similarity Measure to calculate the distance between $\mathbf{d}$ and class c in Naive Bayes based Classifiers, called **Sparse NBNN (SNBNN)**. Define $\mathbf{G}_k = \{\mathbf{F}^0, \mathbf{F}^1, \ldots, \mathbf{F}^c, \ldots, \mathbf{F}^{C-1}\}$ and $\mathbf{F}^c = \{\mathbf{f}_0^c, \mathbf{f}_1^c, \ldots, \mathbf{f}_{n_c}^c\}$, where n_c is the number of STIPs from training video clips within class c. Hence, given $\mathbf{f}_k = \mathbf{d}$, we can obtain nonnegative sparse coefficients $\mathbf{X} = \{\mathbf{X}^0, \mathbf{X}^1, \ldots, \mathbf{X}^c, \ldots, \mathbf{X}^{C-1}\}$ from Eq. (7.10), where $\mathbf{X}^c = \{x_0^c, x_1^c, \ldots, x_n^c, \ldots, x_{n_c}^c\}$. Therefore, we redefine the $\tau^c(\mathbf{d})$ using the nonnegative SIS between $\mathbf{d}$ and class c. In other words, we define $\tau^c(\mathbf{d})$ as a *max* pooling function on the nonnegative SIS

$$\tau^c(\mathbf{d}) = 1 - \frac{\max_{n\in[0,n_c]}\{x_n^c\}}{\max_c\left\{\max_{n\in[0,n_c]}\{x_n^c\}\right\}}. \tag{8.20}$$

According to naive Bayes formulation, we have class conditional likelihood of a video clip ν

$$\begin{aligned} -\log P(\nu|c) &= \sum_{k=1}^{K_\nu}\left(\frac{\tau^c(\mathbf{d}_k^\nu)}{2\sigma_c^2} + \log(Z^c)\right) \\ &= \alpha_c\sum_{k=1}^{K_\nu}\tau^c(\mathbf{d}_k^\nu) + K_\nu\beta^c, \end{aligned} \tag{8.21}$$

where $\alpha_c = 1/(2\sigma_c^2)$ and $\beta^c = \log(Z^c)$. The final decision function is

$$\hat{c}_\nu = \text{argmin}_c \left(\alpha_c \sum_{k=1}^{K_\nu} \tau^c(\mathbf{d}_k^\nu) + K_\nu \beta^c \right). \tag{8.22}$$

Inspired by [1], we learn the optimal α_c and β_c by minimizing a hinge loss of the proposed classifier. Moreover, minimizing the hinge loss can be recast as a linear programming, which is referred to [1] for details.

We would like to point out that the sparse coding-based NBNN is an application of the SIS. Moreover, we describe an adaptation of the NBMIM classifier, where the Sparse NBMIM uses the nonnegative SIS between a descriptor d and class c instead of Euclidean distance.

8.4.2 Sparse Approximated Nearest Points (SANP) Approaches

In this section, we introduce Sparse Approximated Nearest Points (SANP) approaches for visual recognition proposed by Hu et al. [14].

First, we discuss an image set model, an affine hall model [5]. An image set $\mathbf{X} = [\boldsymbol{x}_1, \boldsymbol{x}_2, \ldots, \boldsymbol{x}_N]$ is approximated by the affine halls of training samples

$$\mathbf{H}_0 = \left\{ \boldsymbol{x} = \sum_{n=1}^{N} \alpha_n \boldsymbol{x}_n | \sum_{n=1}^{N} \alpha_n = 1 \right\}, \tag{8.23}$$

where α_n is the affine coefficient. This affine hall can model any affine combination of different instance vectors of one object. This is an approximation model of training samples of one specific class, and is position invariant.

Furthermore, we parameterize the affine hall, by

$$\mathbf{H} = \{\boldsymbol{x} = \boldsymbol{u} + \mathbf{U}\boldsymbol{v}\}, \tag{8.24}$$

where $\boldsymbol{u} = \frac{1}{N}\sum_{n=1}^{N} \boldsymbol{x}_n$ is a reference; $\mathbf{U}$ is an orthonormal basis; $\boldsymbol{v}$ is a coordinate vector for the points within the subspace. Usually, we model training samples per class as one affine hall model. For simplifying the description, we omit the class subscript in both Eqs. (8.23) and (8.24), and $\mathbf{U}$ can be obtained from the Singular Value Decomposition (SVD) of training sample matrix $\bar{\mathbf{X}} = [\boldsymbol{x}_1 - \boldsymbol{u}, \boldsymbol{x}_2 - \boldsymbol{u}, \ldots, \boldsymbol{x}_N - \boldsymbol{u}]$. We can represent the image set as $(\boldsymbol{\mu}, \mathbf{U}, \mathbf{X})$.

Traditional nearest neighbor search could fail when samples could be noisy. To this end, SANP tones two constraints on its formulation: (1) Small Euclidean distance between two points. (2) Sparsely approximate combination of samples of the same class. Given the two data sets $\mathbf{X}_1$ and $\mathbf{X}_2$, we can represent them into the affine hull form as $(\boldsymbol{\mu}_i, \mathbf{U}_i, \mathbf{X}_i)$ and $(\boldsymbol{\mu}_j, \mathbf{U}_j, \mathbf{X}_j)$. The above criterions are incorporated into the following unconstrained problem [14]

$$\arg\min_{\boldsymbol{v}_i, \boldsymbol{v}_j, \boldsymbol{\alpha}, \boldsymbol{\beta}} F_{\boldsymbol{v}_i, \boldsymbol{v}_j} + \lambda_1 (G_{\boldsymbol{v}_i, \boldsymbol{\alpha}_i} + Q_{\boldsymbol{v}_j, \boldsymbol{\beta}_i}) + \lambda_2 \|\boldsymbol{\alpha}\|_{\ell_1} + \lambda_3 \|\boldsymbol{\beta}\|_{\ell_1}, \tag{8.25}$$

where

$$F_{\boldsymbol{v}_i, \boldsymbol{v}_j} = \|(\boldsymbol{u}_i + \mathbf{U}_i \boldsymbol{v}_i) - (\boldsymbol{u}_j + \mathbf{U}_j \boldsymbol{v}_j)\|_{\ell_2}^2, \tag{8.26}$$

$$G_{\boldsymbol{v}_i, \boldsymbol{\alpha}} = \|(\boldsymbol{u}_i + \mathbf{U}_i \boldsymbol{v}_i) - \mathbf{X}_i \boldsymbol{\alpha}\|_{\ell_2}^2, \tag{8.27}$$

$$G_{\boldsymbol{v}_j, \boldsymbol{\beta}} = \|(\boldsymbol{u}_j + \mathbf{U}_j \boldsymbol{v}_j) - \mathbf{X}_j \boldsymbol{\beta}\|_{\ell_2}^2. \tag{8.28}$$

The Eq. (8.26) indicates the distance between $\boldsymbol{x}_i$ and $\boldsymbol{x}_j$. The Eq. (8.27) and the Eq. (8.28) indicate the individual fidelities. The Eq. (8.26) uses sparse modeling in the nearest point search to match two image sets. By doing so, it optimizes the nearest points between two image sets and their affine halls.

8.5 Sparse Coding-Based Deformable Part Models (ScDPM)

8.5.1 *Deformable Part Models*

First of all, we introduce pictorial structures. Pictorial structures represent objects by a set of part in a deformable configuration [10, 11, 19]. Star models are used to represent an object by using a coarse root filter and higher resolution part filters. The root filter represents an enter object in a rectangle, and the part filters represent the parts of the object in a pyramid. An object model is defined as $(F_0, p_1, p_2, \ldots, p_n, b)$, where F_0 is a root filter, p_i is the ith part, and b is a real-valued bias value. Define $p_i = (F_i, v_i, d_i)$, where F_i is a filter of the ith part, v_i is its position w.r.t. the root position, and d_i specifies coefficients of a quadratic function (a deformation cost). Each filter position in a pyramid is defined as $Z = (p_0, p_1, \ldots, p_n)$, where $p_i = (x_{i,i}, l_i)$ is the level and position of the ith filter.

Now, we define the objective function by combining all parts and the layout of each part relative to the root as [10]. The model of an object with n parts is represented by a root filter F_0 and a set of part models $(P_1, P_2, \ldots, P_n)$, where $P_i = (F_i, v_i, s_i, a_i, b_i)$. Here, F_i is a filter for the ith part, v_i is the rectangle position w.r.t. the root position, s_i is the rectangle size a_i and b_i are used to calculate a score.

Now, we define the objective function by combining all filters and the layout of each part relative to the root as [10].

$$s(p_0, p_1, \ldots, p_N) = \sum_{i=0}^{n} F_i \phi(H, p_i) - \sum_{i=1}^{n} a_i \bullet \phi(dx_1, dy_i) + b \tag{8.29}$$

where

$$(dx_i, dy_i) = (x_i, y_i) - (z(x_0, y_0) + v_i), \tag{8.30}$$

$$\phi_d(dx, dy) = (dx, dy, dx^2, dy^2). \tag{8.31}$$

8.5.2 Sparselet Models

Song et al. proposed sparselet models for encoding deformable object models. Sparselets are generic dictionaries of part filters from training samples, where a sparsity constraint is forced into an optimization problem. Mathematically, we have

$$\begin{aligned} \arg\min_{\alpha_{ij}, D_j} \sum_{i=1}^{N} & \|vec(P_i) - \sum_{j=1}^{K} \alpha_{ij} D_j\|_{\ell_2}^2 \\ \text{s.t.} \quad & \|\alpha_i\|_{\ell_0} \leq \varepsilon \quad \forall i = 1, \ldots, N \\ & \|D_j\|_{\ell_2} = 1 \quad \forall i = 1, \ldots, K, \end{aligned} \tag{8.32}$$

where $D = \{D_1, D_2, \ldots, D_K\}$ are sparselets; P_i is a part filter. Equation (8.32) is a NP-hard problem, we can use Orthogonal Matching Pursuit algorithm (OMP) as discussed in Sect. 3.3.1.

8.5.3 The Flowchart of ScDPM

The flowchart of ScSPM is shown in Fig. 8.2. Roughly, we have divided it into three steps. First step is to learn the sparselets from training samples by using Eq. (8.32). Second, the preprocessing step generates the response matrix by convolving testing

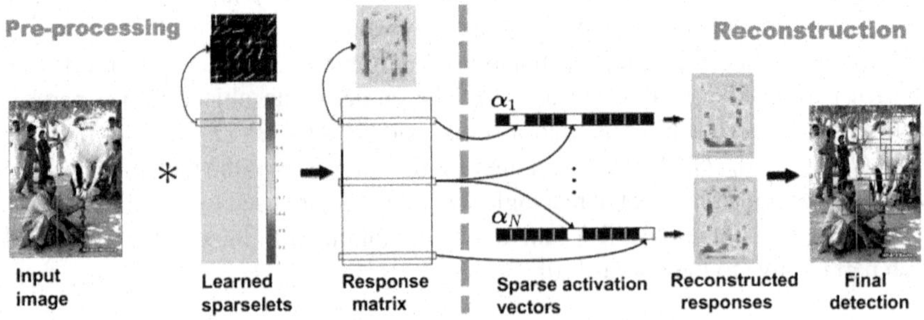

Fig. 8.2 The flowchart of ScDPM [19]

image with learned sparselets. Third, the reconstruction step is implemented by efficient sparse matrix vector multiplications. Thus, we obtain the final detection results.

References

1. Behmo, R., Marcombes, P., Dalalyan, A., Prinet, V.: Towards optimal naive bayes nearest neighbor. In: ECCV. Springer, Heidelberg (2010)
2. Boiman, O., Shechtman, E., Irani, M.: Defense of nearest-neighbor based image classification. In: IEEE CVPR (2008)
3. Boix, X., Roig, G., Leistner, C., Van Gool, L.: Nested sparse quantization for efficient feature coding. In: ECCV. Springer, Berlin (2012)
4. Boureau, Y.L., Ponce, J., LeCun, Y.: A theoretical analysis of feature pooling in visual recognition. In: Proceedings of the 27th International Conference on Machine Learning (2010)
5. Cevikalp, H., Triggs, B.: Face recognition based on image sets. In: IEEE CVPR (2010)
6. Cheng, H., Liu, Z., Hou, L., Yang, J.: Sparsity induced similarity measure and its applications. IEEE Trans. Circuits Syst. Video Technol (2012)
7. Cheng, H., Liu, Z., Yang, L.: Sparsity induced similarity measure for label propagation. In: IEEE ICCV (2009)
8. Cheng, H., Yu, R., Liu, Z., Liu, Y.: A pyramid nearest neighbor search Kernel for object categorization. In: IEEE ICPR (2012)
9. Fei-Fei, L., Perona, P.: A bayesian hierarchical model for learning natural scene categories. In: IEEE CVPR (2005)
10. Felzenszwalb, P., McAllester, D., Ramanan, D.: A discriminatively trained, multiscale, deformable part model. In: IEEE CVPR (2008)
11. Felzenszwalb, P.F., Huttenlocher, D.P.: Pictorial structures for object recognition. Int. J. Comput. Vis. **61**(1), 55–79 (2005)
12. Gao, S., Tsang, I.W., Chia, L.T., Zhao, P.: Local features are not lonely-Laplacian sparse coding for image classification. In: IEEE CVPR (2010)
13. Gao, S., Tsang, I.W.H., Chia, L.T.: Kernel sparse representation for image classification and face recognition. In: ECCV (2010)
14. Hu, Y., Mian, A.S., Owens, R.: Sparse approximated nearest points for image set classification. In: IEEE CVPR (2011)
15. Lazebnik, S., Schmid, C., Ponce, J.: Beyond bags of features: Spatial pyramid matching for recognizing natural scene categories. In: IEEE CVPR (2006)
16. Lee, H., Battle, A., Raina, R., Ng, A.Y.: Efficient sparse coding algorithms. Adv. Neural Inf. Process. Syst. **19**, 801 (2007)
17. Nowak, E., Jurie, F., Triggs, B.: Sampling strategies for bag-of-features image classification. In: ECCV. Springer, Heidelberg (2006)
18. Shi, Q., Li, H., Shen, C.: Rapid face recognition using hashing. In: IEEE CVPR (2010)
19. Song, H.O., Zickler, S., Althoff, T., Girshick, R., Fritz, M., Geyer, C., Felzenszwalb, P., Darrell, T.: Sparselet models for efficient multiclass object detection. In: ECCV. Springer, Berlin (2012)
20. Wang, J., Yang, J., Yu, K., Lv, F., Huang, T., Gong, Y.: Locality-constrained linear coding for image classification. In: IEEE CVPR (2010)
21. Wright, J., Yang, A.Y., Ganesh, A., Sastry, S.S., Ma, Y.: Robust face recognition via sparse representation. IEEE Trans. Pattern Anal. Mach. Intell. **31**(2), 210–227 (2009)
22. Yang, J., Yu, K., Gong, Y., Huang, T.: Linear spatial pyramid matching using sparse coding for image classification. In: IEEE CVPR (2009)
23. Zhang, D., Yang, M., Feng, X.: Sparse representation or collaborative representation: which helps face recognition? In: IEEE ICCV (2011)
24. Zhang, L., Zhou, W.D., Chang, P.C., Liu, J., Yan, Z., Wang, T., Li, F.Z.: Kernel sparse representation-based classifier. IEEE Trans. Signal Process. **60**(4), 1684–1695 (2012)

Part IV
Advanced Topics

Chapter 9
Beyond Sparsity

9.1 Low-Rank Matrix Approximation

9.1.1 Introduction

Both sparsity and low-rank are two basic properties in compressed sensing, and are important structures in images/videos. Therefore, sparse representation and low-rank factorization are widely used in many visual recognitions. Sparsity and low-rank share very similar aspects and also are a little bit different, which are shown in Table 9.1.

In recent years, low-rank matrix factorization has drawn much attention in many visual recognition tasks [2, 14, 21, 26]. There are many matrix approximation approaches by the ℓ_2-norm when all elements of $\mathbf{Y}$ are known, such as singular value decomposition (SVD), principal component analysis. It becomes extremely challenging when the measurement matrix has noisy elements or missing entries. For example, while recognizing objects from images/videos, some feature points may be occluded in some training/testing images, and the measurement noise is also unavoidable [28]. Towards this end, many low-rank matrix approximation with missing entries have been proposed, such as low-rank matrix recovery with structural incoherence for face recognition [2], traffic sign recognition [13], LRSc$^+$SPM [26], RASL [14], structured low-rank representations for image classification [28]. The surrey on low-rank matrix approximation refers to [1, 11]. Moreover, Okatani et al. showed the derivation of the Wiberg algorithm and its implementation is detailed in [11].

9.1.2 ℓ_2-norm Wiberg Algorithm

The low-rank matrix approximations in the presence of missing data can be formulated as the following optimization problem

H. Cheng, *Sparse Representation, Modeling and Learning in Visual Recognition*,
Advances in Computer Vision and Pattern Recognition,
DOI 10.1007/978-1-4471-6714-3_9

Table 9.1 Comparison between sparsity and low-rank

	Sparsity	Low-rank
Object	Vectors/matrix	Matrix
Criterion	Nonzero items	Matrix rank
Convex surrogate	ℓ_1-norm	Nuclear norm
Formulation	$y = Ax + \boldsymbol{\varepsilon}$	$\mathbf{Y} = A(\mathbf{X}) + E$
Unified form	$\mathbf{Y} = A(\mathbf{X}) + B(E) + Z$	

$$\arg\min_{\mathbf{U},\mathbf{V}} \|\hat{\mathbf{W}} \odot (\mathbf{Y} - \mathbf{UV})\|_{\ell_p}, \tag{9.1}$$

where $\hat{\mathbf{W}}$ is an indicator matrix, w_{ij} is 1 if y_{ij} is known, and 0 otherwise; $\mathbf{Y} \in \mathbb{R}^{M\times N}$ is a measurement matrix; $\mathbf{U}$ and $\mathbf{V}$ are the unknown matrices, $\odot$ is the Hadmard product, $A \odot B = [a_{ij}b_{ij}]_{M\times N}$. Moreover, the ℓ_1-norm and ℓ_2-norm of matrix A are

$$\|A\|_{\ell_1} = \sum_{i,j} |a_{ij}|, \tag{9.2}$$

and

$$\|A\|_{\ell_2} = \sum_{i,j} a_{ij}^2. \tag{9.3}$$

The ℓ_2-norm Wiberg algorithm is a numerical one for low-rank matrix approximation with missing data using the ℓ_2-norm.

In practice, given a fixed $\mathbf{U}$ in Eq. (9.1), the ℓ_2-norm Wiberg algorithm is simplified as a linear, least-squares minimization problem over $\mathbf{V}$ by

$$\arg\min_{\mathbf{V}} \|\mathbf{W}\boldsymbol{y} - \mathbf{W}(I \otimes \mathbf{U})\boldsymbol{v}\|_{\ell_2}^2, \tag{9.4}$$

where $\otimes$ is a Kronecker product,

$$A \otimes B = \begin{bmatrix} a_{11}B & \cdots & a_{1N}B \\ \vdots & \ddots & \vdots \\ a_{M1}B & \cdots & a_{MN}B \end{bmatrix}, \tag{9.5}$$

$\boldsymbol{y} = \text{vec}(\mathbf{Y})$ and $\boldsymbol{v} = \text{vec}(\mathbf{V})$; I is an identity matrix; $\mathbf{W} = \text{diag}(\hat{\boldsymbol{\omega}})$, here the $\hat{\boldsymbol{\omega}}$ is the vector with all the elements in the matrix $\hat{\mathbf{W}}$. We can use the alternated least squares (ALS) algorithm to obtain a closed-form solution as

$$\boldsymbol{v}^* = (G^T G)^{-1} G\mathbf{W}\boldsymbol{y}, \tag{9.6}$$

where $G = I \otimes \mathbf{U}$. Similarly, we have the optimization equation given a fixed $\mathbf{V}$.

$$\arg\min_{\boldsymbol{u}} \|\mathbf{W}\boldsymbol{y} - \mathbf{W}(\mathbf{V}^T \otimes I)\boldsymbol{u}\|_{\ell_2}^2. \tag{9.7}$$

Its solution is written as

$$\boldsymbol{u}^* = (F^T F)^{-1} F\mathbf{W}\boldsymbol{y}, \tag{9.8}$$

where $F = \mathbf{V}^T \otimes I$.

In practice, the disadvantage of the ALS algorithms is very slow. Toward this end, Ke et al. proposed the alternated linear programming (LP) and quadratic programming (QP) algorithm in structure from motion [8].

Substituting Eq. (9.6) into Eq. (9.7), we have

$$\arg\min_{\mathbf{U}} \|\mathbf{W}\boldsymbol{y} - \mathbf{W}\mathbf{U}\boldsymbol{v}^*\|_{\ell_2}^2 = \|\mathbf{W}\boldsymbol{y} - f(\mathbf{U})\|_{\ell_2}^2. \tag{9.9}$$

The ℓ_2-norm Wiberg algorithm applied the Gauss–Newton method to the nonlinear least-squares problem in Eq. (9.9) [23]. By contrast, the ALS carries out exact cyclic coordinate minimization.

Thus, δ_k can be obtained by approximating f by its first-order Taylor expansion U_k as

$$\arg\min_{\delta_k} \|\mathbf{W}\boldsymbol{y} - \frac{\partial f(\mathbf{U}_k)}{\partial \mathbf{U}}\delta_k\|_2^2. \tag{9.10}$$

According to the least square algorithm, we have

$$\delta_k = (J_k^T J_k)^{-1} J_k^T \mathbf{W}\boldsymbol{y}, \tag{9.11}$$

where $J_k = \frac{\partial f(\mathbf{U}_k)}{\partial \mathbf{U}}$. Finally, we can update $\mathbf{U}_{k+1} = \mathbf{V}_k - \delta_k^*$.

9.1.3 ℓ_1-norm Wiberg Algorithm

The ℓ_1-norm Wiberg algorithm is the direct generalization of ℓ_2-norm algorithm [8]. The ℓ_1-norm Wiberg algorithms are formulated as the minimization problems

$$\arg\min_{\mathbf{U},\mathbf{V}} \|\hat{\mathbf{W}} \odot (\mathbf{Y} - \mathbf{U}\mathbf{V})\|_{\ell_1}. \tag{9.12}$$

Similar to the derivation of ℓ_2-norm Wiberg algorithms, we can rewrite Eq. (9.12) as

$$\begin{cases} \boldsymbol{v}^* = \arg\min_{\boldsymbol{v}} \|\mathbf{W}\boldsymbol{y} - \mathbf{W}(I \otimes \mathbf{U})\boldsymbol{v}\|_{\ell_1}, \\ \boldsymbol{u}^* = \arg\min_{\boldsymbol{u}} \|\mathbf{W}\boldsymbol{y} - \mathbf{W}(\mathbf{V}^T \otimes I)\boldsymbol{u}\|_{\ell_1}. \end{cases}$$

Both Eqs. (9.6) and (9.7) are linear over **V** and **U**, respectively.

Substituting Eq. (9.6) into Eq. (9.7), we have

$$\arg\min_{\mathbf{U}} \|\mathbf{W}\boldsymbol{y} - \mathbf{W}\mathbf{U}\boldsymbol{v}^*\|_{\ell_1} = \|\mathbf{W}\boldsymbol{y} - \mathbf{W}f(\mathbf{U})\|_{\ell_1}, \tag{9.13}$$

Define $\boldsymbol{v} = \boldsymbol{v}^+ - \boldsymbol{v}^-$, and we reformulate Eq. (9.12) as

$$\arg\min_{\boldsymbol{v}^+,\boldsymbol{v}^-,\boldsymbol{t},\boldsymbol{s}} [\mathbf{0}\;\mathbf{0}\;\mathbf{1}^T\;\mathbf{0}] \begin{bmatrix} \boldsymbol{v}^+ \\ \boldsymbol{v}^- \\ \boldsymbol{t} \\ \boldsymbol{s} \end{bmatrix}, \tag{9.14}$$

$$\text{s.t.} \begin{bmatrix} -G & G & -I & I \\ G & -G & -I & \end{bmatrix} \begin{bmatrix} \boldsymbol{v}^+ \\ \boldsymbol{v}^- \\ \boldsymbol{t} \\ \boldsymbol{s} \end{bmatrix} = \begin{bmatrix} -\mathbf{W}\boldsymbol{y} \\ \mathbf{W}\boldsymbol{y} \end{bmatrix}, \tag{9.15}$$

where $A = \begin{bmatrix} -G & G & -I & I \\ G & -G & -I & \end{bmatrix}$, $\boldsymbol{b} = \begin{bmatrix} -\mathbf{W}\boldsymbol{y} \\ \mathbf{W}\boldsymbol{y} \end{bmatrix}$, and $\boldsymbol{v}^+, \boldsymbol{v}^-, \boldsymbol{t}, \boldsymbol{s} \geq \mathbf{0}$.

Applying the chain rule [6], we have

$$\begin{cases} \dfrac{\partial G}{\partial \mathbf{U}} = (I_{nr} \otimes \mathbf{W})(T_{r,n} \otimes I_m)(\mathrm{vec}(I_n) \otimes I_{mr}), \\ \dfrac{\partial A}{\partial \mathbf{U}} = \begin{bmatrix} -\frac{\partial G}{\partial \mathbf{U}} & \frac{\partial G}{\partial \mathbf{U}} & 0 & 0 \\ \frac{\partial G}{\partial \mathbf{U}} & -\frac{\partial G}{\partial \mathbf{U}} & 0 & \end{bmatrix}, \\ \dfrac{\partial v}{\partial \mathbf{U}} = Q((v_B^*)^T \otimes B^{-1})(Q^T \otimes I_{2mn})\dfrac{\partial A}{\partial \mathbf{U}}. \end{cases}$$

Here $T_{m,n}$ denotes the $mn \times mn$ matrix for which $T_{m,n}\mathrm{vec}(A) = A^T$, and $Q \in \mathbb{R}^{mn \times m}$ is obtained by removing the columns corresponding to the nonbasic variables of $\boldsymbol{x}^*$ from the identity matrix I_{mn}. Combining Eq. (9.1.3) to Eq. (9.1.3), we have

$$J(\mathbf{U}) = \frac{\partial}{\partial \mathbf{U}}(\mathbf{W}\mathbf{U}\mathbf{V}^*(\mathbf{U})) = \mathbf{W}\mathbf{G}(\mathbf{U})\frac{\partial \boldsymbol{v}}{\partial \mathbf{U}} + \\ ((v_B^*)^T \otimes W)(I_n \otimes T_{r,n} \otimes I_m)(\mathrm{vec}(I_n) \otimes I_{mr}). \tag{9.16}$$

We linearizing Eq. (9.1.3) at $\mathbf{U}_k$ and we obtain the following

$$\hat{f}(\delta) = \|\mathbf{W}\boldsymbol{y} - J(\mathbf{U}_k)(\delta - \boldsymbol{u}_k)\|_{\ell_1}. \tag{9.17}$$

Minimizing Eq. (9.16), we have

$$\arg\min_{\delta_k} \|\mathbf{W}\boldsymbol{y} - J(\mathbf{U})(\delta_k - \boldsymbol{u})\|_{\ell_1}. \tag{9.18}$$

Table 9.2 The ℓ_1-norm Wilberg Algorithm [6]

input: $U_0, 1 > \eta_2 > \eta_1 > 0$ and $c > 1$ $k = 0$;
while (!convergence)
  Compute the Jacobian of $\phi_1 = J(U_k)$ using Eq. (9.1.3)– Eq. (9.16);
  Solve the subproblem Eq. (9.19)- Eq. (9.22) to obtain δ_k^*;
  Let $gain = \frac{f(\mathbf{U}_k)-f(\mathbf{U}_k+\delta^*)}{f(\mathbf{U}_k)-\tilde{f}(\mathbf{U}_k+\delta^*)}$;
  if $gain \geq \varepsilon$ **then**
    $\mathbf{U}_{k+1} = \mathbf{U}_k + \delta^*$;
  end
  if $gain < \eta_1$ **then**
    $\mu = \eta_1 \|\delta^*\|_{\ell_1}$;
  end
  if $gain > \eta_2$ **then**
    $\mu = c\mu$;
  end
  $k = k + 1$;
end while

Now we rewrite Eq. (9.1.3) into a linear problem

$$\delta_k^* = \arg\min_{\delta_k, t}[0\ 1^T]\begin{bmatrix}\delta \\ t\end{bmatrix}, \tag{9.19}$$

$$\text{s.t.} \begin{bmatrix}-J(\mathbf{U}) - I \\ J(\mathbf{U}) - I\end{bmatrix}\begin{bmatrix}\delta \\ t\end{bmatrix} = \begin{bmatrix}-(\mathbf{W}\boldsymbol{y} - \mathbf{W}\text{vec}(\mathbf{U}\mathbf{V}^*)) \\ \mathbf{W}\boldsymbol{y} - W\text{vec}(\mathbf{U}\mathbf{V}^*)\end{bmatrix}, \tag{9.20}$$

$$\|\delta_k\|_{\ell_2} \leq \mu, \tag{9.21}$$

$$\delta_k \in \mathbb{R}^{mr}, \boldsymbol{t} \in \mathbb{R}^{mn}. \tag{9.22}$$

Finally, the updated rule of ℓ_1-Wiberg algorithm is

$$\mathbf{U}_{k+1} = \mathbf{U}_k + \delta_k^*. \tag{9.23}$$

The algorithm flowchart is shown in Table 9.2.

9.2 Graphical Models in Compressed Sensing

9.2.1 Inference via Message Passing Algorithm

The Bayesian graphical models are flexible, powerful, and widely used in compressed sensing. We shall introduce the connection between graphical models and sparse modeling as follows. We can use the following linear equation to recover a high-dimensional vector $\boldsymbol{x} \in \mathbb{R}^N$ by

$$y = Ax + \xi \tag{9.24}$$

where A is a known measurement matrix, and $\xi \in N(\mathbf{0}, \beta I)$ is a Gaussian noise vector. Equation (9.24) can be formulated as a graphical model problem whose joint probability distribution on (x, y) [10] is obtained as follows:

$$p(dx, dy) = p(dy|x)p(dx), \tag{9.25}$$

where $p(dy|x)$ models the noise and $p(dx)$ encodes the information on x. We can factorize the joint distribution according to different graph structures. Finally, the $p(dx|y)$ can be used for inferring x given y. Note that $p(dx)$ admits the following density w.r.t. Lebesgue measure dx

$$p(dx) = \frac{1}{\sqrt{2\pi a}} e^{-x^2/2a} dx, \tag{9.26}$$

where a is a bandwidth parameter. The conditional probability is written as [10]

$$p(dy|x) = \left(\frac{\beta}{2\pi}\right)^{N/2} \exp\left\{-\frac{\beta}{2}\|y - Ax\|_{\ell_2}^2\right\} dy. \tag{9.27}$$

Taking the prior $p(dx) = p(dx_1)p(dx_2)\cdots p(dx_N)$, we have the joint distribution

$$p(dx, dy) = \left(\frac{\beta}{2\pi}\right)^{N/2} \exp\left\{-\frac{\beta}{2}\|y - Ax\|_{\ell_2}^2\right\} dy \prod_{i=1}^{N} p(dx_i) \tag{9.28}$$

Thus, factor graphs are used to model the joint distribution. Thus, the posterior distribution of x is

$$p(dx|y) = \frac{1}{Z(y)} \exp\left\{-\frac{\beta}{2}\|y - Ax\|_{\ell_2}^2\right\} \prod_{i=1}^{N} p(dx_i) \tag{9.29}$$

$$= \frac{1}{Z(y)} \prod_{j=1}^{D} \exp\left\{-\frac{\beta}{2}(y_j - A_{j.}^T x)^2\right\} \prod_{i=1}^{N} p(dx_i) \tag{9.30}$$

where $\|y - Ax\|_{\ell_2}^2 = \sum_{j=1}^{D}(y_j - A_{j.}^T x)^2$..

9.2.2 Inference via Approximate Message Passing Algorithm

In previous sections, we have formulated compressed sensing as the problem of inference in graphical models. In a graph, some nodes are known as observed values while we will calculate the posterior distributions of other nodes. Moreover, most of

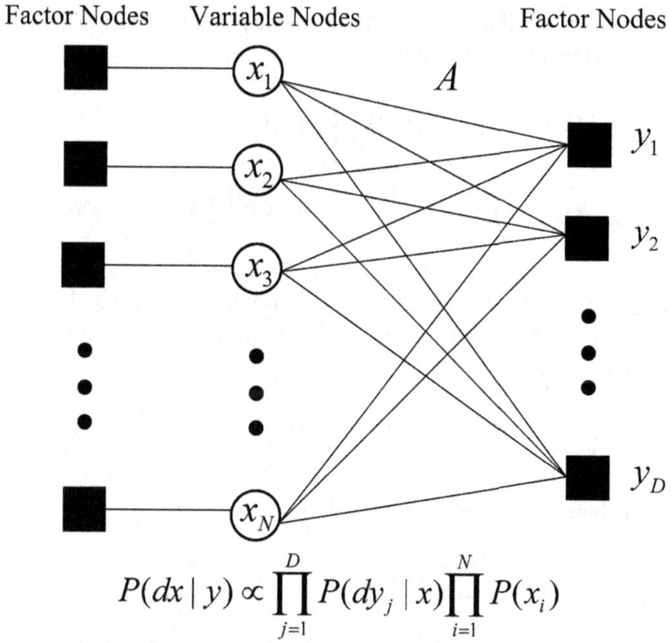

Fig. 9.1 The graphic model of $p(d\boldsymbol{x}|\boldsymbol{y})$

graphical model algorithms are to calculate the propagation of local message around the graph. Belief propagation can be used to calculate the marginal distribution of a posterior distribution. Moreover, a factor graph captures the statistical dependencies between the variables and passed the messages. The messages are passed from variables to factors and then factors to variables (Fig. 9.1)

$$m_{i\to j}(\boldsymbol{x}_i) = p(\boldsymbol{x}_i) \prod_{b\in N(i)|a} m_{b\to i}(\boldsymbol{x}_i) \tag{9.31}$$

$$m_{j\to i}(\boldsymbol{x}_i) = \int_{\boldsymbol{x}_{-i}} p(y_j|\boldsymbol{x}) \prod_{a\in N(j)|i} m_{a\to j}(\boldsymbol{x}_a) d\boldsymbol{x}_{-i} \tag{9.32}$$

For the common LASSO problem in sparse representation is following optimization problem

$$\arg\min_{\boldsymbol{x}} \frac{1}{2}\|\boldsymbol{y} - A\boldsymbol{x}\|_{\ell_2}^2 + \lambda\|\boldsymbol{x}\|_{\ell_1}. \tag{9.33}$$

We can define the joint density distribution on the variable $\boldsymbol{x} = [x_1, \ldots, x_N]$ as

$$p(\boldsymbol{x}; \boldsymbol{y}, A) = \frac{1}{Z} \prod_{i=1}^{N} \exp(-\beta\lambda|x_i|) \prod_{a=1}^{D} \exp\left\{-\frac{\beta}{2}(y_a - A_{a.}\boldsymbol{x})\right\}. \tag{9.34}$$

We can note that this distribution concentrate on the problem of Eq. (9.33) as $\beta \to \infty$. By the sum-product algorithm can get

$$v_{i\to a}^{t+1}(x_i) \propto \exp(-\beta\lambda|x_i|) \prod_{b\neq a} v_{b\to i}^{i}(x_i), \tag{9.35}$$

$$\hat{v}_{a\to i}^{t}(x_i) \propto \int \exp\left\{-\frac{\beta}{2}(y_a - A_{a\cdot}\boldsymbol{x})^2\right\} \prod_{j\neq i} v_{j\to a}^{t}(x_j) d\boldsymbol{x}. \tag{9.36}$$

As Maleki's mentioned in [9], $\boldsymbol{x}$'s third moment is bounded, the messages $\hat{v}_{a\to i}^{t}(x_i)$ are approximate to the Gaussian distribution, which is defined as follows

$$\hat{\phi}_{a\to i}^{t}(x_i) = \sqrt{\frac{\beta A_{ai}^2}{2\pi(1+\hat{\tau}_{a\to i}^{t})}} \exp\left\{-\frac{\beta}{2(1+\hat{\tau}_{a\to i}^{t})}(A_{ai}x_i - z_{a\to i}^{t})^2\right\}, \tag{9.37}$$

where the distribution parameters are given by

$$z_{a\to i}^{t} = y_a - \sum_{j\neq i} A_{aj} x_{j\to a}^{t}, \qquad \hat{\tau}_{a\to i}^{t} = \sum_{j\neq i} A_{aj}^2 \tau_{j\to a}^{t}, \tag{9.38}$$

and the $x_{j\to a}^{t}$, $\tau_{j\to a}^{t}$ are the mean and variance of the distribution $\hat{v}_{a\to i}^{t}$, respectively.

If the message pass from factor nodes to the variable is set to $\hat{v}_{a\to i}^{t} = \hat{\phi}_{a\to i}^{t}$, as defined as in Eq. (9.37), then we can define the message pass from variable nodes to factor nodes as

$$v_{i\to a}^{t+1} = \phi_{i\to a}^{t+1}(x_i)\{1 + O(x_i^2/n)\}, \tag{9.39}$$

$$\phi_{i\to a}^{t+1}(x_i) = \lambda f_\beta(\lambda x_i; \lambda \sum_{b\neq a} A_{bi} z_{b\to i}^{t}, \lambda^2(1+\hat{\tau}^t)). \tag{9.40}$$

The mean and variances of $v_{i\to a}^{t+1}$ are given as

$$x_{i\to a}^{t+1} = \frac{1}{\lambda} F_\beta\left(\lambda \sum_{b\neq a} A_{bi} z_{b\to i}^{t}; \lambda^2(1+\hat{\tau}^t)\right), \tag{9.41}$$

$$\tau_{i\to a}^{t} = \frac{\beta}{\lambda^2} G_\beta\left(\lambda \sum_{b\neq a} A_{bi} z_{b\to i}^{t}; \lambda^2(1+\hat{\tau}^t)\right), \tag{9.42}$$

where, f_β,F_β, and G_β are defined as follows:

$$f_\beta(s; x, b) = \frac{1}{z_\beta(x, b)} \exp\left\{-\beta|s| - \frac{\beta}{2b}(s - x)^2\right\} \tag{9.43}$$

$$F_\beta(x; b) = \mathbb{E}_{f_\beta(\cdot;x,b)}(Z), \qquad G_\beta(x; b) = \mathrm{Var}_{f_\beta(\cdot;x,b)}(Z). \tag{9.44}$$

So, we can get the following iterative message passing algorithm

$$x_{i\to a}^{t+1} = \frac{1}{\lambda} F_\beta \left(\lambda \sum_{b\neq a} A_{bi} z_{b\to i}^t; \lambda^2 (1+\hat{\tau}^t) \right)$$

$$z_{b\to i}^t = y_a - \sum_{j\neq i} A_{aj} x_{j\to a}^t$$

$$\hat{\tau}^{t+1} = \frac{\beta}{\lambda^2 n} \sum_{i=1}^N G_\beta \left(\lambda \sum_b A_{bi} z_{b\to i}^t; \lambda^2 (1+\hat{\tau}^t) \right). \quad (9.45)$$

As we know before, in the limit $\beta \to \infty$ the problem is equivalent to LASSO problem. The iteration of the message passing algorithm Eq. (9.45) can be transformed as

$$x_{i\to a}^{t+1} = \eta \left(\sum_{b\neq a} A_{bi} z_{b\to i}^t; \lambda (1+\hat{\tau}^t) \right)$$

$$z_{b\to i}^t = y_a - \sum_{j\neq i} A_{aj} x_{j\to a}^t$$

$$\hat{\tau}^{t+1} = \frac{1+\hat{\tau}^t}{N\delta} \sum_{i=1}^N \eta' \left(\sum_b A_{bi} z_{b\to i}^t; \lambda (1+\hat{\tau}^t) \right). \quad (9.46)$$

We can call $\lambda\hat{\tau}^t = \gamma^t$ and apply it to Eq. (9.46), then we can get the new form of the AMP algorithm

$$x_{i\to a}^{t+1} = \eta \left(\sum_{b\neq a} A_{bi} z_{b\to i}^t; \lambda + \gamma^t \right)$$

$$z_{b\to i}^t = y_a - \sum_{j\neq i} A_{aj} x_{j\to a}^t$$

$$\hat{\tau}^{t+1} = \frac{\lambda+\gamma^t}{N\delta} \sum_{i=1}^N \eta' \left(\sum_b A_{bi} z_{b\to i}^t; \lambda + \gamma^t \right). \quad (9.47)$$

When compared with the IST algorithm for the LASSO problem, the only difference is the threshold value. We can use the matrix notation to simplify the AMP algorithm as

$$\boldsymbol{x}^{t+1} = \eta(\boldsymbol{x}^t + A^T \boldsymbol{z}^t; \lambda + \gamma^t)$$

$$\boldsymbol{z}^t = \boldsymbol{y} - A\boldsymbol{x}^t + \frac{1}{\delta} \boldsymbol{z}^t \langle \eta'(\boldsymbol{x}^{t-1} + A^T \boldsymbol{z}^{t-1}; \gamma^{t-1}) \rangle. \quad (9.48)$$

The threshold is computed iteratively as

$$\gamma^{t+1} = \frac{\lambda + \gamma^t}{\delta} \langle \eta'(Az^t + \boldsymbol{x}^t; \gamma^t + \lambda) \rangle \tag{9.49}$$

9.3 Collaborative Representation-Based Classifiers

We would like to point out that, sparse representation modeling and learning have been widely used in visual recognition recently. Thanks to the SRC. However, some researchers have started to study the real role of sparsity in visual recognition.

9.3.1 Sparse Representation and Collaborative Representation

As we know, Olshausen et al. found that the first layer of the visual cortex builds a sparse representation of the images [12]. Thus, there has been an increase in imposing sparsity constraints in visual recognition [3, 24, 26]. Many researchers highlight three different aspects of sparsity constraints in visual recognition, feature extraction and learning, and feature pooling and classification. Rigamonti et al. provided both the theoretical analysis and experimental evaluation of sparse representation for visual recognition [15] and claimed that: (1) In feature extraction and learning stages, in general, increasing sparsity constraint can drop the recognition rate. Moreover, feature extraction from a convolution between one image and filters can yield comparable performance. Furthermore, even misusing sparse optimization algorithms degrades the recognition rate. However, sparsity still plays very important roles in learning the filters. (2) In the framework of using pooling steps, sparsity is a temporary condition only in feature pooling stages. As we may know, regardless of the feature extraction and pooling schemes, the corresponding results are dense.

Rigamoni [15] and Shi [18] posed the same question, the relationship between sparse representation and image classification, respectively. Rigamoni et al. analyzed the role of sparsity in classification, and furthermore evaluated it using a shallow modular architecture, adopting both standard filter banks and filter banks learned in an unsupervised way [15]. Moreover, the experiments on the CIFAR-10 and Caltech101 datasets show that sparsity constraints do not improve recognition rate. Shi et al. claimed that sparsity assumption can be supported by the data in many cases (i.e., face recognition [18]). Thus sparse representation may not bring the performance promotion. Moreover, Shi et al. showed a simple ℓ_2-norm approach is even better than ℓ_1-norm approach in robustness, efficiency, and accuracy. Zhang et al. further proposed *Collaborative Representation Classifier (CRC)* to replace the *Sparse Representation Classifier (SRC)*. Also, they analyzed the mechanism of SRC, and indicated that it is not the sparse representation but the collaborative representation that really works in face classification [24].

The efficient way to use the sparse representation is the SRC. From Sect. 8.2, we can see that there are two key points in SRC. First, the coding vector of query sample $\boldsymbol{y}$ is required to be sparse; Second, the coding vector of query sample $\boldsymbol{y}$ is performed collaboratively over the whole dictionary instead of each subset A_i. Suppose that $\boldsymbol{y}$ belongs to some class in the dataset, the sparsest representation of $\boldsymbol{y}$ over A is naturally discriminative and thus can indicate the identity of $\boldsymbol{y}$. In [24], it was claimed that SRC is a generalization of the classical Nearest Neighbor (NN) and Nearest Subspace (NS) classifiers.

Collaborative representation is to use the training samples from all classes to represent a test sample, which was introduced in [27] and was also observed in [18]. Traditional visual recognition algorithms assumed that there are sufficient training samples for each class. However, many visual recognition tasks, such as face recognition, are small-sample-size problems. Toward this end, we can represent each test sample from all classes instead of one class since visual objects of different classes usually share similar parts. By contrast, collaborative representation error could be small thus very stable. Therefore, Zhang et al. claimed that in face recognition, the collaborative representation but not the sparsity really improves its performance [27]. Meanwhile, Shi et al. claimed that no theoretical or empirical evidences show that enforcing sparsity in SRC will improve recognition rate, and also showed a simple least-squares algorithm can outperform many of the existing more complicated algorithms [18].

9.3.2 Collaborative Representation-Based Classification (CRC)

1. Theoretical Analysis

Zhang et al. proposed collaborative representation-based classifier [27], which is described as follows. As we know, the sparse optimization equation in SRC is

$$\hat{\boldsymbol{x}} = \arg\min_{x} \|\boldsymbol{x}\|_{\ell_1} \quad \text{s.t.} \quad \|\boldsymbol{y} - A\boldsymbol{x}\|_{\ell_2} \leq \varepsilon. \tag{9.50}$$

The CRC removes the ℓ_1-norm sparsity term in Eq. (9.50), and becomes a least-squares problem

$$\hat{\boldsymbol{x}} = \arg\min_{x} \|\boldsymbol{y} - A\boldsymbol{x}\|_{\ell_2}^2. \tag{9.51}$$

Then we can obtain its *collaborative representation* and its error as

$$\hat{\boldsymbol{y}} = \sum_{i=1}^{C} A_i \hat{x}_i, \qquad \hat{\boldsymbol{e}}_c = \boldsymbol{y} - \hat{\boldsymbol{y}}_c \tag{9.52}$$

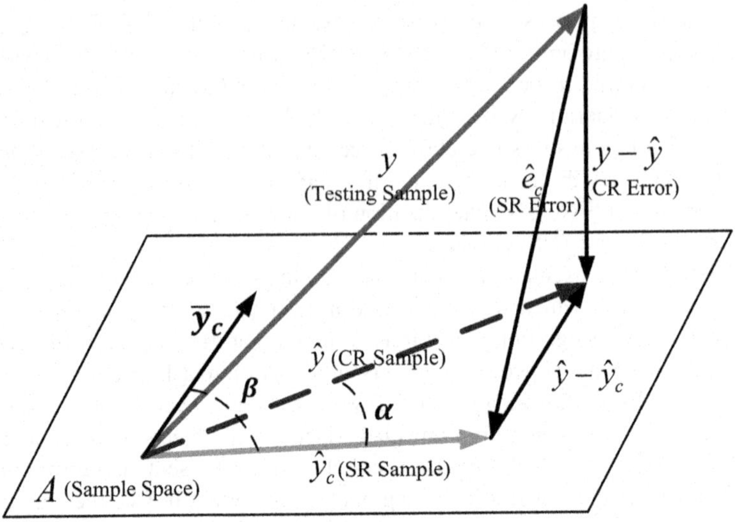

Fig. 9.2 The geometric error analysis of the collaborative representation [27]

Accordingly, we define *separative representation* as

$$\hat{\boldsymbol{y}}_c = A_c\hat{\boldsymbol{x}}_c, \tag{9.53}$$

and its complementary separative representation as

$$\overline{\boldsymbol{y}}_c = \sum_{j\neq c} A_j\hat{\boldsymbol{x}}_j, \tag{9.54}$$

From Fig. (9.2), we further define two angles, the angle α between the collaborative representation (CR) and sparse representation (SR), and the angle β between the CR and complementary SR. Since $\overline{\boldsymbol{y}}_c$ is parallel to $\hat{\boldsymbol{y}} - A_c\hat{\boldsymbol{x}}_c$, we have

$$\frac{\|\hat{\boldsymbol{y}}\|_{\ell_2}}{\sin\beta} = \frac{\|\hat{\boldsymbol{y}} - A_c\hat{\boldsymbol{x}}_c\|_{\ell_2}}{\sin\alpha}. \tag{9.55}$$

Therefore, separative representation error is [27]

$$\hat{\boldsymbol{e}}_c = \|\boldsymbol{y} - A_c\hat{\boldsymbol{x}}_c\|_{\ell_2}^2 = \frac{\sin^2\alpha}{\sin^2\beta}\|\hat{\boldsymbol{y}}\|_{\ell_2}^2. \tag{9.56}$$

Traditional SRC works by calculating class reconstruction error only considering α. From Eq. (9.56), it is easy to think about using both α and β. Therefore, we can consider both small α and big β in classification. Thus, Zhang et al. proposed a "double checking" criterion to provide more effective and robust classification [27].

Table 9.3 The CRC-RLS algorithm flowchart [27]

Initialization: Normalize A with unit ℓ_2-norm columns.
Precalculate $P=(A^TA+\lambda I)^{-1}A^T$.
Main: Projection $\boldsymbol{y}$ onto $P:\hat{\boldsymbol{x}}=P\boldsymbol{y}$.
Compute the regularized residuals
$r_i=\|\boldsymbol{y}-A_c\hat{\boldsymbol{x}}_c\|_{\ell_2}/\|\hat{\boldsymbol{x}}\|_{\ell_2}$.
Classify $\boldsymbol{y}$ by
$c=\arg\min_c r_c$

2. The CRC-RLS algorithm

The CRC-RLS algorithm was proposed by Zhang et al. [27] based on the collaborative representation concept. The CRC algorithm was reformulated as a regularized least square algorithm

$$\hat{\boldsymbol{x}}=\arg\min_{x}\|\boldsymbol{y}-A\boldsymbol{x}\|_{\ell_2}^2+\lambda\|\boldsymbol{x}\|_{\ell_2}^2. \tag{9.57}$$

The analytical solution of Eq. (9.57) is

$$\hat{\boldsymbol{x}}=(A^TA+\lambda I)^{-1}A^T\boldsymbol{y}. \tag{9.58}$$

Note that, $(A^TA+\lambda I)^{-1}A^T$ is independent of $\boldsymbol{y}$, so we can precalculate it as a projection matrix. This is very important for practical applications. Moreover, the advantages of using ℓ_2-norm regularization are two-folded. First of all, the solution is more stable than simple least-squares algorithm. Second, it can enforce sparsity constraints. Of course, its sparsity is weaker than ℓ_1-norm regularization.

The CRC-RLS algorithm flowchart is shown in Table 9.3.

9.4 High-Dimensional Nonlinear Learning

9.4.1 *Kernel Sparse Representation*

1. Kernel Feature Spaces

Kernel tricks have been widely used in computer vision and machine learning. The fundamental idea is to generalize linear algorithms to nonlinear algorithms, such as SVM [22], KPCA [16], KFDA [17], and SVDD [20].

In machine learning, a commonly used strategy is to map feature vectors to another feature space as

$$\boldsymbol{x}=(x_1,x_2,\ldots,x_D)\rightarrow\phi(\boldsymbol{x})=(\phi_1(\boldsymbol{x}),\phi_2(\boldsymbol{x}),\ldots,\phi_M(\boldsymbol{x})). \tag{9.59}$$

when $M \ll D$, Eq. (9.59) is known as dimensionality reduction [7]. By doing so, we can have computation and generalization benefits. However, this can drop the representation performance by increasing the number of features. Toward this end, feature mapping $\phi(\boldsymbol{x})$ is used to increase the dimensions of feature vectors by using kernel tricks.

First of all, we consider a linear function

$$y = f(\boldsymbol{x}) = \langle \boldsymbol{w}, \boldsymbol{x} \rangle + b = \sum_{i=1}^{D} w_i x_i + b. \tag{9.60}$$

Applying a fixed nonlinear feature mapping to a feature space, we have

$$y = f(\boldsymbol{x}) = \sum_{i=1}^{M} w_i \phi_i(\boldsymbol{x}) + b. \tag{9.61}$$

According to a dual representation [4], we have

$$f(\boldsymbol{x}) = \sum_{i=1}^{L} \alpha_i y_i \phi^T(\boldsymbol{x}_i) \phi(\boldsymbol{x}) + b, \tag{9.62}$$

where L is the number of training samples. Here, a Mercer kernel can be expressed as

$$k(\boldsymbol{x}, \boldsymbol{x}') = \phi^T(\boldsymbol{x}) \phi(\boldsymbol{x}'). \tag{9.63}$$

The kernel function is actually a similarity measure function by calculating Euclidean vector inner product between $\boldsymbol{x}$ and $\boldsymbol{x}'$. There are many kernels in machine learning, such as line kernels, polynomial kernels, and radial basis function (RBF) kernels. Moreover, according to symmetric positive semi-definite matrix criterion, we can make kernels from kernels.

2. Kernel Sparse Representation

Rewriting Eq. (9.61), we have

$$\boldsymbol{y} = \sum_{i=1}^{M} w_i \phi(\boldsymbol{x}_i) = \boldsymbol{\Phi} \boldsymbol{w}, \tag{9.64}$$

where $\boldsymbol{w} = [w_1, w_2, \ldots, w_M]^T$; $\boldsymbol{\Phi} = [\phi(\boldsymbol{x}_1), \phi(\boldsymbol{x}_2), \ldots, \phi(\boldsymbol{x}_M)] \in \mathbb{R}^{D \times M}$. For simplicity, we omit the item b in Eq. (9.61). According to traditional sparse representation optimization equation, we have

$$\arg\min_{w} \|\boldsymbol{w}\|_{\ell_1}, \qquad \text{s.t.} \;\; \phi(\boldsymbol{y}) = \boldsymbol{\Phi} \boldsymbol{w}. \tag{9.65}$$

Now the question is how to solve Eq. (9.65) to obtain $\boldsymbol{w}$. Even if Φ is known, the computational complexity of Eq. (9.65) is really high due to introducing nonlinear mapping. Moreover, in case of $D \gg M$, we cannot obtain sparse solution. Of course, in most of those tasks, ϕ is unknown, and then we have to resort to kernel tricks. There are some different ways to incorporate kernel tricks in kernel sparse representation. We shall introduce two basic formulations.

(1) Dimensionality Reduction-based KSR

Considering a very high even infinite dimensionality, we project ϕ into a lower dimensional subspace by multiplying a transformation matrix P in Eq. (9.64)

$$P^T \phi(\boldsymbol{y}) = P^T \Phi \boldsymbol{w}. \tag{9.66}$$

Inspired by transformation matrix in kernel-based dimensionality reduction algorithms, we have

$$P.j = \sum_{i=1}^{M} \beta_{j,i} \phi(\boldsymbol{x}_i) = \Phi \boldsymbol{\beta}_j, \tag{9.67}$$

where $\boldsymbol{\beta}_j$ is the pseudo-transformation vector. We define $B = [\boldsymbol{\beta}_1, \boldsymbol{\beta}_2, \ldots, \boldsymbol{\beta}_D]$, and then we have

$$P = \Phi B. \tag{9.68}$$

By substituting Eq. (9.68) into Eq. (9.66), we have

$$B^T k(\cdot, \boldsymbol{x}) = B^T K \boldsymbol{w}, \tag{9.69}$$

where $k(\cdot, \boldsymbol{x}) = [k(\boldsymbol{x}_1, \boldsymbol{x}), k(\boldsymbol{x}_2, \boldsymbol{x}), \ldots, k(\boldsymbol{x}_N, \boldsymbol{x})]^T = \Phi^T \phi(\boldsymbol{x})$, $K = \Phi^T \Phi$. Finding the solution of the pseudo-transformation matrix B can be referred to KPCA and KFAA [16, 17].

(2) Directive KSR

The general objective function of sparse coding can be written as [7]

$$\arg\min_{\mathbf{U}, \boldsymbol{v}} \|\boldsymbol{x} - \mathbf{U}\boldsymbol{v}\|_F^2 + \lambda \|\boldsymbol{v}\|_{\ell_1}, \text{ s.t. } \|\boldsymbol{u}_n\|_{\ell_2} \le 1. \tag{9.70}$$

Using the nonlinear mapping on Eq. (9.70), we have

$$\arg\min_{\mathbf{U}, \boldsymbol{v}} \|\phi(\boldsymbol{x}) - \mathbf{M}\boldsymbol{v}\|_F^2 + \lambda \|\boldsymbol{v}\|_{\ell_1}, \text{ s.t. } k(\boldsymbol{u}_i, \boldsymbol{u}_i) \le 1, \tag{9.71}$$

where $\mathbf{M} = [\phi(\boldsymbol{u}_1), \phi(\boldsymbol{u}_2), \ldots, \phi(\boldsymbol{u}_M)]$.

Furthermore, we use kernel tricks on Eq. (9.71)

$$\begin{aligned}&\arg\min_{\mathbf{U},\boldsymbol{v}} \quad k(\boldsymbol{x},\boldsymbol{x}) + \boldsymbol{v}^T K_{\mathbf{UU}}\boldsymbol{v} - 2\boldsymbol{v}^T K_{\mathbf{U}}(\boldsymbol{x}) + \lambda\|\boldsymbol{x}\|_{\ell_1} \\ &\text{s.t.} \quad k(\boldsymbol{u}_i,\boldsymbol{u}_i) \le 1\end{aligned} \tag{9.72}$$

9.4.2 Anchor Points Approaches

Definition 9.4.2.1 Anchor points are representative points in feature spaces.

In a high-dimensional space $\boldsymbol{x} \in \mathbb{R}^D$, learning a nonlinear function $f(\boldsymbol{x})$ is an overfitting problem due to the cause of dimensionality when D is larger than the number of training samples. However, it is unusual in many practical applications for the curse of dimensionality, since all features often lie on a lower dimensional structure. In other words, learning an arbitrary Lipschitz smooth function on its original feature space is very difficult due to the curse of dimensionality. However, we often can approximate the function by smaller intrinsic dimensionality than d. Thus, anchor points are representative points in feature spaces, and linearly combined into any point. Anchor points are widely used in high-dimensional nonlinear learning [19, 25]. Local coordinate coding is to embed any points on the manifold into a lower dimensional space with respect to a set of anchor points. By doing so, the advantage is that a nonlinear function on the manifold can be approximated by a linear function. Mathematically, coordinate coding is a pair (r, C), where $C \subset \mathbb{R}^D$ is a set of anchor points [25], and r is a map of $\boldsymbol{x}$ to $[r_v(\boldsymbol{x})]_{v\in C} \in \mathbb{R}^{|C|}$ such that $\sum_v r_v(\boldsymbol{x}) = 1$. Note that we can learn (r, C) only by using unlabeled data which can avoid data overfitting.

Learning local coordinate coding: Given a local coordinate scheme (r, C), we can approximate the nonlinear function by

$$f(\boldsymbol{x}) \approx f_{r,C}(\hat{\boldsymbol{w}},\boldsymbol{x}) = \sum_{v\in C} \hat{w}_v r_v(\boldsymbol{x}), \tag{9.73}$$

where

$$[\hat{\boldsymbol{w}}_v] = \arg\min_{\boldsymbol{w}_v}\left[\sum_{n=1}^{N} \phi(f_{r,C}(\boldsymbol{w},\boldsymbol{x}_n), y_n) + \lambda\sum_{v\in C}(w_v - g(v))^2\right]. \tag{9.74}$$

In Eq. (9.74), $(\boldsymbol{x}_n, y_n)_{n=1}^N$ are labeled data, $\phi(\cdot)$ is the lost function. Ridge regression is used to estimate the coefficients. We define localization measure [25]

$$Q_{\alpha,\beta,p}(r, C) = \mathbb{E}_x\left[\alpha\|\boldsymbol{x} - r(\boldsymbol{x})\| + \beta\sum_{v\in C}|r_v(\boldsymbol{x})|\|\boldsymbol{v} - r(\boldsymbol{x})\|^{1+p}\right], \tag{9.75}$$

where α, β, and p are tuning parameters. Thus, we can obtain $[r, C]$ by optimizing Eq. (9.75) using unlabeled data, since $Q_{\alpha,\beta,p}(r, C)$ is independent with the labeled data. In practice, we reduce Eq. (9.75) into the following objective function

$$Q(r, C) = \mathbb{E}_x \inf_{r_v} \left[\|\boldsymbol{x} - \sum_{v \in C} r_v \boldsymbol{v}\|^2 + \mu \sum_{v \in C} |r_v| \|\boldsymbol{v} - \boldsymbol{x}\|^{1+p} \right], \tag{9.76}$$

we can use alternating optimization to estimate (r, C), where estimating r is a LASSO problem, and estimating C is a least squares problem in case $p = 1$.

9.4.3 Sparse Manifold Learning

In machine learning and pattern recognition, high-dimensional data lie in a manifold with intrinsically low-dimensionality. There are three types of dimensionality reduction algorithms: linear dimensionality reduction approaches, manifold learning-based dimensionality reduction, and sparse learning-based dimensionality reduction algorithms. In recent years, sparse learning became more and more popular based on its efficiency, generality, and interpretation in dimensionality reduction. In this section, we will introduce two sparse learning-based dimensionality reduction approaches, sparse neighbor points [5], and manifold elastic net [29].

1. Sparse Neighbor Points Approach

Ehsan et al. proposed a sparse manifold custering and embedding (SMCE) for both clustering and dimensionality reduction in multiple manifolds at the same time [5].

Assume we have a feature set $X = \{\boldsymbol{x}_i \in \mathbb{R}^D\}_{i=1}^N$ belonging to n different manifolds $\{M_\ell\}_{\ell=1}^n$ of intrinsic dimensions $\{d_\ell\}_{\ell=1}^n$. We consider clustering and low-dimensional representation together.

Here, our goal is to select a few neighbors of each point $\boldsymbol{x}_i$ in the same manifold. First of all, we assume that each point $\boldsymbol{x}_i \in M_\ell$ can find the sparsest solution to some $\varepsilon \geq 0$ by

$$\text{Uniqueness Assumption} \quad \|\sum_{j \in N_i} c_{ij}(\boldsymbol{x}_j - \boldsymbol{x}_i)\|_{\ell_2} \leq \varepsilon, \quad \sum_{j \in N_i} c_{ij} = 1, \tag{9.77}$$

where N_i denotes the set of all data points in the smallest ball of $\boldsymbol{x}_i$ from M_ℓ. Furthermore, we have

$$\|[\boldsymbol{x}_1 - \boldsymbol{x}_i, \boldsymbol{x}_2 - \boldsymbol{x}_i, \ldots, \boldsymbol{x}_N - \boldsymbol{x}_i]\boldsymbol{c}_i\|_{\ell_2} \leq \varepsilon, \quad \mathbf{1}^T \boldsymbol{c}_i = 1. \tag{9.78}$$

From Eq. (9.77), we know that if N_i is small and known, it is easy to solve this equation. However, N_i is unknown usually. Relaxing the constraint causes Eq. (9.78) to be not unique. Therefore, we choose a few neighbors of point $\boldsymbol{x}_i$ into the Lagrange multipliers as

$$\arg\min_{\boldsymbol{c}_i} \lambda \| Q_i \boldsymbol{c}_i \|_{\ell_1} + \frac{1}{2} \| X_i \boldsymbol{c}_i \|_{\ell_2}^2, \quad \text{s.t.} \quad \mathbf{1}^T \boldsymbol{c}_i = 1, \tag{9.79}$$

where λ is a trade-off constant, Q_i is the *proximity inducing matrix*, which is a positive-definite diagonal matrix used to choose the elements close to $\boldsymbol{x}_i$. If the point closer to $\boldsymbol{x}_i$, then its corresponding weight in Q_i will be smaller. X_i is defined as follows:

$$X_i \triangleq \left[\frac{\boldsymbol{x}_1 - \boldsymbol{x}_i}{\|\boldsymbol{x}_1 - \boldsymbol{x}_i\|_{\ell_2}}, \ldots, \frac{\boldsymbol{x}_N - \boldsymbol{x}_i}{\|\boldsymbol{x}_N - \boldsymbol{x}_i\|_{\ell_2}} \right]. \tag{9.80}$$

Note that the first item in Eq. (9.79) is the sparsity constraint, and the second one is affine reconstruction error. By contrast to the nearest neighbors' approaches using the fixed number of nearest neighbors and weight calculation, Eq. (9.79) can automatically choose a few neighbors of the given data point and approximately span a low-dimensional affine subspace at that point.

After obtaining $\boldsymbol{c}_i$, we can calculate the weight $\boldsymbol{w}_i$, which corresponds to neighbors of X_i in the same manifold and its values represent their similarity to X_i. Once we obtain the similarity matrix W, it is easy to build a graph to perform clustering and dimensionality reduction.

2. Sparse Projection Matrix Approach

Alternatively, we can find a projection matrix to project features in the high-dimensional space onto a low-dimensional subspace. Thus, Zhou et al. proposed a *Manifold Elastic Net* (MEN) approach [29], where a sparse projection matrix is obtained for subsequent classification. Mathematically, MEN uses the elastic net to model the loss of a discriminative manifold learning-based dimensionality reduction. MEN consists of two basic steps: The first step is to use the part alignment framework to encode the local geometry. The second step is to use the patch alignment framework to calculate the unified coordinate system for local patches.

Part Optimization Step:

Given a patch $X_i = [\boldsymbol{x}_{i0}^T, \boldsymbol{x}_{i1}^T, \boldsymbol{x}_{i2}^T, \ldots, \boldsymbol{x}_{ik}^T]^T$. ($\boldsymbol{x}_{i1}, \boldsymbol{x}_{i2}, \ldots, \boldsymbol{x}_{ik}$ are related to $\boldsymbol{x}_{i0}$). The part optimization is to find a linear mapping from X_i to $Z_i = [z_{i0}^T, z_{i1}^T, z_{i2}^T, \ldots, z_{ik}^T]^T$.

$$\arg\min_{Z_i} \operatorname{tr}(Z_i^T L_i Z_i), \tag{9.81}$$

where L_i represents the local geometry of the patch X_i.

Furthermore, the k related samples of $\boldsymbol{x}_i$ are divided into two groups, the k_1 ones in the same class with $\boldsymbol{x}_i$ and the k_2 ones from different classes with $\boldsymbol{x}_i$. Then we rewrite X_i as

$$X_i = [x_{i0}^T, x_{i1}^T, x_{i2}^T, \ldots, x_{ik_1}^T, x_{i_1}^T, x_{i_2}^T, \ldots, x_{i_{k_2}}^T]^T, \tag{9.82}$$

and its corresponding low-dimensional representation is

$$Z_i = [z_{i0}^T, z_{i1}^T, z_{i2}^T, \ldots, z_{ik_1}^T, z_{i_1}^T, z_{i_2}^T, \ldots, z_{i_{k_2}}^T]^T. \tag{9.83}$$

Therefore, part optimization is rewritten as

$$\arg\min_{Z_i} \sum_{j=1}^{k_1} \|z_{i0} - z_{ij}\|_{\ell_2}^2 - \kappa \sum_{p=1}^{k_2} \|z_{i0} - z_{i_p}\|_{\ell_2}^2, \tag{9.84}$$

where κ is a trade-off parameter. If we define the coefficient vector as

$$w_i = [1, 1, \ldots, 1, -\kappa, -\kappa, \ldots, -\kappa], \tag{9.85}$$

which have k_1 ones and k_2 K, we can get the part optimization matrix

$$L_i = \begin{bmatrix} \sum_{j=1}^{k_1+k_2}(w_i)_j & -w_i^T \\ -w_i & \text{diag}(w_i) \end{bmatrix}. \tag{9.86}$$

Whole Alignment Step:

Define the global coordinate $Z = \left[z_1^T, z_2^T, \ldots, z_n^T, \right]$, Z_i is chosen from Z. For obtaining a consistent coordinate system, we define a sample selection matrix S_i

$$(S_i)_{pq} = \begin{cases} 1, & \text{if } q = F_i\{p\} \\ 0, & \text{else} \end{cases}. \tag{9.87}$$

Then we have

$$Z_i = S_i Z. \tag{9.88}$$

Substituting Eq. (9.88) into Eq. (9.81), we have

$$\arg\min_{Z} \text{tr}(Z^T S_i^T L_i S_i Z). \tag{9.89}$$

Considering the whole alignment and the difference between Z and $Z\mathbf{w}$, we obtain objective function

$$\arg\min_{Z,w} \ tr(Z^T(Z)) + \beta\|Z - Zw\|_2^2. \tag{9.90}$$

Furthermore, we incorporate the classification error into Eq. (9.90) and then have

$$\arg\min_{Z,w} \ \|Y - Zw\|_2^2 + \alpha tr(Z^T(Z)) + \beta\|Z - Zw\|_2^2, \tag{9.91}$$

where α and β are trade-off parameters.

Finally, we obtain the full MEN by writing Eq. (9.91) into elastic net form

$$\arg\min_{Z,w} \|Y - Zw\|_2^2 + \alpha tr(Z^T(Z)) + \beta\|Z - Zw\|_2^2 + \lambda_1\|w\|_1 + \lambda_2\|w\|_2^2. \quad (9.92)$$

As we know, LARS is efficient and effective to solve the LASSO or elastic net penalized multiple linear regression. Essentially, the MEN is a penalized least square. Thanks to the independent column vectors of the projection matrix **w** in MEN [29].

References

1. Buchanan, A.M., Fitzgibbon, A.W.: Damped newton algorithms for matrix factorization with missing data. In: IEEE CVPR (2005)
2. Chen, C.F., Wei, C.P., Wang, Y.C.: Low-rank matrix recovery with structural incoherence for robust face recognition. In: IEEE CVPR (2012)
3. Cheng, H., Liu, Z., Yang, L., Chen, X.: Sparse representation and learning in visual recognition: Theory and applications. Signal. Process. **93**(6), 1408–1425 (2013)
4. Cristianini, N., Shawe-Taylor, J.: An introduction to support vector machines and other kernel-based learning methods. Cambridge University Press, Cambridge (2000)
5. Elhamifar, E., Vidal, R.: Sparse manifold clustering and embedding. In: NIPS (2011)
6. Eriksson, A., Van Den Hengel, A.: Efficient computation of robust low-rank matrix approximations in the presence of missing data using the l 1 norm. In: IEEE CVPR (2010)
7. Gao, S., Tsang, I.W.H., Chia, L.T.: Sparse representation with kernels. IEEE Trans. on Image Processing **22**(2) (2013)
8. Ke, Q., Kanade, T.: Robust ℓ_1 norm factorization in the presence of outliers and missing data by alternative convex programming. In: IEEE CVPR (2005)
9. Maleki, M.A.: Approximate Message Passing Algorithms for Compressed Sensing. Stanford University (2010)
10. Montanari, A.: Graphical models concepts in compressed Sensing. Compressed sensing: Theory and Applications, pp. 394–438 (2012)
11. Okatani, T., Deguchi, K.: On the wiberg algorithm for matrix factorization in the presence of missing components. Int. J. Comput. Vis. **72**(3), 329–337 (2007)
12. Olshausen, B.A., Field, D.J.: Sparse coding with an overcomplete basis set: A strategy employed by v1? Vis. Res. **37**(23), 3311–3325 (1997)
13. Pei, D., Sun, F., Liu, H.: Low-rank matrix recovery for traffic sign recognition in image sequences. In: Foundations and Practical Applications of Cognitive Systems and Information Processing, pp. 857–865. Springer (2014)
14. Peng, Y., Ganesh, A., Wright, J., Xu, W., Ma, Y.: RASL: robust alignment by sparse and low-rank decomposition for linearly correlated images. IEEE Trans. Pattern Anal. mach. Intell.**34**(11) (2012)
15. Rigamonti, R., Brown, M.A., Lepetit, V.: Are sparse representations really relevant for image classification? In: IEEE CVPR (2011)
16. Schölkopf, B., Smola, A., Müller, K.R.: Nonlinear component analysis as a kernel eigenvalue problem. Neural. Comput. **10**(5), 1299–1319 (1998)
17. Scholkopft, B., Mullert, K.R.: Fisher discriminant analysis with Kernels (1999)
18. Shi, Q., Eriksson, A., van den Hengel, A., Shen, C.: Is face recognition really a compressive sensing problem? In: IEEE CVPR (2011)
19. Silva, J., Marques, J.S., Lemos, J.M.: Selecting landmark points for sparse manifold learning. In: NIPS (2005)

20. Tax, D.M., Duin, R.P.: Support vector data description. Mach.Learn. **54**(1), 45–66 (2004)
21. Turk, M., Pentland, A.: Eigenfaces for recognition. J. Cogn. Neurosci. **3**(1), 71–86 (1991)
22. Vapnik, V.: The Nature of Statistical Learning Theory. springer, New York (2000)
23. Wiberg, T.: Computation of principal components when data are missing. In: Proceedings Second Symp. Computational statistics (1976)
24. Wright, J., Yang, A.Y., Ganesh, A., Sastry, S.S., Ma, Y.: Robust face recognition via sparse representation. IEEE Trans. on Pattern Anal. Mach. Intell. **31**(2) (2009)
25. Yu, K., Zhang, T., Gong, Y.: Nonlinear learning using local coordinate coding. In: NIPS, vol. 9 (2009)
26. Zhang, C., Liu, J., Tian, Q., Xu, C., Lu, H., Ma, S.: Image classification by non-negative sparse coding, low-rank and sparse decomposition. In: IEEE CVPR (2011)
27. Zhang, D., Yang, M., Feng, X.: Sparse representation or collaborative representation: which helps face recognition? In: IEEE ICCV (2011)
28. Zhang, Y., Jiang, Z., Davis, L.S.: Learning structured low-rank representations for image classification. In: IEEE CVPR (2013)
29. Zhou, T., Tao, D., Wu, X.: Manifold elastic net: a unified framework for sparse dimension reduction. Data. Min. Knowl.Discov. **22**(3), 340–371 (2011)

Appendix A
Mathematics

A.1 Linear Algebra

A.1.1 Vector Space

Definition: A vector space consists of the following:

(1) A field $\mathbb{F}$ of scalars
(2) A set $\mathbb{V}$ of objects, called vectors
(3) A rule or operation called *vector addition*, which associates with each pair of vectors $\boldsymbol{v}_1, \boldsymbol{v}_2$ in $\mathbb{V}$, a vector $\boldsymbol{v}_1 + \boldsymbol{v}_2$ in $\mathbb{V}$, in such a way that

   (a) Addition is *commutative*, $\boldsymbol{v}_1 + \boldsymbol{v}_2 = \boldsymbol{v}_2 + \boldsymbol{v}_1$
   (b) Addition is *associative*, $(\boldsymbol{v}_1 + \boldsymbol{v}_2) + \boldsymbol{v}_3 = \boldsymbol{v}_1 + (\boldsymbol{v}_2 + \boldsymbol{v}_3)$
   (c) There is a unique vector $\mathbf{0}$ in $\mathbb{V}$, called the *zero vector*, such that $\boldsymbol{v} + \mathbf{0} = \boldsymbol{v}$ for all $\boldsymbol{v} \in \mathbb{V}$
   (d) For each vector $\boldsymbol{v} \in \mathbb{V}$ there is a unique vector $-\boldsymbol{v} \in \mathbb{V}$ such that $\boldsymbol{v}+(-\boldsymbol{v}) = \mathbf{0}$

(4) A rule or operation called *scalar multiplication*, which associates with each scalar $c \in \mathbb{F}$ and vector $\boldsymbol{v} \in \mathbb{V}$, a vector $c\boldsymbol{v} \in \mathbb{V}$, in such a way that

   (a) $1\boldsymbol{v} = \boldsymbol{v}, \forall \boldsymbol{v} \in \mathbb{V}$
   (b) $(c_1 c_2)\boldsymbol{v} = c_1(c_2\boldsymbol{v})$
   (c) $c(\boldsymbol{v}_1 + \boldsymbol{v}_2) = c\boldsymbol{v}_1 + c\boldsymbol{v}_2$
   (d) $(c_1 + c_2)\boldsymbol{v} = c_1\boldsymbol{v} + c_2\boldsymbol{v}$

A.1.2 Linear Combination of Vector

Definition: A vector $\boldsymbol{v} \in \mathbb{V}$ is said to be a *linear combination* of the set of vectors $S = \{\boldsymbol{v}_1, \boldsymbol{v}_2, \ldots, \boldsymbol{v}_n\}$ in $\mathbb{V}$ provided there exist scalars $c_1, c_2, \ldots, c_n$ in $\mathbb{F}$, not all of which are 0, such that

H. Cheng, *Sparse Representation, Modeling and Learning in Visual Recognition*, Advances in Computer Vision and Pattern Recognition,
DOI 10.1007/978-1-4471-6714-3

$$v = c_1 v_1 + c_2 v_2 + \cdots + c_n v_n.$$

If each vector in vector space $\mathbb{V}$ can be represented as a linear combination of the set of vectors S in $\mathbb{V}$, then the set of vectors S is said to be *spanning* the vector space.

A.1.2.1 Linear Independence of Vectors

Let $\mathbb{V}$ be a vector space over $\mathbb{F}$. A subset S of $\mathbb{V}$ is said to be *linearly dependent* if there exist distinct vector $v_1, v_2, \ldots, v_n$ in S and scalars $c_1, c_2, \ldots, c_n$ in $\mathbb{F}$, not all of which are 0, such that

$$c_1 v_1 + c_2 v_2 + \cdots + c_n v_n = \mathbf{0}.$$

A set which is not linearly dependent is called *linearly independent.*

For a square matrix A, we have the following lemma which shows the relation between invertibility of a matrix and the linear independence of its column vectors.

Lemma 1 *A matrix $A_{n\times n} \in \mathbb{R}^{n\times n}$ is invertible if and only if the column vectors of A are linearly independent.*

On the other hand if matrix A is invertible, then the only solution for the equation $Ax = \mathbf{0}$ is the trivial solution $x = 0$. Let $A = [A_1, A_2, \ldots, A_n]$, where A_i, $1 \le i \le n$ are the column vectors of A. Hence $c_1 A_1 + c_2 A_2 + \cdots + c_n A_n = \mathbf{0}$ implies that $c_1 = c_2 = \cdots = c_n = 0$. Thus the column vectors of A are linearly independent.

A.1.3 Eigenvalue and Eigenvector

Let $A = [a_{jk}]$ be a given $m \times m$ matrix and consider the equation

$$Ax = \lambda x. \tag{A.1}$$

Here x is an unknown vector and λ an unknown scalar. A value of λ for which Eq. (A.1) has a solution $x \neq \mathbf{0}$ is called an *eigenvalue* or *characteristic value* of the matrix A corresponding to the eigenvalue λ.

Equation (A.1) can be written in matrix notation as

$$(A - \lambda I)x = \mathbf{0}, \tag{A.2}$$

where I is the identity matrix. By Cramer's theorem, Eq. (A.2) has a nontrivial solution $x \neq \mathbf{0}$ if and only if its coefficient determinant is zero, that is, $D(\lambda) = det(A - \lambda I) = 0$. The equation $D(\lambda) = 0$ is called the *characteristic equation* of A. The eigenvalues of the square matrix A are provided by the root of the *characteristic equation.*

A.1.4 Diagonalization of Matrix

Lemma 2 *Let A be a square matrix of order m and let A have m distinct eigenvalues. Then the eigenvectors of A are linearly independent.*

Theorem 3 *Let A be a square matrix of order m and assume that A has m distinct eigenvalues. Then A is diagonalizable. Moreover, if P is the matrix with the columns* $\boldsymbol{x}_1, \boldsymbol{x}_2, \ldots, \boldsymbol{x}_m$ *as the m eigenvectors of A, then the matrix* $P^{-1}AP$ *is a diagonal matrix.*

A.2 Matrix Analysis

A.2.1 Matrix Terminology and Notation

* A matrix is a rectangular array of numbers can be written as

$$A = \begin{bmatrix} 3 & -3 & 7 & 0.3 \\ 5 & 3.5 & -2 & 0 \\ 8 & -4.3 & 0 & 8.1 \end{bmatrix}.$$

An important attribute of a matrix is its size or dimension. For example the matrix has 3 rows and 4 columns, so the size of this matrix is 3×4 which is also called an 3×4 matrix.

* A_{ij} denotes the number at the position of row i and column j, for example $A_{13} = 7$.

* The transpose of a matrix, denoted by the superscript T, is a matrix with the rows and columns interchanged, *i.e.*, $A^T_{ij} = A_{ji}$. For example,

$$\begin{bmatrix} 3 & -3 & 7 \\ 5 & 3.5 & -2 \end{bmatrix}^T = \begin{bmatrix} 3 & 5 \\ -3 & 3.5 \\ 7 & -2 \end{bmatrix}.$$

* If matrix A is square, and there is a matrix F that can make $FA = I$, then we can say that the matrix I is *invertible* or *nonsingular* and the matrix F is the *inverse* of A, and can be denoted as A^{-1}.

A.2.2 Basic Matrix Identities

By the definition of transpose, there is the property about it

$$(AB)^T = B^T A^T. \tag{A.3}$$

By the definition of matrix inverse, there is the property about it

$$AA^{-1} = A^{-1}A = I. \tag{A.4}$$

Because $ABB^{-1}A^{-1} = I$, we can get

$$(AB)^{-1} = B^{-1}A^{-1}. \tag{A.5}$$

Because $A^T(A^{-1})^T = (A^{-1}A)^T = I$, we can get

$$(A^T)^{-1} = (A^{-1})^T. \tag{A.6}$$

There is a useful matrix identity about the matrix inverse as follows:

$$(P^{-1} + B^T R^{-1} B)^{-1} B^T R^{-1} = PB^T(BPB^T + R)^{-1}. \tag{A.7}$$

And this identity can be used to get the special case that

$$(I + AB)^{-1}A = A(I + BA)^{-1}. \tag{A.8}$$

Another useful identity is

$$(A + BD^{-1}C)^{-1} = A^{-1} - A^{-1}B(D + CA^{-1}B)^{-1}CA^{-1} \tag{A.9}$$

A.2.3 Traces and Determinants

Definition: Trace is applied to the square matrix A which can be noted as $Tr(A)$, is the sum of the diagonal elements of matrix A.

It has identities as follows

$$Tr(AB) = Tr(BA). \tag{A.10}$$

This identity can be extended to three matrix times as

$$Tr(ABC) = Tr(CAB) = Tr(BCA) \tag{A.11}$$

By the definition of determinant, there has some useful identities as follows:

$$|AB| = |A||B|, \tag{A.12}$$

if both matrices A and B are square.

The determinant of the inverse matrix is

$$|A^{-1}| = \frac{1}{|A|}. \tag{A.13}$$

If both matrices A and B are the same size of $N \times M$, then

$$|I_N + AB^T| = |I_M + A^T B|. \tag{A.14}$$

A special case about this identity is

$$|I_N + \boldsymbol{a}\boldsymbol{b}^T| = 1 + \boldsymbol{a}^T \boldsymbol{b}, \tag{A.15}$$

where $\boldsymbol{a}$ and $\boldsymbol{b}$ are N-dimensional column vectors.

A.3 Linear Programming

A.3.1 Small Size LP1

The LP1 algorithm is undoable for extremely high dimensional problems. Toward this end, we reduce its size by using duality theory. Duality theory in LP plays an important role as a unified theory on building the relationship between a linear programming and its related LP. We have

$$\arg\min_{\boldsymbol{z}} \quad \boldsymbol{y}^T \boldsymbol{z}, \quad \text{s.t.} \quad A^T \boldsymbol{z} = \boldsymbol{c}, \boldsymbol{z} \geq 0, \tag{A.16}$$

where the coefficient relationship between the primal form and the dual form is shown in Table A.1.

Let us derive the primal form (Eq. (3.5)) to the dual form (Eq. (A.16)). From Eq. (3.5), we have

Table A.1 The relationship between the primal form and the dual form

Primal / Dual	u_1	u_2	$\cdots$	u_N	argmax
z_1	a_{11}	a_{12}	$\cdots$	a_{1N}	y_1
z_2	a_{21}	a_{22}	$\cdots$	a_{2N}	y_2
$\vdots$	$\vdots$	$\vdots$	$\vdots$	$\vdots$	$\vdots$
z_D	a_{D1}	a_{D2}	$\cdots$	a_{DN}	y_D
argmin	c_1	c_2	$\cdots$	c_N	Dual $\sum_j y_j z_j$ / Primal $\sum_i c_i u_i$

$$\begin{aligned}\arg\min_{c} \quad & \sum_{j=1}^{N} c_j u_j, \\ \text{s.t.} \quad & \sum_{j=1}^{N} a_{ij} u_j = y_i, \quad i = 1, 2, \ldots, D, \\ & u_j \geq 0, \quad j = 1, 2, \ldots, N.\end{aligned} \tag{A.17}$$

We can rewrite Eq. (A.17) as:

$$\begin{aligned}\arg\min_{c} \quad & \sum_{j=1}^{N} c_j u_j, \\ \text{s.t.} \quad & \sum_{j=1}^{N} a_{ij} u_j \leq y_i, \quad i = 1, 2, \ldots, D, \\ & \sum_{j=1}^{N} -a_{ij} u_j \leq -y_i, \quad i = 1, 2, \ldots, D, \\ & u_j \geq 0, \quad j = 1, 2, \ldots, N.\end{aligned} \tag{A.18}$$

Equation (A.18) can be obtained by using the definition of the duality theory. Define z_i^+ and z_i^- $(i = 1, 2, \ldots, D)$ to be the dual variables. Thus we have

$$\begin{aligned}\arg\min_{z} \quad & \sum_{i=1}^{D} y_i z_i^+ + \sum_{i=1}^{D} -y_i z_i^-, \\ \text{s.t.} \quad & \sum_{i=1}^{D} a_{ij} z_i^+ + \sum_{i=1}^{D} -a_{ij} z_i^- \geq c_j, \quad j = 1, 2, \ldots, N, \\ & z_i^+ \geq 0, z_i^- \geq 0, \quad i = 1, 2, \ldots, D.\end{aligned} \tag{A.19}$$

Collecting terms, we have

$$\begin{aligned}\arg\min_{z} \quad & \sum_{i=1}^{D} y_i (z_i^+ - z_i^-), \\ \text{s.t.} \quad & \sum_{i=1}^{D} a_{ij} (z_i^+ - z_i^-) \geq c_j, \quad j = 1, 2, \ldots, N, \\ & z_i^+ \geq 0, z_i^- \geq 0, \quad i = 1, 2, \ldots, D.\end{aligned} \tag{A.20}$$

Letting $z_i = z_i^+ - z_i^-$, we have

$$\begin{aligned} \arg\min z \quad & \sum_{i=1}^{D} y_i z_i, \\ \text{s.t.} \quad & \sum_{i=1}^{D} a_{ij} z_i \geq c_j, \quad j = 1, 2, \ldots, N, \\ & z_i^+ \geq 0, \ z_i^- \geq 0, \quad i = 1, 2, \ldots, D. \end{aligned} \tag{A.21}$$

Finally, we have another dual form of Eq. (A.16)

$$\begin{aligned} \arg\min_{z} \quad & \sum_{i=1}^{D} y_i z_i \\ \text{s.t.} \quad & \sum_{i=1}^{D} a_{ij} z_i \geq c_j, \quad j = 1, 2, \ldots, N, \\ & z_i \ \text{(unrestricted)}, \quad i = 1, 2, \ldots, D. \end{aligned} \tag{A.22}$$

A.3.2 Solving Linear Programming Problems

In fact, BP is an optimization principle. There are large amounts of developed linear programming algorithms. However, two popular algorithms are used widely in solving the BP optimization: the simplex and interior-point algorithms.

Linear programming lies in the heart of BP. We first briefly introduce its principle. The standard form of linear programming is

$$\begin{aligned} \arg\min_{\boldsymbol{u}} \quad & \boldsymbol{c}^T \boldsymbol{x}, \\ \text{s.t.} \quad & \boldsymbol{A}\boldsymbol{x} = \boldsymbol{b}, \quad \boldsymbol{x} \geq 0. \end{aligned} \tag{A.23}$$

Formally, linear programming techniques are to optimize a linear objective function, subjected to linear equality/inequality constraints. Figure A.1 illustrates linear programming. Each inequality corresponds to a half-space, called polytope. Polytopes are convex, and the optimal solution is at a vertex.

The fundamental theorem of LP: Optimizing a linear objective function $c^T \boldsymbol{x}$ is achieved at the extreme points in the feasible region if the solution set is not empty and the optimum is finite. Moreover, an upper bound on iteration number is simply the number of basic feasible solutions. It can be at most

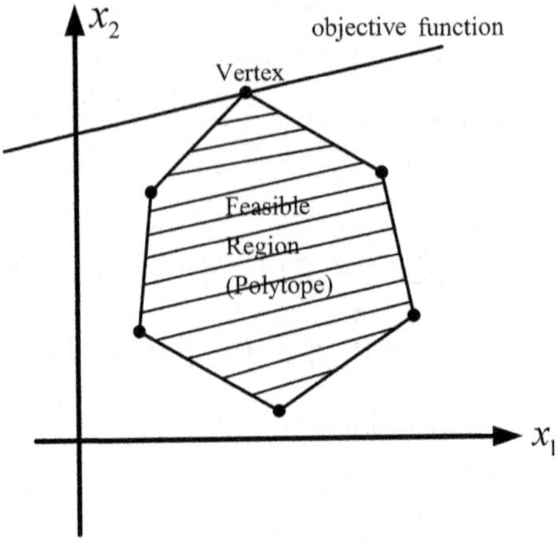

Fig. A.1 Linear programming illustratio

$$C_N^D = \frac{N!}{D!(N-D)!}. \tag{A.24}$$

This equation can be used to evaluate the computation complexity especially for the simplex algorithms.

A.3.3 LP via Simplex

In standard simplex method for LP proposed by Dantzig, we find an initial basis B consisting of N linearly independent columns of A, where $B^{-1}\mathrm{b}$ is feasible. Afterward, we can iteratively improve the current basis by swapping one basis term and one non-basis term, and this improves the objective function. Finally, the simplex method is to give a rule to transfer from one extreme point to another such that the objective function is decreased. We can consider the simplex method as a generalization of standard Gauss–Jordan elimination of linear algebra.

The Primal-Simplex method: The standard LP can be written as

$$\begin{aligned} \arg\min_{\boldsymbol{x}} \quad & \sum_{j=1}^{N} c_j x_j \\ \text{s.t.} \quad & \sum_{j=1}^{N} a_{ij} x_j \le b_i, i = 1, 2, \ldots, D, \\ & x_j \ge 0, j = 1, 2, \ldots, N. \end{aligned} \tag{A.25}$$

Now we introduce slack variables

$$z = \sum_{j=1}^{N} c_j x_j, \omega_i = b_i - \sum_{j=1}^{N} a_{ij} x_j, i = 1, 2, \ldots, D. \tag{A.26}$$

Thus, we can define $(x_1, x_2, \ldots, x_N, \omega_1, \omega_2, \ldots, \omega_D) = (x_1, x_2, \ldots, x_N, x_{N+1}, \ldots, x_{N+D})$.

Appendix B
Computer Programming Resources for Sparse Recovery Approaches

$L1$ Magic
http://users.ece.gatech.edu/~justin/l1magic/

Sparse Lab
http://sparselab.stanford.edu

$L1$ Benchmark Package
http://www.eecs.berkeley.edu/~yang/software/l1benchmark/l1benchmark.zip

GPSR-Gradient Projection for Sparse Reconstruction
http://www.lx.it.pt/~mtf/GPSR

$L1$ Homotopy: A Matlab Toolbox for Homotopy Algorithms in $L1$-norm Minimization Problems
http://users.ece.gatech.edu/~sasif/homotopy/

Linear programming C++ pachage1
http://www.stanford.edu/yyye/Col.html

Linear programming C++ pachage2 (ℓ_p)-solve reference guide
http://lpsolve.sourceforge.net

Bayesian Compressive Sensing
http://people.ec.duke.edu/~lcarin/Bes.html

H. Cheng, *Sparse Representation, Modeling and Learning in Visual Recognition*,
Advances in Computer Vision and Pattern Recognition,
DOI 10.1007/978-1-4471-6714-3

Appendix C
The Source Code of Sparsity Induced Similarity

```
1   void BasisPursuit_LinearProgram_Noise(double *dFeatureTarget, double **dFeatureBasis, double *
2   dSparsityCoeff, int nBasis, int nDim)
3   {
4     int cc,ii,jj,rr;
5
6     // 1 build the model row by row
7     lprec *lp;
8     int Ncol, *colno = NULL, ret = 0;
9     REAL *row = NULL;
10
11    /* We will build the model row by row. So we start with creating a model with 0 rows and 2
      columns */
12    Ncol = 2*(nBasis+nDim+1); //# Variables in the model
13    lp = make_lp(0, Ncol);
14    if(lp == NULL)
15      ret = 1; /* couldn't construct a new model... */
16
17    //build row model
18    if(ret == 0)
19    {
20      /* create space large enough for one row */
21      colno = (int *) malloc(Ncol * sizeof(*colno));
22      row = (REAL *) malloc(Ncol * sizeof(*row));
23      if((colno == NULL) || (row == NULL))
24        ret = 2;
25
26      /* construct row mode: [A I]*alpha = f, alpha>=0 */
27      if (ret==0)
28      {
29        set_add_rowmode(lp, TRUE);  /* makes building the model faster if it is done rows by row */
30        for(rr=0; rr<nDim; rr++)/* [A I]*alpha=f */
31        {
32          for (jj=0; jj<Ncol/2; jj++)/* go through each column*/
33          {
34            if(jj<nBasis) //A
35            {
36              colno[jj] = jj+1; /* first column */
37              row[jj] = dFeatureBasis[jj][rr];
38              colno[jj+Ncol/2] = jj+Ncol/2+1;
39              row[jj+Ncol/2] =-dFeatureBasis[jj][rr];
40            }
41            else //I
```

© Springer-Verlag London 2015
H. Cheng, *Sparse Representation, Modeling and Learning in Visual Recognition*,
Advances in Computer Vision and Pattern Recognition,
DOI 10.1007/978-1-4471-6714-3

```
        {
          if((jj-nBasis)==rr)
          {
            colno[jj] = jj+1; /* first column */
            row[jj] = 1.0;
            colno[jj+Ncol/2] = jj+Ncol/2+1;
            row[jj+Ncol/2] = -1.0;
          }
          else
          {
            colno[jj] = jj+1; /* first column */
            row[jj] = 0.0;
            colno[jj+Ncol/2] = jj+Ncol/2+1;
            row[jj+Ncol/2] =0.0;
          }
        }
      }
      /* add the row to lpsolve */
      if(!add_constraintex(lp, 2*jj, row, colno, EQ, dFeatureTarget[rr]))
        ret = 3;
    }

    //lift-up one dimension for normalization
    double dFeature129;
    //first input nBasis values of A
    for (jj=0; jj<Ncol/2; jj++)/* go through each column*/
    {
      if(jj<nBasis)
      {
        dFeature129=0.0;
        for(int rr=0;rr<nDim; rr++)
        {
          dFeature129+=dFeatureBasis[jj][rr]*dFeatureBasis[jj][rr];
        }
        if (dFeature129>=1.0)
          dFeature129=0;
        else
          dFeature129=sqrt(1.0-dFeature129);

        colno[jj] = jj+1; /* first column */
        row[jj] = dFeature129;
        colno[jj+Ncol/2] = jj+Ncol/2+1;
        row[jj+Ncol/2] =-dFeature129;
      }
      else
      {
        colno[jj] = jj+1; /* first column */
        row[jj] = 0.0;
        colno[jj+Ncol/2] = jj+Ncol/2+1;
        row[jj+Ncol/2] = 0.0;
      }
    }
    colno[Ncol/2-1] = Ncol/2; /* first column */
    row[Ncol/2-1] = 1.0;
    colno[Ncol-1] = Ncol;
    row[Ncol-1] = -1.0;

    /* add the row to lpsolve */
    dFeature129=0.0;
    for (rr=0;rr<nDim; rr++)
    {
      dFeature129+=dFeatureTarget[rr]*dFeatureTarget[rr];
    }
    if (dFeature129>1.0)
      dFeature129=0;
    else
      dFeature129=sqrt(1.0-dFeature129);
```

```

        if(!add_constraintex(lp, 2*jj, row, colno, EQ, dFeature129))
          ret = 3;
      }
      if (ret==0)
        set_add_rowmode(lp, FALSE); /* rowmode should be turned off again when done building the model */
  }

  //set the objective function
  if(ret == 0)
  {
    for(jj=0;jj<Ncol; jj++)//each column
    {
      colno[jj] = jj+1;
      row[jj] = 1;
    }

    /* set the objective in lpsolve */
    if(!set_obj_fnex(lp, jj, row, colno))
      ret = 4;
  }

  if(ret == 0)
  {
    /* set the object direction to minimize */
    set_minim(lp);

    /* just out of curioucity, now show the model in lp format on screen */
    /* this only works if this is a console application. If not, use write_lp and a filename */
    //write_lp(lp, "model.lp");

    /* I only want to see important messages on screen while solving */
    set_verbose(lp, IMPORTANT);

    /* Now let lpsolve calculate a solution */
    ret = solve(lp);
    if(ret == OPTIMAL)
    ret = 0;
  else
    ret = 5;
  }

  // get sparisty coefficients from LP
  if (ret==0)
  {
    get_variables(lp, row);
    for (int jj=0;jj<nBasis;jj++)//note that I only take x_n not take epsilon
    dSparsityCoeff[jj]=row[jj]-row[jj+Ncol/2];
    /*cout<<"Error=";
    for (int jj=nBasis;jj<Ncol/2;jj++)
      cout<<row[jj]-row[jj+Ncol/2]<<"";

    cout<<"\n";*/
  }
  else
  {
    for (jj=0;jj<nBasis;jj++)
    dSparsityCoeff[jj]=100;
  }

  //check if the solution is right
  if(FALSE)
  {
    double *dFeatureRec;
    dFeatureRec=new double[nDim];
    for (ii=0;ii<nDim; ii++)
```

```
        {
          dFeatureRec[ii]=0;
        }
        for(jj=0;jj<nBasis;jj++)
        {
          for(ii=0;ii<nDim;ii++)
          {
            dFeatureRec[ii]+=(dSparsityCoeff[jj]*dFeatureBasis[jj][ii]);
          }
        }


        //Debug
        /*  cout<<"Reconstructed signal:";
        for(ii=0;ii<nDim;ii++)
          cout<<dFeatureRec[ii]<<""<<flush;

        cout<<"\n";
        cout<<"Original signal:";
        for(ii=0;ii<nDim;ii++)
          cout<<dFeatureTarget[ii]<<""<<flush;

        cout<<"\n";*/

    }

    /* free allocated memory*/
    if(row != NULL)
      free(row);
    if(colno != NULL)
      free(colno);
    if(lp != NULL)
      delete_lp(lp);
}
```

Appendix D
Derivations

D.1 Proof of the Theorem 4.3.1

For fixed **A**, Eq. (4.29) is formulated as Eq. (4.31), and we use Eq. (4.31) to prove Theorem 4.3.1.

For $j = 1, \ldots, k$, let $\mathbf{M} = \mathbf{W}^{1/2} \circ \mathbf{X}$,

$$\begin{aligned}
&\left\| \mathbf{W}^{1/2} \circ (\mathbf{X}\boldsymbol{\alpha}_j - \mathbf{X}\boldsymbol{\beta}_j) \right\|_2^2 \\
&= \mathrm{tr}\left\{ (\boldsymbol{\alpha}_j^T - \boldsymbol{\beta}_j^T)\mathbf{M}^T\mathbf{M}(\boldsymbol{\alpha}_j - \boldsymbol{\beta}_j) \right\} \\
&= \mathrm{tr}\left\{ \mathbf{M}^T\mathbf{M}\left(I - 2\boldsymbol{\alpha}_j\boldsymbol{\beta}_j^T + \boldsymbol{\beta}_j\boldsymbol{\beta}_j^T \right) \right\} \\
&= \mathrm{tr}\{\mathbf{M}^T\mathbf{M}\} - 2\mathrm{tr}\left\{ \boldsymbol{\alpha}_j^T\mathbf{M}^T\mathbf{M}\boldsymbol{\beta}_j \right\} + \mathrm{tr}\left\{ \boldsymbol{\beta}_j^T\mathbf{M}^T\mathbf{M}\boldsymbol{\beta}_j \right\}.
\end{aligned} \tag{D.1}$$

Since $\boldsymbol{\alpha}_j^T\mathbf{M}^T\mathbf{M}\boldsymbol{\beta}_j$ and $\boldsymbol{\beta}_j^T\mathbf{M}^T\mathbf{M}\boldsymbol{\beta}_j$ are both scalars, we get

$$\begin{aligned}
&\left\| \mathbf{W}^{1/2} \circ (\mathbf{X}\boldsymbol{\alpha}_j - \mathbf{X}\boldsymbol{\beta}_j) \right\|_2^2 + \lambda_2\|\boldsymbol{\beta}\|_2^2 \\
&= \mathrm{tr}\{\mathbf{M}^T\mathbf{M}\} - 2\boldsymbol{\alpha}_j^T\mathbf{M}^T\mathbf{M}\boldsymbol{\beta}_j + \boldsymbol{\beta}_j^T(\mathbf{M}^T\mathbf{M} + \lambda_2)\boldsymbol{\beta}_j.
\end{aligned} \tag{D.2}$$

For a fixed $\boldsymbol{\alpha}_j$, the above Eq. (D.2) is minimized at

$$\boldsymbol{\beta}_j = (\mathbf{M}^T\mathbf{M} + \lambda_2)^{-1}\mathbf{M}^T\mathbf{M}\boldsymbol{\alpha}_j. \tag{D.3}$$

Substituting it into the Eq. (D.2) gives

$$\begin{aligned}
&\left\| \mathbf{W}^{1/2} \circ (\mathbf{X}\boldsymbol{\alpha}_j - \mathbf{X}\boldsymbol{\beta}_j) \right\|_2^2 + \lambda_2\|\boldsymbol{\beta}\|_2^2 \\
&= \mathrm{tr}\{\mathbf{M}^T\mathbf{M}\} - 2\boldsymbol{\alpha}_j^T\mathbf{M}^T\mathbf{M}(\mathbf{M}^T\mathbf{M} + \lambda_2)^{-1} + \mathbf{M}^T\mathbf{M}\boldsymbol{\alpha}_j.
\end{aligned} \tag{D.4}$$

H. Cheng, *Sparse Representation, Modeling and Learning in Visual Recognition*,
Advances in Computer Vision and Pattern Recognition,
DOI 10.1007/978-1-4471-6714-3

Therefore

$$\hat{\boldsymbol{\alpha}}_j = \arg\max_{\boldsymbol{\alpha}_j} \boldsymbol{\alpha}_j^T \mathbf{M}^T \mathbf{M}(\mathbf{M}^T \mathbf{M} + \lambda_2)^{-1} \mathbf{M}^T \mathbf{M} \boldsymbol{\alpha}_j, \quad \text{s.t.} \quad \|\boldsymbol{\alpha}_j\|_2^2 = 1. \tag{D.5}$$

By SVD $\mathbf{M} = \mathbf{U}\boldsymbol{\Sigma}\mathbf{V}^T$, we have

$$\mathbf{M}^T \mathbf{M}(\mathbf{M}^T \mathbf{M} + \lambda_2)^{-1} \mathbf{M}^T \mathbf{M} = \mathbf{V} \frac{\boldsymbol{\Sigma}^4}{\boldsymbol{\Sigma}^2 + \lambda_2} \mathbf{V}^T, \tag{D.6}$$

Hence $\hat{\boldsymbol{\alpha}}_j = \mathbf{V}(:, 1)$, $\hat{\boldsymbol{\beta}}_j = \frac{\Sigma^2}{\Sigma^2 + \lambda_2} \mathbf{V}(:, 1)$, $\hat{\boldsymbol{\beta}}_j \propto \mathbf{V}_j$.

D.2 Proof of the Theorem 4.3.2

$$\|\mathbf{M} - \mathbf{N}\mathbf{A}^T\|_2^2 = \mathrm{tr}(\mathbf{M}^T\mathbf{M}) - 2\mathbf{tr}(\mathbf{M}^T\mathbf{N}\mathbf{A}^T) + \mathrm{tr}(\mathbf{A}\mathbf{N}^T\mathbf{N}\mathbf{A}^T). \tag{D.7}$$

Since $\mathbf{A}^T\mathbf{A} = \mathbf{I}$, the last item is equal to $\mathrm{tr}(\mathbf{N}^T\mathbf{N})$, hence $\arg\min_{\mathbf{A}} \|\mathbf{M} - \mathbf{N}\mathbf{A}^T\|_2^2$ just to max $\mathrm{tr}(\mathbf{M}^T\mathbf{N}\mathbf{A}^T)$. Since $\mathbf{M}^T\mathbf{N} = \mathbf{U}_1\boldsymbol{\Sigma}_1\mathbf{V}_1^T$ by using SVD, then

$$\mathrm{tr}(\mathbf{M}^T\mathbf{N}\mathbf{A}^T) = \mathrm{tr}(\mathbf{U}_1\boldsymbol{\Sigma}_1\mathbf{V}_1^T\mathbf{A}^T) = \mathrm{tr}(\mathbf{V}_1^T\mathbf{A}^T\mathbf{U}_1\boldsymbol{\Sigma}_1), \tag{D.8}$$

for $\mathbf{V}_1^T\mathbf{A}^T\mathbf{A}\mathbf{V}_1 = \mathbf{I}$. Since $\boldsymbol{\Sigma}_1$ is diagonal, Eq. (D.8) is maximized when the diagonal of $\mathbf{V}_1^T\mathbf{A}^T\mathbf{U}_1$ is positive and maximum. By Cauchy-Schwartz inequality, this is achieved when $\mathbf{A}\mathbf{V}_1 = \mathbf{U}_1$, in which case the diagonal elements are all 1. Hence $\hat{\mathbf{A}} = \mathbf{U}_1\mathbf{V}_1^T$.

Index

H. Cheng, *Sparse Representation, Modeling and Learning in Visual Recognition*,
Advances in Computer Vision and Pattern Recognition,
DOI 10.1007/978-1-4471-6714-3

Printed in the United States
By Bookmasters